FIRST LADY OF THE CONFEDERACY

First Lady
of the Confederacy

VARINA DAVIS'S CIVIL WAR

❦

Joan E. Cashin

The Belknap Press of Harvard University Press
CAMBRIDGE, MASSACHUSETTS, AND LONDON, ENGLAND
2006

Frontispiece: Detail of photo of Varina Howell Davis, circa 1860.
(Museum of the Confederacy, Richmond, Virginia)

Library of Congress Cataloging-in-Publication Data
Cashin, Joan E.
First lady of the Confederacy : Varina Davis's Civil War / Joan E. Cashin.
p.   cm.
Includes bibliographical references and index.
ISBN-13: 978-0-674-02294-2 (alk. paper)
ISBN-10: 0-674-02294-7 (alk. paper)
1. Davis, Varina, 1826–1906. 2. Presidents' spouses—Confederate States
of America—Biography. 3. United States—History—Civil War, 1861–
1865—Biography. 4. United States—History—Civil War, 1861–1865—
Social aspects. 5. Confederate States of America—Social conditions.
6. Davis, Jefferson, 1808–1889—Family. I. Title.

E467.1.D27C36 2006
973.7'13092—dc22   2006042734
[B]

For Michael

CONTENTS

ILLUSTRATIONS

FIRST LADY OF THE CONFEDERACY

INTRODUCTION

 IF SHE HAD TO HAVE A BIOGRAPHER, Varina Davis once remarked, she would prefer someone like Agnes Strickland, the Englishwoman who described the marriages of Mary Queen of Scots as "so many holocausts of herself." These were Davis's words, not Strickland's, in 1862. Mrs. Davis was having a bad summer. Her doubts about the Confederacy's ability to win the war had gotten into the newspapers, and she had to assure her husband she had faith in his success, which was not entirely true. Davis nonetheless invited her future biographer to focus on the war and the sacrifices she made for her marriage, and the evidence leads ineluctably to those themes. This book focuses on the war and the marriage, as well as other topics she would not have wanted a biographer to address.[1]

Like most biographers of my generation, I try to portray Davis as a figure in historical context, not floating in a void like the subjects in Strickland's work, and I do not share Strickland's conservative political views, or those of Varina Davis. Because historians of the Civil War are often asked what their ancestors did during the conflict, I should say that I, like Varina Davis, had relatives in both armies. One of my ancestors fought for the Confederacy, being from Georgia; and one fought for the Union, being from New York; after 1865 a Northerner crossed the Mason-Dixon line to take a new job. Some of my relatives did not serve in either army, and at least one left the United States rather than take sides.

We should not make too much of connections or lack thereof between biographer and subject, however, because scholars have to do research to write books and the research trail always leads in unexpected directions. The research and writing for this volume took the better part of fourteen years, and I, like most biographers, came to appreciate how alien Davis's experience is from mine or that of anyone alive today. When I first came across her correspondence, I was struck by the vivid prose; her letters have pith. Beyond that, I knew nothing about her, including how to pronounce her name (rhymes with "Marina"). I soon learned that Davis's life did not conform to most of the paradigms of Southern history, women's history, or the Civil War, and that she was a complex human being, by no means easy to understand. Tall, dark, and smart, she could be affectionate, forgiving, and generous. Her peers described her as one of the great conversationalists of her time, and she had physical courage, for she probably saved her husband's life when federal soldiers captured the couple in Georgia in 1865. She had her full share of faults, and she could be demanding, cutting, possessive about people she loved, and loyal to people who did not deserve her loyalty.

But her greatest shortcoming to a modern reader was her reluctance to follow through on the unorthodox comments she made about the times through which she lived. She found it hard to face the conclusions that flowed logically from her observations that slaves were human beings with their frailties; that the South did not have the material resources to win the war and white Southerners did not have the qualities necessary to win it; that her husband was unsuited for political life; that maybe women were not the inferior sex; that perhaps it was a mistake to deny women the suffrage before the war; and that everyone was a "half breed" of one kind or another. Instead she usually fell silent, or apologized, or uttered the platitudes that her contemporaries expected her to say. She made a significant breakthrough in her old age, however, when she declared in print that the right side won the Civil War.

The question arises, why did she make these unorthodox statements in the first place? The key seems to lie in her childhood—in her excellent education and her father's bankruptcy, both of which unfitted her for the conventional role of a Southern "lady." She became detached from some, but not all, of the values of antebellum white society, and she could never resign herself completely to the status quo, as many white Southern women did. This gave her personality a restlessness and a keenness of perception that was unusual among white women of her generation. Both her father and her husband failed to provide for her as men of the nineteenth century were expected to do, and she had to take on many responsibilities beyond those that were expected of a woman of her generation.

The next question, why she was unable to follow through on her observations, is easier to answer. She once said it was better to press forward with the business of life and not look back, and that is how she survived, hurtling forward to meet the task in front of her. Furthermore, she thought duty to the family was more important than self-fulfillment, and her family obligations were often overwhelming. Her marriage to Jefferson Davis also inhibited a certain kind of honesty, because he expected her to conform to his wishes, as did her residence in a slave society, where no white person was encouraged to speak bluntly about the power arrangements upon which that society rested. Her fame, too, was an inhibition. Her public image went through several phases between the 1850s and her death in 1906, and she learned to adopt different voices, or personas, in different situations. She tacked back and forth, making contradictory, oblique remarks about the events she lived through.[2]

In a long, complicated life filled with incident, several themes recur. Her regional identity was never firmly fixed, for she grew up in the South, was educated in the North and the South, had kinfolk in both regions, and spent most of the fifteen years before the Civil War in Washington, D.C., giving her a cultural outlook that was broadly American. Her class identity is also hard to fix, because her affluent father went bankrupt when she was a girl and her wealthy spouse lost his fortune in the war. During the war, she told her husband she would work for a salary if necessary, and in her widowhood she supported herself. Her racial attitudes were conventional for much of her life, although she formed some attachments to individual black people and made some unorthodox comments about race. She sometimes felt frustrated by traditional ideas about gender, without knowing what to do about it, but she was also protected by her gender during the war, when her some of her actions could have landed her in prison. She cannot be described as a representative figure, since most people do not lead lives of such operatic extremes; it is hard to generalize about someone who met Prince Kropotkin and Booker T. Washington on the same day. Yet her biography does suggest the many constraints on nineteenth-century women, even white women who married into the planter class.

For her, as for most women of her generation, marriage was destiny, and after she wed Jefferson Davis, his decisions determined the course of her life. Although we have to be careful in charting the emotional history of any marriage from this distance in time, a few points seem clear. When Varina Howell was very young, she fell deeply in love with a rich, handsome older man. She discovered that he insisted on deference from his wife, and after a crisis in the 1840s, she realized she had to subordinate herself if she wanted to stay married to him. They had a difficult relationship, fraught with passionate outbursts of love, regret, and resentment and marked by several terrific power struggles, most of which she lost. She did not have the companionate marriage she wanted, but she tried to accommodate, to overlook, and to forgive, as did most women of her generation. The Davises were in some ways incompatible, as is evident in her remark that the happiest time in her life was in Washington before the war and his that the happiest days of their marriage were spent at their Mississippi plantation.[3]

Jefferson Davis is just as compelling a figure as she is, although for different reasons. He was the champion of a slave society and embodied the values of the planter class, and thus was chosen Confederate President by acclamation in 1861. Figures as diverse as William Yancey and W. E. B. Du Bois portrayed him as a representative man, although neither Yancey nor Du Bois was interested in gender. In fact, Jefferson Davis had highly conventional ideas about gender, which were, simply put, that white men should provide for everyone else and exercise power over them too. In adulthood he lost his vision in one eye, which creates a flatness of perspective that lends itself easily to metaphor, for he could not "see" many things. The indulged youngest son of a large family, a military man, a slaveholder, and before the war a rich man even by planter-class standards, he acquired the habit of telling other people what to do. Domesticity meant little to him, and he believed that a man's duty to his country was just as important as duty to the family. Yet he had a devastating charm, and some of his letters, including those to his wife, have a surpassing sweetness. Many of his contemporaries responded to that ineffable quality. During the Civil War a white man remarked on his "indescribable charm" which "leads you captive and holds you so." Mrs. Davis was captive, and captivated, until his death in 1889.[4]

Because she was married to Jefferson Davis, Varina was linked forever to the Confederacy, and she had to go along with the public role thrust upon her. Elizabeth Blair Lee, the sister of a member of Abraham Lincoln's cabinet and the wife of a U.S. naval officer, said in 1861 that Varina was "one of the victims of this war," which was not quite on the mark. Mrs. Davis occupied the middle of the political spectrum of her time, for she was pro-Union, pro-slavery, and in favor of states' rights. In Richmond, she found herself held up as an exemplar of values about which she was herself ambivalent. She tried intermittently to do what was expected of her, but she never convinced people that her heart was in it, and her tenure as First Lady was for the most part a disaster. Her story sheds light on the debate on whether white women supported the Confederacy,[5] for she articulated the argument historians made later, that the South could not win the war, even as she demonstrated by her behavior the many divisions within the white population. We now know that there were Unionists in every Southern state and all social classes, as well as Southerners who went along reluctantly with the Confederacy, or changed their minds during the war, or gave up. If Varina Davis—a white woman who benefited personally from slavery, who was married to the Southern President, who believed in family duty—did not enthusiastically support the Confederacy, then perhaps the whole project was doomed from the start.[6]

As for her counterpart in Washington, Varina Davis made no comment in writing about Mary Todd Lincoln, and Lincoln said nothing in writing about her. Although the two women never met, their lives nearly intersected several times. In the winter of 1847–48, when Lincoln lived in Washington, Davis happened to be absent from the capital, and in the winter of 1860–61, they employed the same seamstress, Elizabeth Keckley, and they had a friend in common, Elizabeth Blair Lee. Mary Lincoln's half-sister Martha Todd White visited the Confederate White House in 1864, when the Davises received her politely. After the war's end, Mrs. Lincoln visited the Davis residence in the Southern capital with Keckley, and in the 1890s U. S. Grant's widow Julia became friends with the widow Davis. But if either First Lady asked Keckley, Lee, White, or Grant about the other, there is no record of it.[7]

Their peers sometimes designated one or the other as the superior "lady," but Davis and Lincoln actually hailed from similar backgrounds. Both came from town-dwelling families that owned slaves, the Howells in Natchez and the Todds in Lexington, and both were well educated by the standards of the time. The term *First Lady,* which was coined to describe Dolley Madison upon her death in 1849, came into widespread usage in the 1850s, and it was used to describe both Davis and Lincoln. When their husbands became heads of state, both women received a lukewarm welcome from elites in the respective capitals, and their peers criticized their clothes, their manners, and their so-called western origins. Just as Harriet Beecher Stowe called Mrs. Lincoln "fat, & frank," Confederates pondered Mrs. Davis's girth and her candor. Both women had kinfolk in the other army, and both found their patriotism questioned. The war made both of them famous, and after 1865 they remained controversial. No one accused Davis of being insane, as Lincoln was accused of being, but white

Southerners attacked her fiercely when she moved to the North in 1890.[8]

The two women differed, however, on several important points. Varina Davis was more resilient than Mary Lincoln, and she had a talent for friendship that Lincoln lacked. She lived longer, dying when she was eighty; Lincoln died at age sixty-four. Davis's life is also better documented. Each woman wrote about six hundred letters, but Davis drafted an autobiographical sketch and published a memoir of her husband and a number of articles, none of which Lincoln did. Moreover, Davis lived in the national capital for most of the fifteen years before the secession crisis, and she was deeply ambivalent about her husband's rise to the post of Confederate President, while Mary Lincoln, who had been languishing in Illinois, was thrilled by her husband's election to the White House. Varina Davis did not fully support her husband's cause and was a wavering Confederate patriot, while Mary Lincoln firmly believed in her husband's cause and was a staunch Unionist.

After 1865, the war was text and subtext for the rest of Varina Davis's life. Because her husband served two years in prison and was unemployed most of the time until his death in 1889, she was repeatedly thrust into situations where she had to depart from traditional gender roles. She endured years of turmoil, scandal, and financial trouble, and she adapted, pushed along by circumstance, not ideology, and even though she was interested in reforms such as woman suffrage and temperance, she did not openly support either cause. Her husband sometimes treated her so badly that he seemed to be taking long slow revenge for her lack of Confederate patriotism, and he fell in love with another woman whose political views more closely resembled his own. Much of Varina Davis's travail was covered in the national press, yet her fame was a double-edged sword, for even though she lost her privacy, she and her husband acquired a retinue of people who helped them out, and her celebrity allowed her to begin a new life in New York as a widow. There she became a pivotal figure in the reconciliation between North and South, and the qualities that made her ill-suited to be the Confederate First Lady made her well-suited for this role. In her old age she reasserted her nationalism and took an oath of allegiance to urban life. Her widowhood suggests that there is something called the "self," a vital, autonomous core that endured throughout her life. She lived in a state of friction with her times, but she was never completely sanded down.[9]

Because this book is the first biography of Varina Davis by a professional scholar, it contains a great deal of material that has never before appeared in print. Two recent biographies of Jefferson Davis, both of them fine books, focus naturally on his experience, and because her life has been obscured for so long, I have quoted liberally from some hitherto-neglected sources. Regarding the use of language, I call Varina Davis the "First Lady" because that is what contemporaries in both regions called her, and I refer to the military conflict as the "Civil War" because that too was common usage. I have tried to be fair to Jefferson Davis, who is easy to dislike, and to Varina Davis, who is the product of another time and place. They were human beings, not icons, and their story looks different from her perspective.[10]

1

HALF BREED

MRS. JEFFERSON DAVIS HAD JUST RETURNED, much refreshed, from her daily drive through Central Park. The shimmering contrast of colors, figures, shapes, and sounds in *fin de siècle* New York lifted her spirits, as always. She took special pleasure in the lawns studded with white and gold blossoms, the swan boats gliding across the lake, the smartly dressed people darting by on bicycles, and the laughter of children at play, which sounded, she said, like the plucking of a harp. This was Decoration Day, and the park was covered with maypoles, wreaths, ribbons, and American flags. She had never seen the park looking so beautiful, she told a granddaughter. Even as she exulted in the scene, she was herself part of the urban tableau, for passersby often recognized the former Confederate First Lady. She had been a public figure for more than forty years, but savvy New Yorkers, accustomed to seeing Mrs. George Custer and Mrs. Ulysses Grant on the streets, did not bother her. So Davis's buggy passed through the streets to the Hotel Gerard on West Forty-fourth Street, where she heaved her bulky frame out of the carriage, hobbled with a cane into the lobby, and took the elevator to her apartment. She liked to gaze out the window at the human pageant on the streets below, but one day in the mid-1890s she sat down at her desk and spread out some paper before her. She had already published a memoir of her husband, but people had been urging her for years to write her own story.[1]

Varina Howell Davis moved to the metropolis after her husband died, arriving, in the last irony in a life bursting with them, in the Northeast where her ancestors had flourished a century before. Tall and slim as a girl, she had grown into a voluptuous woman and had gained weight as she aged until she had become, to put it plainly, fat. Always dressed in black, she favored the conservative fashions of an earlier age, floor-length fitted dresses with long sleeves, silk shawls, and a black veil over her white hair, which she wore in a chignon. She had ordinary features, an olive complexion, an infectious laugh, and tiny hands. Many people thought the old lady was striking. Her large dark eyes looked back at the world with much sadness, some wisdom, and considerable reserves of stamina.[2]

Her suite at the Gerard Hotel was comfortable, reflecting her love of beautiful objects. Pillows covered the sofas, quilts were draped over the chairs, thick rugs lined the floor, and Tiffany vases and a Dresden tea service adorned the tables. She had a piano, in tune, and a sewing machine, in working order. The apartment was filled with the souvenirs she had managed to keep through years of wandering— scrapbooks, photographs, calling cards, and paperweights—with yet more mementos stored in her trunks, and the bookcases contained titles in history, poetry, fiction, and biography. Having run out of storage space, she had taken to tying bundles of letters together with ribbons in a sort of primitive filing system. The range of her correspondence, including dozens of friends and hundreds of acquaintances, can be glimpsed in the names on her letters: Mary Boykin Chesnut and Frances Willard, Jubal Early and Francis Preston Blair.[3]

In her Manhattan aerie, surrounded by relics, she started her autobiography, or, as she termed it, a "sketch" of her "self." She began with her birth on a Louisiana plantation, rendered a paean to her grandparents, skipped her parents, and then described her student days in Philadelphia. After listing the offices held by Jefferson Davis— congressman, cabinet member, senator—she recalled that she had known two Presidents, Franklin Pierce and James Buchanan, as personal friends. As her husband accumulated political honors, she was absorbed with running a household and raising children. When the

Civil War erupted, she went to Richmond with a "very heavy heart," believing that the South could not win the war, and she feared she might never see her Northern relatives and friends again. The years after 1865, a period when the family wandered from Montreal to London to Paris and back to the States and two of her sons died, she summarized with a sentence fragment: "narrowing circle of boys." She concluded after a few pages with the observation that she had "tried to bear many trials" as best she could, and put her pen aside. A quick writer who wrote easily on a host of subjects, she would never finish this project.[4]

Very few women in Varina Davis's generation published autobiographies, since men and women alike thought it improper for a woman to write a book about herself, and as of the 1890s no President's wife had published a personal memoir. Among Davis's contemporaries, Julia Dent Grant composed an autobiography, but it was published long after she died. Davis was not only a woman and the widow of one of the country's most controversial politicians, she had to grapple with some especially acute dilemmas that grew out of her divided regional identity. She had relatives in both the North and the South, and in her old age she called herself a "half breed," Yankee on one side and Confederate on the other. A few miles away across the Hudson River, her father's father had been the governor of New Jersey and mixed with the most accomplished men of his time. Both Varina Davis and her husband hailed from large tumultuous clans, but her family was more distinguished than his and had been for several generations.[5]

THE HOWELLS, impulsive, hard-driving Welshmen, left their native country in the early eighteenth century and settled in Delaware, where Varina's grandfather Richard, one of many children of Ebenezer and Mary Bond Howell, was born in 1754. The family then moved to Shiloh, New Jersey, and purchased sizable tracts of land; Ebenezer Howell also owned a few slaves. He practiced law, and after Richard came of age, the son too studied law.[6] Both became outspoken supporters of the Patriot movement. In the War for Independence,

Richard embarked on what proved to be a brilliant military career. "Hearty" even in the thick of danger, he was dedicated to the cause and had a strong desire to bring honor to his family. He fought at Brandywine, Germantown, and Monmouth, endured the winter at Valley Forge, and developed a close friendship with George Washington. By the war's end Howell had attained the position of major. His relatives were just as patriotic: one of his brothers died in the service, and his cousin George Read of Delaware signed the Declaration of Independence.[7]

After the war Richard Howell entered politics, where his achievements were stellar. He joined the Federalist Party and in 1793 was elected to the first of four terms as governor. He was quite popular for most of his tenure, and the citizens of Monmouth County named the town of Howell in his honor. The governor dominated his party by force of his personality and by dint of his friendship with George Washington. After the Whiskey Rebellion took shape in Pennsylvania in 1794, Howell led New Jersey troops against the so-called insurrection alongside his old chief. In Howell's last year in office, the Jeffersonians charged him with mishandling state funds, and the investigation was incomplete when he passed away in 1802 after leaving his post. During his governorship, there was little controversy about woman suffrage, even though New Jersey was the only state that granted women the right to vote. Enfranchised in 1776, female property-owners lost the vote in 1807 in the wake of an election dispute, but in the interim Howell approved two procedural bills that confirmed female suffrage; whether any of his female relatives voted is unknown.[8]

Richard Howell's personality was just as memorable as his career. Even though he married a Quaker and was buried in a Quaker cemetery, he wore the beliefs of the Society of Friends lightly. A man of convivial, sometimes mercurial temperament, he partook of the flowing bowl and before he married was known to enjoy female companionship. He was also unpretentious, and while he was governor liked to pitch quoits in an alley near his office. Howell had some musical talent, and one of his works, "Jersey Blue," became a popular melody in the state.[9] His wife, Keziah Burr, the daughter of a well-to-do landowner, was literate, when many women were not, and Varina described her as a person of "education and refinement." The Howells had eight offspring, and William Burr Howell, Varina's father, was born in 1795. William acquired a good education, judging by his fluent letters. He left home to join the navy, and he matured into a tall blond with a taste for adventure. Most of his brothers stayed in New Jersey and Pennsylvania, where they prospered in banking, the law, and agriculture. His sisters married men from prominent families, Sarah a doctor in Pittsburgh and Beulah a merchant in Philadelphia who moved to what is now northern Germany.[10]

The legacy for Varina Howell from these ancestors was a significant one. She knew a lot about the New Jersey Howells, much of the information garnered from her female kinfolk, and she carried on a lifelong correspondence with her Yankee cousins. She was proud of her illustrious grandfather, tending to overlook the sour end of his career, and she was just as proud of her other kinfolk in the North. Her parents had eleven surviving siblings between them, and Varina had thirty-four first cousins, most of whom lived north of the Mason-Dixon line. She described herself as having a lot of "family feeling" and once declared that a large family is a treasure more valuable than any fortune. She believed that kinfolk should assist each other, and in middle age she observed that families should "hang together" for another reason, so they can make an impression on others. The idea that power derived from the family and that individuals had to present a public self to others came not just from her marriage but also from her family of origin.[11]

In his service in the War of 1812, her father, William Howell, seemed to be well on his way to adding to the family's distinction. In the Great Lakes campaign, where he was a second lieutenant, he was commended for bravery. After the war, William traveled down the Mississippi and decided to live in Natchez. Settled almost a century before, the town had passed from the French to the Spanish to the United States by 1798, when the county was named for President John Adams. Other settlers arrived via the river or overland by the

Natchez Trace,[12] and by the early nineteenth century, cotton had become the foundation of the economy. The Natchez district contained extremely rich soil, and the demand for the crop from English cotton mills proved to be inexhaustible. As the plantation economy took off, the number of slaves skyrocketed from a few hundred in the 1790s to fourteen thousand in Adams County in 1840. Some of the local planters, deemed the "nabobs," soon ranked among the richest men in the United States.[13]

Natchez was firmly a part of transatlantic culture, however, and had been since its colonial origins. Foreigners made up nearly half of the town's residents in the 1810s, and by 1850 they still constituted a third of the population. Furthermore, the town contained a mix of ethnic Catholics and Jews, and it attracted literary talent from abroad, such as John J. Audubon, who taught school there in the 1820s. The place also had a raffish frontier quality with the ambiance of a man's town. From the start of the nineteenth century into the 1840s, men constituted the majority of its white population. Members of the gentry carried weapons and spent much of their time drinking, boasting, and fighting, and fights there were aplenty, as misunderstandings easily escalated into duels.[14]

When William Howell arrived in 1815, Natchez was a thriving settlement of some two thousand people, with most of the businesses clustered around the courthouse and the villas and gardens of the nabobs on the outskirts of town. Howell found a position as a clerk at a mercantile firm and struck up a friendship with Joseph E. Davis, a lawyer from Kentucky who also owned land on the Mississippi Delta. Davis, who had a brother named Jefferson, did well at his law practice, and the two friends considered purchasing some land together in the low country, but Howell decided against it because the place was unhealthy. Joseph Davis would grow rich in a few years even as Howell's fortunes would peak and irrevocably decline. But all that lay in the future. In the late 1810s, when prospects seemed bright, Davis introduced Howell to the woman he would marry, Margaret Kempe.[15]

Jefferson Davis once characterized the Kempes as "wild people," or, as another relative described them, passionate people who liked laughter, good fellowship, and creature comforts. Margaret Kempe's father, James, was a Protestant Irishman from one of the northern counties (probably Donegal), and his family included barristers and landowners. Despite the legend that he attended Trinity College, Dublin, the university records are innocent of his name, and the story that he befriended the nationalist Robert Emmett is probably untrue, because he emigrated to Virginia before 1800. He served in the Patriot army as a teenager, and by the 1790s he moved to Prince William County, Virginia, where he worked as a merchant and edited a newspaper sympathetic to the Jeffersonians. Kempe had quite a presence, and his portrait shows a handsome, knowing face. He fell in love with Margaret Graham, the illegitimate daughter of George Graham and Susanna McAllister.[16]

George Graham, another wandering Celt, had done well for himself in the new country. The son of a titled Scottish family, he studied medicine at the Universities of Glasgow and Edinburgh, and in the 1760s left for America, where he supported the Patriot movement in his new home, Prince William County. At the dawn of the new century he owned about a dozen slaves and an estate he styled Graham Park. Nothing is known about his relationship with McAllister other than that they had at least one child and never married.[17] Said to be a beauty, their daughter Margaret Graham had a sharp wit and a dislike for affectation, which may have appealed to a self-made man like James Kempe. They married in 1801, and their daughter Margaret Kempe, one of six children, was born in 1806. In 1809, after he killed one of his in-laws in a duel over politics, James Kempe moved his family to Natchez, perhaps because of the fabled richness of the soil. The town remained his home until his death a decade later.[18]

Kempe soon rebounded from his scandalous exit from Virginia. Outside of Natchez he constructed a fine house he named Kempeton, and he purchased a plantation, Marengo, in Concordia Parish across the river in Louisiana. The land was extremely productive, and the parish would become one of the richest in the state. Kempe enjoyed the trappings of wealth: he often entertained at his house, where he played the flute for guests, and he bought a pleasure carriage. Both Mr. and Mrs. Kempe emerged as community leaders. He was instrumental in driving gamblers out of the town slum, Natchez-Under-the-Hill, and she helped found the local orphan asylum. As Varina Davis liked to recall, James Kempe "held large sway" in Natchez.[19] When another contest with Great Britain broke out in 1812, Kempe served in the Battle of New Orleans under the command of General Andrew Jackson. After the war, Kempe continued to prosper. His daughters Jane and Frances, who attended a private school in New Orleans, were strong-willed young women, comely and fond of fashion. In 1818, the year Mrs. Kempe died, Jane wed the merchant Francis Girault, scion of a renowned local family. Five years later Frances married Sturges Sprague, a lawyer from the North. Unlike her sisters, Frances protected her dowry with a marriage contract, which roughly resembled the modern prenuptial agreement. Margaret was milder by temperament than her older sisters, but she remained close to them both all of her life.[20]

When James Kempe died in 1819, Margaret's share of the estate—some sixty slaves and more than two thousand acres of land—made her a wealthy young woman. She had what William Howell called a "cheerful animated laugh," and she was tall and stately with dark eyes. The couple fell in love and married in 1823 at Trinity Episcopal Church in Natchez, with Joseph Davis attending as best man. The newlyweds then moved to Kempeton. When their first child was born there in 1824, they named him Joseph after Davis, and two years afterward, when a daughter was born at Marengo plantation, they named her Varina for one of Margaret's friends. The baby had the olive complexion of her Welsh ancestors, and the name Varina was supposedly Irish in origin. With its continental ring, it perfectly suited this time and place.[21]

⚜

IN THE EARLY 1830s, after Kempeton was destroyed by fire, the Howells moved to a new home in Natchez, the Briars, named for the thick undergrowth nearby. The house, located on about fifty acres of land, was built in the Federal style of the early nineteenth century, with a long veranda, Doric columns, and a roomy interior with high ceilings and a wide hall. Although the Howell family resided at the Briars until 1850, William Howell rented the place the entire time. Why he never bought it, even when he was making a good living, is unclear.[22] In the 1830s he formed a merchandising partnership with his brother-in-law Sturges Sprague, and from their office on Commerce Street they began speculating in property all over the Mississippi Valley. They opened an auction house in Natchez, did estate sales, and sold goods on consignment. Even though he was five years younger than Howell, Sprague seems to have been the leading partner, possibly because he was a lawyer, and he bought part of Marengo plantation and a comfortable mansion in Natchez.[23]

The other partner in Sprague and Howell also did well. William bought a fancy carriage and owned about a half-dozen house slaves. Though Howell was a New Jersey native, he accepted the institution of human bondage with no apparent qualms and was happy to profit from it. He developed some expensive habits—he liked to play cards, and he liked to hunt—and he needed a good income to support his numerous children.[24] Of the eleven children born to Margaret and William, seven lived to adulthood. Mrs. Howell found motherhood deeply fulfilling, calling the children her "treasures." Most of the children grew to be tall and lanky, with extroverted personalities. The Howell children studied with their cousins, and sometimes the large clamorous tribe traveled en masse to visit their relatives across the river in Louisiana. Varina developed especially close ties to her cousin Margaret, or "Missy," Sprague, two years her senior, who would one day name a daughter after her. Mrs. Howell took in two girls from a neighboring family, Anna and Louisa McCants, in the 1840s after their mother died, a true act of charity, for by that time the Howell fortunes had capsized.[25]

Margaret Howell was not entirely consumed by her domestic duties, for she loved books, and she communicated to her eldest daughter a lasting pleasure in the written word. William Howell was known to read a book, and he counted Joseph H. Ingraham, a local writer, among his acquaintances, but it was her mother whom Varina described as "eloquent," and her adult letters to Mrs. Howell are filled with literary references from Samuel Taylor Coleridge to Charles Dickens. When Varina was a girl, books provided the key to another realm. The Howell children read Sir Walter Scott's novels *The Talisman* and *The Betrothed,* and Guilhem de Castro's play *El Cid,* and acted out scenes on a makeshift little stage for the household. Mrs. Howell knew the *Odyssey* well, which was unusual among women of her generation, and read aloud to her children from such works as Dickens's novel of 1839, *The Life and Adventures of Nicholas Nickelby.* Books also taught moral lessons, such as Hannah More's *Hints towards Forming the Character of a Young Princess,* which Varina remembered for its emphasis on the overriding importance of duty, and John Bunyan's *Pilgrim's Progress,* which she read throughout her childhood. From that classic Puritan tale of spiritual struggle, Varina seems to have absorbed the concept that life is full of tests with many a "hill difficulty," a phrase she quoted all her life. Mrs. Howell did not neglect the other arts, for the children studied piano and learned French. When Varina's brother Joseph enrolled at an academy in Princeton, New Jersey, the siblings exchanged letters in the language.[26]

One of the most important constituents of this household, and one of the most important influences in Varina's life, was George Winchester of Salem, Massachusetts. Born in 1794, he graduated from Yale University and settled in Natchez, where he became an attorney, then a judge, and a well-known political figure. Although he lost races for governor in 1829 and for the U.S. Senate in 1846, Winchester ran successfully for the Mississippi legislature and was a stalwart of the Whig Party. He was Sturges Sprague's law partner and did legal work for the firm of Sprague and Howell, and he became closely involved in the family's finances. In the 1830s Winchester began living at the Briars with the Howells, and the children called him "Uncle." He was a touch eccentric, but his erudition and dedication to his profession inspired great loyalty among his friends.[27]

George Winchester tutored the young Varina, probably as a form of payment for lodging at the Briars, and she was his only pupil from the time she was a young girl until she married, an unusual arrangement in the Old South, where boys, not girls, typically had individual tutors and children rarely worked so intensively for so long with a single instructor. Moreover, Winchester was a learned man and a hard teacher. Varina studied languages, including Latin, and the classics of Anglo-Irish literature. Works by Laurence Sterne, Samuel Johnson, and Richard Sheridan made a deep impression on her, and her agile prose owed something to a childhood immersion in these authors. Winchester's political influence was also considerable, awakening in her an early interest in public affairs. He embraced the Whig outlook on the world—wise rule by elites, preservation of the social structure, and use of the government to address social problems—and he read the Whig newspaper, the *National Intelligencer*. The teenage Varina developed "Whig proclivities" and wore an anti-Democrat cameo on her collar. Winchester was also a devout Episcopalian, and Varina thought his most important lesson was his belief in doing what was right. In adulthood, she described him as one of her best friends, but he more closely resembled a surrogate father. At age ten, she sent her love in a letter to all of her relatives, "particularly Mr. Winchester," and as an adult she called him "Great Heart."[28]

Her education continued with a brief term in 1836 at a girls' academy in Philadelphia, which she attended for several months while her parents visited relatives in the area. Her father had some happy memories of his Yankee boyhood that he liked to share with his children, and the school, run by Deborah Grelaud, was one of the better-known female academies. Grelaud, a refugee from the French Revolution, had a high opinion of Miss Howell's abilities, praising her as "very smart & capable." Small numbers of pupils attended the academy, in some years fewer than a dozen, and the students included Protestants, Catholics, and Jews from privileged families all over the eastern seaboard. Varina spent a single term at the school and returned a few years later.[29]

By this time the contours of Varina's personality had begun to emerge. She was a tomboy, and she liked to roam the grounds of the Briars with her brothers. She was also courageous. When Kempeton caught fire in the early 1830s, she ran into the burning house and carried two of her siblings out to safety, an exceptionally brave act for a little girl. Like all of the Howell children, she was "proud and sensitive," as her father remarked, and she had grown up in a household of personalities who expressed their emotions freely. She had many friends, and in 1839 she was crowned May Queen at a local dance. Most of the tyro monarchs included daughters of the richest families, but Miss Howell did not win because of her father's wealth, which even in the good times did not compare with those fortunes, nor did she win for her looks. She had liquid eyes and glossy hair, but her features were plain and her olive complexion and slender build did not conform to standards of beauty in the Old South, where a lily-white complexion and a plump figure were considered attractive. More likely she won for her generous nature and her sense of humor, for she had inherited her grandmother Kempe's wit.[30]

She was also deeply attached to her mild-mannered mother. All of their lives, Varina and Margaret Howell exchanged tranquil letters predicated on unconditional love. Their unique bond was probably intensified by living for some years in a household of men and boys. Varina had four surviving brothers—Joseph, two years her senior, William, eight years her junior, Becket, fourteen years younger, and Jefferson, a full twenty years her junior. Three sisters died as babies before Varina reached her teens, and until a surviving girl named Margaret was born in 1842, Varina and her mother had been the only white females in the household for sixteen years. Like many oldest daughters in large families, Varina was expected to help raise the little ones, including Jane, born two years after Margaret. As an adult, she said that mothers and daughters should be able to depend on each other, and she was an affectionate big sister, giving her siblings nicknames such as "Maggie bighead" and "Jinny sassbox," and she remembered their childhood antics for years. She could also be quite possessive. In the 1850s Varina became Margaret's legal guardian and later said she wanted to keep her sister close by, all to herself.[31]

BENEATH THE NOISY bustle of the Howell ménage, serious financial trouble loomed. Varina once commented that the Howells seemed to be cursed with bad luck and a "fatal want of system, and order." Her father's financial collapse in the 1830s might be explained by both bad luck and a certain lack of system. Inflation soared in the decade, based in part on President Andrew Jackson's monetary policies, and cotton prices rose too, creating what one Mississippian called a "bloated abundance." The bubble burst with the Panic of 1837. As the American banking system crashed in the spring of that year, Sprague and Howell went under along with thousands of businesses all over the country. The Natchez courts were soon clotted with bankruptcies. William Howell's personal debts mounted, and by October 1838 the sheriff sold the family's furniture at a public auction. Fortunately the principal buyer was Thomas Kempe, Mrs. Howell's brother, who returned the belongings to the family.[32]

But William Howell's downward spiral was not over. The Natchez chancery court announced that the firm of Sprague and Howell owed more than one hundred thousand dollars to banks, mercantile firms, and individual lenders, and Howell contracted yet more debt by borrowing against the firm's profits. After Sturges Sprague died en route to Texas, the firm was dissolved and most of its assets seized. Howell's personal property went on the block again, and Thomas Kempe purchased some land, a few slaves, and several buildings for him. The rest of Howell's merchandise then burned in a mysterious fire. William began digging into his wife's dowry to pay his debts, although he did not take advantage of the state's Married Woman's Property Act of 1839, designed to let married men shield their property from creditors by deeding it to their wives. When the cyclone had passed, Sprague's widow Frances survived with much of her property intact, thanks to the marriage contract she had signed in 1823, and Thomas Kempe went on to acquire great riches as a Louisiana planter as William Howell sank in a mire of debts. His brother-in-law's death seems to have hurt Howell, as did the fact that he had no profession to fall back on, and, it seems, he already had a reputation as a poor businessman. As he grimly acknowledged, when things went wrong he "*helped* them *along* a *little*." He tried one scheme after another to recoup his fortune, but by the mid-1840s he had to rely on loans from relatives to make ends meet.[33]

Her father's bankruptcy was one of the most painful moments in Varina Howell's life, and she was haunted forever after by the spectacle of a man going broke and taking his family down with him. Of more immediate concern, however, were the ways the bankruptcy affected her responsibilities at the Briars. As the slaves were sold off, Margaret Howell and her firstborn daughter had to do more of the housework themselves, so that Varina learned to cook and sew, as most planter daughters did not, and she became highly skilled at both. As the family continued to grow, her duties as mother's helper grew. Mrs. Howell gave birth to five surviving children between 1839 and 1846, even though the family had less and less money, and the horizons for the children began to shrink. Varina's brother Joseph did not attend college after he left the Princeton academy, and a few years later he began working as Jefferson Davis's overseer. The children's clothing grew shabbier and the holiday gifts more meager. Her father withdrew from the family, perhaps out of shame. The adult Varina remarked that William Howell did not like children, and in old age she stated that she had always been sure that mothers, not fathers, played the chief role in raising children.[34]

William Howell's bankruptcy had another salient consequence for his oldest daughter by making it impossible for her to conform to the role of the Southern "belle." This image has had such staying power in American culture that it is easy to forget its origins in the economic conditions of the 1830s. As the cotton market boomed and planters grew richer, the "belle," with her beauty, poise, and porcelain-white complexion, became the symbol of the family's status. According to stereotype, she had nothing to do but flirt with men, and when she married and became a "lady," she enjoyed a leisurely existence on the plantation, reading about the arts. Like all stereotypes, these images are misleading. For most girls, marriage had as much to do with family alliances as romantic love, and most plantation mistresses rarely enjoyed complete leisure, if only because they had large numbers of children, and many were too badly educated to appreciate the arts. But the images of the "belle" and the "lady" outlasted the 1830s because they represented the power of the planter elite. The prerequisite was wealth, and the Howells, who had never been full-fledged planters, were not rich as Varina entered her teenage years. Nor was she suited for the role of the "belle," being a town dweller and a merchant's daughter with a raft of kinfolk in the North. Yet few white girls could be indifferent to these images, which were held up as the norm of femininity for the generation before the Civil War. As another white woman recalled, "ladylike" was the universal term of praise.[35]

Yet more scandals lay ahead for the Howells, involving Varina's aunt Jane Kempe Girault, who went through an especially lurid divorce. After her first husband died, she owned a plantation in Louisiana and more than a hundred slaves, and she sent her daughter Anna to Emma Willard's academy in Troy, New York. As Jane's second marriage to a younger man, Charles Rowley, ended in 1840, Rowley killed a judge in a duel over the case, and Jane's brother Thomas Kempe distributed handbills in Natchez denouncing his former brother-in-law. The divorce prompted another wave of lawsuits over Rowley's financial conduct, who had evidently mismanaged his wife's money. Jane kept most of her fortune, but the Kempe siblings sued Rowley and one other, and the cases dragged on for years. The only saving grace for Margaret and William Howell was that they no longer had enough property to be drawn into fights with her wealthy kinfolk. Varina may not have known about her grandmother Kempe's illegitimate birth in Virginia, but she knew about her aunt Jane's debacle in Louisiana, and even though she loved her aunt, it left her with a permanent, lifelong horror of scandal.[36]

Miss Howell escaped these embarrassments with another term at Madame Grelaud's academy in Philadelphia in the early 1840s. Because William Howell could not afford the tuition, her godfather George Guion or one of her uncles may have paid it for him. This second term seems to have made a deeper impression on Varina, undoubtedly because she was old enough to appreciate fully the city's splendors. Philadelphia was a true metropolis, a mecca for writers and artists, and the Declaration of Independence, with her cousin George Read's signature on it, was on display at the statehouse. The citizens enjoyed a rich menu of lectures, plays, concerts, and operas, much of it available a few blocks from Grelaud's school downtown. The city was also home to prominent abolitionists and woman's rights activists, but Deborah Grelaud was quite conservative politically, and Varina never mentioned the reformers at her doorstep. She had warm memories of the "sweetest ways" of her Philadelphia kinfolk, especially the women, and it was probably during this school term that she received an heirloom, a recipe book from a great-grandmother on the Howell side. Through the Northern branch of the Howells, she met the Reads, Stocktons, Rushes, and other distinguished persons who had married into the family.[37]

Varina's education diverged from the usual pattern among white Southern girls in another respect: she did not undergo a conversion experience. The Howells worshipped at the Episcopal church, and as was true for many couples Mrs. Howell was more religious than her husband. She read the Bible to the children every morning, and she seemed to be motivated by a profound religious belief. But Varina did not make the emotional commitment to God that many teenagers made, even though it was a coming-of-age ritual among Protestant girls in the Old South and expected of them, as it was not expected of boys. She may have abstained because such conversions were less prevalent among Episcopalians. For whatever reason, she remained secular-minded until the trials of adulthood began to turn her thoughts toward her faith.[38]

WHEN SHE RETURNED home after her second term with Madame Grelaud, Varina was seventeen and old enough to think about marriage, since white women married young in the South, on average at the age of twenty, and many wed at even younger ages in the Mississippi Valley. Miss Howell understandably had some rather contradictory attitudes on gender, race, region, and riches, arising from both the society she lived in and the circumstances of her own family. Gender would remain the central dilemma. She had absorbed the principal idea that the sexes were profoundly different and, as she said in her old age, "incongruous," and a girl growing up in the Howell family might draw those conclusions. From her mother she learned that the family was a woman's greatest responsibility, and Margaret Howell

*Varina Howell, 1840s. The merchant's daughter in Natchez.
(National Portrait Gallery, Smithsonian Institution;
gift of Varina Webb Stewart)*

was an exemplary wife, sister, and mother, never faltering in her loyalty to her feckless husband or the melodramatic Kempes. After Varina married, Mrs. Howell advised her to control her emotions and do her duty to God and her husband, as she herself had learned to do.[39]

Gender relations in the Old South were in fact built upon the assumption that the sexes had different natures and therefore had to play distinct roles in the family. These ideas were written into the law and permeated every aspect of social custom. White women in the region were expected to marry young, have many children, and devote themselves exclusively to the family. They had the nation's highest fertility rates, as well as the highest rates of death in childbirth. Women did not attend universities or enter the professions, and in Mississippi, unlike New Jersey, they had never voted and were not expected to have the faintest interest in public life. Respectable women were not even supposed to travel from home without a male escort. In return for such self-denial, women were supposed to receive security; they gave up autonomy in exchange for protection. As an adult, Varina Davis believed that men, especially kinfolk, were obligated to protect women, and she, like most women, believed marriage was a lifetime commitment. The law reflected that belief, for divorce was very difficult to obtain in Southern courts, and it had such a stigma that most women would rather endure the most acute unhappiness than get a divorce.[40]

Within Varina Howell's immediate family, however, gender relations did not conform to received wisdom. In the wake of his bankruptcy, William Howell still could not give his full attention to his responsibilities as a provider. He bet twenty-five dollars on a shooting match even though he was bankrupt and his wife was pregnant with their sixth child. As an adult Varina believed that her father's intentions were good, but her youthful letters brim with longing to break through his indifference. When she was nineteen years old, she wrote that she wanted to help him somehow, if only to fan him while he rested, but added, "I know you cannot need me." Only once did she quote an aphorism by her father, his observation that familiarity breeds contempt.[41]

So the teenage Miss Howell was left to ponder a series of bewildering questions: If a man did not honor the sacred vows of marriage, if he neglected his wife, or failed to provide for her, what should she do? Should she defy social convention as her aunt Jane Kempe did, even at the cost of scandal, or should she submit, endure, and hope for the best, as her mother did? And how was it that her divorced aunt remained a rich woman, while Mrs. Howell lived at the edge of poverty, dependent on the kindness of her relations? How should a woman strike a balance between devotion to others and her duty to herself? What, if anything, did a woman owe herself, in addition to what she owed family and household? These questions lingered as she approached adulthood, for she identified strongly with women but wanted the security that men, and only certain men, could deliver.

A white girl growing up in Natchez would be confronted with even more bewildering ideas about marriage and sexuality. Despite the dogma that sexual relations between white masters and slave women was anathema, that it never happened and never should happen, of course it did happen, almost always because white men forced sex on black women. Mulattos constituted at least 10 percent of the slave population, and the phenomenon of interracial sex dated back to the beginnings of slavery in the New World and occurred in every slave society in the Americas. While there is no evidence that Varina's father or grandfather sired children with slave women, Natchez contained many people of mixed race. A few white men in Adams County defied convention and freed their mulatto offspring in their wills, but that was rare. White men who abided by custom and kept silent about their slave children found themselves accepted into respectable society.[42]

By contrast, the strictest rules of conduct governed white women. In the world Varina inhabited, girls were closely chaperoned during courtship, and they were expected to marry as virgins; chastity was essential for women before marriage, and fidelity within it was required. If a married woman was known to commit adultery with any man, white or black, her reputation would be destroyed. Living with such an extreme version of the double standard that prevailed in the rest of the country could be very difficult for white women. William Wells Brown, an ex-slave, wrote that miscegenation made planters' wives miserable, and in the privacy of their diaries a few white women denounced it. Mary Boykin Chesnut, a South Carolinian who would become one of Varina's friends in the 1860s, raged that slavery was a *"monstrous"* system and that white men who sired mulatto children with slaves were no better than tyrants. But most white women dealt with this hypocrisy by looking the other way, pretending not to know, or resigning themselves to it. For most people, it was easier to keep quiet than to face the deceits, evasions, and self-deceptions that governed gender relations in the Old South.[43]

The young Varina Howell learned another simple yet stark lesson about race, that whites exercised power over blacks. Slaveowning was embedded in American history from colonial times and in part of her own family's history, going back three generations among the Howells. In the early nineteenth century, New Jersey had more slaves than any Northern state, and it adopted a gradual emancipation law only in 1804. Her great-grandfather Ebenezer Howell freed a slave in his will in 1785, a common gesture in the altruistic post-Revolutionary years, but William Howell's New Jersey relatives continued to own bondsmen well into the nineteenth century. Her maternal ancestors on the Kempe side owned bondsmen in Virginia, where African American slavery had its start in North America two hundred years before Varina was born. Other whites in her circle, such as her Yankee tutor George Winchester and her teacher Madame Grelaud, owned slaves. Many whites in Philadelphia abhorred the anti-slavery movement, so much so that a mob burned down a building in 1838 when it became known that activists were meeting inside. By that time, almost all whites nationwide had retreated from the ideals of racial equality that the most idealistic thinkers articulated after the Revolution.[44]

During her girlhood, Varina Howell nevertheless experienced the

paradoxical intimacy with black people that so often marked race relations in the antebellum South. From the time she was a child, she
had contact with slaves, including an unnamed black nurse in the
Briars household, and as a young wife she sometimes sent greetings
to the few house slaves still working for the Howells. The basic features of race relations were nonetheless very clear. Slave auctions
took place in Natchez on a daily basis, and the state's Black Code,
which restricted the latitude of the few free blacks in Mississippi,
only grew tougher over the decades. When rumors of slave uprisings
swept the Mississippi Valley in the 1830s, whites retaliated swiftly,
and in 1841, when Varina was fifteen years old, a self-appointed vigi-
lance committee drove some free black residents out of Natchez.
Throughout her youth, white supremacy was deeply engrained in
American culture, and only the most high-minded white people in
any region questioned the assumptions behind slavery. None of the
adults in Varina's circle were among those noble souls. Dissenting
voices came from the printed page, for both Charles Dickens and
Hannah More supported the abolitionist movement, but Varina never
referred to their views on slavery. When she was growing up, she evidently did not question the racial values of her time.[45]

She sensed some puzzling contradictions on regional identity, however, which came to the fore in national life when she was a girl. In
the 1830s and 1840s, as Varina was coming to know and love her
Yankee kinfolk, Northerners began to criticize slavery in particular and Southern society generally as undemocratic and backward.
White Southerners counterattacked, describing the North as chaotic
and unstable. After the Nullification Crisis some people in both regions started to perceive those in the other as alien and increasingly
threatening. Because Varina Howell grew up in a household where
the adults read the newspapers, and her tutor George Winchester
had been elected to public office, she was probably more aware than
most teenagers of these political debates. As a native of the South
with a Yankee father and many Yankee relatives, including the most
eminent person in her lineage, her grandfather Howell, she was also
probably more reluctant than most teenagers to take sides.[46]

Finally, the young Varina Howell had learned some harsh truths about the transient nature of riches. When her father's business failed in 1838 she was twelve, old enough to remember prosperity, as her parents, themselves the children of wealthy people, fell far in a town of the very rich. She grew up at the fringes of the planter gentry, not as a member of it. By the time she was in her teens, she knew that fortune was capricious. More responsible than most teenagers, she was, it would turn out, the most competent of the Howell children, and acutely aware of what her father's collapse meant for the family's future. She badly wanted to compensate somehow for everything they had lost. In 1845 she told her mother that she wanted her siblings to have "*plenty* of everything." But she had learned another lesson from his failure, that catastrophes could be survived.[47]

As for her marriage prospects, there were no budding romances with the young swains of Natchez. She had some strikes against her, being highly intelligent with a fine education, a destitute father, and some well-publicized scandals in her family. Nor did she think of herself as pretty. In December 1843, Varina Howell received an invitation from her father's friend Joseph Davis, who lived some seventy miles north of town at the Hurricane plantation in Warren County. The year before, Davis had asked Margaret Howell to allow her daughter to visit, but the invitation had been declined because Varina was completing her studies in English and Latin. This time her parents said yes, so George Winchester accompanied Miss Howell on the steamboat *Magnolia* upriver the week before Christmas in 1843. Years later she remembered the boat, with its flowery interior and delicious food, as a floating palace of "luxury," perhaps because it symbolized the escape from poverty that marriage to Jefferson Davis seemed to promise.[48]

THIS MR. DAVIS

 MISS HOWELL DISEMBARKED at Diamond Place plantation, about twelve miles from Joseph Davis's residence,
and the next day George Winchester returned to Natchez,
leaving Varina in the care of Joseph's daughter Florida Davis McCaleb.
The house was small with modest white pillars, but the plantation,
with land as flat as a pancake, was immensely fertile; thus the name.
The fields were at rest between cotton seasons, and the landscape was
bursting with life, raw, abundant, and menacing. Only a generation
removed from the wilderness, much of the place was still forested.
Hunters scared up huge flocks of geese from the woods, the marshes
of iridescent water were constantly in flux, and alligators swam in
the ditches. The family topography was just as complex. For miles
around, the land belonged to the Davises, or, more properly, to Joseph Davis. As Varina Howell would discover, this was his domain.[1]

The Davis clan, like the Howells, had traveled vast distances in
their quest for the good life, but their origins are as obscure as the
Howells' are crisply delineated. About his ancestors Jefferson Davis
observed that none of them had been hanged, and he was so uninter-
ested in genealogy that he sometimes confused his great-grandfather
Evan Davis, who emigrated from Wales to Philadelphia in the eighteenth century, with his grandfather of the same name. About his
grandfather, little is known, other than the fact he lived in Georgia,
but we know that Jefferson's father, Samuel, joined the Revolutionary

army. After the war, Samuel married Jane Cook, probably a South Carolinian, and they had ten surviving children. In the 1790s the Davises moved to Christian County, later renamed Todd County, in Kentucky. Samuel owned a few slaves, although he did manual labor himself, as did his sons and his wife. Here Jefferson was born in 1808 or 1809 (probably 1808, although he gave both years as his birthdate) and named for his father's hero, the Virginian in the White House. In about 1810 the family moved to what was then called the Southwest, Wilkinson County in the Mississippi Territory. Three of the Davis sons fought in the War of 1812, two of them serving under Varina Howell's grandfather James Kempe, and after the war the clan settled in the Mississippi Valley, where most of them farmed.[2]

Jefferson was singled out for special treatment, perhaps because he was the youngest son. Samuel Davis regretted his own limited education, and the family seems to have determined that Jefferson would have the best opportunities. Although some of his brothers did not attend college, Jefferson went to a Catholic boarding school in Kentucky and attended both Jefferson College in Mississippi and Transylvania University in Kentucky before he enrolled in West Point Military Academy. When he was traveling to Kentucky in 1816 to start boarding school, he stopped at the Hermitage, the Tennessee home of war hero Andrew Jackson. The visit made a lasting impression on Davis, and all of his life he venerated Jackson. Jefferson's oldest brother, Joseph, some twenty-four years his senior, guided Jefferson's education, even as he built the family fortune, first by his legal practice in Natchez and after 1827 with his plantation. Called the Hurricane after a memorable storm, the place grew to over five thousand acres; the stretch of land along the river became known as Davis Bend. In 1840 Joseph owned 226 slaves, whereas Samuel owned only 6 slaves when he died in 1824. The neighboring plantation, called Brierfield, was approximately nine hundred acres in size and would become Jefferson's place.[3]

But soldiering, not planting, was Jefferson's first occupation. He was just old enough to recall troops leaving to fight in the War of

1812, and Joseph, whom Jefferson described as standing to him "in loco parentis" after their father died, decreed that he would have a career in the military. So Jefferson went to West Point in 1824. His record was mediocre at best. Several times he was nearly expelled for student pranks and misadventures with alcohol, and he graduated twenty-third in a class of thirty-three, although he made some lasting friends. In 1829 he began serving on the rugged frontiers of the Old Northwest, where he hunted deserters, guarded Indians, and helped construct forts. He advanced to second lieutenant in 1833. When he was posted at Fort Crawford in the Michigan Territory (now in Wisconsin), Jefferson met the woman who became his first wife, Sarah Knox Taylor.[4]

Called "Knox" by her intimates and "Sarah" by everyone else, she was the daughter of Lieutenant Colonel Zachary Taylor, Davis's superior at Fort Crawford. Petite, pretty, in her late teens, she fell in love with Davis, and he with her, but Zachary Taylor opposed the marriage because he did not want his daughter to endure the long separations from her husband required of military couples. Then Taylor gradually became disenchanted with Davis himself. The two men argued over whether soldiers should wear full-dress uniform at a court-martial—after which Davis briefly considered challenging Taylor to a duel—and later Davis was charged with insubordination toward another officer. Davis was acquitted, but he was already thinking of becoming a planter, so he resigned from the military in the spring of 1835. He and Knox Taylor wed in June 1835 at the Kentucky residence of her aunt and uncle. The bride's parents consented, although they did not attend the ceremony, which must have embarrassed Jefferson because he denied it years afterward. The couple went to Mississippi to visit relatives, defying folk wisdom about the dangers of summertime travel, when fevers were thought to be abroad. They stopped at Locust Grove plantation in Louisiana to visit Jefferson's sister and brother-in-law, and there both newlyweds contracted malaria. Sarah Knox Davis expired in her husband's arms, singing in her delirium a song called "Fairy Bells." She was buried at Locust Grove, at age twenty-one. The Davises had been married less than three months.[5]

Nearly crushed with grief, Jefferson moved into a cottage at Brierfield and threw himself into working on the plantation. He labored alongside the slaves, sometimes chopping down trees himself, and in his spare time read books on government and history, which he discussed with his brother Joseph. This hermetic existence lasted for almost eight years. In the interim, his personality seems to have undergone a permanent transformation. His youthful recklessness evaporated, and he began to show the capacity for sustained concentration on a task that would characterize him for the rest of his life. Reserved, somewhat aloof, and apparently content to remain a widower, he might not have remarried without his older brother's intervention. Joseph stayed in touch with his Natchez friends, and when he invited Varina for a visit in December 1843, he probably had her in mind as a mate for his brother.[6]

❦

VARINA HOWELL met Jefferson Davis when he rode up to Diamond Place to hand-deliver the invitation to visit the Hurricane mansion. He was about six feet tall, with grey eyes, high cheekbones, and thick curly hair, and although his features may be a bit sharp for modern tastes, many women of his time thought him exceedingly handsome, much more so, they said, than portraits or photographs managed to convey. He had a melodic speaking voice, and he was always well dressed, yet he was intensely masculine by the standards of the day, an accomplished rider, hunter, and marksman. A man of honor as white Southerners understood the term, he was respected by other men, conscious of their opinion, and quick to defend his reputation, with perhaps the extra edge of touchiness characteristic of white men in the Old Southwest. Varina remembered him as the picture of autonomy and competence, "so free and strong" on horseback.[7]

The couple talked for some time, long enough for Miss Howell to make some astute observations before Davis rode to Vicksburg to attend a Democratic Party caucus. That evening she shared her thoughts with her mother by letter:

> To-day Uncle Joe sent, by his younger brother (did you know he had one?), an urgent invitation to me to go at once to 'The Hurricane.' I do not know whether this Mr. Jefferson Davis is young or old. He looks both at times; but I believe he is old, for from what I hear he is only two years younger than you are. He impresses me as a remarkable kind of man, but of uncertain temper, and has a way of taking for granted that everybody agrees with him when he expresses an opinion, which offends me; yet he is most agreeable and has a peculiarly sweet voice and a winning manner of asserting himself. The fact is, he is the kind of person I should expect to rescue one from a mad dog at any risk, but to insist upon a stoical indifference to the fright afterward. I do not think I shall ever like him as I do his brother Joe. Would you believe it, he is refined and cultivated, and yet he is a Democrat![8]

She misjudged Joseph, whom she would grow to dislike intensely, but she was right about Jefferson. He was indeed a remarkable man, and she would suffer from his temper and his iron will, just as she would always be attracted to his physical beauty, his charm, and his polished manners. He was the quintessential Southern gentleman, even though the teenage Whig found it hard to believe that such a man could be a Democrat. Davis's young-old quality must have appealed to her as well, for he could be both suitor and protector.

The next morning Varina proceeded to the Hurricane mansion, a brick house of three stories with a driveway lined with oaks. The interior was furnished with great luxury, containing a large dining room and an extensive library. The music room included a harp, when that was a rare instrument in a private home. The deep closets in the house, filled with all kinds of household goods, were open to everyone. The grounds included a separate building for Joseph's office, a garden, a carriage house, stables with some top-grade thoroughbreds, large herds of cattle, and a pack of hunting dogs. The Hurricane was renowned as a seat of hospitality, and Zachary Taylor, who visited in the 1840s, called it a little paradise. The scale and prosperity of the place awed William Howell's daughter.[9]

Joseph E. Davis, her host, was a small man in his fifties with bushy eyebrows and penetrating eyes, well mannered, well spoken, and possessed of an enormous ego. Varina described him as very intelligent and used to having his way, and a relative observed that Joseph did as he pleased and never deferred to anyone else. His racial attitudes were more progressive than those of many planters. Inspired by a chance meeting with the Scottish reformer Robert Owen in 1825, Davis created a jury system for slaves accused of wrongdoing, at which he presided as judge. He allowed a favorite slave named Ben Montgomery to become literate and run a mercantile business. His views on gender, however, were highly traditional, as was his marriage. In 1827, at age forty-three, he married Eliza Van Benthuysen of New Orleans, whose mother ran a boardinghouse. She was sixteen, black-eyed, and tractable; as she grew older she became more sickly and neurotic. The marriage was childless, but Joseph and Eliza hosted a cast of nieces, nephews, and relatives of unspecified origin called "cousin."[10]

Not that Varina Howell thought very much about this household's secrets, for she was falling madly in love with Jefferson Davis. They talked in the music room and took walks in the garden with what she called his "sweet voice" sounding in her ear, and she said later he was her first love and the only man she ever loved. As one of her relatives noted, she had a capacity for deep attachments. She fell in love in "an unreasoning way," Varina recalled, with all the fervor of a teenage girl. For his part, Davis seemed ready to fall in love again, and her high spirits and affectionate nature had a galvanizing effect on the brooding widower. Dispassionate observers would have noted that they were both better educated than most of their peers. Jefferson once described Varina as "gifted," and she was probably one of the few women he had met who could hold her own in conversation with him. He could have courted any one of a number of heiresses, but he fell in love with the daughter of a bankrupt merchant who had no dowry to bring to the marriage. In 1844 Joseph Davis explained his holdings to Varina, most likely during a visit to Natchez in the spring, when he said that Brierfield belonged to his brother. She was definitely in love, but with conflicting expectations of marriage, wanting both romantic fulfillment and economic security.[11]

The romance moved so quickly that the couple had agreed to marry by the time Varina went home in February 1844, but the engagement had a rocky start. She did not write for some days, probably because her mother had reservations about the match. The age difference was much greater than the five- or six-year gap typical among married couples in the Old South, and it was already clear that they did not think alike. Jefferson traveled throughout the state in 1844 giving speeches on behalf of the Democratic Party, and he served as an elector for presidential candidate James Polk, but Varina thought his political activities kept him on the road too much. She did not want to live at Brierfield or the Hurricane, preferring Natchez for their first home. Varina sometimes found it hard to confide in Jefferson, although he urged her to do so, even if, as he admitted, he was prone to "censuring" her sometimes. Yet George Winchester approved of the engagement, Margaret Howell's doubts subsided, and William Howell was apparently pleased with the match.[12]

On February 26, 1845, Varina and Jefferson were married by an Episcopal minister at the Briars as Varina's parents, siblings, and cousin Missy Sprague looked on; no one from the Davis family was there. Miss Howell was nineteen years old. When the newlyweds left for their honeymoon in New Orleans, they stopped at Locust Grove plantation in Louisiana, where Jefferson took Varina with him to visit the grave of his first wife, Knox Taylor Davis. This is not as unkind as it might appear, since husbands in the nineteenth-century made similar visits to the graves of their first wives. Calvin Stowe, for one, instructed Harriet Beecher Stowe to do the same and go by herself when he could not accompany her. Nevertheless, it must have stung the bride just a little. Varina was gracious about the first Mrs. Davis, whom she never met, calling her "refined, intelligent, sincere," but she was often confused with the first wife, and according to her great-granddaughter, she wearied of being compared to the "sainted Sarah."[13]

∿

THE DAVISES spent their honeymoon at the St. Charles, the premier hotel in New Orleans, and the indirect references in Varina's correspondence, which are themselves unusual for a woman of her generation, suggest that the honeymoon was a prelude to a satisfactory physical relationship that lasted much of the rest of their lives. After they set up housekeeping in Brierfield, Varina could hardly write a letter without her yearning husband tapping at the door, and she awoke in the morning thinking of his warm kisses on her lips. They read together, visited their neighbors, and took long rides down the country roads, where, Varina said, giant lilies floated in the lagoons. An ex-slave observed that Mr. Davis seemed to be an indulgent husband and added that Mrs. Davis talked, and talked a lot. Jefferson was indeed generous, buying Varina some fine new clothes. Yet he already seemed intent on subduing his wife's personality, for he informed Mrs. Howell that her daughter was growing "calmer" every day, as he wished. Varina assured her mother she would learn "self control" to win her husband's approval. She called him, in all unselfconsciousness, "Uncle Jeff."[14]

Having never lived on a plantation before, Varina was naive about her duties as the plantation mistress. She expressed surprise that the slaves required so much of her time. In the early 1840s Jefferson owned about seventy-four adult slaves (the average for whites in Warren County was fourteen), and much of the responsibility for superintending the feeding, clothing, and medical care of those slaves fell to the mistress. Some obligations were relatively easy, such as making the slaves' clothes, since Davis already knew how to sew. She rose at dawn to cut out material to make clothing with two slave women and then helped distribute it to the bondsmen. She was the amateur doctor in residence, treating slave children who required her attention "constantly." After some months she learned the names of

Mr. and Mrs. Davis, 1845. Stern husband, demure bride.
(Museum of the Confederacy, Richmond, Virginia)

all the slaves, and a handful of them had positive memories of her. James Lucas said of the Davises that "he wuz good but she was better," and another, Florida Hewitt, described her as a "fine" mistress who could be very particular about the fare on the table. She could indeed be demanding. When a house slave did not work to her satisfaction, Mrs. Davis sent her into field labor. She punished another slave who took cooking utensils from the house, and she had several maids before she found one she liked.[15]

She did a small share of physical labor herself, although it never approached the hard work a yeoman farmer's wife performed or the burdens a slave woman shouldered every day. She cooked occasionally, knitted frequently, and mended her own clothes, and, because she still felt a strong obligation to her own family, made clothing for her siblings. When Margaret Howell offered to help with her wardrobe, Varina gently declined, saying she did not want to add anything to her mother's duties. She sent her family packages of food (preserves, sugar, hams) and once decided not to buy a piano for herself and instead sent the money, 450 dollars, to her parents.[16]

As for her own childbearing prospects, Davis said in 1845 that she did not need a "comfortable" dress, meaning maternity clothes, and she worried that she might never need one. Like many women of the time, she expected to become pregnant immediately after marriage. The medical knowledge of the day provided women with much misinformation about infertility, and Varina had painful, irregular menstrual periods, for which she took uva ursi leaf; she was reed thin, which may also reduce a woman's chances of becoming pregnant. Her husband was in his late thirties, when male fertility begins to decline. Varina probably had a miscarriage in 1847 or 1848, and she consulted Charles D. Meigs, an eminent Philadelphia doctor, but she did not become pregnant, which disappointed her very much. Her mother's fecundity—she conceived almost every two years into her forties and had a son in 1846, the year after Varina married— mystified her. Varina thought a "successful" woman had many children, and although she did not know it, seven years would pass before she would bear her first surviving child.[17]

Other hints of future difficulties appeared with the in-laws. In 1845 Varina reported that she had been "affectionately received" by all members of the huge Davis family. At first that included Joseph's wife, Eliza, with whom she passed some agreeable visits, and she became fond of her niece Mary Jane, or "Malie," Bradford, who was actually a year older than Varina, and of her sister-in-law Lucinda Davis Stamps. (Her mother-in-law, Jane Davis, died in 1845.) But gradually she began to perceive how different most of her in-laws were from the Howells, so self-contained. Later she advised a kinswoman that the first year of married life is difficult for "two people born with a different strain of blood, educated differently, and compelled to make constant compromises of temper and mode of life." The newlywed Varina began to wish for less visiting with the in-laws and more privacy. When she looked back from old age, she observed that it is essential to keep other relatives at bay during the first year of marriage so a couple can get to know each other.[18]

These problems derived at least partly from age differences, for Varina was a full generation younger than her sisters-in-law. Amanda Davis Bradford, the youngest of Jefferson's sisters, was twenty-six years older than Varina, and Eliza, Joseph's wife, was some fifteen years her senior. All of the Davis women could read and write, but they were born too soon to benefit fully from the swift rise in literacy among antebellum women. Few of them were at ease with a pen, and on the frontiers where most of them had grown up, books were scarce. Although Eliza Davis perused the occasional novel, the love of books, especially serious books, was foreign to them. Varina never openly ridiculed her in-laws, but she admired well-read women, equating a knowledge of books with feminine refinement, and she believed that poorly educated women were prone to "desuetude." The combination of beauty, virtue, and brains was most admirable in women, she thought.[19]

Jefferson's political career also presented dilemmas—not problems exactly—as he pursued his ambitions. After the state Democratic Party nominated him as their congressional candidate in July 1845, he left immediately to campaign, and in November 1845 he won. Varina worried that she would never acquire the "fortitude necessary to be a Politician's wife" and bear his long absences. She may have already sensed that politics came first, for she dreamed that she had to kiss her husband good-bye in front of a crowd. Yet his career was undeniably exciting. After the election, the Democratic Party invited him to give a speech in Vicksburg to honor the deceased president Andrew Jackson, so he dictated the draft to his wife, and she accompanied him to the river city, where she met John C. Calhoun. After her husband introduced the old man, the South Carolinian gave a speech about a citizen's duty to his state. Calhoun talked afterward to Mrs. Davis, and he told Varina's brother Joseph that she was talented with pleasing manners.[20]

The nation's capital was just as exciting for the bride when Congressman and Mrs. Davis arrived in December 1845. The town itself, home to some thirty thousand people, was not prepossessing. Charles Dickens named it the "City of Magnificent Intentions" for the plain wooden buildings marooned in frowsy fields. With its barnlike hotels and rude boardinghouses, it lacked Philadelphia's beauty. Omnibuses clanged down the streets, in danger of running over pigs and loafing dogs, but every spring the Capitol grounds came alive with flowering trees, and the White House was of course imposing. The Davises moved into a boardinghouse on Pennsylvania Avenue with other Democratic couples. Varina relinquished her Whig loyalties to become a Democrat like her husband, and she wrote some of his letters for him. She proudly mailed copies of his speeches to her parents, and she was thrilled when former president John Quincy Adams, then a congressman, predicted a bright future for Jefferson Davis.[21]

After her niece Malie Bradford joined her in Washington City, as it was sometimes called, the two women explored the town together. The social season followed the congressional calendar, opening in December and closing in March, and despite the vaulting ambitions of so many politicians concentrated in a small place, Washington was friendly to new faces. Varina had letters of introduction to Robert J. Walker, Secretary of the Treasury, whose wife, Mary Bache Walker, was her mother's friend in Natchez. In the mid-1840s, before slavery moved front and center as a political issue, it was easy to have friends from all over the country. Varina enjoyed meeting "grand" people from all regions, such as Mary Woodbury Blair of New Hampshire, nicknamed "Minna" and wife of Montgomery Blair, and all the women in the Bache family, whose dinner parties Varina called the most scintillating in town. She also met the Whig leader, Massachusetts Senator Daniel Webster, whose speeches in the *National Intelligencer* she had read as a girl. Her training with George Winchester stood her in good stead as she discussed Byron, Wordsworth, and Dante with Charles Ingersoll, chairman of the House Committee on Foreign Affairs, and George Dallas, Vice President of the United States. She felt "brilliant" talking with George Bancroft, the New England historian who served as Polk's Secretary of the Navy. Not every public man was so impressive in person. Sam Houston's showy greeting reminded her of a fencer going through his paces. She was learning to be flexible, however, playing the role of gracious hostess when guests dropped by unexpectedly.[22]

Adaptability was a good quality to have in Washington, for the town was a laboratory of social custom, filled with educated people of both genders who were keenly interested in public issues. Here women could discuss politics with men, which was not deemed acceptable on the plantation or in most of rural America. Politicians such as John C. Calhoun, Charles Ingersoll, and James Buchanan had relatively advanced views on the parity of the sexes and pioneered this behavior, speaking to women as their equals and listening in return, a quality that Varina Davis especially appreciated. In the Jacksonian era the new practice of shaking hands upon being introduced became routine here, and women could make social calls without a male escort, contrary to custom in the Deep South. A few women went far beyond traditional gender roles and crafted their own careers, such as the daughters of Supreme Court Justice Roger Taney, who became professional artists.[23]

Varina Davis's sojourn in Washington was brief, because the United States went to war with Mexico in the spring of 1846, prompted largely by the expansionist dreams of President James Polk, who hoped the institution of slavery would spread all over the West. Jefferson promised her that he would not volunteer to serve in the army, then changed his mind and joined up. She forgave him, she told Margaret Howell, because he was so good to her. As he left for the front that summer, she returned to Mississippi. She took up gardening to calm her nerves, and when a captain took care of Jefferson after an injury, she sent her effusive thanks to his wife.[24]

WHILE JEFFERSON was in the army, Varina became embroiled in a struggle with her brother-in-law Joseph. At some time in 1846 her in-laws told her that Jefferson depended on Joseph for his fortune, and Caroline, Joseph's daughter, taunted her that Jefferson had to rely on her father's "bounty." Because this was contrary to what Joseph had told her before she married Jefferson, she flew, considerably exercised, to ask her brother-in-law who owned Brierfield. They spoke alone with no witnesses, and he made the cagey reply that he had "given" the land to Jefferson and said nothing about the title, which was still in his hands. Years later the family would debate Joseph's intentions regarding the property, and one of his friends claimed that Joseph did not want anyone in the Howell family to inherit Brierfield. Nor is it clear how many of the Davis relatives knew that Joseph had not given the Brierfield title to Jefferson. Whatever Joseph's true intentions regarding the property, this exchange made Varina Davis distrust her brother-in-law for the rest of her life.[25]

The explanation for Joseph's actions—that he did not want the property to go to the Howells—does not make much sense. Joseph had known Varina's parents for three decades, and he was well aware of William's bankruptcy. William tried to ingratiate himself with the Davis family, running errands in Natchez for his son-in-law, and the Howells named their last child, born in 1846, after Jefferson. Varina's father, who was responsible for the Howells' financial woes, would probably predecease her. In fact, he died in 1863, forty-three years before Varina Davis and seven years before Joseph Davis. Nor did Joseph Davis object to floundering in-laws per se, for he sometimes paid their debts, even though he groused about it, and he delivered what Varina called "philippics" toward most of his relatives. Perhaps there were other reasons: Joseph may have been disappointed that Varina had no children, or he may have seen her as a rival for his brother's affections. She described herself as "defiant and plainspoken," as the other Davis women were not, and another relative observed that Joseph could be "too masterful" when dealing with other people. Maybe the best explanations came from Joseph's kinfolk, one of whom said that Joseph tried to control all the property because he had a strong desire to be regarded as the head of the entire family. A kinsman agreed that Joseph Davis had the "peculiarity" of rarely giving deeds to his relatives when they bought land from him. This was indeed peculiar, especially for a lawyer—the statutory term being *fraud*—and the American economy would have ground to a halt if other landowners had followed the practice.[26]

Varina hoped that her husband would protect her interests in this situation, but he did not. When Jefferson came home on furlough in the fall of 1846, he agreed with his brother's actions. He later gave some revealing counsel to a niece whose property was being mismanaged by her parents: yield and accept the wrongdoing. Maybe this man who rarely felt intimidated by anyone felt intimidated by his brother, for he once said that he owed more to Joseph than to any other man. Whatever his motives, for Varina it meant a double betrayal by her brother-in-law and her husband. She and Jefferson quarreled before he returned to the army, and the recriminations continued by mail. He informed his wife that he had stopped in New Orleans to see several "female acquaintances" he had known while he was in the army, including an officer's wife who was able to rise above "annoyances" and write cheerful letters to her husband. He stayed at the front, fighting one war, and she stayed home, fighting another. New Year's Day of 1847, by tradition a day for making social calls on friends and family, she spent alone at Brierfield doing housework in a kind of purdah. After her mother and siblings came to visit in February 1847, she returned with them to Natchez for five months.[27]

Another issue soon inflamed relations between Varina and her husband's family: who would live at Brierfield. Joseph decreed that his widowed sister Amanda Bradford and her seven children should reside at the plantation with Jefferson and Varina. After her husband died in 1844, Mrs. Bradford moved her family to the Hurricane, which had nine bedrooms and a guest cottage, but some kind of difficulty arose between Amanda and her sister-in-law Eliza. Sometime in 1847 the family told Varina that they were coming to Brierfield, which she opposed. Jefferson tried with little success to mediate between his wife and his brother about these disputes, and soon the Davises shut Varina out of their discussions altogether. "Some decision has been arrived at about the house," she indignantly told her mother, but no one had thought it "proper" to "inform" her of it.[28]

Varina once observed that no household was large enough for two women, which was the working assumption in the Old Southwest, including Mississippi, where the majority of white households contained one nuclear family each. Moreover, common sense would suggest that it was unwise to move a widow with seven children into a house with newlyweds. Nor did Amanda Bradford especially want to go to Brierfield, but she was willing to acquiesce because Joseph wanted it. Even though Varina was fond of Malie, the other Bradford children were prone to having food fights at the table, and after witnessing one such contest, she observed, "Woman was made to live alone if man was not." Then Joseph tried to tell her how to design the kitchen at Brierfield. Varina replied that it was her kitchen and she should design it herself. Afterward he brought up this comment as evidence of what he perceived to be her unreasonable nature.[29]

❦

BOTH OF THESE fiery controversies about Brierfield—who owned the land and who would live at the house—struck at the question of who was considered part of the family and indirectly raised questions about Joseph Davis's private life. If Varina did not know his secrets before, she must have discovered by now that he had some illegitimate children. Some years later she described him as a "libertine." Henry Foote, a Mississippi politician who hated the whole Davis family, archly pointed out that Joseph left behind a "number of children," and estimates by more impartial writers range from three to nine illegitimate white children. In Kentucky he fathered a child out of wedlock with a white woman, and mother and child both left the state. In Mississippi he had at least four white children, Florida, Mary, Caroline, and a son known only as "W." who died in Vicksburg in 1838, all of them apparently born out of wedlock. Jane, often called a "cousin," was probably his daughter, according to another relative, and Julia Lyons, another "granddaughter," "cousin," or "adopted daughter" who

Joseph E. Davis. Varina Davis's nemesis in the Davis family.
(Museum of the Confederacy, Richmond, Virginia)

lived near Vicksburg, was said to be his daughter. The gossip about Joseph Davis's offspring probably made it impossible for him to go into politics.[30]

The mothers of these children have never been identified, and Joseph's marriage to Eliza Van Benthuysen in 1827 was barren. This was his only marriage recorded in Natchez, his home from 1820 to 1827, even though Caroline was born in 1823 and Julia in 1826. The Howells did not mention a wife when they knew Joseph in Natchez, and the land deeds he signed between 1821 and 1827 did not include a spouse's signature, which was required under state law. Mississippi law also provided that the biological father would receive custody of all illegitimate children, and the age gaps between the sisters would seem to indicate more than one mother. Finally, there is Eliza Davis's strangled cry in the 1850s that her husband *"ought to have married"* someone else.[31]

In Varina's dealings with the in-laws, there was one more unpleasant surprise in store. Sometime in the winter of 1847 she discovered that her husband had written a will, probably during the previous year. No copy of this will survives, but by all accounts Jefferson chose to leave Brierfield and a share of income from the property to his wife for her lifetime only and did not allow her to dispose of the property upon her death. Instead he gave that right to someone else, probably Joseph. Jefferson composed this will as he literally conferred with his brother behind closed doors in the Hurricane library, and Varina believed that he followed Joseph's "advice" as he wrote it. Since Brierfield supposedly belonged to his brother, it did not make much sense to compose a will, but Jefferson did it anyway. The fact that she would not be allowed to own Brierfield after her husband's death disturbed her, Varina said, as the rest of the will's contents did not. Joseph's wife and other relatives would have land and financial security, but she would not. She believed in fact that Joseph was trying to deprive her of her "legal rights."[32]

The law codes of the 1840s did not actually prohibit such conduct, for any man who wrote a will could dispose of his property as he wished so long as he provided for his minor children. He could leave his wife little or no property, and if he left her property, he could bequeath it to her for her lifetime only; he could also deny his widow the right to dispose of property in her own will. Nor did he have to explain his reasons. If a man died intestate, or without a will, the Southern courts typically gave the widow one-quarter to one-half of the estate, the premise being that a husband owed his wife some compensation for her contributions to the household. Since 1821, Mississippi law required that the widow receive half of the estate when a childless man died without a will, with the rest of his property distributed among his siblings. The Married Woman's Property Act, passed in Mississippi in 1839, allowed men to deed property to their wives but did not require it. So Joseph's daughter Caroline was correct: because Brierfield still belonged to Joseph, he could dispose of it as he wished. Or, if we suppose that Jefferson owned it, then he had the right to deny his wife permanent ownership of Brierfield in his will. Whether this was wise or just is another question, and, as Varina realized, it was unusual. Planters who wrote their own wills typically left a third or more of the estate to their widows, and some allowed them to dispose of the property as they wished.[33]

Varina's husband came back to Mississippi in June 1847, a national hero from his military service, even as the marriage was entering a crisis. In August, Jefferson was appointed to a vacant seat in the United States Senate, and when he left Brierfield in November his wife did not accompany him. She felt restless at the "monotony" of plantation life, and she expected her husband to contact her in a few weeks, but the invitation did not come. At one point she wondered if he was "ashamed" of her, and in the new year the inheritance issue erupted in their correspondence. In January 1848 Jefferson wrote a furious missive, denying her charge that he had robbed her of her *"rights as a woman and a wife"* and insisting that she wanted Amanda Bradford to live with them. No one in his family was capable of a "mercenary" motive, he said, and he could not bear her reproaches. He would not return to Mississippi until he was sure that she had changed for the better. She wrote at least two more letters that spring, both of them angry by his lights, which have disappeared.

Varina was trying to do what was right regardless of her husband's "displeasure," she told her mother. About her in-laws she added, "When attacked I can fight."[34]

In April 1848, Jefferson Davis responded to her fighting letters. Her "habits, education, combativeness" made her challenge him, which, he repeated, he could not bear. He knew that she did not wish to drive him to "temporary stupefaction," probably meaning drink, and "vicious associations," a nineteenth-century euphemism for prostitutes, but he might have to resort to those behaviors if she did not stop. In fact, he said that he was not sure they could live together. He expected her to abide by his wishes, which he said was demanded by her "duties as a wife." Meanwhile, she could spend the summer in the North with a family friend if she wished. He concluded by saying, "I need not say that (because I love you) it would always make me happier to be with you" if she were "kind and peaceful." His farewell included the admonition, "Truth & Love ever attend upon you." Her reply to this letter has not survived.[35]

This was his manifesto of married life, and it reveals that Jefferson did not see marriage as a partnership. Wives had many duties, he believed, and not many rights. He did not seem to grasp that these conflicts were about dignity and privacy, as well as property, and he seems to have expected her to acquiesce, as women in the Davis family usually did regarding Joseph's wishes. In fact, he seems to have taken his cue from his older brother and thought little else about the matter. Here he demonstrated the poor judgment about human beings that would surface in his political career and the disregard for social custom that his brother displayed. One of Jefferson's friends in Mississippi called him a brave, capable man with bad judgment. It could also be said that he was used to having his way, habituated to command on the battlefield and on the plantation. Varina had a different vision of marriage. She wanted a reciprocal relationship, a companionate marriage in which husband and wife both had obligations. At the very least she expected her husband to protect her legal interests and respect her wish for a home of her own.[36]

None of her letters have survived from this crisis phase in 1848,

but she must have passed some sleepless nights at Brierfield wondering if her marriage was over. The depth of her feelings can be guessed
from her later denunciations of wealthy men who took their wives
for granted or mistreated them. Senator Stephen Douglas was the
subject of an outburst in 1856 when he wed Adele Cutts, his second
wife and a great-niece of James Madison. The undeserving Douglas
"buys" his second wife, Varina said, only because "she is poor." In
1885 Varina told her friend Mary Boykin Chesnut that old men inflicted "miseries" on women with their inequitable wills, and she declared that the world would condemn such practices if the sexes were
reversed. She paraphrased the Declaration of Independence and said
all family members had the right to "'liberty and the pursuit of happiness.'" In 1903 she rebuked the husband of Frederike Quitman Smith,
a friend from Mississippi, after the couple argued over their property
holdings. When Frederike's spouse threatened to leave her, Varina
Davis unleashed a torrent of indignation. "You expose her to scandal,
stab her in the heart and leave her," she cried, "and for what," an honest disagreement over property. She reminded Smith that his wife
was alone in her misery and he should remember his vows to love and
protect her.[37]

IN 1848, as the summer wore on, relations between the Davises did
not improve. Jefferson came to Mississippi in the summer during
the congressional recess but left for Washington in November, while
Varina stayed behind, in low spirits. If during this unhappy passage she
considered divorcing her husband, she would have realized that the
obstacles were insurmountable. Mississippi granted divorce for big-
amy, desertion of five years, and impotence—none of which pertained to the Davises—as well as adultery, and she probably could not
have proved whether Jefferson Davis visited "female acquaintances" or
engaged in "vicious associations." Divorce could also be allowed on
grounds of "extreme cruelty," which was left to a judge to determine,
and Mississippi's courts were the most conservative in the region on
defining cruelty, dismissing petitions from white women who alleged

verbal or emotional abuse. Even if divorce was possible, it was expensive, and her husband was rich, the owner of seventy-nine slaves in 1848, while she had no property of her own. Just as important, divorce carried a dreadful stigma, with the blame attaching to the woman, and Varina did not want another family scandal like her aunt Jane Kempe's divorce. Later she observed that an unhappily married woman was trapped like the starling in Laurence Sterne's *A Sentimental Journey through France and Italy.* In the novel, a traveler hears a starling call from a courtyard, "I can't get out—I can't get out," but sees that he cannot open the cage without destroying it. In her old age, Davis wrote that marriage was a lifetime contract and that all Southern women considered divorce a disgrace.[38]

Now she decided to act on those beliefs, and she gave in, the only choice if she wanted to stay married to Jefferson Davis. As a kinswoman remarked, Jefferson was the "master in his house, in his life, in his marriage," and Varina had to accept that if she was going to be his wife. She chose to follow her mother's example rather than that of her aunt Jane, and she confided to Mrs. Howell that she would keep silent on the "miserable" subject of her conflict with Joseph and accept her husband's decrees. The marital quarrel, almost three years in duration, was over. In January 1849 she wrote her husband a groveling letter, calling herself his "thoughtless, dependent wife" and describing him as her "nobler self." In the summer of 1849 Jefferson was back at Brierfield, and he and his wife began to exchange warm letters when he traveled from home. Both of the wills—Joseph's and Jefferson's—remained unchanged, but Varina had accomplished a few objectives. She would live at Brierfield without the Bradfords, and she would design her own kitchen. Yet she made a conscious effort to subordinate herself, reading Sarah Ellis's *Guide to Social Happiness,* which counseled wives to submit to their spouses. She accompanied Jefferson on a speaking tour in the fall of 1849, even though she did not enjoy such events.[39]

As Varina made peace with her spouse, her family of origin could hardly assist her. Her mother sympathized with her situation, but she had no property of her own, since everything she owned became her husband's when she married, and by 1849 all of Margaret Howell's dowry was gone. Nor did William Howell try to protect his daughter's interests. In fact, she tried to help him more often than he helped her. She asked Secretary of the Treasury Robert J. Walker in 1846 if he might have a government post for her father. Despite a pleading letter from her father to Walker, he did not receive a job. Varina watched her family's plight with growing anxiety. She brought her sister Margaret to Brierfield for several months to tutor her because the Howells could not afford it, and she sent more clothes to her siblings. Varina did not want to add in any way to her mother's burdens, and she longed to do more to help her family, exclaiming to her parents, "I wish I could turn out, and work for you myself."[40]

Not surprisingly, the conflagration over the wills and the house permanently affected her relations with her in-laws. Her friendships with Malie Bradford and Lucinda Stamps survived, but she never could bring herself to forgive Joseph Davis, and their interactions had what she called a "varying character." Joseph grumbled that Varina and Jefferson spent too much money on Brierfield, although this wealthy planter spent money freely himself. Still, Varina tried to stay on civil terms with him, and he with her. When other members of the Davis family came to Brierfield, they were usually polite to Varina, and she to them. Gamely she tried to draw some wisdom from this brutal lesson about power in the family, telling her mother that she had decided that a person's attitude, not external circumstances, determined one's happiness. In December 1849 she was allowed to return to Washington with her husband, escaping the plantation at last for the city.[41]

3

FLATTERED AND COURTED

AFTER THE DAVISES ARRIVED for the start of the congressional session, they rented a house with Mr. and Mrs. Armistead Burt and other couples from the South. Varina enjoyed sitting by the window and looking out on the street; as she told her mother, she liked "to see the bustle." It was already clear that she was an urban personality and much happier in Washington. The town had a pleasing openness, and, as the young Henry Adams observed during a visit, a swagger. Varina attended a reception at the White House on New Year's Day 1850, when the rich attire of the other guests dazzled her. She was a guest at another party with Howell Cobb, the Georgian who was the Speaker of the House of Representatives; Senator Stephen Douglas of Illinois and his first wife, Martha; William Corcoran, a merchant who became one of the town's wealthiest bankers; and William Seaton, one of the town's most influential editors, and his wife, Sarah Gales Seaton, one of the chief arbiters of society, who took a liking to Varina. She gave a few parties herself, hosting one for a granddaughter of the Virginia governor. She continued to have friends from all parts of the country: the Speaker's wife, Mary Ann Lamar Cobb of Georgia, whom she liked and respected from the first time they met; Mary Bache Walker, descendant of Ben Franklin; Julia Kean Fish, a New Jersey native married to Senator Hamilton Fish, the Whig from New York. Mrs. Senator Davis easily blended back into the social life of the capital.[1]

The marriage was patched up, too. Varina forgave her husband for the trouble over the wills and happily assisted him with his work, taking dictation for letters to constituents and correcting proofs for his speeches, and he reported to her parents that she was a "good girl." She readily took on other family obligations as needed. When the Davis nieces came to town, she chaperoned them, and as her niece Malie Bradford, who married Democratic congressman Richard Brodhead, prepared to give birth to her first child in 1850, Varina went to Pennsylvania and stayed with Malie, since none of the other relatives could come. Back in Washington, she disapproved of a young woman who declared that only fools considered the norms of society when determining their conduct.[2]

In keeping with her position as a senator's wife, Varina acquired some expensive clothes. Even though a contemporary thought she was "plain," she was young, married to a wealthy man who noticed how women dressed, and she was beginning to love beautiful clothes as an expression of femininity. Although she did not say so, such attire has always symbolized elite social status as well. Her wardrobe included a watered poplin dress with short sleeves and a high neck, a green and gold satin, and a sky-blue ruffled silk with rosettes in the bodice and a train, all of which she described in exquisite detail to her mother. Married women in the capital had dropped the Southern practice of wearing caps, and Varina adopted the local custom of wearing plumes and flowers in her hair and dangling earrings. Like other women in Washington, she followed international fashion, and when the French introduced hoop skirts to the world in the 1850s, she redesigned her dresses to fit over the hoops.[3]

The Davises had personal entrée to the White House because Jefferson had decided to make peace with his first father-in-law, President Zachary Taylor, a Whig and the second President from that party. Jovial, blunt, and disdainful of ceremony, Taylor seemed to many people unsuited for the nuances of political life, but Varina liked him, and she liked his wife, Margaret Smith Taylor, who was so reclusive that there is no surviving portrait of her face. Their daughter Betty Taylor Bliss hosted many White House functions for her.

The gossips clucked that Mrs. Taylor was really quite crude, but Varina recorded that the President's wife shone at small gatherings with family and friends. The First Lady did feel isolated, however, as Varina understood when she visited her after an official dinner and found Mrs. Taylor shivering by a fireplace and feeling "wretchedly lonesome." Davis talked to her as long as she could before she had to leave.[4]

In 1850, the Congress had to decide what to do with the territory acquired during the Mexican War, the central question being whether

Zachary Taylor. Varina Davis was at the President's deathbed with his family. (Beinecke Rare Book and Manuscript Library, Yale University)

the land would turn into slave states or free states. In January, Senator Henry Clay introduced resolutions with features designed to please the slave states, especially a stronger fugitive slave law, and some features for the free states, most importantly the admission of California as a free state. The debate over his compromise was raucous, because slavery was by now a chief engine of the American economy and the subject of vociferous criticism from abolitionists and adamant defenses by politicians who believed slavery should expand into the West. Jefferson Davis would emerge as one of the most determined advocates of slavery's expansion. After the Mississippi legislature re-elected him to his Senate seat in February, he spoke numerous times against the compromise. For a politician in a rough-and-tumble place like Washington, Jefferson easily took offense, and he nearly fought a duel with Representative William Bissell of Illinois over the congressman's statements about the Mississippi regiment's performance in the Mexican War. At times Davis appeared to seek out political conflict. When he encountered Henry Clay on the Capitol grounds, and the Kentuckian said his proposals could buy peace for another generation, Davis tartly replied that he did not want to postpone the crisis. Announcing that he was able to meet the trial, he walked away.[5]

VARINA DAVIS WAS PROUD of her husband's eminence, but she did not always agree with his truculent approach to politics. She cautioned him that a speech against anti-slavery Congressman John Hale was "a little too violent," although she thought Hale deserved criticism, and she described Jefferson's exchange with another political foe as "too fierce for my taste." Her instincts seemed to be those of a consensus builder, or at least more moderate than those of her spouse, but he never liked what he called "political" women, that is, women who brought up political topics and tried to discuss them with him in a straightforward manner. His wife rarely discussed politics in her letters, making one brief reference to "this compromise bill" in June

1850, saying only that it was occupying a lot of her husband's time. She devoted the rest of the letter to her parents' financial problems, family news, the neighbors, and the like.[6]

For Varina, Zachary Taylor's death was also principally a family matter. When he died, probably from cholera, at the White House on July 9, she was at the bedside with his relatives, and she watched Mrs. Taylor clinging to her husband's body as bells began to toll the President's death. Varina returned the next day to sit with the bereaved, and she tried to comfort the widow on the day of the funeral. The family soon left Washington, and Margaret Taylor died two years later. Although Varina did not say so, the political consequences of Taylor's death were enormous. He had opposed the compromise for several reasons, preferring to admit California and then let its citizens decide about slavery, but the ascent of Vice President Millard Fillmore, an ally of Clay and Webster, meant that a bill would probably pass. By the fall of 1850, Congress had enacted most of the elements of Henry Clay's compromise, each part guided through on separate votes by Senator Stephen Douglas and most of them opposed by Jefferson Davis. Indeed, Jefferson had already mentioned the possibility of disunion as the South's last resort. As this political battle played out, Varina saw little of her husband. Jefferson told Mrs. Howell that summer that his wife had to spend a lot of time alone because he was so busy.[7]

The Howells left Natchez in 1850 to make a new start in New Orleans. William Howell had landed a position as a federal timber agent, most likely with his son-in-law's assistance, and the family settled in Tunisburg on the city's south side, where they opened a dairy. Margaret Howell presided over a household of her children plus the McAnts girls, and she called herself a member of the "working class," which was not quite the case, since the family could still hire servants. But she did manual labor at the dairy herself and eventually began to take in work as a seamstress. She told Varina that any amount of money would keep the wolf from the door. Mrs. Howell kept her sense of humor, for she thought no woman was poor who had three dresses—one on her person, one in her trunk, and one in the wash—

and she told her daughter that she would try to be as happy as circumstances allowed.[8]

Varina felt mortified by her family's exit from Natchez, but she did not openly blame her improvident father. She wanted others to think of her parents as genteel people, and she was desperate to help them. She still made clothes for the family, and she sent them cash, which she apparently set aside from an allowance her husband gave her; she told her mother she would send much more "if the money I enjoy were *my* money." When the Howells lost some of their belongings in a fire at Tunisburg, she replaced them. Varina's father opened a commission house in New Orleans, but the business faltered, and Jefferson Davis had to buy the Tunisburg house for the family. Varina's older brother Joseph could barely look after himself, much less contribute to the family's welfare. He read law, practiced briefly in Texas, and then roamed around out west, taking a job as a clerk in the Mexican Territory, but his true occupation was "wild" man, according to Abner Doubleday, who met him there. A skilled marksman when he was sober, Howell was frequently drunk and took part in public brawls, one of which left a jagged scar across his face. In 1852 he joined an expedition to conquer Mexico, which failed. When he came back to the United States, his mother deplored his absurd ideas about "glory" and hoped that he would start making an honest living.[9]

By September 1850, Jefferson Davis's work for that congressional session was done. He claimed to be disgusted with politics, but after the Davises reached Mississippi he left on another speaking tour for several weeks. Varina occupied herself with furnishing a new, eight-room house at Brierfield, and the couple spared no expense to adorn the house and the grounds. Varina looked back on the years before the war as a time of "ease and plenty," and her husband indulged her love of creature comforts. She bought some costly furniture, including a sofa finished in velvet, a piano, many books for their library, and a sewing machine; having heard of this newfangled device before she left Washington, she soon found it indispensable. When Jefferson returned to Washington for the congressional session in November, Varina remained at Brierfield because she was pregnant. She was by herself in December when she miscarried. Her husband returned to Brierfield in March 1851, but in May and June he embarked on another speaking tour in Mississippi on behalf of candidates in the "Southern rights" wing of the Democratic Party, explaining that although he missed her he had to attend to party business.[10]

Jefferson Davis was emerging as a leader of the pro-slavery states' rights wing of Mississippi's Democratic Party, and in September 1851 the Democrats in his state convinced him to stand for governor. After he resigned his Senate seat, he began campaigning on an anticompromise ticket. In one of his speeches Jefferson declared that white women supported the Southern rights cause, just as their mothers supported their fathers during the Revolution, but in private his wife sensed the futility of the campaign. Varina told her mother in October that the extreme Southern rights position could not win, as everyone but her husband and his allies knew, although she thought it might rebound if more "aggressions" against the South occurred. She helped him anyway, taking dictation and nursing him when he was sick. Jefferson lost the race to the pro-Union candidate Henry Foote by 999 votes. Most secessionists did badly in the Mississippi elections, and over the next year the disunion movement fell apart. Varina was relieved. She confessed to her parents that she might lack the aplomb to be a governor's wife, a role that consisted, she believed, of holding her tongue when necessary and making conversation with various and sundry strangers, no matter how rude, gossipy, or uninteresting they might be.[11]

SO THE DAVISES settled down at Brierfield. The plantation was generating 350 to 450 bales of cotton a year from the mid-1840s into the early 1850s. Jefferson's landholdings in 1850 were worth twenty-five thousand dollars. He grossed some thirty-five to forty thousand dollars a year in the 1850s, the amount declining each year that Davis spent in Washington and could not attend to the plantation himself, but he purchased slaves throughout the decade, so that his slaveholdings increased from 72 bondsmen in 1850 to 113 in 1860, putting him in the top 6 percent of slaveholders in the state. The Davises could afford all kinds of luxuries. They bought a pleasure carriage, and Jefferson hired slave musicians to play the occasional concert. Brierfield became known as a showcase plantation. In 1851 Charles, the nineteenth Earl of Shrewsbury, made a point of visiting it during a tour of the South.[12]

Like many white men who prospered on the southwestern frontier, Jefferson Davis believed utterly in slavery and would not admit that anything could possibly be wrong with it. His brother's financial success may have confirmed these opinions, and he tried to emulate what he called his brother's "patriarchal care" of slaves. Jefferson asserted that the Bible supported the view that blacks were inferior to whites and that slavery benefited African Americans, and he liked to tell what he thought were amusing anecdotes about slaves who made mistakes or said foolish things. His bondsmen had an adequate diet and adequate housing, as one ex-slave recalled, and after the Civil War some former slaves corroborated Varina's statements that Jefferson did not allow his bondsmen to be whipped. Black preachers came to Brierfield to give the occasional sermon, and every year the slaves had dances at harvest time. One ex-bondsman said that the neighbors referred to them as "Jeff Davis' free niggers [sic]."[13]

Yet Brierfield witnessed the abuses of power that took place on every plantation. The Davis slaves, most of whom were under age forty, worked very hard, picking cotton by moonlight, and Brierfield and the Hurricane produced corn yields that were much higher than those on other Mississippi plantations. Slaves experienced intrusions in their personal lives, as when Joseph Davis's daughter Florida insisted a bondswoman come to Diamond Place and leave her son behind at Brierfield. Nor was daily life absent other indignities, for the slave children ate breakfast every morning from a trough. Nor was there ever any question about who had the ultimate authority. After James Pemberton died in 1852, Jefferson Davis went through a series of white overseers, one of whom lasted only four months. The master, irritated at finding a gate locked at Brierfield, once ordered a slave to tear it down, declaring it was his gate and he could do as he wished.[14]

From September 1851 to March 1853, for nineteen months, Varina Davis became mistress at Brierfield again, her longest continuous residence on a plantation. She still related to slaves as workers who should assist her in whatever needed to be done in the household, and she took it for granted that slave labor allowed her to order expensive items for the household. She usually did not object to the separation of family members through the slave trade, and she once admitted that she had no "tact" in dealing with house slaves. Yet it may be significant that she typically used the word *Negro* rather than *nigger* in her writings when the latter term was common usage among white Americans. Certainly she dealt with slaves in the household on a daily basis, as her husband did not. She sometimes worked alongside them in her vegetable garden, whereas he was not even sure what ought to be planted in it, and she handed out clothes to the bondsmen in the fall. James Lucas, a teenager, was responsible for meeting her at the river landing when she returned from a trip and briefing her on plantation matters. She practiced the female version of paternalistic race relations, what we might call maternalism, playing a mediating role between whites and blacks. After a slave allegedly threatened an overseer with a knife, she went to talk to the slave and discovered that he did not have a knife after all.[15]

After Jefferson's defeat in the gubernatorial race, Varina enjoyed a period of true companionship with her husband at Brierfield. They worked in the flower garden together and went for rides down the shady lanes. A little before Christmas, Mrs. Davis discovered that she was pregnant again, with a baby due in July. She tentatively remarked that her husband seemed satisfied staying at home, and she needed him close by more than ever, but he left in June and again in July on speaking tours for Democrats in Mississippi and Tennessee. Even though she did not want to be "selfish," she asked him, "Can you not come home." As she waited, Varina poured her heart into letters to her mother, sometimes writing every other day. She confided her fear

that she might die in childbirth, as many women did in her generation, and Margaret Howell assured her that nothing could keep her
from her daughter's side.[16]

In the spring of 1852, when Varina was about five months pregnant, she made an extraordinary comment about one of the Davis
slaves, Ferdinand. He worked in the garden at Brierfield, and he had
labored for the Davises for at least five years. She told her mother
that spring that kind treatment would make him a good worker and
added that she did not agree with "the doctrine of grinding down
young people to the earth because they are human beings, with their
frailties." She did not say who might have been grinding Ferdinand
down—possibly an overseer, her husband, or her brother-in-law Joseph—but very few plantation mistresses ever made such remarks
about slaves. Then she abruptly changed the subject, adding, "I don't
know what set me off on this track," perhaps feeling uncomfortable
with the implications of recognizing the frailty of African Americans
in bondage. She obviously did not agree with the scientific racism on
the rise in that decade, as American and European intellectuals began
to argue that black people were not human beings, or her husband,
who said on the floor of the Senate in 1848 that he had no more fear
of his slaves than he did of his cattle.[17]

Varina gave birth to a son in July 1852, and she and her husband,
who had given up hope of becoming parents, were overjoyed. They
named him Samuel after Jefferson's father. Jefferson showered the
baby with gifts, but three weeks later he left for Natchez for a political meeting, and soon more trouble brewed up with the in-laws. Joseph's daughter Caroline thought she overheard Margaret Howell
criticize her father; Mrs. Howell had reasons to be displeased with Joseph, but exactly what she said is unknown. Joseph fired off a letter to
Jefferson, who thought the original report untrue, and after Jefferson's biting reply came back by messenger, the brothers considered
fighting a duel. Instead they did not speak for three years. For the first
time, Jefferson defied his imperious brother. He destroyed his will
from the 1840s and composed a new document giving most of his
property to his wife and child, even as Joseph vowed that none of his

property would ever go to the Howell family. Varina Davis received her due as a wife when she became a mother, proving herself, as it were, after seven years of marriage.[18]

⚜

SHE DID NOT LIVE on the plantation much longer. The Democrat Franklin Pierce won the presidential race of 1852, and he recruited Jefferson Davis, whom he had known since the 1830s, to serve as his Secretary of War. The President-elect, a New Hampshire native, preferred a balance between North and South in his cabinet, and Davis had campaigned hard for him. The appointment also rescued Davis from political oblivion. So in the spring of 1853 Varina returned to Washington, where the family rented a house on Thirteenth Street. Again the Davises were on close terms with the first couple. Franklin Pierce was a conservative, in favor of slavery's expansion and opposed to abolition, and he was sociable, suggestible, and easily dominated by strong-willed men in his cabinet such as Davis. Varina loved what she called Pierce's guileless nature and fine manners, and she honestly did not understand why others thought him weak.[19]

Varina also struck up a friendship with the First Lady, Jane Appleton Pierce, the daughter of a Congregational minister from New England. Mrs. Pierce had been unalterably opposed to her husband's political career and had prayed that he would lose the presidential race. When her prayers went unanswered and she had to move to Washington, she avoided the capital's social life as much as possible. Shy by nature, she missed her husband's inaugural because she was grieving over the death of their only child a few months before, and she held séances in the White House to communicate with her son. Although Varina did not share the First Lady's taste for séances, she discovered that Mrs. Pierce had depth and "lived much within herself." The two women began visiting and exchanging gifts. Much of their conversation centered on books. Varina thought Jane resembled the poet Elizabeth Barrett Browning, also delicate and erudite, and she admired the First Lady's wide reading.[20]

As a cabinet officer's wife, Varina Davis had demanding social obligations of her own. She no longer did secretarial work, because her husband had his own staff, but she was expected to entertain frequently and on a large scale. She invited each of the sixty-two senators and 234 congressmen to her house at least once a year for four years, in addition to holding weekly receptions on Tuesday afternoons that attracted dozens of people. Mrs. Davis had invitation-only

Franklin Pierce. The charming, gullible President.
(Library of Congress)

receptions for various guests, such as military officers leaving to witness the Crimean War. One night twenty-two guests came to dinner. If the Pierce administration was trying to win votes of particular congressmen, they were invited over for a friendly conversation or a meal. Visitors also appeared unannounced at the house at all hours asking for the secretary. A group of senators and congressmen once called on the Davises on a Sunday morning to discuss the Kansas-Nebraska Act with Jefferson, and another day a soldier's wife arrived at seven o'clock in the morning with her children to ask for a pardon for her husband. It was a hectic life. Occasionally Varina retreated upstairs to sit quietly and collect her thoughts.[21]

She nonetheless became a renowned hostess. In the midst of the bruising, full-throated political debate in Washington, a pleasant social life was necessary to soothe ruffled feelings and preserve friendships, and as Varina once observed, people need enjoyment as much as they need food. She could make small talk on a range of subjects, because in Washington "every body is well read, and well informed," as Mrs. Howell noted, and Varina realized it was important to speak to every guest at a party. She mastered Washington etiquette, a streamlined version of European court etiquette pioneered by Dolley Madison. Mrs. Davis learned where the hostess should stand at a reception (near the door), when evening dress should be worn (after six), and how to serve a five-course meal and with which wines. Just twenty-six years old when her husband became a cabinet secretary, she had to learn to put on an official persona. She was civil to obnoxious guests, and, as custom dictated, she was meticulous about returning social calls to politicians' wives, because a blunder could hurt her husband's career. Even though Jefferson was a Democrat and Varina had adopted his political views, Washington social life was fully bipartisan. She socialized with Whigs, and after the Whig Party disintegrated over the slavery issue in the mid-1850s and the Republican Party was founded, she added Republicans to her guest list.[22]

Varina Davis was married to a powerful public figure, and she knew some of the city's most eminent residents. She traded quips with Democratic editor Duff Cooper at a dinner party, she liked the Republican Senator William Seward of New York, a wiry man with a fondness for banter, and she knew the Republican Senator Charles Sumner of Massachusetts, whose verbal "pyrotechnics" sounded rehearsed, she thought. She became acquainted with Charles King, president of Columbia University, the naturalist Louis Agassiz, the chemist Benjamin Silliman, the astronomer Maria Mitchell, and Joseph Henry, the director of the Smithsonian, who regaled her with a discourse on tidal motions as they rode the ferry to Virginia one day. She met young people who would make their mark in the world, such as James Whistler, who worked for the government as a cartographer before leaving for Paris. Varina boasted to her mother that she gave some of the finest dinners in town, and she enjoyed her social position. But she knew that there was a lot of polite artifice in society. She was so "flattered and courted," she told Margaret Howell, that sometimes she longed for a little down-home bluntness.[23]

Being married to a cabinet officer, Varina had some indirect political influence. Although she recalled her interest in politics in the 1850s as "intense," she rarely campaigned with her husband after their children were born and her letters scarcely mention policy, legislation, or her husband's constituents, even though Jefferson controlled the Democratic Party in Mississippi. For her, politics was about the scrimmage in Washington. After James Buchanan was elected President in 1856, she knew six men who wanted to become his Secretary of State. She practiced the cheerful, open nepotism widespread in Washington, and she said that if she held elective office, assisting her friends would make it tolerable. She tried to aid relatives and friends by lobbying her husband or government officials for favors, such as helping a Howell kinsman gain an appointment to the U.S. Military Academy. She wrote Franklin Pierce asking that an army officer be allowed to delay his departure for California because his wife requested it; the President agreed, with the teasing remark that she had a man's handwriting (an angular script with the extrovert's slant to the right). As Pierce implied, women were not supposed to be too forthright. Sometimes Davis may have gone farther than her husband wanted. When she tried to find a job for her brother Beckett, she told her mother, "I did it without Jeff's consent and without help."[24]

But women did not have power, which is different from influence. They did not hold office in Washington or anywhere else, they did not vote in national elections, and they had not voted in state elections since New Jersey disenfranchised women at the dawn of the century. Antebellum women could attend political rallies, and in a few instances they wrote political pamphlets; the Whig Party, and later the Republican Party, were somewhat more welcoming than the Democrats, so long as women confined themselves to supporting the party leadership. Democrats typically portrayed themselves as upholding traditional gender roles and protecting the household from the government. Therefore they were not eager to include females in the political process, even in these secondary activities. Most citizens dismissed female abolitionists and suffrage activists as hopelessly naive or outright lunatics. Women were relegated to the sidelines of public life, and Varina Davis knew that. When women were invited to sit on the floor of the Senate to listen to a speech, she knew they were there "on sufferance," effectively and symbolically at the margins.[25]

She focused much of her energy on her domestic responsibilities, central among them her son. She rejoiced in his first words, his good looks, and his winsome temperament. When Franklin Pierce rode by one day on horseback, Samuel blew the President a kiss. Jefferson was just as devoted to his son, and he called him "le man," a Celtic endearment for "little man." Varina worried over Sam's every illness, and in the spring of 1854 he came down with the measles. Despite his parents' anxious nursing, he died on June 13, a few weeks before his second birthday, and was buried in Georgetown. Varina wrote the necessary letters informing her relatives and shut herself up at home. Her husband could hardly bear the sound of a child's voice, and Varina was still depressed that fall. At the end of the year the Davises moved to a new house between F and G Streets a few blocks west of the White House. Called the Everett House after the Massachusetts politician who once lived there, the mansion had twenty-three rooms and was one of the grandest houses in town.[26]

The Davises' fertility problems, whatever the cause, were over, for they had another child in February 1855. The girl resembled her grandmother Margaret Howell, for whom she was named, and she grew up to share her mother's olive complexion, as would all the Davis children. The baby was high-spirited, and she once bit a dog on the nose after the canine snapped at her first. The Davises spoiled Maggie more than a little, giving her a coral necklace and some gorgeous outfits. From the beginning she was her father's daughter. When her mother tried to discipline her, Maggie declared that her father would let her do as she wished. Both of the Davises were lenient parents by the standards of the time, preferring to send their children away from the table or slap them on the hand when they misbehaved, only spanking them as the last resort.[27]

Varina's younger siblings, who lived with her in Washington, became virtually a second set of children. Margaret and Becket arrived in 1853 and stayed for the rest of the decade, and Jeffy D. and Jane lived with her for months at a time. Varina promised her parents she would do her best for them all, and she spared no effort, hiring a governess and selecting the finest schools. Her husband paid their tuition and most of their expenses. He helped the children with their homework, but he sometimes intimidated the young Howells, for Margaret said "the slightest fault never escapes his notice." Their sister Varina, however, was truly a second mother. She delighted in their witticisms, and the teachers wrote to her, rather than her parents, about their conduct. During the holidays, the Howell siblings usually visited relatives in Pennsylvania and New Jersey or stayed with Varina. As she told her father in 1857, "God only knows" how little the passage of time had "weaned" her from her parents and siblings. Sometimes she thought their happiness should be her first obligation.[28]

She lavished special attention on Margaret, who was then entering her teens, and tried to inculcate in her a love of books, asking her to read aloud from Sir Walter Scott's *Ivanhoe* and Agnes Strickland's *Queens of England*. In 1853 she hosted a party for her sister attended by Pierre Soulé, a former senator and American ambassador to Spain; Sidney Webster, the President's private secretary; and some cabinet officers. Varina chose carefully which invitations her sister could accept, and she was a vigilant chaperone, because Margaret, a slender brunette, already took a keen interest in the opposite sex. Varina tried to protect what she candidly described as the teenager's "draggled tailed chastity" and make sure her sister was "pureminded." Margaret was sometimes flippant with Varina, responding to her plea that she think about her duty to God and other people by asking about a party hosted by the British ambassador. Varina worried that her sister had not yet learned to be unselfish, something she believed all women had to learn. Margaret was baptized into the Episcopal church, and in the 1850s the Davises became her legal guardians. More or less abdicating his own responsibility, William Howell called the Davises her "natural protectors." Varina had become the balance wheel for the entire family.[29]

While she lived in Washington, Varina kept up friendly relations with her Northern kinfolk. She was very fond of her uncle Joseph Howell, a thoughtful, deliberate man who owned a sizable farm in New Jersey and a house in Philadelphia, where he worked at the U.S. Custom House. His political views were those of a moderate Democrat. She liked his children, whom she invited to visit her in Washington, and she saw them when she visited Philadelphia. After Varina sent her siblings to an academy in Burlington, New Jersey, in 1858, she made sure that they spent time with their kinfolk, and her brother Jeffy D. corresponded with his New Jersey cousins. The Northern Howells were just as swift as other relatives, however, to ask the Davises for help in obtaining government jobs. Franklin Glaser, the German-born son of Varina's aunt Beulah, came to New York in the 1850s, and this earnest young man, popular with his American kin, asked for letters of introduction from Jefferson and Varina both, although he sometimes misspelled her name. She usually complied with these requests. Her uncle Joseph praised her "uniform kindness" to all of her relatives, which continued to 1861.[30]

❦

MRS. HOWELL DECLARED in 1852 that a successful pregnancy would make the Davis marriage happier, and her prediction came true to some extent. Varina must have been gratified at her husband's revised will in 1852, and she basked in her new status as a mother, because at last she was doing what a woman of her time was supposed to do. Motherhood made her more attractive by antebellum standards, for she gained weight and her figure filled out. She stopped calling her husband "Uncle Jeff" and adopted a Celtic endearment, "Banny." Jefferson's letters became markedly more affectionate for "Winnie," one of his nicknames for her. She always loved his polished manners, and he was sober most of the time, unlike a number of his colleagues on Capitol Hill. His conversation could be elegant, and he was considered so handsome that strangers on the street turned to look at him.[31]

His physical health was not very good, however, and Varina did her best to care for him. She sent lunch to his office to make sure he remembered to eat, and she served him dinner when he came home from work after midnight. When he fell ill, which was often, she nursed him herself. After he came down with a chill one day, she sent for a doctor and impulsively ran over to the Blairs' house to tell them he was sick. His left eye had been bothering him since the 1830s, and by the early 1850s he was partially blind, possibly because of a fever or a riding accident, and when he could not read, his wife stepped in to help him. He once said her tender care had saved his good eye, which she called the highest compliment anyone ever gave her, suggesting how important this interaction was in the marriage. They enacted the roles of nurse and patient dozens of times, and this seemed to fulfill emotional needs for them both, hers to take care of him, and his to be taken care of, sometimes, by his wife.[32]

Jefferson still made all of the key decisions in the marriage. Like his brother Joseph, he never discussed finances with his spouse, and he controlled the family budget, giving Varina an allowance to pay household bills. He was quick to scold her when she spent too much money. Even though he traveled frequently on party business, he decided if and when she could go South to visit her family. When she asked his permission in the spring of 1854, he replied that she "could not possibly do it," after which, Varina told her mother, "I can't understand," but she had to abide by his decision, since no respectable woman traveled without a male escort. Nor did the Davises always share their deepest feelings with each other. She told her mother in 1850 that she found it difficult to tell her spouse about her family's money woes, and she observed in 1854 that her husband's "alien-

Jefferson Davis, 1850s.
Considered a handsome man.
(Filson Historical Society)

72

ation" from his brother Joseph "preys upon his mind—but he never speaks of it."[33]

Her friendships therefore loomed large in her emotional life, and in Washington she had many friends of both sexes. She liked their neighbor Judah Benjamin, the brainy senator from Louisiana, and the debonair Dudley Mann, Pierce's Assistant Secretary of State who was very popular in Washington. But her closest friends were women, all of whom lived within walking distance in the residential neighborhoods near the White House. (The Blairs lived across the street from the executive mansion.) Varina believed that Washington developed a woman's innate character, for good or for ill. Some of these women she had known since the mid-1840s, such as Minna Blair; Minna's sister-in-law Lizzie Blair Lee; Mary Bache Walker; Mary's sister Matilda Bache Emory, married to U.S. army officer William Emory; Mrs. Henry Wayne, an army wife and a neighbor on F Street; Margaretta Hetzel, a widow whose husband, a Pennsylvanian, had died during the Mexican War; and Mary Ann Cobb, wife of Congressman Howell Cobb of Georgia.[34]

These friends were well-educated, middle- or upper-class women from all regions of the country whose husbands were affiliated with one political party or the other, or with neither, or who had changed parties. Varina liked all of these women—affectionate, congenial, and reliable—very much, and they liked her. Matilda Emory later called her a "courtly" woman with a "lovable disposition." With them Varina could have candid talk that went beyond the politesse that a cabinet officer's wife had to engage in so often. She relished these conversations, once arriving early at a levee so she could see the Blair women privately before the other guests came. They were not only confidantes but allies in the prosaic duties of running a household. Varina nursed her friends when they were ill, and, she said, when her daughter was sick a friend kept her "courage up." In the last weeks of a difficult pregnancy, when Varina had to remain in bed, one of her friends moved in to assist her, and when she was nursing a baby, they took turns breast-feeding after her milk gave out. When she came

Minna Blair, wife of Montgomery Blair. One of Varina Davis's closest friends. (Library of Congress)

down with a fever, Varina said that her friends "did everything in the world" for her.[35]

She also developed a rich inner life. In her free time, she pursued literary culture, attending dramatic readings by the British actress Fanny Kemble, who did the soliloquies from *Macbeth* to perfection, Davis thought. She found time to read, often late at night. Although she enjoyed music and the pictorial arts, she had a literary sensibility, and in the 1850s she became a voracious, eclectic reader. Her letters are filled with literary references from Shakespeare to popular novels, and she was steeped in the culture of her time. Characters from literature took deep root in her imagination; "like household friends," they became a source of solace, she said. In her old age, she said that if she were still wealthy she would spend all of her money on books, and in Washington the Davises could afford all the books she wanted. When she traveled out of town, she wanted plenty of books, including titles in history and fiction, so long as they were well written. She read the works of Maria Edgeworth, Charles Dickens, George Sand, and Lord Byron at a time when some of their books, such as *Don Juan,* were considered quite daring for proper ladies.[36]

Reading was not just a solitary pleasure but a social activity. In Washington, unlike rural Mississippi, Varina knew many people who loved books, and with these friends she debated the merits of characters in Scott's *Rob Roy* and Pope's *Rape of the Lock,* and she received books from her friends by then-popular writers, such as the Anglo-Irish poet George Darley. Reading also gave her a code for communicating with other literate women. With her closest friends, she began to use literary references as shorthand to express unpalatable feelings of loneliness, fatigue, or disappointment. She told Jane Pierce that she felt exhausted after moving to a new house while her children were sick and supervising an auction of some of her furniture; now, like the "weary knife grinder" in George Canning's eighteenth-century poem, she had no tale to tell. In a letter to Pierce two years later, she paraphrased Dickens's Mr. Micawber to describe her labors in Mississippi, where the summer had been hot and she had been acutely bored, as "honorable but not remunerative." Sometimes her reading veered in a subversive direction. After she read Dinah Mulock's novel of 1856, *John Halifax, Gentleman,* a coming-of-age story about an English abolitionist, she pronounced it a charming book and urged her parents to read it. Her husband read books, of course, and his letters contain some allusions to Jonathan Swift and Charles Dickens, but literature did not seem to play much of a part in his inner life, or in the marriage.[37]

JEFFERSON DAVIS'S TERM as Secretary of War ended in 1856. He missed serving in the U.S. Senate, and after he discreetly lobbied the Mississippi legislature, that body elected him to the position. The new President was James Buchanan, a Pennsylvania Democrat who over his long career had accrued many political debts without achieving anything especially notable. Like Pierce, he accepted slavery and was on friendly terms with politicians from the party's powerful Southern wing. Buchanan's administration would be filled with increasingly acrimonious clashes over slavery, such as the Dred Scott decision, the Brooks-Sumner caning, and John Brown's raid at Harper's Ferry. Nervous of confrontation, Buchanan struck many of his peers as too timid for his responsibilities. He stated repeatedly, once in Varina's presence, that he hoped the sectional crisis would not come on his watch. "Pulpy" by one description, aged far beyond his years, he had never married, and his bachelor status was the subject of pointed comment. Varina was fond of him, however, and enjoyed his wit. She was on friendly terms with Buchanan's niece Harriet Lane, who served as his official hostess. An impeccable dresser, Lane was interested in the arts and had acquired distinctly European manners during her residence abroad. Her regal detachment put some people off, and an acquaintance called her smiles rare and cold. Watchful, careful, and correct, Lane said as little as possible and maintained a polite social discourse despite the regional tensions in the capital.[38]

In 1857, Varina Davis gave birth to another child, which nearly killed her. After Jefferson Jr. was born in January, she contracted puerperal fever and lay at death's door for several weeks. Medical science had no effective treatment for the illness, and she suffered a great deal. Her husband and her women friends looked after her, and when a snowstorm kept Margaretta Hetzel from the Davis residence, William Seward arranged for a sleigh to take her there, a gesture Varina never forgot. After some weeks she fought off the illness, and when she was strong enough to sit in the parlor, she received calls from both Franklin Pierce and James Buchanan. Amid the joy that the baby brought to the house, however, Varina's father sent a brief mes-

Harriet Lane Johnston. The glacially composed
First Lady, niece of President Buchanan.
(Smithsonian American Art Museum)

77

sage of congratulations to Jefferson and expressed no sympathy about his daughter's brush with death. When Varina read his "short, mercantile note" she burst into tears.[39]

After Mrs. Davis recovered, her social duties resumed at a breakneck pace. Before James Buchanan was inaugurated in March 1857, she hosted four dinners and a reception, her last as a cabinet member's wife, and then returned the visits she owed her callers. By this time the feuding Davis brothers had made peace. Joseph told his brother that he may have made a mistake, and when he visited Washington Varina hosted a party in his honor. But when her brother-in-law offered in princely fashion to buy her a new dress for the inaugural, she demurred. On Inauguration Day, she joined her husband for the long procession to the Capitol, where the President took the oath of office, and on the same day Jefferson Davis was sworn in as the new senator from Mississippi. The Davises led a glamorous life in the capital, but the mundane reality of the plantation was waiting. After the family returned to Brierfield that spring, Varina found the locks broken, the cooking utensils missing, and the sheets cut up for napkins, probably by the overseer. She sat down and cried for a moment, then brought out her sewing machine and began making summer clothing for the slaves. Her husband left to attend a political meeting in Vicksburg, and, feeling "right lonely," she asked her mother to send her sister Jane for a visit.[40]

She was still looking out for the Howells. Her father managed to buy some property in New Orleans, but he acknowledged that he had not been able to learn perseverance in his business affairs. When Varina asked him to be candid about his money problems, promising to give him everything she had, he would not confide in her. Once again, her brothers did not provide much assistance. Joseph fought in several duels, one of which appeared in the national press, and he may have sustained a permanent head injury, for he was listed in the New Orleans census of 1860 as "idiotic." For whatever reason, he could not hold a job for very long. William enrolled in a small college in Mississippi, quit, then worked for Jefferson's cotton merchant in New Orleans. In 1859 he married Mary Leacock, a minister's daughter, and took a job at the Custom House in New Orleans, but he was prone to idleness, as his big sister realized. Over the course of the decade, her relationship with her mother began to shift, as Varina took the lead and advised Mrs. Howell on family matters. But it was still her mother to whom Varina opened her heart, longing for her visits so they could talk, and she tried to follow her teachings on the supreme importance of duty.[41]

4

FIRST LADY

IN THE LATE 1850s, Washington society reached such heights of extravagance that residents compared it to the court at Versailles or the reign of Louis Napoleon. Whatever historical analogy applied, new arrivals, such as Mary Cunningham Logan, the wife of an Illinois congressman, were taken aback by the "ostentatious display." Hostesses vied with each other for creative ways to amuse their guests, one of them installing movable panels in the ceiling over the dinner table and showering her guests with flower petals between courses. Fashion became just as ostentatious. Varina Davis employed a dressmaker and had an extensive wardrobe of conservative taste—conservative for the late 1850s. She attended a White House event wearing a black lace bertha and a golden silk gown trimmed with black velvet and small lemon-colored bows. She continued her high-profile social life, dining one evening with Senator John Bell, the Tennessean who would run for President in 1860, and the Baroness de Stoeckel, the American-born wife of the Russian envoy. She told Jane Pierce in 1858 that she had never seen anything like the hectic round of parties, breakfasts, oratorios, matinees, and riding parties, and that it would take the pen of Laurence Sterne or Jonathan Swift to portray the turbulence of society, the new faces, new fashions, and competition for status.[1]

In this environment, Davis stood out for her erudition and her bracing wit. The word that many residents of Washington associated with her was *cultivated.* In old age, she said that conversation was an art, and if she talked as she wrote—her letters full of literary allusions and comic thumbnail sketches of people she met—then she must have been a superb conversationalist. She could bring a dinner party to life, and she knew how to defuse an uncomfortable situation with humor. When Varina received several callers one day, including Mrs. Clement Clay Sr., wife of the former senator from Alabama, the elderly Mrs. Clay did not recognize one of the guests and began to sulk. Davis coaxed her back into the conversation with "bright flashes" of wit. Varina hugely enjoyed wit in other people, relating with pleasure a bragging contest between Britons and Americans at a dinner party. An American journalist who found Senator Davis polite but rather austere believed that Varina's "amiability" won her husband many friends.[2]

Yet she did not suffer fools gladly. She played a practical joke on Winfield Scott, commanding general of the U.S. Army, who had feuded with her husband over promotion and other issues since the Mexican War. Many people found Scott vain, and Varina thought him a bit grandiose, so she decided to take advantage of his well-known fussiness about food. While he was a guest at her table he disparaged the soup, whereupon the hostess sweetly informed him that it had been prepared by his own chef, whom she had hired for the evening. The story was repeated with hilarity throughout Washington, which did not endear her to General Scott. Her humor could be cutting. At a costume ball in 1858, she appeared as Madame de Staël, the author of *Corinne,* who might best be described as an iconoclast who wanted to escape from convention even as she conformed to it. Varina acted in character, delivering repartee in English and French to anyone who would "cross swords" with her. The guests danced until dawn, and a newspaper listed Mrs. Davis as one of the "prominent" ladies there.[3]

She was still largely indifferent to the regional tensions on the rise in the late 1850s. Varina considered enrolling her sister Margaret in music school in New York, then decided against it only because it was too expensive. By some astute lobbying, including speaking to President Buchanan, she secured her brother Becket's appointment to the

Winfield Scott. Subject of a practical joke by Varina Davis.
(National Portrait Gallery, Smithsonian Institution)

U.S. Marines Corps. In the summer of 1858, the Davis family went to New England, where Bowdoin College awarded Jefferson Davis an honorary degree, and the family took a holiday in Maine, attending clambakes and a picnic, gazing at the dramatic coastline, and visiting their friends, the Woodburys and the Porters. Varina made friends with several local women, some of whom she corresponded with for years. When Alexander Bache, the brother of Mary Bache Walker and head of the U.S. Coast Survey, invited the Davises to go camping, she was enthralled by the rocky landscape, the flowers sprouting in the green moss, and the stillness of the night air, so different from the "insect clamor" in the South. In the evenings, the party pitched tents and listened to Verdi on a hand-cranked music box under the stars.[4]

During the Davises' return trip to Washington, the family stopped in Boston, and while they were staying at the Tremont House a quint-essential Yankee saved the life of one of their children. Jeff Jr. came down with the croup, and just when it seemed that he might die, Mrs. Harrison Gray Otis appeared at the hotel. A member of the dis-tinguished Boston family, Otis knew homeopathic medicine and vol-unteered to help, even though she had never met the Davises. She sat up all night with mother and child, treating the baby and, what was probably just as important, radiating calm and confidence. The child recovered, and Varina never forgot that this lady had saved her boy's life. After Jefferson made a speech at Faneuil Hall, the family stopped to see Varina's kin in Philadelphia. Lizzie Blair Lee said that her friend returned to Washington full of enthusiasm for New England hospital-ity and homeopathic medicine.[5]

IN THE FALL OF 1858, while Varina was in Washington, a great wave of unhappiness swept over her. What precipitated this *cri de coeur* is unknown, but suddenly she felt trapped in her duties. Her life had be-come a "weary pilgrimage," she told her mother, and she wondered if she would ever be able to do as she pleased. Even though she believed this was the lot of all humankind, she exclaimed, "Oh it would be lovely sometimes to cut duty, and go on a *bust*." She wanted to be carefree, if only for a few days, and said that her cares had worn out her youth. Then she pulled back. She observed that duty refined one's character, and her flights of fancy were "lame efforts" anyway. It was better, she wrote to Mrs. Howell, to say no more of it. Varina's religious faith, which had gradually deepened in her late twenties, may have provided her with some comfort. At age thirty, she had been confirmed in the Episcopal church. Afterward she attended services regularly, although she never had a typical conversion experience. Instead she followed the high church tradition, with its emphasis on reason and a lifelong effort to follow Christian teaching. When she urged her sister to concentrate on her "duties to her God, and fellow beings," that seems to be what her faith meant to her, an inspiration to do her duty.[6]

Varina Davis mentioned her unhappiness in 1858 only once to her husband, telling him she would refrain from a "series of useless regrets" about their long separations. When they were apart again in the summer of 1859, she said she looked forward to the future when they could spend more time together. In fact, they lived apart for almost ten months during the three years between the start of his Senate term in March 1857 and the end of the 1859 calendar year. Jefferson gave many speeches for the Democratic Party every year, and in 1859 he spent weeks at Brierfield trying to salvage a crop from floods that plagued the plantation. The Davises wrote to each other with affection when apart, but when they both were in Washington and living in the same house, they did not have the kind of companionship she wanted. Her work made the day pass quickly, she told her mother, but she yearned for more time with her husband, who sometimes came home from the office at one o'clock in the morning. He still made all of the important decisions, including those about money, and she still had to ask his permission to see her own family. In the fall of 1858 she admitted to her mother that she had been "begging" Jefferson to let her visit her family in the South, but "he does not say yea or nay."[7]

When a couple spends so much time apart, the possibility of adultery arises, at least in theory, and Washington provided plenty of opportunities for those so inclined. Gossip circulated about various politicians in town, such as the unmarried Thaddeus Stevens, or about couples who lived apart, such as Mr. and Mrs. Winfield Scott, or Judah Benjamin, whose attempt to reconcile with his wife, then living in Paris, failed. Rose Greenhow once said half-jokingly that Mary Chesnut's husband was one of the few blameless men in the capital. Whether Jefferson Davis ever strayed during the months apart from his wife is not known. That he had an eye for the ladies was long remembered, and he had a flirtatious correspondence with Anna Carroll of Maryland, one of the first women journalists. (They had a falling out during the secession crisis.) Varina once told Mary Ann Cobb that because both of their husbands flirted with other women, they should take their staffs in hand "and go, and surprise them." But in the busy gossip circuits in Washington, Jefferson's name was never linked with anyone in particular.[8]

Neither was Varina's. Her letters contain no hint of infidelity, where we might not expect it, or in the writings of the many people who knew her, where it might surface. Mrs. Davis received a lot of polite attention from men, but she assured her mother that she was "not fond of their admiration," and she had the good sense to avoid the appearance of impropriety, rebuffing a popinjay who approached her at a ball to ask if he could kiss her. She may have had no desire to seek affection elsewhere, for she still felt a strong physical attraction for her husband, longing to have him in her arms whenever they were apart. Moreover, she was a harsh critic of adultery committed by other women. When Congressman Daniel Sickles murdered attorney Philip Barton Key on the street in February 1859, Varina Davis felt as shocked as everyone else, but after Teresa Sickles admitted to having an affair with Key, she was appalled. She did not know Mrs. Sickles but condemned her infidelity and called the scandal "filth—filth."[9]

For both of the Davises, the children helped bond them together. Varina called them the greatest happiness of their lives. She tried to spend time with them every day despite her other duties, writing letters with the children "stirring round like mad." When Jefferson was at home, he was an informal, affectionate father. A neighbor once found the senator flat on his back in his library with the children climbing all over him. He loved hearing about his offspring when he was away from home, and his wife supplied vignettes of them standing hand in hand in their new clothes, Maggie a pretty girl with a quicksilver temperament and Jeff an athletic boy who resembled his grandfather Howell. But they did not see their father very much. Maggie missed him during his long absences and asked if she could go to Mississippi with him. Jeff Jr. liked to sing a tune of his own invention called "I Want Daddy Home." Once he offered to send two dollars he had in his possession so his father could come back.[10]

Varina knew another child was on the way by the fall of 1858, and because the doctor said she could contract puerperal fever again, she prepared calmly for the possibility that she might die. She made clothes for the baby and chose not to share the doctor's warning with her spouse, who was at Brierfield; instead she sent him instructions on what to plant in the garden, and then, with the assistance of a clerk, mailed two thousand copies of one of her husband's speeches. She later told her mother, "If I had to die it was useless to make you all wretches." But when she had a son on April 18, 1859, all went well, and after she gave her husband the joyful news, she gingerly brought up an idea he had proposed earlier, that the baby be named after Joseph E. Davis. She preferred naming him William after her father, and, although she did not say so, her older brother was named for Joseph Davis, her sons Samuel and Jefferson Jr. were named for men in the Davis family, and seven boys in the Davis clan had already been named for her brother-in-law, including Joseph Davis Brodhead, Malie's son, born in January 1859. Her in-laws pointedly suggested that she follow her husband's wishes anyway, which annoyed Varina so much that she threatened to call the boy Deuteronomy. To her mother she said that naming a child was the "highest compliment in a woman's power," and she could not pay tribute to a man who had treated her with "injustice and unkindness" from her youth "up to middle age." She resented her brother-in-law's fell maneuvers more as she grew older and understood all of the consequences, and in 1859, she told Mrs. Howell, she came close to hating him.[11]

But she gave in to her husband's wishes, as he expected, and the boy was named Joseph Evan Davis. Soon afterward, her brother-in-law asked her to go with him to Europe because he needed a traveling companion with whom he could discuss the great sights he would encounter in the Old World. His own wife was too badly educated to converse with him on these subjects, so he offered to pay the passage for the Davis children and a nurse if Varina would travel with them. To this stupefying request, she said no, but Varina forgave her husband, who had suggested naming the boy Joseph in the first place. By now she had learned the central lesson, that her husband's wishes usually prevailed, and a related lesson, that the couple would spend a good deal of time apart. She passed most of the summer with her children at a Maryland farm, where some of her friends congregated, while her husband visited occasionally between trips to Washington and the Deep South. Her views of marriage she expressed obliquely in the late 1850s in the guestbook of her friend Catherine Thompson. Jacob Thompson, a Mississippi Democrat, was Secretary of the Interior in the Buchanan administration, and the couples met often in society. Mrs. Davis inscribed this passage, apparently her own composition, about her "good husband":

> He's managed to offer both love, and esteem,
> The latter by far the best feeling I deem,
> Though to disperse them between the sexes,
> The Wise, the Great, the Good still perplexes.

The distribution of love and esteem between the Davises appears to have been somehow unsatisfactory, but these rueful lines, done with a wistful touch, suggest that Varina had taught herself to accept it. She may have thought it was a feature of other marriages as well. Otherwise she had the comforts of life in Washington: friends she cherished, children she adored, and the opportunity to launch her siblings in the world.[12]

She enjoyed Washington for yet another reason, the town was relatively tolerant of unorthodox behavior by women. After one occasion when Jefferson upbraided her for spending too much money, Varina earned some cash by selling a story to a New York magazine. The publication paid her fifty dollars, a hefty sum, and offered her a regular assignment, which she declined. She published the story under a pseudonym sometime in the 1850s and unfortunately left no surviving copy and no hint as to the subject or the magazine's title. We know of its existence only because she mentioned it later to a friend. More unorthodox behavior occurred. When she was pregnant with Joseph, she attended the theater alone, even though custom dictated that an expectant mother should not appear in public. In September 1860 she endorsed a sewing machine in *Harper's Weekly,* stating that she used a Grover and Baker model, one of the first portable machines, and she liked its stitching capacity. She probably did the ad for the money—the Davises were renting a modest house on I Street—and because Jefferson almost certainly would have vetoed the idea, she probably did not consult him in advance. The other endorsements came from four men whose wives liked the machine, and Varina was the only woman quoted by name. Married women, especially politicians' wives, rarely behaved in such a way, but Varina did not hear a ripple of criticism from her peers.[13]

<hr />

IN THE LAST YEAR of President Buchanan's term, as slavery moved to the center of political discourse, Washington society began to fragment along regional lines, but Varina Davis maintained her friendships, and her civility, to the very end of the decade. Women both led and followed in the polarization—in 1859 Mrs. Stephen Douglas stopped visiting the White House because of her spouse's disputes with Buchanan—and Mrs. Davis lagged behind her peers in hating citizens from other parts of the country. Mary Logan, wife of the Illinois congressman, remembered her "cordial greeting to all callers," and Davis continued to socialize with Northerners and Southerners, Republicans and Democrats. She related that two Republicans she met at a dinner party were pleasant company, and despite her husband's animosity toward Stephen Douglas and her own dislike for the Illinois senator, whom she described as a "party trickster," she graciously ceded Adele Douglas the seat of honor at a party because she ranked Varina, meaning that Adele's husband had been in the Senate longer than her husband. Varina recognized that the Republicans had talent and thought William Pitt Fessenden, a moderate elected from Maine in 1859, the most capable. In 1860 she attended a ball with one of the Blair women and a White House dinner for the Prince of Wales, the future Edward VII. She confided to Jane Pierce that she did not understand why others thought British aristocrats superior to "our own people," meaning the American people.[14]

The Blairs, longtime residents of Washington, were among Varina's closest friends. Democrats who changed parties in the 1850s to become Free-Soilers and Republicans, the Blair menfolk were admired and feared in equal measure for their combativeness. Even though Francis Preston Blair, the head of the clan, never held national office, he was perceived as one of the most influential behind-the-scenes figures in town, and his son Montgomery, who had what Varina called a "thoroughly American" face, was, she said, puritanical, fearless, and outspoken. The Blairs' political views were somewhat inconsistent, for Francis Preston opposed the westward expansion of slavery without believing in racial equality or freeing his own slaves, even though Montgomery served as legal counsel for Dred Scott in 1857. Francis Preston's daughter Lizzie, married to Samuel Phillips Lee of the U.S. navy, was an ardent Unionist even though she too did not believe in racial equality. Varina continued to be fond of Lizzie Blair Lee and Minna Blair, although the sisters-in-law did not care for each other, and she liked Francis Preston Blair, who was a warm, devoted friend to people he liked.[15]

Although the Blairs had become convinced that slaveholding politicians were trying to take over the Democratic Party and destroy the Union, and some of them had privately hoped that Henry Foote would beat Jefferson Davis in the Mississippi governor's race in 1851, they maintained their friendship with Varina Davis. In 1859 she wanted to spend the summer in Maryland with the Blairs, because, Jefferson said dryly, paraphrasing the Republican party slogan, she had "'free

soil' proclivities." In the spring of 1860 Varina invited Lizzie Blair Lee
to have lunch at her house and called her "the best woman in the
world," and the two women continued their easy friendship that fall,
Lee borrowing food from Davis's kitchen when she could not go to
the market. As they discussed making a visit to Silver Spring, the
Blair residence outside Washington, Lee anticipated that her friend's
"agreeability" would depend on how the state elections went in October, meaning how they went for the Democratic Party in general, because Jefferson Davis was not up for reelection to the Senate.[16]

Varina Davis's mood was indeed apprehensive as election season
approached. As the nation considered the presidential candidates, the
Republican Abraham Lincoln, Democrats Stephen Douglas and John
Breckinridge, and the Unionist John Bell, she knew that some Southern politicians were planning to leave the Union if Lincoln was
elected. She had known since the summer of 1860, if not earlier, that
her husband was being talked about as the chief executive of the seceded states. In October 1860 in a letter to Jane Pierce she expressed
a range of conflicting opinions: fear, love of the Union, racial prejudice, a willingness to consider war, and hope that the sectional crisis
could be resolved without war. Political matters looked "very dark,"
she said, and threatened the Union—"under which," she said, "we
have lived like the scriptural birds in the cedars of Lebanon," a reference to the book of Isaiah, with the connotation of living safely under
God's protection. Each night she prayed for peace but feared her
prayer would not be answered. After predicting that Lincoln would
probably win the election, she declared that the country might be
"buried" under "negrodom," which suggests that she feared he would
emancipate the slaves. If so, she had begun to feel for the first time
that armed resistance might be best and that the "Southern men"
would resist. Yet Davis also wished she had lived sixty years earlier,
when the nation was at peace. Then she sent her "affectionate remembrance" to Franklin Pierce and concluded the letter "Very sincerely and affectionately your friend." The last seven weeks of the
campaign Davis spent apart from her husband, who left on a speaking
tour of the Deep South in mid-September. From Washington she an-

Varina Howell Davis, circa 1860. On the eve of leaving Washington, the city she loved. (Museum of the Confederacy, Richmond, Virginia)

swered some of his routine correspondence for him, and she wrote to him, but her letters did not reach him and are now lost. Nor is there any evidence of her immediate reaction after the votes were tallied on November 6. Her husband voted for Breckinridge, as did most voters in Mississippi.[17]

BETWEEN LINCOLN'S ELECTION on November 6, 1860, and her husband's resignation from the Senate on January 21, 1861, Varina wrote four letters, which are filled with contradictory, strangely jarring elements about the political crisis unfolding around her. In the first letter, written to her husband on November 15, she hoped that newspaper reports about his good health were accurate, because she had not heard from him in a month, and after relaying news of their children, she related that there was "intense" interest in Washington as to what he was going to do. "I always say I don't know and can't guess," she wrote, and when anyone talked "impudently" of disunion in her presence, she denied that her husband was a secessionist. The town was gloomy, with the politicians trying to decide what to do. *"Everybody is scared,"* she said, especially President Buchanan. Senator Louis Wigfall pontificated, Senator Robert Toombs considered resigning his seat, Secretary Jacob Thompson waited to see what the public wanted, and editor William M. Browne "rings the true metal" for secession, repudiating Buchanan, even though Browne's newspaper had been the official administration organ. She closed with a prayer that God would direct him "right." The phrase "true metal" could be interpreted as support for secession, whereas the adverb "impudently" applied to talk of disunion could have the opposite connotation. On November 27, her husband arrived in Washington.[18]

Sometime in December 1860, Varina Davis penned a one-paragraph note that appears to be both self-conscious about region and strongly pro-Southern. To the sergeant-at-arms in the Senate she recommended Margaret Coleman for a patronage job as attendant in the "ladies' apartment" in the Senate. Even though Coleman was not a relative or friend, Davis had already mentioned it to him before, and this time she added firmly, "I know you could not appoint a northern woman" and Coleman's appointment would give her "great satisfaction." Another one-paragraph letter, composed on Christmas Day 1860, to James Buchanan is quite friendly, with no references to the secession crisis. She sent her holiday greetings to the President and a gift, some slippers she made for him, and assured him of her "sincere affection" and "great regard." She signed it "faithfully your friend" and stayed on good terms with him although her husband broke all social contact after assailing Buchanan's policies in January 1861. As the Davises prepared to leave Washington in January, she went alone to the White House to bid him what she called an "affectionate" farewell. Finally, she wrote a short note to an unidentified friend on the first of the new year, 1861, describing the town as a "great mausoleum" filled with "gloom," with no dinners and no parties. The "Southern men" no longer called on Buchanan, feeling that he had misled them about reinforcing Fort Sumter, but she said, "I love the dear old man & would like to forget that I do." This does not sound like a true believer in the secessionist creed.[19]

The evidence from her contemporaries in the winter of 1860–61 is just as contradictory. Her friend Lizzie Blair Lee was not sure of Varina's views. According to Lee, Davis announced in December 1860 that she would no longer associate with Republicans, even as she showed "extra civility" to Lee herself, whose family was full of Republicans. Lee started calling her "Queen Varina," even though Mrs. Davis might "pretend to be mad." (Lee once accused Jessie Fremont, whom she thought too ambitious, of holding "court.") Lee suspected that Jefferson Davis "plays the calm game & evidently looks to being Dictator" and huffed that she would avoid both of the Davises in the future, but a few days later in December the two women attended a party together. During the festivities, Davis asked if Lee was coming to the South to "fight" against her. As people clustered around them to listen, Lee replied no, she would not let Davis "break any *bonds*" between them. The crowd burst into applause, but Davis's response is not recorded.[20]

Other people believed that Varina Davis supported secession and

burned with ambition for her husband's success and her own prominence. In December 1860 the Blairs quoted Senator Albert Gallatin
Brown, a Democrat from Mississippi, as saying that he did not want
to see Varina become an "Empress" and Jefferson a "Dictator." In his
postwar memoir, Brown described Jefferson as a man with poor
judgment, not a fiend, and said nothing about Varina. In 1865 David
Dixon Porter imparted to Gideon Welles, Lincoln's Secretary of the
Navy, a conversation he had with Varina in December 1860. She had
called South Carolina's secession "glorious news" and hoped that the
seceded states would create a monarchy in the South. Davis also said,
Porter alleged, that President Buchanan had secretly encouraged the
secessionists. In his memoir of 1885 Porter repeated the anecdote but
left out Davis's name, calling her a "magnificent" lady married to an
unnamed Southern man, and he gushed that she shone in Washington
society like the planet Venus, brighter than all women. Robert Dale
Owen of Indiana, son of the famous reformer, wrote in 1863 that
Varina Davis claimed in January 1861 that she was not worried because the Middle States and the Old Northwest would be the South's
allies if secession took place; his source, Owen said, was an unnamed
"friend" from Pennsylvania. Other Washingtonians, some anonymous
"ladies" quoted in the *New York Tribune,* had the impression that Davis
wanted to be First Lady of the United States, not the Confederacy.[21]

Another witness, Elizabeth Keckley, a free black woman who worked
for Varina Davis, published a memoir after the war filled with another set of contradictions. Keckley was in her mid-thirties and an
accomplished seamstress, and after Margaretta Hetzel recommended
her, she worked in the Davis household from November 1860 to January 1861. She perceived that Mrs. Davis was "warmly attached" to
Washington. Davis said that she did not want to break off her "old associations" and go to the South for "trouble and deprivation," and
Keckley overheard Davis tell a friend that she would rather stay in the
national capital and "be kicked about" than go to the South and become "Mrs. President." Davis also claimed that there would be a war
over abolition, which she, Davis, opposed, that the South would win
the war, and that she, Davis, would eventually become First Lady of

the United States. Keckley said that Davis invited her to come to the South and work for her, but she declined, even though she liked Mrs. Davis, because she believed that the South would lose the war. After the couple left town in January 1861, Keckley never saw them again. Yet other witnesses had diverging memories of Varina Davis's opinions. Mary Chesnut recalled that Varina told Mrs. Benjamin Huger in the summer of 1860 that the South would secede if Lincoln was elected and Jefferson Davis would be made President of the new country, but, Varina reckoned, "The whole thing is bound to be a failure." At some time before the Chesnuts left Washington in December 1860, Mary said Varina appeared at the White House wearing a badge on her lapel saying that her husband was "no seceder."[22]

All of these statements about the secession winter may be biased in different ways, starting with Varina Davis's own remarks. In the winter of 1860–61, she may have been undecided about secession, or she may have made different comments to different individuals, dissembling as a politician's wife often had to do. The witnesses may have misrepresented or misunderstood her views, due to their feelings of friendship or ill will for one or both of the Davises, the benefit of hindsight, or their own fallible memories. They all had prejudices: the Blairs were close friends and Unionists, and Chesnut, who became a close friend in Richmond, was a secessionist. David Porter and Elizabeth Keckley liked Mrs. Davis, but both were staunch Unionists. Albert Brown's relationship with Jefferson Davis had cooled during their long association in politics, and his assertions, and those of David Porter, are accompanied by dubious claims, given that Jefferson Davis became a president, not a dictator, and James Buchanan was a weak president, not a secret secessionist. (Brown joined the Confederate army and later served in the Confederate Senate, while Porter remained in the U.S. navy.) Porter is the only witness who claimed that Varina Davis had monarchist views, and Keckley the only one who said Davis confidently predicted the South would win the war. Robert Dale Owen was a Unionist, and his Pennsylvania "friend" could have been anyone, with any kind of motive. The anonymous "ladies" quoted in the *New York Tribune* may or may not have known Davis, and they too could have had a host of motives. And there is always the possibility that Varina's contemporaries projected their fears and hopes onto her that fateful winter, sometimes conflating her views with those of her husband, sometimes not.

In fact, Varina Davis had a number of misgivings about secession that were the natural product of her life experience. Her family history was intertwined with the nation's history, and she felt very proud of her grandfather Howell, who had fought alongside George Washington in the Revolution, and her grandfather Kempe, who also served. Her relatives in both regions, her New England tutor, her Philadelphia schooling, and her residence in Washington had prevented the development of the crude stereotypes that many white Southerners had of Yankees. Her travels in the North, most recently her New England holiday, had the same leavening effect. She was better traveled and better educated than most white Southerners and understood more fully the resources the North could bring to bear on a war, and she knew it would pit her friends, neighbors, and kinsmen against each other, and some of them could die. The threat to her immediate family was dire. The political crisis came in the midst of her childbearing years, and she had three children to raise. Her husband could be arrested, imprisoned, or killed if he headed the new government.

Furthermore, public position, in and of itself, no longer had great appeal for her. After meeting the Prince of Wales at the White House in the fall of 1860, she told Jane Pierce that she was "deficient in reverence for rank—perhaps because [she had] tested thoroughly the hollowness of position, on a small scale." Her friendships with Jane Pierce and Margaret Taylor alerted her to the loneliness of being a First Lady, and she knew that even the composed Harriet Lane had her detractors. Varina realized when her husband ran for the governor's chair in 1851 that she probably was not temperamentally suited to be a governor's wife. She once told Lizzie Blair Lee that being a senator was the best job in Washington, with the implication that being a senator's wife was the best job for a politician's spouse. Varina had been comfortable in Washington as one of an ensemble of politicians' wives, not alone in the spotlight.[23]

At the same time, she had motives to support secession, and they too were the product of her life experience. She believed in states' rights and opposed what she believed to be the concentration of power at the federal level, telling a friend after the war, contra Gideon Welles, that she feared that the federal government might turn into something like a monarchy. She supported slavery, and Lincoln's election threatened the expansion of slavery into the West. She later declared that emancipation was unconstitutional and denounced abolitionists for their attacks on the Constitution. She apparently found it hard to believe that politicians who opposed slavery were sincere in their convictions. In the 1850s she asked William Seward if he believed his public statements against bondage, and when the New Yorker smilingly replied that he uttered them only to get votes, she could not tell if he was joking. Slavery as an economic system had saved her from the poverty that gripped her parents, and the labor of the Davis bondsmen in Mississippi had created her husband's fortune. The work of the house slaves in Washington gave her the leisure to go to parties, host parties, and read late into the night. Through the 1850s, minstrel shows performed at the White House, and slaves worked in the executive mansion, and all of this Varina Davis took for granted. Her views on race placed her in the middle of the spectrum of opinion among whites of her generation, far to the right of all abolitionists and to the left of her husband. Despite her admission in 1852 that slaves were human beings with their frailties, she did not support emancipation.[24]

As we sort through Varina Davis's own statements and the testimony of the various witnesses from the winter of 1860–61, the wisest conclusion appears to be that she was both pro-Union and pro-slavery; that she believed the states had the right to secede and thought armed resistance might be necessary, but the *casus belli* were not yet sufficient; that she wanted the states to remain in the Union and try to effect another compromise; that she loved life in Washington and did not want to leave. She was ambivalent about secession in the dictionary sense of the word, holding contradictory opinions. Her ambivalence would surface during the war and for much of the rest of her life, as she teetered back and forth. If women had the suffrage in 1860, she almost certainly would have voted for the slaveholding Unionist John Bell. But Bell lost and Lincoln won, so she wavered in the middle of the spectrum, hesitating as did some of her Washington friends, such as First Lady Harriet Lane, former President Franklin Pierce, former Vice President George Dallas, and Robert J. Walker, former Secretary of the Treasury. Most of these people in the middle, such as George Dallas and Robert J. Walker, supported the Union. Families in Varina's circle differed on secession. Of Jefferson's relatives from his first marriage, his former brother-in-law, surgeon Robert C. Wood Sr., was an unconditional Unionist, but the sons Robert C. Wood Jr. and John Taylor Wood chose the Confederacy.[25]

In Varina's own family, her relatives divided on secession and war and not always in predictable fashion. Her Northern-born father William Howell supported the Confederacy, as did her brothers and many of her cousins in her mother's family; Margaret Howell's political views remain unknown. The majority of residents in Varina's hometown of Natchez voted for John Bell in 1860, and Josiah Winchester, husband of Varina's cousin Missy Sprague, voted against secession in the state's convention in January 1861, calling it suicidal. Her Northern relatives also disagreed on the crisis. Some of the Howells supported the Union, the Republican Party, and the abolition cause, some supported the Union but were indifferent to abolition or opposed to racial equality, while others supported the Union and the right to own slaves, as did her uncle Joseph Howell, who lost his job at the Philadelphia Customs House in 1861 partly because of his political views. Two of her Yankee cousins who expressed tepid support for the war avoided military service, probably by hiring substitutes, but most of her Northern kinfolk who were of draft age fought for the Union. People knew she had relatives in the North, and her uncle Joseph received an anonymous hate letter during the secession winter asking if "Mrs. Verina [sic] Davises cousins of Philadelphia" would fight for the Union. One of her Howell cousins, whose son fought all four years in the federal army, denied in 1865 that he was related to Varina Davis.[26]

During the secession crisis, she, like most people in Washington, was riveted by the political drama, but like most women Davis had no way to express her views in a public forum. Women were deeply interested onlookers, be they undecided, ambivalent, or strongly partisan on one side or the other, but they could not vote in the District of Columbia or in any state, participate in the secession conventions, or hold public office anywhere in the country. In private discussions between most married couples, when spouses differed on the issue, men probably made the final choice. Anna Lee, wife of Sydney Smith Lee and sister-in-law of Robert E. Lee, had to be "dragged" out of Washington. In a few cases women prevailed. Varina's friend Matilda Emory had her husband William reinstated in the Union army after he quit in May 1861, probably by retrieving his letter of resignation herself. In a very few cases, women chose to separate from their husbands rather than support the Confederacy, as did Margaret Conway, a plantation mistress whom Davis had never met. Conway left her Virginia home and moved to Pennsylvania because she opposed secession.[27]

There is no hint in the evidence, however, that Varina Davis considered leaving her husband during the secession winter. She accepted the fact that Jefferson would choose for both of them, and that it was her duty as a wife to accompany him; if he decided to stay with the Union, she would have stayed too, but he chose to follow Mississippi out of the Union, and she had to go with him. That was the unforgiving logic of the situation. Most white women in the South probably felt the same way; as one of them said, "My husband is my country," and Varina's husband was being touted as the head of the new country. In 1859 Varina tried to remind her spouse that he was only one of a host of members of the Democratic Party but everything to his wife and children. For Jefferson politics came first, however, and he expected her to subordinate her wishes to his. In 1865 an anonymous Northerner condemned her in a pamphlet for sticking with her "arch-traitor" husband even though she was Richard Howell's grand-daughter, but it is highly unlikely that Varina Davis could have per-suaded her spouse to remain in Washington if he did not want to do it.[28]

☙❧

AS THE CRISIS DEEPENED that winter, President Buchanan seemed completely unable to deal with the awesome challenges before him. At one cabinet meeting he trembled with fear as he asked his col-leagues what he should do, and some of them believed he was engag-ing in treason of some kind. One politician's wife said that the denun-ciations heaped on Buchanan by Southerners were "fearful," and the story spread that the president would be kidnapped; according to Varina, he thought he might be harmed before his term ended. The hostility toward the President spilled over onto the First Lady, in gos-sip, untrue but widely repeated, that Harriet Lane was stealing por-traits from the White House. On December 20, 1860, South Carolina left the Union, and Washington's social life ground to a halt. At the Davises' house on I Street, the family had a secluded holiday with few callers. Jefferson served on the Committee of Thirteen with William Seward, Robert Toombs, and other congressional leaders in Decem-ber and January, but the committee failed to resolve the crisis with new compromise proposals, and now secessionists were calling on Davis to lead the new government taking shape.[29]

Jefferson Davis had been a leader of the Democratic Party's South-ern wing for most of the last decade, and his name had been bruited about as a presidential candidate in 1860. Many of Davis's contempo-raries were not eligible to serve as head of state because like Louis T. Wigfall they had scandalous private lives, or like Robert Toombs they drank too much, or like Alexander Stephens they did not yet support secession. Davis was well educated, industrious, devoted to states' rights and slavery, and a veteran of the Mexican War with a long résumé in national politics. He looked the part of a president, being tall and handsome by the standards of the time, with his ineffable charm. Although some of his contemporaries dismissed him as arro-

gant or thought he enjoyed power too much, others believed him to
be the ablest politician in the South, and he was probably the best that
an inegalitarian political system like the Old South could have produced. Moreover, since the early 1850s he had been saying in the
harshest language that honorable men had to defend the South and
slavery at all costs. He appeared to be the perfect representative of
the planter class, which helps explain the stampede toward him as the
only candidate for the job. After the war, Davis said that he opposed
secession and did not want to be the Confederate President; he stated
in his memoir that he did not want to be a candidate for President of
the United States in 1860 and instructed his allies not to put his name
forward. But he did not give them the same instructions regarding
the post of Confederate President. He could have insisted forcefully
that he would not accept the position under any circumstances—
what another generation would call a Shermanesque refusal—but he
did not.[30]

In 1861, the juggernaut of secession lurched forward, as Mississippi voted to leave the Union on January 9, followed within three
weeks by other states in the Deep South: Florida, Alabama, Georgia,
Louisiana, and Texas. Perhaps it would be more accurate to say that
the states were hijacked out of the Union, for the votes in the secession conventions in South Carolina and elsewhere took place in an atmosphere of violence and mounting hysteria, with public opinion
among whites deeply divided and only one state, Texas, putting the
question to a popular vote (the voters endorsed secession). Jefferson
Davis resolved to follow his state out of the Union, and then he fell
ill, as he often did under stress, and went to bed, so his political
friends came to talk to him at the Davis home. Varina said she did not
know what they were saying, and her husband did not discuss any of
those conversations with her. The night before her husband resigned
his Senate seat in January, she stayed awake pondering the horrors of
war that probably lay ahead. She was in the Senate gallery on the
twenty-first as he resigned. He expressed his love of the Union and
his desire for peace, and then asserted the right to own slaves and the
right of each state to secede.[31]

His wife started packing right away for their departure for Mississippi. She released the servants, including Elizabeth Keckley, who went to work a month later for another couple, Mr. and Mrs. Abraham Lincoln, and she sold most of the household furniture. As Varina said goodbye to her friends, it was so hard to "wrench" herself away, she recalled, that it felt like death. Their last night in Washington, the Davises stayed up until three in the morning talking with their friends Senator William Gwin of California and his wife, Mary, a native Southerner who a few weeks before had said that she was *"not yet a secessionist."* No one has described the content of that night's conversation, and the Davises left town at the end of January. They had been gone for almost a month when Abraham Lincoln arrived.[32]

The Davises' trip southward was difficult, a harbinger of trouble to come. Crowds waited at the railroad stations to watch them pass, and when Jefferson stopped to speak to them, telling them to prepare for a lengthy, deadly war, Varina stayed in the train. Not all of the faces were friendly. When the party stopped at a Chattanooga hotel, a white man leapt on a table and made a speech in favor of the Union, to which Jefferson Davis briefly replied. Varina described the entire journey as "very unpleasant." When the family reached Brierfield in the first week of February, Jefferson began planning for a long absence, although he hoped that the country might somehow be reunited. The couple talked late into the night, and Varina asked her husband how the sections might be "pacified"; he replied that the rights of the South would have to be guaranteed and possibly some kind of dual presidency might be created. Years later she said that her husband wanted to serve in the military, and she thought he was suited for the army because he "did not know the arts of the politician," by which she seemed to imply that he did not have the ability to compromise, and "would not practise" those arts if he had known them. If she asked him to decline the position that seemed to be in the offing, one he said he did not want and she thought him unsuited for, again there is no record of it. They were tending the rose garden when a messenger arrived on February 9 informing him that he had just been chosen provisional President of the Confederacy by a caucus of seven states in Montgomery. He stumbled into the house, asking her to look after the messenger, and soon left for the capital of the seceded states, Montgomery. His wife would gladly have stayed at Brierfield, she told James Buchanan that spring, but she packed and left to join Jefferson in late February. When she stopped to visit her parents in New Orleans, a crowd gathered to serenade her. She felt too "depressed" to speak but took a bow and gave them some flowers and a flag.[33]

Varina Davis's brother-in-law Joseph traveled with her to Montgomery and tried to make amends for what he called their "estrangements" since the 1840s. When the Davises named their son Joseph after him, he said, the hostilities ended on his side. In reply, she thanked him for his assistance to her husband but said that Jefferson chose the boy's name, and she reminded Joseph that he attempted to deprive her of her legal rights with his will in the 1840s. Joseph left her in the "first flush of youth" on a plantation where her only close neighbors, at the Hurricane, were hostile to her. She owed Joseph nothing, she insisted, and she now understood the will's inequity more fully. He responded with some heat that Jefferson owned Brierfield and the will was her husband's decision. Moreover, he assumed that Jefferson thought she would remarry in her widowhood and wanted to keep the property in the Davis family. So here was yet another explanation—that Jefferson owned the property, not Joseph—for the family quarrel, offered some fifteen years later.[34]

Varina arrived in Montgomery some two weeks after her husband had been sworn in as acting Confederate President on February 18, and she set up housekeeping again, this time in a clapboard house a few blocks from the capitol. Local residents gave the Davises a friendly welcome, sending flowers to the residence, and Varina received from some South Carolinians a white satin case containing a bouquet woven of strands of human hair—a nineteenth-century practice that now seems rather morbid—with the inscriptions "C.S.A, 1861" and "To Mrs. Jefferson Davis." Her new home was a market town with some handsome residences, a courthouse, and a population of about nine thousand. The political and military leaders of the

South burst into town and converged on the Exchange Hotel, where the new government had its headquarters.[35]

Jefferson Davis, the new head of state, was of course the center of attention. One onlooker, William Yancey, proclaimed that "the man and the hour have met." Another contemporary called him the perfect "gentleman-President," and, as one politician discerned, something about Davis "captivated" people. Whether he had real leadership qualities remained to be seen, but he took the obligations of his office seriously, laboring into the night, just as he had done in Washington. His wife was also a center of attention. Although she was sometimes called "Mrs. President Davis," her usual title was "First Lady," and she like her husband drew stares when she appeared in public. When she held her first reception in early March, newspapers all over the region covered the event, and her weekly receptions attracted big crowds. William Russell, the English journalist, described her as attractive, well dressed, and clever. Preston Johnston, who would join Jefferson Davis's staff, liked Varina, whom he called "blunt, but friendly." He described Jefferson as a "great man" with one fault, "a personal bitterness" toward his political foes.[36]

With the Union sundered, Varina Davis had a new part to play as First Lady, but far from reveling in it, she found it hard to adjust to her role. She was a conscript, not a volunteer, and her ambivalence was clear from the beginning. Referring to the lack of ceremony in Montgomery, Davis told a friend, "We are Presidents in embryo here, shorn of much of our fair proportions." Both Howell Cobb, the Georgia secessionist, and Mary Chesnut could tell that she missed Washington. Cobb added that Mrs. Davis smiled and said nothing when he told her she could return to the old capital after the South won the war. With others Davis talked openly of her warm feelings for her Washington friends, which made her "somewhat unpopular" in Montgomery, as Margaret Sumner McLean allowed, because such comments could be used "to her disadvantage." Davis's friendship with McLean soon became controversial, for she was the daughter of Bostonian Edwin V. Sumner, the U.S. General who escorted Abraham Lincoln to Washington. Even though her husband, Eugene, fought for the South, Mrs. McLean felt a lingering attachment to the Union, for which Mary Chesnut later denounced her as a "villain," but Mrs. Davis remained devoted to Margaret McLean. Varina told Mary Chesnut that she still adored Matilda Emory, who managed to send her some embroidery from Washington. Davis obviously could not dissemble when it counted most, now that her husband was the Southern President, and she was living in a town where a person's Confederate patriotism would be questioned for doubting that victory might take longer than a few months. Across the South, other white women expressed a burning hatred for Northerners, some of them wishing that they could join the army and kill Yankees themselves.[37]

If a Confederate enthusiast read Varina's letter of March 1861 to James Buchanan, now retired in Pennsylvania, he or she would have been even more concerned. The ex-President had done nothing as the country broke up, leaving it all to Abraham Lincoln, and he departed Washington on March 4 for Wheatlands, his country estate. Varina Davis may have mailed the letter to him, since the United States postal service was still functioning throughout the country, or she may have asked a friend to deliver it for her. Buchanan said in January that he wished her well, "wherever your lot may be cast," and in her letter of March 18 she related that she thought of him often and remembered their friendship with pleasure. She assured him that the public respected him as much for what he had accomplished as for what he tried to do, and she described her new position with dry humor, stating that she would try to "perform the lady civil to everybody" and hoped to strike the "juste milieu," if only to conform to Buchanan's onetime description of her as a true politician. Montgomery had so many refined people, she teased Buchanan, that Congress now seemed no better than Botany Bay. In a more sober tone, she observed that most politicians in town opposed rejoining the Union and that peaceful relations between the United States and the Confederate States could not last much longer. She told the former President that he might be the last in an "illustrious line" and thought that children treat their stepmothers just as "Republics treat politicians, use and abuse them," by which she apparently meant Buchanan rather than her husband, although the comment is ambiguous. She sent her best regards to Harriet Lane and asked them both to write to her. Davis closed the letter, "Believe me my dear Sir in all time, and under any circumstance, your attached friend Varina Davis." She did not send any greetings from her husband, who may not have known about the letter. No reply survives from Buchanan. This was not the last time that the Confederate First Lady corresponded with people on the other side.[38]

5

NO MATTER WHAT DANGER
THERE WAS

ON APRIL 14, the day after Fort Sumter surrendered to the Confederates, Varina Davis was returning to Montgomery from Brierfield, where she had gone to fetch more of the family's belongings. Whatever thoughts she had about the attack or the Union commander at Sumter, Robert Anderson, with whom she had been on friendly terms in Washington, she kept to herself at the time. President Lincoln called for volunteers to put down the rebellion, four states from the Upper South left the Union, and preparations for war commenced in earnest. Three of Varina's brothers joined the Confederate armed services: Becket after some hesitation resigned from the Marines and became a lieutenant in the Southern navy, Jeffy D. became a midshipman in the Navy, and William served as a second lieutenant in the Louisiana infantry before resigning in 1862 to become an agent for the Commissary Department. Her father eventually landed a job as a Confederate naval agent in New Orleans. Many of her cousins from the Sprague and Kempe families and more than a dozen of her kinfolk from the Davis family joined the Confederate military. Her vagabond brother Joseph evidently did not serve in uniform.[1]

After Fort Sumter, Varina Davis seems to have tried harder to become a Confederate patriot. When she received an embroidery box from some young women in Petersburg, she wrote a gracious letter of thanks and congratulated Virginia on joining the Confederacy, noting that her mother hailed from the state. She accompanied her husband and other Confederate officials to Pensacola to view some defense works. At a public reception she told guests that she was inclined to believe reports that the Union had put a price on her husband's head. The Confederate navy named a ship the *Lady Davis* in her honor, although she never mentioned it in her letters. In May 1861 she mused to a friend, "My patriotism oozes out, not unlike Bob Acres' courage," a reference to the fearful country squire in Sheridan's play *The Rivals*. Most likely she meant that her American patriotism was oozing out, but the comment is so perfectly ambiguous that it is impossible to tell if she meant her loyalty to the Confederacy or the United States.[2]

When the Confederate government moved to Richmond in May 1861, she packed again, and during the train trip to Virginia she maintained a good front, for a soldier who traveled with her found her agreeable company. On June 1 she arrived in Richmond, the state capital since 1779 and home to ironworks, mills, and tobacco factories. Jefferson was waiting at the station in a carriage, and hundreds of people cheered in the streets. At their hotel, the Spotswood, the Davis suite was decorated with a Confederate coat of arms. As politicians and journalists thronged the city, the spotlight on the First Lady only intensified. Crowds came to the hotel to serenade the Davises, and Varina received bouquets from friends and strangers. Fifteen or twenty callers arrived at the presidential suite every evening. Much of the Confederate leadership in Richmond, self-selected for its fervor, was filled with a sense of giddy exhilaration.[3]

Varina Davis did not share the exhilaration, however, and in June 1861 she confided her true feelings to her mother. She told Mrs. Howell that she found the constant attention exhausting, and again she expressed her doubts about the South's ability to wage war. The region was not ready to fight, she said, and the North's advantage in population and manufacturing power was immense. (The Union's population of twenty-two million far outnumbered the Confederacy's nine million, four million of whom were slaves, and the North had much of the country's industrial capacity.) She informed her mother that nonetheless she had made up her mind to "come here & to be happy no matter what danger there was, & to run with the rest if needs must be." Varina's tone was one of resignation, a desire to conform, and a determination to endure, with none of the fiery enthusiasm for the cause that her peers might hope for from the First Lady. Her father, who was visiting Richmond, added a postscript to the letter saying that the Confederacy was "well supplied" and Varina's "fears must have led her into an error." In a few years, however, she would run with the rest.[4]

During the first battle of the war, at Manassas, Virginia, Jefferson Davis insisted on going to the battlefield to watch the action, thereby putting himself in physical danger, something he did during other battles despite the remonstrances of Confederate officials. After Varina learned of the Southern victory in July, she told a friend about it in a "desperate calm way" and said that her husband led troops in battle, an early report that turned out to be false. In conversation later, Varina diplomatically gave credit to Generals Johnston and Beauregard for the victory. Because she was the First Lady, frantic army wives flocked to the hotel to beseech her for information about their menfolk, and when she learned of Confederate Colonel Francis Bartow's death in battle, she told his wife the news herself. She also slipped out of the hotel that weekend to attend a funeral for the infant son of one of her friends.[5]

In August 1861, Mrs. Davis moved again, to a house at the intersection of Clay and Twelfth Streets, her sixth place of residence in as many months. She liked the building, which was leased by the Confederate government. Three stories tall, the house had high ceilings, wide hallways, and furnishings in rococo revival style; statues of Athena and Hera, the goddesses of war and marriage, looked on from niches in a stairwell. An Englishman waggishly termed the residence the "Gray House" for the building's gray finish, but the Confederate public called it the White House. The family lived on the second floor and the staff on the third floor, with the rooms on the ground floor reserved for public functions. Varina hired an Irishwoman from Baltimore, Mary O'Melia (also spelled O'Malla) to run the household.

She met her neighbors on Clay Street, including Anne Grant, a Quaker and merchant's wife who became one of her lasting friends, and she already knew Margaret Stone, daughter of the Washington editor Thomas Ritchie.[6]

That summer Davis had her first sustained contacts with Richmond society. Unlike Washington, where the social calendar followed the congressional calendar, here society functioned year-round, and the First Lady was expected to entertain year-round. She did so, holding receptions that were open to the public. This Washington practice was criticized by some Richmonders because what they called the "hoi polloi," such as government employees, attended a levee with John Tyler, the former president who served in the Confederate Congress. The protocol officers in the Confederate State Department apparently did not give Mrs. Davis advice on how to en-

Confederate White House, 1865. Where Varina Davis spent the worst years of her life. (Library of Congress, copy courtesy of Museum of the Confederacy, Richmond, Virginia)

tertain, as their counterparts in the U.S. State Department did for Mrs. Lincoln; in Washington, protocol officers suggested that Lincoln host open receptions and small private dinners. Lincoln did not follow the advice, but Davis, probably because of her long residence in Washington, did exactly that.[7]

Local society proved nonetheless to be something to reckon with, for the city had an intricate network of families related by blood and marriage. In Richmond, family status mattered more than education, wit, accomplishment, or wealth, and the clannish "three hundred" gave a wary welcome to the new people flooding into the city. They were, as Varina Davis delicately put it, "full of enthusiasm for their own people." The city was different from heterodox, striving Washington, and although Davis did not quite say so, some of the leaders of Richmond society were deeply provincial. The preeminent hostess was Martha Pierce Stanard, a widow renowned for her hospitality. She invited some of the new arrivals to her grand house, but the talk must have been less than stimulating, because she boasted to natives and newcomers that she had not read a book in her adult life.[8]

Varina Davis was not only a First Lady, but the Confederate First Lady, and because the South was fighting for its survival from the beginning, she encountered great pressures to follow conventional gender roles. This was no time for experimentation. The role of the Southern "lady," although it was only a generation old, had great political valence, and the Confederate elite expected Davis to conform to it; she should embody the values of the planter class, as her husband seemed to do. As has often been the case with politicians' wives, people paid a lot of attention to her looks. She was judged to be handsome rather than pretty, or, as one politician put it, a "good-looking lady with plenty of flesh & blood." Many believed that her eyes, dark and expressive, were her most arresting feature. She spent a good deal of time on her appearance. Every day she took an hour to make her coiffure, wearing her long hair in a chignon. She employed her own seamstress and received some fabulous gowns from abroad despite the Union blockade. She favored rich fabrics in solid colors, and she wore earrings, brooches, and some bracelets, appropriate attire for a middle-aged woman. A Virginian probably summed up the opinion of most people when she judged that Davis dressed "plainly, but well."[9]

Yet in other respects Mrs. Davis did not look the part of a First Lady, starting with her olive complexion and her height. In the matter of skin tone—an obsession in a society in which whites enslaved blacks—she did not have what her peers considered to be the right color. The First Lady was a dark lady in the literal, not Shakespearean, sense, and whites commented on it more during the war than at any other time in her life. Her contemporaries, including people who liked her, noticed her "dark" skin and her "brunette" complexion, while a Richmond editor who disliked her called her "tawny" and said she looked like a mulatto. Moreover, she was taller than most American women of her generation, at five feet six or seven inches. The Northern press described her as tall, and other women of that height considered themselves tall. She apparently elicited the anxiety that tall women can inspire, for one acquaintance called her not only tall but "commanding." She towered over Mary Chesnut, who stood about five feet, and she was about the same height as Confederate leaders Vice President Alexander Stephens and General Pierre Beauregard.[10]

She did not talk like a First Lady, either, for she was too well-read, too smart, and too blunt. Unlike Martha Stanard, Mrs. Davis had read many books, and she could not hide it in her conversation. One Southern officer enjoyed her "entertaining cleverness and keen perception," and a friend portrayed her as witty and capable of withering sarcasm when crossed. In the spring of 1861 the Confederate press lauded her cerebral qualities, depicting her as no less intelligent than her husband, and Chesnut, who had a dexterous wit of her own, observed that "clever people" gravitated toward Mrs. Davis. But a lively mind and a quick tongue, which had been assets in Washington, did not wear well in the salons of Richmond. Often, too often for the wife of a head of state, she said what she was thinking. She had what her friend Constance Cary described as a "warm heart and impetuous tongue" in an environment where blandness was at a premium. Her emotions showed in her face, as Chesnut noted, which was undesirable, as Chesnut well knew, because other people scolded her for the same reason.[11]

Davis's sense of humor, which was evident in her debut summer in 1861, also became a liability. She was a good mimic, and after she did some impersonations at a party that summer, one onlooker thought she should make such demonstrations in private. She had a keen sense of the absurd, and, as a contemporary noted, the "unfitness of things" provoked her to laughter. Secretary of the Navy Stephen Mallory, who did not like her very much, called her sense of the ridiculous "perfectly riotous." In her first summer in the Confederate capital, she made jokes that people remembered for the wrong reasons. During a dinner party, when a guest said that the underdrawers for an entire Confederate regiment had been made with two left legs, Davis laughed out loud, much to the horror of the other guests.[12]

In Richmond, for the first and only time in her life, some whites called her crude. Here refinement had nothing to do with books or literary culture, as Varina Davis believed, but with iron self-control. Several of her peers described her as brilliant but unrefined. William Blackford, a blue-blooded Virginian, overheard Varina Davis scolding a slave for mistreating a horse and said he had never heard such language from a woman before. He believed that the arrival of people from the "Cotton States" shocked Richmond society. Charlotte Cross Wigfall called Davis a "coarse western woman," even though her own husband had been a U.S. Senator from Texas. A schoolteacher's wife liked her "unpretending" manner, and another Virginian said that she was pleasant "without any airs of superiority," but that was minority opinion.[13]

The Confederate elite might have overlooked Mrs. Davis's shortcomings—the wrong appearance, the wrong sense of humor, the wrong manners—if she had fully supported the Southern cause. To borrow some examples from English history, Jane Austen was described by her peers described as intelligent but unrefined, and unconventional hostesses such as Nancy Astor have won over their contemporaries. But Mrs. Davis had one strike against her that could not be overcome: citizens of Richmond, the hub of the new empire, doubted her devotion to the cause. They wanted to believe that everyone had closed ranks to support the Confederacy, and many of the townspeople became fanatical Confederates after Virginia seceded on April 17. Most of the city's papers supported secession, and in the spring of 1861 mobs threatened citizens believed to harbor Unionist loyalties. Throughout the conflict, white Richmonders reviled Northerners and suspected whites of espionage if they were born in the North or had relatives there. Even cabinet officers, such as Attorney General Thomas Watts, were targets of rumors that they had Unionist sympathies.[14]

Varina Davis's enduring friendships with the spouses of highly placed figures in the Lincoln administration naturally disturbed the Confederate elite. In June 1861, Richmonders said that Mrs. Davis sent a baby dress for the infant son of Minna Blair, whose husband Montgomery was now the Postmaster General in Lincoln's cabinet, and Minna Blair was said to have written in reply that even if the men killed each other, her friendship with Varina Davis would last as long as she lived. Mary Chesnut was not sure the story was true, but it was true, for Nicholas Hill, a Blair kinsman with relatives in Virginia, had taken Varina's gift and message personally to the Blairs. According to Minna's sister-in-law Lizzie Blair Lee, Hill passed on the Confederate First Lady's "unaltered" regards. Lee told her husband, a U.S. naval officer, that Varina Davis was "one of the victims of this war"—an excessively sympathetic remark from a friend—and added, "I shrink from looking her future in the face." The United States government halted mail delivery to the South on June 1, 1861, coincidentally the date the Confederate postal service began operations, but many other people smuggled letters and goods in and out of Washington D.C., as Varina did, or to other parts of the North, since the boundary with the United States covered thousands of miles, most of it rural and much of it unpatrolled. Julia Tyler, the wife of John Tyler, corresponded with her Northern friends and relatives, as did Mary Sumner Long, the wife of Robert E. Lee's military secretary Armistead Long, sister of Varina's friend Margaret McLean, and daughter of

U.S. General Edwin Sumner. But Davis was the wife of the Confederate President, and she was writing to a powerful family in the other
capital.[15]

Furthermore, Varina Davis had at least one visit in the summer of
1861 from a Yankee relative. According to a tantalizing diary entry by
Mary Chesnut, "Mrs. Davis' *own* niece of those Philadelphia Howells"
appeared at a Richmond dinner in July, although Varina did not mention it in her letters. There is no clue as to Miss Howell's identity,
how she arrived in the Confederacy, or how long she stayed, but she
was a living reminder that the First Lady had Northern kinfolk. What
is just as surprising, Mrs. Davis corresponded with at least one of her
Northern relatives in 1861. In October she somehow smuggled two
letters by means unknown—possibly the mysterious niece—to her
cousin Franklin Glaser, now working as a bookkeeper in New York.
Glaser was a pro-slavery Unionist, and he thought Jefferson Davis
sincere but mistaken in his political convictions. The originals of her
letters have disappeared, but Glaser shared the contents with his uncle Joseph Howell. Varina was in good health but "much worn out
with sorrow about this terrible war and her dear ones." She said "the
fear of bloodshed is all prevailing," Glaser related, but he declared
that she was still a "secessionist." He probably did not reply to Davis's
letter, for in the same letter he scolded Joseph for sympathizing with
the Confederacy because Varina was married to its president. Glaser
thought it wrong to let *"individual Sentiment"* for those who are "dear
to us" affect political opinion. By contrast, Varina's father and brothers stopped writing to their Northern kinfolk after the war started.
Varina's Yankee relatives burned some of their wartime correspondence because, one of her aunts said, it might fall into the wrong
hands. Yet Mrs. Davis communicated with people north of the Mason-Dixon line at least eleven times—including her letters to them
and their letters to her between February 1861 and April 1865.[16]

This was indeed risky conduct. In the spring of 1861 the Southern
government began opening the mail of white Richmonders suspected
of having Northern sympathies, and authorities arrested other whites,
including women, for writing to relatives in the Union. Throughout

the South, the Confederate government arrested Union sympathizers, put them in prison, sequestered their property, and sometimes executed them. Increasingly concerned about security, the Confederacy adopted a passport system in the fall of 1861. Yet no one tried to arrest the Confederate First Lady, who was protected, ironically, by her social status and by her gender. There was no formal investigation of her conduct, possibly because of the weakness of the Confederate Congress, which handed much of its authority to the executive and included some politicians who had their own doubts about the Southern cause.[17]

⚜

THE FIRST LADY PRESIDED over a crowded household, and she paid the expenses out of her husband's annual salary of twenty-five thousand Confederate dollars. She hosted visitors from her husband's family and her own, some of whom stayed for weeks or months at a time. Her sister Margaret lived with her through most of the war, while her sister Jane worked as a governess in Louisiana. Davis was in charge of a household staff of about twenty, men and women, blacks and whites, free people and bondsmen, including slaves from Brierfield, such as James Dennison, and slaves who had worked in the Washington household, such as Betsey. Varina occasionally shopped at the market herself, but other people did the hard physical labor of running the household. She met with Mrs. O'Melia, planned the menus, received callers, hosted luncheons, receptions, and dinners, and wrote letters. In her free time she read, did needlepoint, and went for a drive in her carriage. She spent most of each day at the mansion, while her husband spent most of his day at his office in the Custom House building.[18]

Davis tried to remain involved in rearing her offspring, nursing them herself when they fell ill, and she sometimes turned callers away, explaining that her offspring needed attention as much as other children. Maggie, age six, was a black-haired girl with a dimpled chin, and Jeff Jr., age four, was, according to his mother, a good-natured, energetic boy who liked to dress in a miniature Confederate uniform. They both studied at home with private tutors, and as they played together their laughter could be heard ringing from the second floor. The youngest—gentle, affectionate Joe—gave Varina much joy. She gave birth to another son on December 6, 1861. This boy was named William after her father—the name she had wanted to give Joseph—and he received some extravagant gifts, such as a quilt from George Washington's nephew said to be the handiwork of the first First Lady. Varina was bedridden for more than a month after the birth, so on New Year's Day 1862 her sister Margaret stood in as the official hostess.[19]

The Confederate First Lady had recovered by the time of her husband's inaugural on February 22, 1862, when Jefferson was sworn in as President of the Confederacy. The previous November, after holding office as a provisional president, he had been elected to a six-year term. The ceremony started at noon at Capitol Square, a few blocks from the White House. Varina felt "depressed" by an incident that morning, when four black men who were to accompany the carriage came dressed as pallbearers, telling Mrs. Davis that this was the local custom for funerals. After she arrived, her husband took the oath in front of a cheering crowd. In his speech, he invoked the example of the Founders, denounced the North's "barbarity," and said it was impossible to make peace with the Union. As Varina recalled, when she watched her husband take the oath, he seemed like a "willing victim going to his funeral pyre." Abruptly she made an excuse and took a carriage back to the residence. In Washington, presidents' wives did not always attend the inaugurals, but Mrs. Davis must have known it was inappropriate to leave during the ceremony. Her behavior again reveals the depth of her fears and her inability to control them. At a reception at the White House the next day, she greeted the guests in an affable manner, although one of them said that she was not a fit partner for her husband. She remains one of the only American women who has ever left her husband's inaugural. Perhaps the only one.[20]

As Mrs. Davis embarked on her second year as the Confederate First Lady, she still would not relinquish her ties to her Northern

The Davis children, 1860s. The rambunctious offspring. (Beauvoir)

friends, and early in 1862 she managed to slip more letters to a Mrs. Taylor, unidentified, who shared the contents with the Blairs in Washington. Again, the means of delivery cannot be determined, but the Blairs quoted her missive in correspondence with each other, including her exclamation that her memory "overleapt the horrid Gulf now between us" to the happiest part of her life, her days in the nation's capital. In her heart, Davis said, she clung to Lizzie Blair Lee, Minna Blair, and Matilda Emory with unchanged affection, and all three women, so different and so clever, would be dear to her all of her life. Later in 1862, Union forces intercepted more of her correspondence with Northerners—the recipients unnamed—and a naval commander gave the letter to the Blairs. The Northern press also reported that authorities confiscated dresses sent to Varina Davis from unknown persons in Washington and Baltimore. She obviously did not agree with her husband's statement in his inaugural about the North's barbarism or his other statements that Northerners were "evil" or that they were "savages."[21]

Into 1862, the First Lady tried halfheartedly to conform to her role, displaying in the executive mansion some knickknacks sent to her by Confederate soldiers, but the criticism of her appearance, her demeanor, and her friends continued. In the spring Marion T. Myers, wife of Quartermaster Abraham Myers, took note of Mrs. Davis's "very dark" complexion and called her a "squaw," nineteenth-century slang that connoted an overt sensuality. When the report reached Varina Davis, a "high scene" took place with Mrs. Myers. Some of the criticism became increasingly irrational. A Virginian objected because Mrs. Davis called her husband by his first name and, even worse, he thought, hired an Irish servant and went by carriage to the girl's residence to pick her up. Confederate Congressman William Porcher Miles mocked the First Lady's attire and rejoiced when some of her dresses were lost at sea. He believed that she disliked South Carolinians, overlooking Mary Chesnut, and added that she was not very smart. The "'best people'" in Richmond did not like her, he averred, only a few "fast women," including, possibly, the Quaker Anne Grant.[22]

Attacks on presidents' wives were nothing new; they predated the Civil War and would outlast it. Since the dawn of the Republic, the press and the public have criticized these women, often as surrogates for their husbands, sometimes because they did not conform to conventional ideas of feminine behavior or physical beauty, or because their conduct raised anxieties about other cultural issues. First Ladies were tasked for their looks (Mrs. James Polk), their haughty manners (Mrs. James Monroe), their flirtatious manners (Mrs. James Madison), their fine educations (Mrs. John Quincy Adams), their poor educations (Mrs. James Madison), their partisan views (Mrs. John Adams), their supposed domination of their husbands (Mrs. John Adams, Mrs. James Madison, the second Mrs. John Tyler, Mrs. James Polk), their western ways (Mrs. Zachary Taylor), and for using snuff (Mrs. Madison). The wives of other Confederate politicians probably would have been criticized had their spouses become the head of state. Mary Chesnut had enthusiasm for the Southern cause, but she was highly literate with a slashing wit plus an opium problem that exacerbated her mood swings; Mary Breckinridge was probably too openly ambitious for her husband's success; and Mary Ann Cobb too shy. All of them fell short of the rigid standards for First Ladies.[23]

Varina Davis must have expected some criticism, because she knew three previous First Ladies, the vulnerable Margaret Taylor, the grieving Jane Pierce, and the silent Harriet Lane, all of whom had their detractors. But if she took any of these women as a model, it does not seem to have worked, for she was more visible in Richmond society than Taylor or Pierce had been in Washington, and she had a more exuberant personality than any of them. Davis did little during the war to improve her image, other than trying intermittently to express support for the Confederacy. She never had a secretary, and she did not try to cultivate the press, as other First Ladies, such as Julia Tyler, did. In old age Varina observed that individuals who flouted society's codes and stated their opinions too frankly risked "social death." Yet she could not seem to absorb the Confederate code or accept the fact that she was no longer a senator's wife but a different kind of political figure, almost always on stage and expected to camouflage her political views and, when necessary, say things she did not mean, as other wives of heads of state have learned to do. She was a First Lady of doubtful loyalty surrounded by *echt* Confederates, a reminder, perhaps, of the political divisions within the white Southern population.[24]

DESPITE THE UNEASINESS about her loyalty, Varina Davis had friends in Richmond, including Mary Chesnut, whom she had met in Washington in the 1850s when Mary's husband, James, was the Democratic Senator from South Carolina. Talkative, febrile, with deep-set eyes, Chesnut read widely and used many of the literary references Davis favored, such as that of the trapped starling in Sterne's *Sentimental Journey*. They had a few tiffs, such as the time Varina kept Mary waiting too long for a seat at a tea, and they had political differences, for Davis was not deeply troubled by doubts about slavery as Chesnut was, and Davis, having been in Washington for more than ten years before Chesnut arrived, was more jaded about politics. Moreover, Chesnut was a fervent Confederate, as Davis was not. Chesnut's contradictory views—doubting slavery while supporting the Confederacy—may have allowed her to tolerate Davis's heresies. In any case, these two vivid personalities became good friends. The First Lady told Chesnut how much she missed Washington, and she confided that Jefferson Davis was not suited to be President and should have served in the army. Chesnut related that the First Lady was extremely pleasant "when she is in the mood" and "awfully clever—always." She enjoyed watching Davis deploy her wit against the pompous and thought her so full of "spice" and "so warmhearted and considerate" that other people seemed banal by comparison. Chesnut was not as comfortable with the President, who scolded her for fleeing at the sound of his footsteps, and she was a little afraid of him.[25]

Judah Benjamin also became good friends with the First Lady. She had known him since 1853, when he became the Whig Senator from Louisiana. A descendant of Sephardic Jews, he grew up in South Carolina, attended Yale University, and journeyed to New Orleans, where he opened a law practice and bought a plantation outside the city. He married Natalie St. Martin from a Creole family, but the couple lived apart for most of their lives. In the 1850s Benjamin switched parties to become a Democrat, but he was not as fanatically pro-slavery as Jefferson Davis and did not believe that the institution was divinely ordained. He worked hard in the Senate, and at one point he declined a seat on the Supreme Court. Benjamin was not in the vanguard of the secessionist movement, but he left the Union with his state. More than most figures in the Southern elite, he understood Jefferson Davis's large ego and sensitivity to criticism—the two men once had a brusque exchange in the U.S. Senate—and now he did his best to convince the Mississippian that he was loyal to him and to the Southern cause. After serving in two positions in Davis's cabinet, Benjamin was elevated in March 1862 to the post of Secretary of State. He was probably the most talented of the men who served in the cabinet.[26]

Soon Benjamin became one of Varina Davis's favorite guests at the executive mansion. He must have decided to overlook the gossip on her doubts about the Southern cause and focus on what they had in common, such as their love of books. Benjamin had more enlightened views on gender than most men of his time, and he talked to Davis as his peer. He was a short man with a suave, merry manner, and Varina found his company was so refreshing that decades after the war she recalled their talks with pleasure. He kept up a serene front in the face of trouble, as she usually could not, and he told her that he was a fatalist and thought it useless to fret about destiny's workings. He could be supremely tactful, once going out of his way to speak to a young woman wearing a shabby dress at a dance, which touched Varina, no doubt because it evoked memories of her impoverished youth.[27]

Benjamin understood Varina Davis's dilemma as a public figure better than most people, for he was an outsider in Richmond by virtue of his ethnicity. Even though he was highly assimilated like many Southern Jews and did not attend temple, his contemporaries called him a "pilfering Jew," Jefferson Davis's "pet Jew," and Judas Iscariot. Varina, by contrast, was free of the anti-Semitism that gentiles North and South expressed during the war. Other Confederates jested about his private life, deeming him a "brevet bachelor," or a "eunuch," but she did not mind. He was more worldly than many Confederates in Richmond, just as she was. Years afterward a white Southerner reported the gossip that Varina Davis and Judah Benjamin "ran" the Confederate government. This was untrue, of course, but she gave Benjamin some correspondence sent to her by Rosine Slidell, the daughter of the Confederate emissary to France, about diplomatic matters, the contents undescribed. She apparently did this as a personal favor to Benjamin, but it was not widely known in Richmond and did nothing to change her image as an unreliable Confederate.[28]

At the end of April 1862, federal forces captured New Orleans, fulfilling part of the Union's plan to seize the Mississippi River and split the Confederacy in half. When Varina Davis learned of the fall of New Orleans from an officer on the street, she exclaimed that everything she had was there and the Confederacy was almost finished. The First Lady told Mary Chesnut, "I live in a kind of maze: disaster follows disaster—guns—powder—numbers fail" and quoted the Victorian poet Thomas Hood regarding the Confederate ship of state: "Ships spars are mangling her / cables entangling her / mermaids carnivorous / Good Lord deliver us." She felt as if she were living on a Louisiana prairie, with nothing certain underfoot, and added, "This dreadful way of living from hour to hour depresses me more than I can say." She told Chesnut that she wished her husband were a dry goods clerk so that they could dine in peace, take a quiet Sunday drive, and live wherever they wished. After New Orleans fell, Varina's family escaped to Georgia, although she did not hear from them for several weeks.[29]

That spring the Union army captured Brierfield. Jefferson warned his brother in February 1862 that both of their plantations were in danger, but Joseph remained at the Hurricane until April, and then became a refugee, his vanity unaffected as he gave his brother advice about military strategy. He left most of the bondsmen behind, including Ben Montgomery, whose family fled to Cincinnati, where the sons Isaiah and William volunteered to serve in the federal navy. Other bondsmen ran away, some of them looting both mansions beforehand, and the overseers did not stop them. In May the flotilla of Union gunboats advancing up the Mississippi was led by none other than Samuel Phillips Lee, husband of Varina's friend Lizzie Blair Lee. In June 1862 Brierfield was sacked and the Hurricane torched. Jefferson bought another plantation in Mississippi in 1862, and Varina later claimed to be indifferent to Brierfield's capture, but at the time she was anguished at the loss of her personal belongings, including her letters, which would resurface in private collections and museums as war souvenirs.[30]

THE WAR is the most underdocumented period of the Davis marriage, and the most puzzling. The couple was together most of the time, and neither kept a diary or confided in other people about their relationship, so its inner workings remain mysterious. Jefferson may have spoken to Varina privately about her lack of enthusiasm for the Confederate effort, or possibly he overlooked it because she sometimes acted as a First Lady should, or maybe because he was preoccupied with other matters; there is no evidence either way for the first year of the war. If Jefferson objected to or knew about his wife's correspondence with Buchanan, the Blairs, or Franklin Glaser, or if he reproached her for leaving the inaugural, there is no evidence of that either. It is clear that they still cared for each other. The few times they were apart in 1861, he wrote her affectionate letters, and his courtly manners could still charm her; he once gravely asked permission to come into her sitting room and smoke his pipe. In the spring of 1862 Jefferson joined St. Paul's Episcopal Church in Richmond, inspired, he said later, by his wife's example. Both of the Davises became jealous on occasion. When Virginia Clay, wife of the Alabama politician, gave Jefferson a friendly kiss, one of the President's aides knew that Varina would not like it, and Jefferson did not like it if anyone flirted with his wife or behaved toward her in a way he deemed too familiar.[31]

Varina loved him despite his faults, and she knew he had faults. She said later that he was abnormally sensitive to criticism and expected fealty from his friends, yet was unwilling to flatter anyone in public life. At times a poor judge of personalities, he could react to criticism by developing a "repellent" manner, and he easily became depressed. He admitted to Varina during the war's second year that he wished he could ignore both the "cats" and the "snakes" in politics, but he had not yet learned to do so. Disappointing news from the battlefield profoundly affected his emotional state, and when he was unhappy, she looked after him. In 1862, when prospects for the Confederacy looked dim, he came home one evening and told her that his responsibilities were almost too much to bear. She decided to read aloud from George Lawrence's novel from the 1850s, *Guy Livingstone,* a character study of an Englishman who after various adventures learns something about himself and dies young. It was not a cheery story, but it was well written and absorbing, and Jefferson forgot his troubles as he listened. The book is more than three hundred pages long, and she stayed up all night reading to him.[32]

As George McClellan's army drew closer to Richmond, Jefferson Davis sent his wife and children out of the city. Varina did not want to leave and had a "hard cry" with her niece Helen Keary, but Jefferson insisted on it. Raleigh was chosen as the destination because it was a day's journey by train and still in Confederate hands. Varina left with her brood on May 10, taking some twelve thousand dollars in Confederate money. On the eve of her departure, Jefferson told her, "I belong to the country but my heart is ever with you," and then, thinking in practical terms, he sent her a pistol and told her to learn how to use it. In Raleigh the party stayed most of the time at St. Mary's, a school for girls. People immediately appeared at Davis's door asking for help, and polite acquaintances made social calls. A local journalist praised her unostentatious manner.[33]

Varina Davis was nevertheless a public figure, and her flight from the capital was sharply criticized. Even though other Confederate women left Richmond that spring, the press attacked the First Lady for showing a lack of faith in the Southern army, one newspaper comparing her to Marie Antoinette. At least a few white Southerners agreed that she set a bad example. Malicious report followed her from Virginia to North Carolina, where a planter's wife who had never met her said that Davis's clothing was shabby, adding the novel criticism that she wore too many bracelets, and objected because Mrs. Davis employed a white woman, Mary O'Melia, to run her Richmond household. (While in Raleigh she also hired a free black man, James H. Jones, to work for her.) Last of all, this planter's wife alleged that Varina Davis was from the North, Philadelphia to be specific, and unworthy of her husband, who needed a "truehearted Southern woman" for his wife.[34]

While Davis was in North Carolina that summer, she sustained a more serious blow to her public image. The Davis's coachman, a slave named William Jackson, ran away to the Union lines on April 27, and after army officers and Secretary of War Edwin Stanton questioned him, he gave an interview that appeared on page 1 of the May 12 issue of the *New York Tribune*. Other Northern papers, with both white and black readerships, soon picked up the story. Jackson called Jefferson sickly and irritable and Varina a "termagant," a "scold," and a "d——l" to the household staff, the word "devil" being unsuitable for a family newspaper. Twelve days later the *Tribune* published a more extensive interview, and again Jackson portrayed Jefferson Davis as chronically ill and depressed and the Confederate leadership as riven with infighting. Again he cast Varina in a bad light. Not only did she blurt out what she was thinking, according to Jackson, she was pessimistic about the Confederacy's prospects. After the fall of New Orleans, he claimed, she stopped caring about the war's outcome, and she told one of her friends that she wanted to escape to Europe. Jackson said that her doubts about the Confederacy's chances dated from the first weeks of combat, when she told another friend that the South would probably never capture Washington because troops had failed to pursue the Northern army after First Bull Run in 1861, and she had ceased to believe by early 1862 that any of the foreign powers would assist the Confederacy.[35]

William Jackson was a fugitive behind federal lines, so it was in his interest to portray both the Davises and the Southern cause in the worst possible light. Parts of the story are simply wrong. He said that Varina Davis criticized Richmonders for being Unionists and that her only friends hailed from the Deep South, overlooking Margaret McLean and Anne Grant. He revealed some biases of his own by deriding "women politicians" in Richmond. When Northern periodicals reprinted the story, the narrative varied slightly: in *Harper's Weekly* Jackson quoted Varina Davis as saying that the Confederacy should not endeavor to hold the Upper South states such as Virginia. He also related that Davis told her friend Becca Jones, wife of Confederate General David R. Jones, that she should not worry about visiting her child in Washington because the Yankees would take Richmond and then she could go. Some of Jackson's claims are dubious, such as his allegation that Mrs. Davis visited government offices and hotels to trawl for news, but his account of her underlying hopelessness about the Confederacy's prospects, the most explosive aspect of the story, conforms to the First Lady's own writings and to her comments in Richmond's drawing rooms.[36]

6

HOLOCAUSTS OF HERSELF

THE WILLIAM JACKSON INTERVIEWS were bad press indeed for the First Lady, for they made her look foolish as well as unpatriotic. Jackson embarked on a lecture tour of the North and then Great Britain, and his interviews seem to have inspired other stories in the Union press that Mrs. Davis was actually a native of the North. After the interviews appeared, the prominent Preston family ignored broad hints from mutual friends that they invite Varina to visit them in South Carolina. The Confederate First Lady did not respond publicly to Jackson's comments, but her husband immediately asked her to be more cautious about what she said, no matter how she might feel. He must have had some ongoing doubts about her support for the cause, for a few weeks later she had to assure him in a letter, "Yes I have faith in your success."[1]

That was not a completely honest statement, but his reproaches did matter to her and she tried harder to play her part. When her brother William asked her to find lodgings for his wife in case the Union army captured Richmond, she was reluctant to do so because she might be accused of taking a dim view of the Confederacy's chances. After Stonewall Jackson won a signal victory in the Valley campaign in 1862, she congratulated her husband. She felt sorry to hear the rumor that U.S. General Edwin Sumner, Margaret McLean's father, had been captured, though she told Jefferson she "would not say so" to anyone but him. In a letter to her husband, Varina described the Confederate cause as "our side" and the federal army as "the enemy." Perhaps because she was saying what was expected, Jefferson Davis evidently forgave her for the Jackson interviews.[2]

Their correspondence that summer, some thirty letters in all, was mostly concerned with family matters, and much of it was highly affectionate. She missed her "precious" husband, and he missed her, sending her a "long, long kiss." They both loved their children, of course. When Billy's health suddenly declined in June, Jefferson came to Raleigh for a few days until the boy recovered, and in July and August Varina made flying visits to Richmond with the children. Jefferson wrote to his wife that he could sacrifice everything for the Confederacy except his family. She asked him not to expose himself to physical danger, but several times that summer he rode so near the battlefields that he risked his life, earning rebukes from Confederate officers, including General Lee himself.[3]

Yet Varina's underlying pessimism about the Confederacy's prospects did not change. In July 1862 she told Jefferson that the North's greater resources, as well as its "habits of discipline" and "perseverance," might render it invincible, almost exactly what she said to her mother in June 1861. She observed that if the South failed it would be because God decreed it, and she admitted that for every prayer she said for the Confederacy she said ten thousand for her husband. She told him that she did not mind if he failed so long as he came back to her safe and sound. Her realism about life after the war was unchanged, for she wrote to Jefferson that she would take a paying job if necessary when the conflict ended. Such a prospect would have been unthinkable for a woman in the antebellum planter class, but she realized that the old way of life was crumbling with the war.[4]

Her discomfort with her public role seemed to be unchanged, as well. She confided to her husband a disturbing dream, that they had to say farewell in front of a laughing crowd, which bore an uncanny resemblance to a dream she had in the 1840s. When Robert E. Lee drove McClellan's army back from Richmond in late June, in the Battle of the Seven Days, it did not reassure her much. In August she told a friend that she was dreading the next campaign to take Richmond, although she attempted to conceal her anxieties from other people. She was trying to keep her spirits up, she told Rosa Johnston, wife of Jefferson's aide Preston Johnston, and she took comfort—what kind is not clear—from paraphrasing Friedrich von Logau's epigram that the "mills of God grind slowly, yet they grind exceedingly small." She also told Mrs. Johnston that someone in Richmond was opening her mail, yet she continued to express her thoughts rather freely at the expense of her image. An officer who met her that summer called her "very smart, intelligent, and agreeable," as well as "quite independent, says what she pleases and cuts at people generally."[5]

In August 1862, there was another round of negative press. On the eighth, the *New York Tribune* published one of Helen Keary's letters to her relatives. The letter, written in May, had miscarried and fallen into Northern hands. Keary portrayed Jefferson as miserable and overworked, and Varina as weeping on the eve of her departure from Richmond. Joseph Davis then wrote to Jefferson "the less W——— knows of public affairs the better," "W" for *Winnie,* Jefferson's nickname for his wife. In fact, she did not know much about Confederate policy or strategy. Her spouse told her about preparations for Richmond's defense and disparaged generals such as Pierre Beauregard, whom they both disliked, but he made a point of not discussing details of military campaigns then under way. He was probably even more reluctant to do so after the Jackson interviews appeared. Other newspapers published the correspondence of well-known figures, as each side waged psychological warfare against the other, and in 1864 the *New York Times* would publish a letter by Jefferson Davis instructing his brother to hide his valuables from Yankee troops. But no one in Richmond doubted Jefferson's dedication to the Confederate cause, as they did doubt Varina's.[6]

Her letters in August 1862 illustrate the chronic tensions regarding the war and her marriage, as she was whipsawed back and forth by her lack of faith in the Confederacy and her love for her spouse. She confided in Rosa Duncan Johnston, a New Orleans native in her thirties who had been educated in the North and had beloved relatives there. She too doubted that the South could win the war, telling her husband Preston so at the very start of the conflict. On August 13 Varina informed Rosa that her friends, like Pharaoh's host, had been engulfed, and that with her "usual luck" she had to defend Margaret McLean from many critics. Yet McLean was "one of the few in this Confederacy who love me," and in her isolation, Davis admitted, that meant a great deal. She was tired of seeing new faces and yearned to talk to friends with whom she had a shared history, but, she added somewhat unconvincingly, she did not miss the "Yankee fleshpots." She would stay in Raleigh because her husband told her to, and she worried about the "immense masses to be hurled upon us in [the] future." Again she fretted that some unknown Confederate official was reading her mail.[7]

Davis had been reading Agnes Strickland's history of the queens of England, she told Johnston in the same letter, and if she had to have a biographer, she hoped it would be someone like Strickland who wrote about the marriages of Mary Queen of Scots as "so many holocausts of herself." Since her death in 1587, Mary has been a potent symbol, most often serving as an emblem of Scots nationalism. In the nineteenth century, the reading public throughout the Anglo-American world was fascinated by her. Although recent authors have criticized Mary's private life and political judgment, Strickland's biography of 1844, which was enormously popular with female readers, depicts the queen as a well-meaning woman who adhered to most of the tenets of Victorian propriety. Varina seems to have been drawn to Strickland's portrait of a highly educated, courageous, and impetuous figure who strove to find happiness in her turbulent life. Davis, married to a head of state, had further reasons to be absorbed by the story. Maybe she wondered if her part in the civil struggle of her own time would end, as Mary's had, in prison and death. Perhaps she saw aspects of her spouse in all of Mary's husbands: the devoted Francis, the companion of her youth; the handsome Darnley, with whom Mary fell in love only to be deeply disillusioned; and the arrogant Bothwell, whose ambition betrayed her in the end.[8]

Holocausts of herself. This phrase, so different in tone from Varina Davis's "love and esteem" poem in the 1850s, suggests that the accommodation she had made with herself about her marriage was no longer working. The bleak analogy to the Scottish queen raises other questions: If Varina thought someone might write her biography one day, why did she not play the part of First Lady as her husband and the Confederate elite expected? Given that she had adapted to being a politician's wife in Washington, why could she not adapt to the role of First Lady? On the practical level, if she had begun to see herself as a historical figure, and she thought someone was reading her mail, why did she make such statements in writing? The answer seems to be that her doubts about the Confederacy—unscripted, sincere, and uncalculating—had not gone away, and now she was using a literary reference to convey unpalatable feelings, just as she had before the war: anger at her husband for bringing them to Richmond, and horror at so many deaths in what she believed to be a doomed cause.

And now that her husband was the Confederate head of state, there was little she could do about any of this. If she wanted to leave the South, where would she go—the North? Canada? Europe? With her children or without? How would she pay for it? If she reached the North, would she be arrested? Her mother's example and her previous experience as a politician's wife seemed to furnish the answer: there was no choice but to stay with her husband, make whatever sacrifices her marriage required, and endure whatever the war brought. On the same day, August 13, 1862, that she made these astonishing comments to Rosa Johnston about her marriage and the war, she sent a lighthearted note to her husband about their children—diverting, pleasant, nothing at all grim. Before the war she had learned to conceal some of her deepest emotions from her husband and to confide in her friends, and during the war she apparently chose to do the same. Two weeks after she sent the "holocausts" letter to Rosa Johnston, Rosa's husband Preston saw the First Lady at a dinner. Putting on her official persona, Davis gracefully endured a conversation with what Preston called "five stupid senators."[9]

Varina Davis's public embarrassment and private discomfort that summer may have inspired her to send a message from Betsey, a slave in the Raleigh household, to Betsey's husband, James Dennison, who worked in the Richmond household. Before the war she occasionally sent such messages, and now she asked her spouse to relay Betsey's love and news of her good health to Jim. Possibly for the same reasons, she made some humane comments about the Davis slaves in Mississippi. In June 1862, when she heard that the bondsmen still at Brierfield had contracted the measles, she told her husband that a "competent person"—meaning someone other than her brother-in-law Joseph—should look after them. "Even if the Negroes never make us a cent," she remarked, "I can't bear to think of them in utter destitution." But she said nothing in her letters when Lincoln issued the Emancipation Proclamation in September 1862.[10]

BY OCTOBER 1862, with the prospect of another federal invasion past, the Davis family returned to Richmond and Varina took up her public duties again. She paid social calls on the Richmond mandarins, and she could impress others with the force her personality, such as the officer who described her as "one of the smartest and wittiest people I ever met." But she was still out of her element. While talking at a reception with Mrs. Stephen Mallory, Davis made a jest about "Mr. Hawkins' Wives," alluding to an eighteenth-century English comedy about marriage. Angela Mallory, who did not understand the literary reference, thought Davis was joking about her own marriage, and an exchange of sharp notes resulted. The First Lady was still too irreverent. Chief of Ordnance Josiah Gorgas called her a person with "much more than ordinary cultivation," yet he was not amused when she told dinner guests in October 1862 that the next time everyone had to flee Richmond, they would all go to Raleigh together, proof that Mrs. Davis lacked "refinement," he thought. She tried to rein herself in sometimes. That winter she told Mary Chesnut that it was better to refrain from drollery or dry wit in Richmond society, for people loved gossip, no matter how outlandish, and they were so humorless they took literally every word she said.[11]

Varina Davis departed from her expected role in even more daring fashion, however, when she "frequently" visited Union prisoners of war in a Catholic hospital in Richmond. According to a local history, she brought the prisoners tobacco, soap, razors, and small gifts. She told the nuns that the sick and wounded Confederates were well supplied, suggesting that these visits took place in the first two years or so of the war. She asked the sisters not to reveal her identity, and she apparently believed that most of the Union soldiers would not recognize her. The nuns agreed, although at least one federal soldier did recognize Davis, for he told a clergyman after the war that she had nursed him in a Richmond hospital. In this brief newspaper account from 1865, the anonymous veteran described Mrs. Davis as an attentive nurse and said nothing more. This was nonetheless risky behavior for a Confederate First Lady, especially in Richmond, where white civilians, including women, taunted federal prisoners as they arrived in town in 1861. Again it is unclear if Jefferson Davis knew of his wife's visits to Union prisoners, but it seems that most of the city's populace did not know that Mrs. Davis visited federal prisoners in the Southern capital.[12]

Her critics focused instead on what they thought were her insufficient visits to the city's twenty-odd Confederate hospitals. Davis went often enough to be remembered clearly by a few Southern veterans, and one matron recalled that the First Lady went to the Confederate hospitals on a regular basis. Davis also sent food from her kitchen to those hospitals, and she worked with other women from St. Paul's Church who ran a charitable home in Richmond, which received no publicity during the war. Some of her peers nonetheless believed she should do more hospital work, but Varina said later that her husband did not want her to do much nursing, and he with his many illnesses was her chief patient. Furthermore, her distaste for what she called the "odors" from the sick and dying had grown worse since the campaigns of 1862. For both reasons, she apparently stopped nursing soldiers from either army, most likely after 1862.[13]

Yet it seems that no one tried to recruit her to spy for the Union. Stranger things have happened in wartime. In World War II and in modern wars for independence, married women engaged in espionage and acts of resistance without their husbands' knowledge or approval. In the American Civil War, white Southern women were known to assist anti-Confederate guerillas and deserters, and at least one white woman passed information to the Union even though her son served in the Confederate army. Since the start of the conflict, Union spies made their way into Richmond, including one Mr. E. H. Stein, who stood near Jefferson Davis at the inaugural and must have witnessed Varina's exit from the ceremony. Richmond's Union spies also included Elizabeth Van Lew, a member of a wealthy family who may have placed a black servant, Mary Bowser, in the executive mansion. Someone could have pieced it together: the First Lady who left the inaugural, who doubted the South could win the war, who no longer cared about the outcome, who had well-placed friends in the North, who nursed soldiers from both armies, and who wanted to escape to Europe.[14]

But if anyone considered Varina Davis to be spy material and sounded her out, there is no reliable evidence of it. She refused to plead for the life of the Union spy Timothy Webster despite a personal request in 1862 from a white woman, Hattie Lawton, who was, unbeknownst to Davis, herself a Union spy and posing as Webster's wife. Lawton allegedly asked Davis to consider the sacred ties of family—evidently between herself and Webster, not between Davis and her Northern relatives—and Davis, while "fully sympathizing" with Webster's fate, said she would rather not interfere in matters of state. Detective Allan Pinkerton, who heard this story from Lawton, included it in a book published in 1886. Varina Davis never mentioned the incident, however, and when someone asked her in 1905 if a black woman had worked as a spy in the Confederate White House, she rejected the idea out of hand. Moreover, her surviving letters to the North divulge nothing about Confederate policy. Barring the discovery of any new evidence, it seems that the First Lady's unhappiness did not translate into espionage for the Union cause.[15]

After Jefferson Davis left town in December 1862 to tour the western half of the Confederacy, Varina spent the holiday in Richmond with her family, reading and writing letters. When Jefferson wrote to her, he as usual shared nothing of substance about military strategy or government policy. She wrote to him that they had been "granted another brilliant victory" at Fredericksburg, and she urged him to look forward to peace and promised again that she would love him even if he did not succeed. A missive she composed on Christmas Day to Preston Johnston strikes, yet again, another tone. She related that when they opened their gifts the children shouted with joy, the kind of joy that "we poor war-torn veterans would fain offer up upon a proclamation of peace." She compared the "world of Secessia" to the "world of chance" in a German folktale in which everything was uncertain, and regarding local society she told him that her "Richmond carols" were "blank." What Johnston thought of this letter, or what he may have said to other people, is not recorded. She either trusted Johnston implicitly or was so unhappy that she did not care what he thought. After the New Year, Varina told Mary Chesnut that many civilians were depressed about the South's prospects and longed for peace and reunion. Although she had been surrounded by "terror stricken wives" begging her for information about their husbands, she felt as "helpless" as they did. Davis wondered whether the Confederacy was an experiment in "self government" or "self immolation."[16]

In the spring of 1863, family duty took her away from Richmond, this time to care for her ailing father. He was running a Confederate commissary in Montgomery, so the Howells congregated there in late 1862. Varina's father urged everyone to be "rational" about their troubles, but she had been helping the family since the war began, and since none of them seemed capable of looking after their father, she went to Alabama. He died on March 16 while she was en route. Varina was overwhelmed when she learned of his death, according to her escort, Preston Johnston. William Howell was buried at Oakwood Cemetery, and Varina put on mourning clothes in his memory. Mrs. Howell insisted that her oldest daughter stay in Montgomery to care for her, saying no one else could do it, so the First Lady sat by her bedside as Margaret Howell talked about her grief and wept. Varina dispatched her sisters to stay with relatives and found an odd moment to read the newspaper and dash off some letters to her husband. She had to "choke down" her own sorrow, she said, and wrote, "Nothing but my sense of duty performed keeps me from going quite wild." During her forays into town, she thought local whites appeared interested only in the western theater of the war, or in making money from speculation, or in nothing at all.[17]

She assumed a different persona, the polite official self, when she received some visitors in Montgomery. She saw William Owen, an artillery officer from New Orleans who was engaged to her sister Margaret; he found the First Lady and her family to be charming. She received Lydia Johnston, the wife of Confederate General Joseph E. Johnston, who interrogated Varina for the latest military news. When Lydia Johnston exclaimed that no one had been so mistreated as General Braxton Bragg, Davis asked innocently if there was anything the matter with him. She then observed that generals' wives knew all the gossip, at which Johnston blushed, and the visit ended. Davis also saw Priscilla Cooper Tyler, the daughter-in-law of former president John Tyler, who came away highly pleased with Mrs. Davis, calling her warm, witty, and "extraordinarily gracious." Priscilla Tyler conveyed to her family Davis's compliments about Julia Tyler, whom Davis had met in Richmond. Tyler had been First Lady in the 1840s, and even though her family was from New York, she had embraced the Confederate cause. Varina described Mrs. Tyler—a vivacious brunette— as her "beautiful stepmother," the same sort of metaphor she used with James Buchanan in 1861.[18]

While the First Lady was in Montgomery, she had an unexpected colloquy, rich in symbolism and very sad, with a slave woman. As she was running errands one day, Davis passed a slave auction, where a young woman either recognized her or had Davis pointed out to her. She appealed directly to the President's wife to buy her so she could escape her occupation working at a tavern. The young woman was tired of being sold from one master to another, she called out, and in Davis's account, she begged Varina, "If you have a little girl, as they say you have, I will wait upon her until I die if she will only be good to me." After this heartbreaking appeal, Davis felt a pang of what she called "sympathy," so she stopped to inquire about the woman's character. When she heard mixed reports from whites nearby, she walked away. Then she reproached herself, telling Jefferson that she had felt too much sympathy for a slave woman, and soon afterward she bought a slave boy to work for her brother Jeffy D., who was serving in the Confederate Navy.[19]

In mid-April 1863, she returned to the Confederate capital and her household duties. With her husband's permission, her mother and her sister Margaret came to Richmond, while William and his wife moved to Augusta, Georgia, where he was assigned to the Commissary Department, and Jane Howell accompanied them. Varina invited her husband's relatives to stay at the White House whenever they needed lodging, and she found rooms for her other kinfolk if they had no place to stay. She hosted her sister Jane, who arrived in Richmond in November to marry William Waller, a grandson of John Tyler who served with the Confederate Ordnance Bureau. The city was more crowded than ever, the streets thronged and hotels filled with guests, theaters playing to packed houses, gambling dens doing a booming business, and society overrun with lavish parties.[20]

The Davis household had been spared most of the shortages created by the Union blockade, as Varina admitted. Into 1863 she had new clothes when they were a rare sight in Richmond. The Davises received gifts from friends and strangers, and they had writing paper, books, and coffee when those items were becoming increasingly scarce. The First Lady received more exotic items, such as pineapples smuggled in from Bermuda. Although Varina was in Montgomery on April 2 when hundreds of white women broke into stores in Richmond searching for food, she made no comment about the riot or the hunger now widespread in the Confederate capital. By mid-1863, however, even she had to make do and sometimes do without. She started making gloves out of her husband's old suits, and because Jefferson's salary did not cover all of the family's expenses, Varina began managing the household with strict economy.[21]

Regarding the crucial battle of Gettysburg that summer, we see her now well-established ambivalence about the war. After news of the Union victory reached the Confederate capital, Jefferson fell ill and Varina looked after him, and after her husband's nephew Isaac Stamps perished in combat she comforted his widow Mary. Yet within a week of the battle, the Confederate First Lady received by means unknown a letter from Margaretta Hetzel, her Washington friend who had a son in the Union army. To Preston Johnston, Varina read aloud some doggerel composed by Hetzel about "old Abe" Lincoln and the "rebs" that depicted the war as pointless and absurd, much like work composed by popular humorists in both regions. When Johnston looked offended at what he called this "trash," she refused to read the rest of the letter. Johnston chalked it up to an unfortunate lapse by a woman of "talent, taste, and wit," and they soon reconciled. He may have no longer been surprised by her views. One can only wonder what, if anything, he said to his employer, the Confederate President.[22]

BY 1863, DAVIS'S POSITION as First Lady cost her the friendship of Lydia Johnston, wife of the Southern General Joseph E. Johnston, not because of Varina's unreliable Confederate patriotism but because of anxieties about her influence over Jefferson Davis. In the late 1850s the two women had been friends in Washington, and into 1861 they remained on good terms. Yet Mrs. Johnston came to believe that the Davises were deliberately hurting her husband's career, and she began to despise them both, calling the First Lady a "western belle." When Lydia started boarding with Charlotte Cross Wigfall, wife of Confederate Senator Louis T. Wigfall, that only seems to have stoked their shared hostility for the Davises until it became a fixation, despite overtures from the First Lady, including a dinner invitation to the White House. Charlotte Wigfall distrusted Varina's Northern friend Margaret McLean, who more than returned the sentiment after Mrs. Wigfall, a Rhode Island native, nevertheless wished aloud that all Yankee generals were dead. By the end of the war, Lydia Johnston called the Davises "my *Skeletons*" and wished they too were dead. She imputed an influence to the First Lady that Varina did not have, for Jef-

ferson did not consult his wife about military matters, and General
Johnston's career path had little to do with his wife's friendships and
much to do with his own shortcomings.[23]

The question of Varina Davis's influence over her husband remained an issue, not only with the Johnstons. Most people did not
seem worried, oddly enough, about whether she was a Union spy.
Richmond had no political parties of the antebellum type, only temporary coalitions formed around specific issues, and there was no real
meritocracy either, since Jefferson Davis could not easily tolerate
honest differences of opinion and promoted his favorites even if they
did not deserve it. In this environment, personal connections seemed
all the more important, and because Varina Davis was the First Lady,
much attention focused on her. She had access to information that
most other people could not easily obtain, such as newspapers from
all over the country and occasionally from abroad, whereas some
Confederate papers refused to publish news about battlefield re-
verses. She must have overheard information when her husband held
meetings in the residence or was sick at home. Jefferson stayed home
for a total of six weeks in the first seven months of 1863, and he
sometimes left official papers lying on tables in the family quarters,
much to the frustration of his staff.[24]

From the beginning of the war, whites asked Mrs. Davis for help of
various kinds. In 1861 a Texas soldier published a letter in a Richmond newspaper asking her to exclude dishonest businessmen from
polite society and help stop government corruption, to which she
made no reply. Women asked for information about their husbands in
the Confederate service, or if she could help their menfolk get discharged from the service or assist them in obtaining passes to leave
the Confederacy. The requests kept coming after the William Jackson
interviews were published, suggesting that some white Southerners
did not believe his claims or may not have read them in the first place.
One refugee from Missouri appealed to what she called Mrs. Davis's
"generous nature" to help her find a job. She could indeed be compas-
sionate with other women. When a stranger, obviously agitated,
asked the First Lady for help in obtaining a pardon for her husband,

Davis agreed to do it. On another occasion, she took pity on a woman on the street because of her downcast expression and brought her to the mansion to help find her husband among the city's wounded soldiers.[25]

Her friends and relatives asked for assistance too, and she responded as she had in Washington. She tried to help them obtain appointments in the military or in the Richmond bureaucracy, and she sometimes asked her husband to assist them. She promised an acquaintance that she would ask Jefferson to make sure an officer was exchanged from the North if the Confederate President forgot to do it. Kinfolk in Jefferson's family and her own importuned her for help, and they were quick to complain if they did not get what they wanted. Before 1861 she said that one advantage of being in politics was being able to assist one's friends, but the volume of requests and their urgency surpassed anything she had experienced before. People could be very demanding, she told Mary Chesnut.[26]

Some Confederates believed she had so much power that officers whose wives "toadied" to Mrs. Davis would get promoted, as one disgruntled man put it. A plantation mistress heard that Samuel French, a New Jersey native who fought for the Confederacy, became a major general because his wife was Varina's sister (false), which was evidence of "curtain influence," she thought. Others believed she was able to "indoctrinate" her husband or that she "governed" him so thoroughly that she made Quartermaster Myers resign. There is no evidence, however, that she had that kind of influence. One day in 1864 she sent a brief note to Josiah Gorgas about the delivery of some rifles, passing on information that was evidently meant for her husband's staff. None of the aides were in the house, she explained, and she asked Gorgas to excuse her "exceeding ignorance of business details." In fact, Jefferson rarely discussed his work with his wife, who did not know what he was doing much of the time, and he made it clear to the war's end that policy questions were none of her business. Her doubts about the Confederate cause may have made him even less likely to confide in her.[27]

The impression lingered in some circles nevertheless that Varina

Davis was strong and her husband was weak, or rather that she was stronger than he was. The American public has occasionally perceived other politicians' wives in the same way and resented them, and in Richmond some people thought the First Lady had as much physical courage as her husband, possibly more. In the fall of 1863 the couple took a carriage ride outside the city and on their return at twilight walked past Libby Prison, where the sentinel did not recognize the Confederate President. He challenged Davis, which angered the President so much that he pulled out a weapon, whereupon the soldier pointed his gun at Jefferson. According to one witness, Varina said that this was indeed the President and "threw herself," or by another account "flung herself," between the two men. Another informant asserted that Mrs. Davis said that her husband had been drinking. In any case, the sentinel decided to let them pass. The incident appeared in the Northern press in 1865, and Henry Foote and Edward Pollard, both of whom hated Jefferson Davis, wrote about it after the war.[28]

For the First Lady, the year 1863 ended on a happier note than it had begun, for she knew by November that she was expecting another child. As she hosted holiday parties at the White House, the First Lady seemed cheerful by one description and displayed her usual "wit and learning." On the first of January, 1864, she held her annual reception at the mansion. All comers were welcome, and for three hours she exchanged polite salutations with scores of people as they filed through the parlor. But the shadowboxing in Richmond society did not stop for long. Among the guests at another reception in January 1864 was William Munford, scion of one of Virginia's oldest families, who had written a satire about the First Lady and Mrs. Abraham Myers. Intended for a small audience, Munford's composition had fallen into the First Lady's hands, and she pointedly asked him about his work as a poet. Munford turned scarlet with embarrassment, and after an awkward silence someone changed the subject. Mary Chesnut thought he deserved it, but Davis had demonstrated again that she could not hold her tongue. Nor could she accustom herself to the repressed manners of local society. In another conversation a Virginia dame intoned that a lady such as herself did not raise her voice for any reason, even when she was being robbed, and in private afterward Chesnut and Davis shouted with laughter at the latest specimen of what Mary called "ponderous Richmond society." In early 1864 another Confederate secretly corresponding with the Blairs apprised them that Mrs. Davis still talked about how much she missed her Washington friends and had become "very unpopular" in Richmond.[29]

In 1864, some of the Davis slaves, like thousands of other bondsmen in the wartime South, ran away to the federal lines. In early January two of them fled from the Richmond household down the James River to the Union forces. The fugitives were none other than James Dennison and his wife Betsey, both of whom had worked for the Davises for years, Betsey as Varina's maid. Betsey took eighty dollars in gold and over two thousand Confederate dollars in cash. After the war, Varina claimed that the slave woman hinted broadly that she was leaving, and, moreover, that Betsey only followed her husband. She also persuaded herself that whites and "disaffected" blacks paid the Davis slaves to run away during the war. Then another bondsman fled. On January 19, while the Davises were hosting a reception, a fire started in the basement, and during the confusion the house was robbed. The fire was soon extinguished, but the next day Henry, a butler whom the Davises had hired a few months before, was gone.[30]

Northern journalists interviewed James Dennison when he arrived at Union lines, and his story did not add any luster to Varina Davis's reputation as First Lady. In January 1864 the *New York Herald* and the *Chicago Tribune* published his observations that Varina Davis "pines" for "those good old days" in Washington, and that she had told her women friends the Confederate cause was "hopeless." Dennison claimed that the family had already secreted some money in a bank in England and was planning to flee overseas if necessary. In Washington, Secretary of War Edwin Stanton interviewed an unnamed fugitive from the Davis household—possibly James Dennison, possibly Henry—and shared the information with Gideon Welles, who recorded it in his diary. This black man claimed that Varina Davis slapped him several times, but Welles did not believe it, maybe because he liked Mrs. Davis, or perhaps because a number of impostors had stepped forward since William Jackson's escape, claiming to be runaways from the Confederate White House.[31]

A few Southern newspapers reported James Dennison's escape, and although the story was not as widely published as William Jackson's interview, Dennison's further comments were just as damaging. He claimed that Jefferson Davis's temper was so "violent" that he threw chairs when angry, and he snapped at his family members. After Varina asked her husband to have the roof fixed, Jefferson retorted, "You will be out of this"—meaning either the house or the war—"before another rainstorm" and told her not to bother him with small matters. Dennison also claimed that the President's health was so bad he was suicidal. One day in January 1864 a pistol accidentally discharged in Davis's room, and the household rushed in to make sure he had not killed himself. In these articles, Dennison repeated his claim that the First Lady believed the Confederate cause to be "hopeless." Some white readers in Dixie discounted his remarks because of his race, and Dennison was probably wrong on a few points. No one else claimed that Jefferson threw furniture or felt suicidal, just as no one else claimed that Varina slapped one of the bondsmen. But once again a fugitive slave had described accurately the First Lady's nostalgia for Washington and her honest assessment of the Confederacy's chances. Among the other household workers, only Mary O'Melia shared her thoughts on President Davis, saying that his ambition rivaled that of Napoleon, but that was in a private conversation after the war, and she made no reference to Mrs. Davis.[32]

In February 1864, the Northern press printed another story about Jefferson Davis: that he had fathered children with other women, including an Indian in Wisconsin and a slave in Mississippi, and that his mulatto son, now an adult with the surname Davis, was a purser in the United States Navy. The London *Times* broke the story, based on an anonymous source in the U.S. Senate and an interview with the alleged mother in Mississippi, and newspapers across the North, including those with sizable readerships such as *Frank Leslie's Illustrated Newspaper*, carried the story. The account varied in the different papers, some of them portraying Davis's supposed miscegenation as proof of slavery's barbarism, others, of Davis's own hypocrisy. The story appeared again in the press after 1865. Jefferson never made any public comment on the allegation, and Varina, who must have heard this widely circulated story, did not discuss it in writing, in 1864 or at any other time. She did what other white Southern women, and other politicians' wives, of her generation did: she kept silent about it.[33]

In her own household, Varina related to black people much as she had before the war, as laborers who worked for her. One possible exception was Ellen Barnes, a mulatto slave who took over Betsey's duties caring for the Davis children and working as the First Lady's maid. Barnes was in her mid-twenties and a native of Richmond; her previous owner was a Richmond druggist, and her husband, a slave, had fled the city. She could not read or write, but she was highly observant, and Varina Davis expected house slaves to be "attentive," as she told an acquaintance, and she described Ellen as "faithful." Some genuine regard developed between the two women, for after Barnes was free she told a reporter that she felt "great affection" for Mrs. Davis.[34]

That winter Varina Davis made an unexpected humane gesture toward a black child. During a carriage ride through Richmond one February day, when she saw a black man beating a boy, she halted the carriage and bolted into the street to stop the assault. The boy, James Limber, was five or six years old, the orphaned child of a free black woman. His youth may have inspired her to act, as the plight of the slave woman in Montgomery had not; in any case, she had never done anything quite like this before. Varina took the child back to the mansion, and her husband had James's freedom papers registered with the city. He sometimes called himself James Brooks, the surname of several families in the local black community. Varina intended to find a job for James, but her children took a liking to him and he began living in the household. He even joined with Joe and Jeff Jr. as a member of the Hill Cats, a boys' gang. Varina said he did no labor in the household, and he seemed to occupy a distinctive status as a playmate for the Davis children.[35]

The relentless, devouring pace of events went on, and in March 1864 U.S. Colonel Ulric Dahlgren launched his raid on Richmond. Someone in Washington, possibly Secretary of War Edwin Stanton, rather than Lincoln himself, authorized Dahlgren's plan, which was

Ellen Barnes and the infant Winnie Davis. Barnes worked at the Confederate White House. (Museum of the Confederacy, Richmond, Virginia)

to open the prisons, burn the city, and kill Jefferson Davis and his cabinet. As Dahlgren rode toward Richmond on February 28, alarm bells rang and soldiers gathered to defend the city. Dahlgren had to turn back, and on March 2 he was killed north of the Confederate capital. Witnesses claimed that Dahlgren's plans were taken from his body, and those plans, apparently genuine, appeared in the Richmond newspapers. The colonel's body was mutilated and displayed in public before it was buried. When news of Dahlgren's death reached the Confederate White House, Varina Davis was horrified. She had known the family, including Ulric and his father, Admiral John Dahlgren, before the war, and she found it hard to reconcile her memory of a blond-haired boy with the man who led the raid. Still she, like most white Southerners, including her husband, thought the plans to kill Jefferson Davis were probably genuine.[36]

DEATH CAME SUDDENLY into the household in the spring of 1864 for one of the Davis children. On the afternoon of April 30, Varina left the mansion to take lunch to her husband, and while she was at his Custom House office a messenger ran in to say that five-year-old Joseph had fallen off a balcony at the residence. His brother Jeff found him on the pavement, and the boy was still breathing when his parents reached his side. He died about forty-five minutes later, his skull fractured, whereupon Varina gave way to a "passionate" outburst of grief while Jefferson began pacing the floor and praying aloud. Someone handed the Confederate President a dispatch, so he asked his wife to read it to him, then tried to write a response before saying in a broken voice that he had to have this day with his child. The parents were then left alone with their dead. The lights in the mansion blazed through the night as the curtains billowed into the darkness.[37]

The boy's death transfixed much of Richmond and brought on a wave of sympathy for the family. On the first of May, a huge crowd attended the funeral at Richmond's Hollywood Cemetery, as the stricken parents stood by, Varina Davis's tall figure stooped with heartbreak. Since 1861 she had been surrounded by death in what she believed to be a hopeless struggle, and now her son had died in a freak accident in her house. A week after the funeral she felt so stunned she could hardly command her thoughts, and a few days later she wrote to her mother, who happened to be out of town. She was trying to accept her loss, she told Mrs. Howell, and be grateful for her blessings. Her husband had gone back to work a few days after Joe's death, and he spent much of his time surveying the battlefields near Richmond. She was thinking about sending the children away from the city, she said, "if events take the turn I expect." The scale of human suffering and the ever-growing numbers of the dead and dying haunted her as never before. While the battle raged around the city, she, like other civilians, could hear the rattle of gunfire at all hours.[38]

During the spring of 1864, Varina Davis seemed to start longing outright for peace. Later she reflected that disaster seemed to be the norm for the Confederate armies by 1864, and regarding her own emotional state, she believed that this calendar year had marked the beginning of a lengthy bout of depression. In April 1864 Mary Chesnut described the First Lady as "utterly depressed" about the federal army's attempt to capture Richmond, and in May 1864 a panic swept the capital that federal troops were approaching—although they did not take the city, not yet—and in June the inhabitants could hear the cannons roaring from the battle at Cold Harbor. Varina observed that the defense of Richmond, like the destiny of humankind, was in God's hands. Speaking more elliptically, she told her husband's secretary Burton Harrison that the imagination "is a more powerful limner than Rosa Bonheur," the French artist noted for her realistic paintings of country life, and said she could not foresee what "blue ruin"—slang for complete ruin—might befall the Confederacy. She felt exhausted and looked it, for an acquaintance thought she looked "grey & forlorn." Just as she had done in Washington, she sometimes found a quiet room in the house to compose herself. "It is my only comfort," she told her mother that spring, "to sit alone."[39]

This terrible year brightened at last with the birth of her daughter, Varina Anne, on June 27. The mother adored the baby, nicknamed Winnie, from the first, thinking her sweet-tempered, pretty, and delightful in every way. Perhaps because Winnie arrived in what her mother recalled as the war's darkest hour, after Joe's death, she lavished love on this baby and with her recreated the primordial bond that she had with her own mother. The other Davis children were "precocious" with "unbroken wills," according to Mary Chesnut, and being the children of the Confederate President they received gifts from strangers as well as the occasional catcall. When Jeff Jr. was out riding his pony one day in 1864, a crowd of local boys hooted as he

Varina Davis and her daughter Winnie. A powerful bond developed between mother and child. (Museum of the Confederacy, Richmond, Virginia)

went by. William was a dutiful boy, much loved by his kinfolk, but easily startled, and whenever he heard the city's alarm bells he ran to find a hiding place in the house. Maggie appeared to be the most un-affected by the turbulence of a Richmond childhood. She had a natu-ral flair for the dramatic, and her performance at a theatrical for chil-dren charmed the audience. All of her offspring were "infinitely precious" to her, Varina Davis said, probably more than ever after Joe's death.[40]

Her closest companions in the household remained her mother and sister, although neither afforded her much solace anymore. She called herself Mrs. Howell's "devoted child," but most of the time she took care of her mother. The old lady had lost faith in the Confeder-ate cause by 1864 and began hoping that the war would end. After she ridiculed Joseph E. Johnston in conversation, a kinsman wrote to Varina warning her about Mrs. Howell's reckless talk. Varina also worried about her sister, whose behavior had become more unre-strained. Margaret twitted Mary Chesnut about her loyalty to all South Carolinians, and that spring she insisted that Mrs. Robert E. Lee leave the Davis pew at St. Paul's Church, for which Jefferson had to apologize. Varina called her sister "my most assailable point" and sent her out of town on a visit. For companionship the First Lady turned to her friends, as she had in the past. That fall she confided in Mary Chesnut that she found the rote predictions of a Southern vic-tory unconvincing, and she expected another significant attack on Richmond in the spring but was trying not to be "disconsolate." The town was rife with gossip about women, much of it concocted, she thought, by idle men. As for her position as First Lady, she said that people did not bother to snub her because she resembled a dead lion, not worth kicking. In her diary, Chesnut remarked that she did not like to think of the troubles that lay ahead for Mrs. Davis.[41]

By the end of 1864, Richmond had a worn, dilapidated look, and food shortages began to afflict much of the civilian population. Bur-glaries were increasing and prostitution was rampant, as the "Cary Street women" traveled all over town plying their trade. Refugees poured into the city, and beggars scoured the streets for food. Confederate morale probably hit a new low after Sherman's March to the Sea concluded in December, with his army's arrival in Savannah. Davis remembered the Christmas holiday of 1864 as unfolding amid a sense of impending catastrophe and desperate want. She received gifts of food, which she turned over to some poor families, and she made some presents for her children. One of her friends gave her a collection of works by Swinburne, which she thoroughly enjoyed. Her public duties did not recede, and when someone told the Davises that orphans at the Episcopal home had been promised some Christmas gifts, the First Lady collected some toys, stitched together some rag dolls, and with her mother and sister made a dollhouse, and on Christmas Day she gave out the presents to the orphans. Resourcefulness of a different kind would be required in the next year.[42]

7

RUN WITH THE REST

EIGHTEEN SIXTY-FIVE began with unseasonably cold temperatures and heavy snows. Richmond was full of "people, and suffering, and crime," as one resident described it, the sidewalk hubbub punctured by the wails of the bereaved in their houses. In the midst of this compounding misery, one of Varina's friends from Washington, Francis Preston Blair, suddenly appeared. His son Montgomery, a moderate Republican, had alienated so many Radical Republicans that he resigned from the cabinet the previous fall, but after President Lincoln's reelection, the elder Blair conceived his own plan to end the war: the Confederacy would surrender so the reconstituted United States could invade Mexico and overthrow Maximilian, the Austrian prince installed by the French government. The plan was as impractical as it was audacious, but Lincoln allowed the elder Blair to go to Richmond to discuss it, and on January 12 he arrived. Jefferson Davis agreed to a conference to discuss the possibility of ending the war.[1]

Francis Preston Blair dined with the Davises at the Confederate mansion, where Varina greeted him with the exclamation, "Oh you Rascal, I am overjoyed to see you." In reply Blair supposedly gave her a kiss on the cheek. After he called her son William a "little Rebel," Varina "wept bitterly," with what feelings of regret or shame we can only guess. Later, when they had a quiet moment together, she asked Blair about Ulric Dahlgren's orders to kill her husband. He made a "laughing remark of disbelief," and after she pressed him on the point he said he would rather not know. Blair returned to Washington, then hastened to Richmond again to convey Lincoln's approval for a meeting. Back in the Northern capital, he told his family that Mrs. Davis was stout, well-dressed, and an "even better talker." In a letter that was probably hand-delivered by Blair in mid-January, Varina told Margaretta Hetzel that "all of dear Mr. Blair's efforts," she feared, would "prove useless."[2]

Mrs. Davis sent another letter to Eliza Gist Blair, Francis Preston Blair's wife, this one certainly hand-delivered by Blair. Varina wrote it even though in November 1864 the Confederate Congress had made communicating with the enemy a treasonable offense punishable by fines and imprisonment. Whether Jefferson Davis, who signed the bill, knew of his wife's latest letter to a Northerner is a mystery. Varina thanked "my dear old Liz" for her recent missive—which has since disappeared—and confessed that she felt the keenest "deprivation" being apart from her Washington friends. She was disappointed that only Margaretta Hetzel and Liz Gillespie, aside from the Blairs, had written to her since the war started. (Gillespie's husband, Archibald, who had a long career in the Marines, was dismissed from the federal service in 1863, but nothing else is known about his wife, and her correspondence with Davis is lost.) She had also heard by methods unknown about another friend from Washington she simply called "Neighbor C." Those who lived in peace surrounded by friends could not understand how she felt, Varina said. She wanted to write earlier to Mrs. Blair but thought the government might intercept a letter from what she acidly called a "moral detrimental" like herself. She called the previous four years the "weariest, and most trying" of her life.[3]

She closed with the most unambiguous burst of Confederate patriotism she expressed during the war, although it would prove to be fleeting, and it coexisted with her enduring love for her Washington friends. "Ours has been the invaded country," Davis told Blair, and she would endure anything to obtain the "liberty" the South was contending for, even the possibility that she would never see Blair again.

What kind of liberty, she did not say. She wanted the Confederacy, which she now called "my own country," to succeed. She gave up her personal happiness when she left Washington, she said, and much blood had been shed during the war. All of it—her own sacrifices, the thousands of deaths—was for nothing if the Confederacy failed, she told Blair. So let us pray for peace, she said, and hope to meet in Heaven, where "no public differences of opinion can alienate us for eternity." She asked Blair to write again if possible and promised to write "'innocent'" letters in reply. She sent her love to Blair and her family, including Montgomery Blair and the Emorys, and she signed, "as ever yours, V." What prompted this political lurch in the Confederate direction is unknown; maybe her husband read the letter; perhaps she really believed these ideas at last. If she did believe them, it is unclear why she chose to share them with a friend in the other capital, which of course had no impact on her reputation in Richmond or on Southern morale.[4]

In any event, at the Hampton Roads peace conference on February 3, the Confederate representatives could not agree with their counterparts on fundamental assumptions. The U.S. representatives, led by President Lincoln himself, insisted that reunion was the precondition for further talks, which the Confederate commissioners would not grant. To end the fighting, Lincoln was apparently willing to offer almost anything, including deferred or compensated emancipation, but his own cabinet in Washington balked at the terms. The Confederate cabinet also rejected the terms, as Varina Davis listened in an adjoining room. So the war went on.[5]

In the Confederate capital, rumors abounded through February and into March that the government would leave town or the Yankee army was about to invade. The cannons roared at all hours, even as refugees flocked to Richmond, one of the last places still in Confederate hands. The city's manic social life at last began to wind down, Vice President Stephens left for his home in Georgia, and the Confederate Congress shut down. The First Lady started preparing for the worst, packing some household goods and selling others for cash. She made these sales without consulting her husband, who was, she said, too busy to pay attention to her affairs, but when he discovered that she used the money to buy flour for the family, he insisted it be left in Richmond to feed the army instead.[6]

As she waited for it all to end, Varina plunged into absolute despair. A Confederate officer quoted her as saying she would rather "*die*"than go on living in this way, and the man added that she was not only fat but "ill-tempered." Davis informed a Confederate congressman that she could give her husband better advice than the Congress had, and she was "very bitter" in conversation with Thomas Conolly, an Irish visitor. He called her a "tigress" and thought she would damage any cause. In the last weeks of the war, Davis was thinking a lot about death. Two of her relatives had died in battle—a nephew in the Confederate army and one of the New Jersey Howells in the Union army—and several of her women friends had passed away. That spring she gave Ellen Barnes a present that some of those women had given her in 1861, a bouquet mounted on a satin cloth, telling Barnes she no longer wanted to have it around her. Davis also predicted to Barnes that a great battle would be fought for Richmond and that the result would be starvation for the people even if the South won. According to Barnes, Mrs. Davis very much wanted to leave the city.[7]

Her unhappiness prompted her to question, if only for a moment, received wisdom about gender. On March 13, Davis wrote to Confederate Colonel Alexander R. R. Boteler in Petersburg to thank him for a gift—probably a horse for her carriage—and then ruminated about the war winding to its conclusion. Boteler, a Virginian congressman, had opposed secession and joined the Confederacy at the last hour, and his wife, Helen Stockton of New Jersey, was distantly related to Varina. The First Lady told the colonel that she hoped the "storm" would soon be quelled and asked if the white Southern people had the capacity to keep fighting. Would they be swallowed up, as Jonah was swallowed by the whale? Would they follow the "pillar of cloud" (an allusion to the book of Exodus, when God guides people to safety)? Or would they keep fighting until the firstborn son in every household was slain? She went on, inserting question marks after two of the adjectives—"Serene in the conviction that the wise and brave of our land were absorbed in the great works of patriotism," she "like the rest of the inferior? and weaker? sex," had been busy with her "individual cares." The times looked so dark, she said, that she was "startled" into these thoughts. After paraphrasing the Irish poet Thomas Moore, "'Tis heart alone, with steel, and stone, That keeps men free forever,'" she asked, "have the hearts of men not failed," meaning the word *men* literally, not as a synonym for humankind. "To you who fight, hope, and die, these questions are not so portentous," she told him, as they were for women like herself "who watch, pray, wait." Then she apologized for her letter, hoping it would not bother him. Boteler did not respond, so we cannot know what he made of this message, in which Mrs. Davis appeared to be blaming white men for losing the war.[8]

She drafted her last letter from Richmond in the small hours of April 1, as the family packed to leave town. Now, like the handful of white women who criticized how Southern men conducted the war, she swerved back toward orthodoxy. Varina told a General Preston (probably William Preston) that the future seemed so dark she could hardly put her ideas into words. She expected her husband would never give up, but the men in the Southern armies were faltering from hunger, and the Union forces, "our enemies," as she now called them, were legion, and the Confederate public, or what was left of it, seemed demoralized. Even Robert E. Lee looked dejected. She thought a "strict construction of our constitution is incompatible with the successful prosecution of a war," and then seemed to recoil from all schools of political thought. She no longer believed in "popular sovereignty," the Democratic Party's stance on slavery in the territories in the 1850s, or "state sovereignty," but at the same time thought they were the only "guarantees" of "Republican liberty," meaning, apparently, the values of a Republican society. After declaring, "We had a right to indulge our own theories, and I do not regret the separation," she apologized for wasting his time with these "womanly, therefore, I fear, weak dissertations" on politics, which should not be taken seriously; her emotions and not her reason were dictating her words, she said. After praising her husband as an honest man, she apologized again for discussing politics "like a 'neophyte.'" She concluded, "Excuse this scrawl. I am so depressed." The letter was evidently never mailed, forgotten as the family left town.[9]

Jefferson Davis had in fact decided it was safer for his wife and children to leave Richmond. Citizens on both sides thought it would have been more dignified for the Southern leadership to surrender in the Confederate capital, and a few Confederates blamed the First Lady for the fact that her husband fled Richmond, but, like most decisions in the marriage, the final decision was his. Varina packed quickly, taking about two thousand dollars in gold, a revolver, and some books. She left most of her household possessions or gave them away, presenting the tea service to Mary O'Melia. Her sybilline warnings about the region's ability to wage war had come true, and she told one of the servants that she was going out into the world "a wanderer without a home."[10]

✵

THE DAVISES SELECTED Charlotte, North Carolina, as her first destination because it was still in Confederate hands. Jefferson told his wife to make her way from North Carolina to the Florida coast and then to some other country, while he would go to Texas and keep fighting. Burton Harrison, Varina's sister Margaret, and James Morgan, a soldier who was also a kinsman, accompanied her. Varina took Ellen Barnes and also James Limber, the boy she found on the street in 1864, apparently without giving the matter much thought. They left on the night of March 30, and when Varina's party arrived in Charlotte a few days later, a crowd of Confederate deserters was waiting for them at the station. They "reviled" her in "shocking" language, Morgan said, and when some men tried to push their way into the car, Harrison forced them back. Eventually the throng dispersed, and the Davis party disembarked and went door to door seeking lodging until a Confederate officer prevailed upon a family to take them in. "How the mighty have fallen," a white woman observed.[11]

On April 2, Jefferson Davis received a telegram from General Lee stating that Richmond would have to be evacuated, and that night he left the city with his staff for Danville, Virginia. The looting began immediately, and parts of the city were in flames when federal troops arrived on April 3. President Lincoln, whose leadership skills had outmatched those of Jefferson Davis in every respect, toured the city on April 4 with David Dixon Porter. Admiral Porter noted that Mrs. Davis's "refined" taste was evident in the mansion, and Mrs. General Ord, wife of the U.S. General stationed in Richmond, appropriated what was left of Varina's wardrobe. Other household objects became instant souvenirs to be collected, traded, bought, and sold for years afterward, and the building began drawing visitors curious about the Confederate White House. That spring Mrs. George Custer toured the residence and spent the night in the Davises' bedroom.[12]

When Varina learned that the capital had been evacuated, she asked her husband, in a letter probably delivered by courier, if her friend Margaret McLean had escaped unharmed. She also assured Jefferson that she had faith in his strength and was praying for God to deliver them all from their travail. Then she wrote to Mary Chesnut, a refugee in the Carolinas. Paraphrasing *Macbeth,* she said she could sleep now after the "fitful fever" of Richmond, and she felt numb, relieved, and hopeless by turns. She trusted God to protect what she called "our cause," but hoped to have no more troubles "of a public nature." Davis left Charlotte in mid-April after she heard that federal troops might attack the town, and then the Confederate specie train, filled with the contents of the treasury, appeared from Richmond; the military escort, including her brother Jeffy D., offered to travel with her. (Becket was likely in England where many Confederate sailors landed after the *Alabama* sank in 1864, William was probably in Augusta, and Joseph's whereabouts were unknown.) Varina accompanied the treasury train to Chester, South Carolina, and there she met James and Mary Chesnut. Davis cheered up in her friend's presence, but she was afraid federal troops might be nearby, so they left again with the specie train headed south. Recalling Davis's prediction in 1860 that the whole thing would fail, Chesnut said that her worst enemies had to grant her the gift of prophecy.[13]

As the party bumped along the country roads, the skies opened and the rain fell. One night when the wagon stuck in the mud and no one else would get out, Davis got out to walk. As she trudged ankle-deep through the muck carrying her baby, she heard the occasional cry of "Yankees" sounding faintly in the darkness. Federal soldiers were indeed in the area and fought some skirmishes with Confederate troops, but none of them crossed her path. At night the party slept in abandoned churches and vacant houses. In a few days they arrived at Abbeville, South Carolina, a village with little food and sporadic mail service. Armistead and Martha Burt, with whom the Davises had rented a house in Washington in 1849, invited her to stay at their residence. On April 19, Varina wrote to her husband asking what she should do, assuming that the report about Lee's surrender was correct. She prayed that God would keep Jefferson safe and protect "our bleeding country."[14]

After waiting five days for someone to deliver her letter to her husband, she added a postscript that the "dreadful news" about Lincoln's assassination had been confirmed and said she felt "wretched." Years later Varina Davis claimed that she wept for Lincoln's family and because she realized this was bad news for the South. Although she did not know it in April 1865, the federal government believed that Jefferson Davis was involved in Lincoln's death, and the new President abandoned Lincoln's policy of letting the Confederate leaders escape. On May 2, Andrew Johnson offered a reward of one hundred thousand dollars for Davis's capture and accused him and other Confederates of having planned the assassination. Many Northerners believed Davis guilty of the murder, and now they called for him to be executed.[15]

At the end of April, Varina left Abbeville by wagon, parting company with the specie train, which was still headed for Florida. She was spending a lot of her own money on necessities, but the children were doing well under the circumstances, and she sent her husband some quick notes with prayers for his safety; some of her letters were intercepted by federal troops and later published in the *New York Times*. At the start of May 1865 she arrived in Washington, Georgia, a village full of refugees, the stores looted and the avenues strewn with garbage. The Davis party stayed with a local family. When residents called on her, she seemed grateful for their politeness and worried that federal troops might be nearby.[16]

As Jefferson Davis rode by horseback through the Carolinas, several dozen miles behind his wife's party, he told his companions that he did not feel like a beaten man and that he could never desert his post as head of the Confederate government. He moved so slowly that one white Southerner thought that he did not understand that he was in danger. At last he began to falter in his dedication to the cause, and in mid-April he sent an aide to find his wife and children. He dismissed his escort and rode on with a small party, federal troops trailing him, as his cabinet broke up, the men leaving singly or in groups. These developments prompted Jefferson to write to his wife that this was not the fate he had envisioned for them in better days. In her reply of April 28 she told him that he had not invited her to a "great Hero's home, but to that of a plain farmer," which was of course untrue, but she wanted him to save himself, and she now suggested that he put aside what she called his "'strict construction' fallacy" if he organized a new government in the west. The only consistency, perhaps, was that she still loved him.[17]

Varina left the village of Washington, traveling south, with her children, her sister Margaret, her brother Jeffy D., Ellen Barnes, James Limber, and a few soldiers who volunteered to go with her. As they headed across Georgia, they feared that they were being shadowed by thieves, so at night they set up guards around the tents and Varina started using the pseudonym Mrs. Smith. People nonetheless recognized her from time to time. One night a group of Confederate veterans appeared, intending to rob the party. They changed their minds after they saw her by the campfire; she had nursed the group's captain when he was wounded in Richmond. They suspected she had the whole Confederate treasury with her, but after she blurted out that she had only two thousand dollars in gold, something in her demeanor—maybe her candor or her desperation—persuaded them to leave, and the party kept moving. As Davis passed through the landscape of abandoned farms and scarecrow chimneys, she was unable to conjecture what the future might hold.[18]

She had run with the rest, as she predicted to her mother in 1861, and her flight from Richmond, nearly six weeks in duration and covering over five hundred miles, was almost done. By early May her party reached the piney woods not far from the Florida border. She hoped that her husband would make it to Texas, and when he and his aides found her party one night near Irwinville, she was greatly alarmed, thinking he had already gone west. After traveling with his family for a short time, Jefferson was satisfied that they were safe and planned to leave again the next morning. Varina was ready for the ordeal to end. That night she told her sister she dreamed they would be caught at a camp in Georgia, and this was the place in her dream. When Margaret anxiously inquired if they should camp somewhere else, Varina said no, they should stay where they were. The party, which numbered some fifteen adults and five children, pitched tents by the roadside, and on May 10 they were surrounded by two U.S. cavalry units that had been following them by separate routes. When the troops burst out of the forest at dawn, they surprised the Davis party, which had posted no sentries. Varina woke up to the sound of soldiers yelling at the top of their lungs.[19]

Much has been said about what happened next, but this is certain: Jefferson Davis tried to escape. He slept in his riding clothes, and by most accounts, including his own, Varina tried to disguise her husband by throwing a raincoat, called a raglan, around him and draping a shawl over his head. Believing that he might not be recognized in the morning light, she begged Ellen Barnes to walk with him into the woods as a decoy, crying, "For God's sake, don't refuse me Ellen." Barnes decided to do it, so the tall white man and the petite black woman walked into the forest, Barnes carrying a bucket as if going to a stream, but a corporal called out for them to identify themselves just as other soldiers realized that the tall person wore boots. Varina answered that it was her mother, but the men recognized Jefferson and ordered him to halt, and one soldier raised his gun. Jefferson wheeled around as Varina rushed over in her nightclothes and threw her arms around her husband. The soldier lowered his gun. Varina had probably saved her husband's life, since federal officers on the scene were determined to take him dead or alive.[20]

Jefferson Davis did not appreciate her efforts at the time. He told Preston Johnston that he would have heaved the soldier off his horse, but "*she* caught me around the arms," to which Johnston sensibly responded that an escape attempt was futile. In his memoir Jefferson stated that the opportunity for escape "had been lost" and said nothing about Ellen Barnes, who disappeared from most accounts of the capture or was sometimes confused with Varina's sister Margaret. Other people did not appreciate Varina's efforts, either. One white Southerner believed that if she had halted during her flight and stayed in one place, Jefferson could have escaped. This seems improbable, because a huge reward had been issued for his capture and federal troops were scouring the region for him. John Taylor Wood, Jefferson's nephew who was traveling with him, also blamed her for what he considered to be the undignified attire. Varina with her usual pragmatism said she would have used any disguise to help her husband escape.[21]

The story began to spread immediately that Jefferson Davis tried to escape dressed as a woman. Similar stories have attached themselves to other politicians who had to flee for their lives, such as Prince Metternich, who departed Vienna under duress in 1848, and during the Civil War political cartoonists in the North had sometimes depicted Jefferson Davis in female attire. In 1865 an officer present at the capture recorded in his diary that Davis was dressed in women's clothes, a "fit ending for such a cause," and another officer who was present informed Secretary of War Stanton by letter three days after the capture. The account appeared right away in the Yankee newspapers and spread like wildfire through the entire country.[22]

The Northern press jubilantly noted the contrast between Varina's behavior and that of her husband. The *New York Times* claimed that she "put on the breeches" because her spouse tried to run off in petticoats, and the *New York Herald* thought she was "more of a man than her husband." For the rest of his life, Jefferson denied that he was dressed as a woman, and technically speaking he was not, since he had on men's attire beneath the raglan and shawl. White Southerners vociferously denied the story, realizing that it held up to ridicule the Confederate cause, Jefferson Davis, and all white Southern men. Regardless of how Jefferson was dressed, however, he was trying to escape, and he relied on the mettle of two females, one white and one black, to do it.[23]

THE TROOPS INFORMED EVERYONE in the Davis party that they were federal prisoners. Jefferson, sans his disguise, kept his composure, the women and children began sobbing, and John Taylor Wood slipped into the forest, ultimately making his way to Canada. Soldiers confiscated the party's belongings, including, apparently, Varina's gun. Someone cut a piece of cloth from the dress she was wearing, and it eventually turned up in a museum in Chicago. Clement Clay Jr., another Confederate who was under arrest, joined the party, as did his wife, Virginia. The prisoners were put in wagons and taken to Savannah, as crowds watched them pass, many of them jeering. Varina looked like a "wreck," said a journalist. In Savannah, they boarded the steamer *William P. Clyde* to the catcalls of passengers on ships nearby. As the *Clyde* steamed out of the harbor on May 15, Varina nursed some family members who had fallen ill, while her husband moved restlessly about the boat or stared at the shore. The vessel stopped at Hampton Roads, Virginia, and most of the prisoners were dispersed. Varina's brother Jeffy D. was taken to Fort McHenry, and on the morning of May 22 Jefferson Davis and Clement Clay were taken to Fort Monroe. Varina's request that she be permitted to accompany her husband was refused.[24]

As Jefferson Davis said goodbye to his wife, he repeated that he had nothing to do with Abraham Lincoln's death, which he had already told her during the trip from Irwinville, when she learned that he was accused of taking part in the Lincoln assassination. She knew that Walker Taylor, Jefferson's kinsman from his first marriage, had broached the idea in 1862 of kidnapping Lincoln. Jefferson had told his wife about Taylor's plan, which, she said, he refused to take seriously.[25] John Wilkes Booth had contact with low-ranking members of the Confederate government, but much of the evidence against Jefferson Davis turned out to be perjured or false, and it has not been proven that Davis or other high-ranking Confederates participated in or knew of Booth's plan to kill Lincoln. Davis was indicted for treason but never formally charged with Lincoln's death. In any case, Jefferson wanted his wife to believe he was innocent, and she did. In the summer of 1865 she told Francis Preston Blair that the accusation was false, and she asked Horace Greeley what her husband could have gained from the death of a "kindly man" such as Lincoln and the substitution of a "bitter enemy" such as Andrew Johnson in his place. In old age she repeated that it was "most unfortunate" for the South that Lincoln was killed, and she dismissed a Confederate officer's statement that Jefferson knew about the murder in advance, because, she said, if there had been any proof of her husband's involvement it would have been produced while he was in prison.[26]

In 1865, while her party stayed on the *Clyde* at Hampton Roads awaiting orders, two white women wearing garish clothes and lots of rouge came to their cabins. Varina Davis said they were "detectives," and Virginia Clay, who was with her party, thought they were prostitutes. Whoever they were, they strip-searched Davis, Clay, and Margaret Howell for treasonous documents while several guards and an aide to U.S. General Nelson Miles, the commander in charge of Fort Monroe, stood by. After they discovered no papers, they left. Clay found Davis sitting in her lingerie, crying, "Oh, Ginie! What humiliation!" The search was probably intended to shame all three of them, since no one strip-searched Jefferson Davis, Clement Clay, or Jeffy D. Howell, all of whom served the Confederacy in office or in the military.[27]

Varina then learned that the *Clyde* was going back to Savannah, where she would be placed under house arrest. Ellen Barnes left, Varina claiming that she went only because her husband made her go, but Barnes told a journalist that although Mrs. Davis was good to her, she would "rather be free, much rather." The soldiers insisted that James Limber had to leave too, so Varina sent him to U.S. Brigadier General Rufus Saxton at Beaufort, South Carolina. One witness said that the boy wanted to stay, and a weeping Varina promised she would come back for him, but another witness recalled that Davis gave him to Saxton as an insult because the general, whom the Davises knew before the war, was now a Radical Republican. Virginia Clay merely commented that Mrs. Davis gave her "pet Negro" to an officer after a "great scene." Saxton sent Limber to the North, where he learned a trade, and Varina never saw him again. She called him a "fine boy" and denied the allegation after the war that the Davises had mistreated him.[28]

When the rest of the party reached Savannah at the end of May, they walked onto the docks only to meet a large crowd waiting to see Jefferson Davis's wife. Varina stopped in her tracks, astonished, until a stranger came forward and took the party to the Pulaski House, where she was formally arrested. Virginia Clay was allowed to go. Varina stayed at the hotel, where she paid her own board out of the thousand or so dollars she had left. Feeling uncomfortable at what she called the "gaze of the crowd," she seldom left the hotel except to take walks late at night accompanied by Robert Brown, a black man employed by the family. After some name-calling between the federal soldiers and the Davis boys, she sent the three oldest children with her mother and sister to Montreal. She was allowed to receive visits from some friends she had known in Washington, members of the Cohen, Phillips, Levy, Yates, and Myers families who landed in Savannah at the war's end, and she grew especially fond of Martha Phillips. A federal soldier guarding Davis at the hotel related that she hoped to leave the country eventually with her husband. He described her as "very intelligent & quite ladylike," demonstrating again that ladyhood was in the eye of the beholder.[29]

AT THE SUMMER'S END, the military authorities allowed her to leave Savannah, and she and Winnie moved to a plantation near Augusta at the invitation of George Schley, a family friend who put them up free of charge for the rest of the year. Varina could not go beyond the state of Georgia, but she could correspond with relatives and friends. A neighbor remembered her as a "big lady" who could be entertaining in conversation, but her inner life was one of great turmoil. She told Mary Chesnut, "You know I bleed inwardly." She could not sleep, even though she felt exhausted and nearly "unhinged" because of the separation from her husband and most of her children. Sometimes she could do nothing but sit and stare into space. She passed the time reading, devouring the newspapers and returning to her favorite authors, among them Elizabeth Barrett Browning and Charles Dickens. She explored new books, such as Charlotte Yonge's *The Clever Woman of the Family*, and older titles, such as Robert Burton's *Anatomy of Melancholy*.[30]

That summer she was very angry about everything that had happened to her, and she directed—or displaced—most of her fury at General Miles and President Johnson. Miles, who had authorized her strip-search and was now in charge of her husband's incarceration, she hated more. When she discovered that the authorities had placed manacles on her husband, she was beside herself. Even though the government was rightly worried about a rescue attempt, and the constraints were removed after about a week, she called Miles a "brute." Andrew Johnson, she claimed, was exacting personal revenge on her husband, and she wrote to the President demanding that she be allowed to visit Jefferson, which naturally offended him. Now she erupted with animosity for the North that went far beyond anything she said during the war. "There is no bond uniting us to the Northerners," she declared, and she said that "a great gulf of blood" rolled between the regions and "my spirit shrinks appalled from attempting to cross it." Because so many men had died, and so many homes been destroyed, she felt "bitter" against the Northern people.[31]

Her hatred of Yankees was pitched at the abstract level, however, for she quickly resumed correspondence with individual Northerners, such as her friends Lizzie Blair Lee, Lizzie Gillespie, and Minna Blair. Minna, who followed Varina's fate in the newspapers and wanted "one long uninterrupted talk" with her, assured her that Matilda Emory had been misquoted in a recent article to the effect that they were no longer on good terms, and she signed the letter "ever yr friend." A group of Varina's Washington friends, including Margaretta Hetzel, offered to help obtain Jeffy D.'s release from prison. Varina also heard from her Richmond friends Margaret McLean, Anne Grant, and the Ritchies, and her niece Malie Brodhead, now a widow in Pennsylvania. In the fall of 1865 she exclaimed, "Never woman had such friends" and few women, she said, had ever "loved and trusted" their friends as much as she loved and trusted hers. Her circle of close friends had survived the war intact.[32]

Davis now reasserted the moderate states' rights opinions she had voiced intermittently since the secession winter. To an attorney she remarked that the Constitution protected states' rights and the federal government had broken the "grand old compact" with the states, but she thought the structure of the government was basically sound. When Francis Preston Blair proclaimed, "I know that your eagle-eyed intellect was never shut to the true glory" of her country—meaning the United States—nor her "honest heart severed from its worship," she made no reply; she did not hear from her other wartime correspondents, James Buchanan and Franklin Glaser. Yet she told Mary Chesnut in the fall of 1865 that she did not take a dim view of the future as most Southern politicians did. She reasoned that they could make their case once they rejoined the Union, which provided "great scope" for men to try to persuade others of the states' rights cause by exercising their rights of speaking, writing, and making use of the press. South Carolina, she believed, had caused the secession crisis by its "hasty action" in 1860. In September 1865 she told John W. Garrett, the railroad magnate whom she had known in Washington, that she "never *believed* in the Southern people" because they were "too self indulgent" and "unwhipped of justice," quoting *King Lear* about villains who conceal their wrongdoing and are then discovered. She may have told Garrett because he was a Unionist but fundamentally apolitical and most interested in his business concerns. Yet she did not specify what kind of justice or what kind of self-indulgence—maybe something related to slavery, secession, or rural life itself.[33]

Then she retreated, abjuring any serious interest in politics, an interest that was, she told Chesnut, unfeminine. Women were "*insufferable*" when they tried to generalize about politics, she said, adding, "I think I see the beard sprout." She still accepted conventional gender roles, despite the fleeting doubts expressed to Colonel Boteler that

John W. Garrett. The businessman to whom Varina Davis confided her thoughts about the war. (Maryland Historical Society, Baltimore, Maryland)

spring and her bravery at the capture, and she still saw herself as a woman first and foremost. That summer she was astonished to learn that a Union officer said that she "injured" the government by not taking the oath of allegiance to the United States, as women in some parts of the former Confederacy were required to do, and she called herself an "unprotected" mother with four children in her charge. Moreover, she had done what she thought a wife should do. She told Francis Preston Blair that she had been "punished" for "being Mr. Davis'[s] wife and born in the South."[34]

Perhaps because she saw herself as a woman, a mother, and a wife, she did not face her husband's responsibility for the events of the last four years. She was profoundly unhappy, and as the leaden days went by she had more free time than she had had in years, certainly time enough to reflect on how this had come to pass. She was primed, as it were, for a breakthrough. Moreover, she was better educated, more observant, and capable of more insight than most of her peers. To her friend Martha Phillips, she quoted Milton's *Paradise Lost,* "what in me is dark / illumine, what is low raise and support," but she had no illumination, no catharsis, no epiphany. She did not face the hard truths that all the bloodshed was in vain because, as she told Mrs. Blair in January, the South lost the war; that her husband, who headed the Southern government, bore much of the responsibility for the bloodshed; and finally, that his political choices had brought a storm of calamities upon his family. Nor did she face her own complicity. She may have hurt the Confederate cause as much as she helped it with her vacillating political opinions, not to mention nursing Union prisoners, but she conveyed messages for Judah Benjamin, she nursed soldiers in the Confederate hospitals, and she said earlier in 1865 that the South was contending for "liberty."[35]

As for slavery, the chief cause of the war, she had not learned much. She did understand that a new racial decorum was in place, and she felt relieved that the local "Negroes" were "civil" to her. She tried scrupulously to avoid offending black people she encountered. She observed that the Georgia countryside was full of homeless African Americans and commented, "This is no Utopia," although she thought that something good might come from this "chaos" in the distant future. In 1865 a few white Southerners made the conceptual breakthroughs prompted by the war and faced the fact that slavery was wrong. This could have been such a moment for Varina Davis, who said in the 1850s that slaves were human beings with their frailties, but it was not. Instead she predicted that black laborers would not abide by work contracts or support themselves. Whether she believed that they were as self-indulgent as white people, she did not say.[36]

She tried to stay in touch with a small number of black people she had known in the past. In 1865 she asked her relatives about some of the former Davis slaves by name, and she hoped she might meet Betsey, who had run away in 1864, but Betsey did not contact her and Varina never saw her again. When Ellen Barnes remarried in Virginia in 1867, Varina helped make the wedding dress, and she and Mary O'Melia, who had moved to Baltimore, were apparently the only white people who attended the ceremony. In 1865 Davis's assumptions about gender still informed her views on race. She believed that African American women, like white women, had to abide by their husband's wishes. When a black woman left the Schley farm, it was only because her husband insisted on it, Varina said, much as she believed that Betsey left in 1864 only because her husband ran away and that Ellen left in 1865 because her husband made her do it. The idea that these black women or African Americans in general wanted to be free was too much for her. On race, slavery, and secession, she did not have the intellectual courage at this point in her life to match the physical courage she demonstrated at the capture.[37]

8

THREADBARE GREAT FOLKS

VARINA DAVIS NOW FOCUSED on the immediate task at hand, helping her family. In mid-August 1865, General Nelson Miles allowed the couple to begin corresponding, with the stipulation that they discuss family matters only. After sending her his love and prayers, Jefferson reminded her of her duty to the children, suggesting that she join them in Canada. In reply, she explained why she sent them there and furthermore that her desire for his approval guided all her decisions. She said she did not know what she would do without him, but, as it turned out, she did a great deal. She told Mary Chesnut, "I never report unfit for duty"—family duty, that is. Somehow she arranged for two Northerners—one Alfred T. Barnes, probably no relation to Ellen, and Thomas Buckler, a Baltimore physician whose patients included James Buchanan—to have her letters sent unopened to correspondents in the region. Possibly these men had delivered her wartime letters as well. She remained in Georgia, and after consulting Horace Greeley and others by mail, she hired Charles O'Conor, a prominent New York attorney she had known before the war, to represent her husband.[1]

For the first time she started managing the Davis finances. The federal government confiscated Brierfield and the Hurricane, and because they could no longer make the payments, the Davises gave up the Mississippi plantation they bought during the war. If Jefferson took part of the Confederate treasury, as some of his enemies alleged, the money was gone by now. In the summer of 1865 Varina had about a thousand dollars in cash, but Judah Benjamin, now living in London, lent her a little over twelve thousand dollars, and she received several thousand dollars from friends and strangers, including Charles Farrar Browne, alias Artemus Ward, the editor of *Vanity Fair*. Varina thought it undignified to take cash from people she did not know, but she swallowed her pride and took it. She learned to invest, and by the fall of 1865 she had enough money to make loans to friends and relatives, including her brother-in-law Joseph. Probably acting on her husband's instructions, she gave Joseph several hundred dollars.[2]

Varina's mother and six siblings, who gathered in Montreal, consumed much of her energy. In fact, they got into more trouble than ever. The Howells boarded in the city's hotels and spent money freely, while Varina's brothers, who could not find or keep jobs, passed their time hunting in the countryside. Even though Mrs. Howell was eligible for a federal pension from her husband's service in the War of 1812, she did not apply for one. A charlatan named Mr. Stuart insinuated himself with the Howells and bilked them out of some money, and Varina's brother William may have embezzled money from some ex-Confederates in Montreal. Jeffy D., after he was let out of prison, was arrested and then released again. Varina sent the Howells what she could spare from her own funds, but they began to try her exemplary patience. She cried to a friend, "By the Lord Harry they will leave me nothing to carry."[3]

She kept helping them anyway. After Margaret Howell left her watchful older sister, she became pregnant and would give birth to a son, Philip, in June 1866. Margaret was engaged to yet another man in 1865 before the match was broken off, but she did not name the baby's father, who could have been one of several men: her ex-fiancé, Mr. Stuart, or one of the ex-Confederates who visited Montreal. Varina learned of the pregnancy by the start of 1866, when she said the "new addition to the family circle" made her and "all parties" unhappy. She knew that an out-of-wedlock pregnancy could make a respectable marriage impossible for her sister, and she was determined to salvage Margaret's prospects. The Davis children may have been

Margaret Howell. Varina Davis's wild sister.
(University of Kentucky, Lexington)

told that the boy was their brother, the son of Varina and Jefferson, and the family maintained its silence forever after on Philip's paternity. Varina's unbreakable love for her siblings had survived the war.[4]

At Fort Monroe, her husband's condition was deteriorating. President Johnson retreated from his initial desire that Jefferson Davis should be executed, partly because of the influence of the Blairs, and by the fall of 1865 Varina believed that her husband would probably serve a long term in prison or be exiled from the country. The authorities still feared a rescue attempt, so Jefferson remained under tight security, and he had no visitors aside from Charles Minnegerode, a Richmond clergyman. He tried to read but he often felt sick, and he became sensitive to noise, complaining about the footsteps of soldiers guarding him. The isolation began to affect his judgment. He became concerned that baby Winnie's hair was not growing fast enough, although he had not seen his daughter in months and had no way to measure the growth of her hair.[5]

His wife, the only relative allowed to correspond with him regularly, did her best to brace him up. She assured him that he was the only man she had ever loved or wanted to marry. Regarding their future, she was eager to return to private life. Varina wanted what she called a "real home life" and a "sunny green bank upon which we might rest and pray, and work and see its fruition." Misrepresenting much of their marital history, she proclaimed that she had been happily dependent upon him throughout their union. She took the blame for their conflicts and asked his forgiveness for being "willful." She asked him, however, if she meant half as much to him as he did to her.[6]

Jefferson did not answer that question, but he admitted that he had focused on his political career rather than his family. Now he wanted to repay her for his long absences on public business. He said his love for her was undiminished, and he appreciated the times she "soothed" his suffering and "anticipated" his wants. In February 1866 he thanked her for throwing her body in front of his when he "refused to surrender," as he put it, at the capture in 1865. Neither of them touched on issues relating to the late war, such as her doubts about the Confederate cause, but Jefferson had some Olympian advice for his spouse on family matters. He told her again, "You were reminded of the importance of your presence with the children," so she explained once again why she sent them to Canada. She had done the best she could do under the circumstances, he said, although she was a "nervous woman." He concluded, "I can only hope that you will be able to address yourself to current demands upon you."[7]

VARINA DAVIS was still a public figure, and the next phase in her mutating celebrity was about to begin. In 1866 the federal government gave her permission to visit Canada, and in February she set off, going first to New Orleans. Burton Harrison, recently out of prison, was her escort. A friend warned that she might meet hostility from some white Southerners during the journey, but individuals sought her out to praise her husband. Now she was the wife of a prisoner whom many white Southerners saw as a martyr for his cause, which mitigated much of the animosity toward him, and her. At her New Orleans hotel, she was inundated with callers, and shopkeepers would not accept her money. The outpouring overwhelmed her. The Richmond complaints about her "crudeness" vanished, and her lack of enthusiasm for the Southern cause was forgotten or overlooked. She had become, in the latest incarnation, a symbol of the Confederacy.[8]

Davis had been in Montreal only a few days when the U.S. government allowed her to visit her husband, and she arrived on May 3 at Fort Monroe, a compound of buildings at Hampton, Virginia. She had to swear that she would not help her husband escape, and after General Miles interviewed her to ascertain that she had no weapons, she spent the day with her husband. Jefferson was very glad to see her, although he still thought she should have remained in Canada with the children. She decided to stay at the fort anyway and lodged at the apartment of the prison doctor, Samuel Cooper, and his wife. Her daily visits to her husband convinced her that his health was in danger, and the doctor agreed, telling Miles that Jefferson could die in prison.[9]

She swung into action, marshaling her energies on his behalf. Literally on familiar ground again, in the United States, she began working through her contacts in Washington, showing the political skills she had not displayed as Confederate First Lady. She gave interviews to journalists about her husband's situation, thanking white Southerners for their concern even as she praised federal officers for their kindness, and she asked Andrew Johnson, politely this time, for a personal interview, and, if it was feasible, a parole for her husband. Partly as a result of her efforts, Secretary of the Treasury Hugh McCullough visited Fort Monroe. Jefferson's diet improved, and he was allowed visits from his attorney and his friends. Varina cultivated good relations with two officers at the fort, Lieutenant J. A. Fessenden, kinsman of the Maine senator she had known in Washington, and Colonel Henry DuPont, whom she had known before the war. Because Jefferson was allowed to write only to his relatives, she took over his legal correspondence and continued to manage their money.[10]

After President Johnson agreed to see her in May 1866, she hurried to Washington. Clement Clay Jr. had been released from Fort Monroe in April, so she had hopes for Jefferson's release. This was her first visit to the White House since January 1861, when she went to bid farewell to James Buchanan, and it would be her last. When she saw the President on the 25th, the conversation was brisk. She asked him to withdraw the assassination charge against her husband, which he refused to do. He was in fact under strong pressure from some congressmen and members of the public to try Jefferson Davis or have him executed, and in the midst of a fierce struggle with the Republican Party over his Reconstruction policies. She glimpsed Johnson's peril when a Republican senator barged in during the interview, browbeat the President while ignoring her, and stormed out. Johnson then hinted that the prisoner should request a pardon, but she said Jefferson would not do that. At least they parted on civil terms. She stayed with the family of Thomas Miller, the Davises' doctor in the 1850s, and the press noted that her arrival at the F Street residence caused a "sensation" in "certain circles." She was overjoyed to see the Blairs, among others, and received a call from Senator Lafayette Foster, a Republican from Connecticut. He listened politely as she asked him to help her husband obtain a parole. Mrs. Davis's "dignified" manner fascinated him, especially when she lost her self-control for a moment. She began to cry and explained that his kindness had made her weep. If he had been harsh, she said, she could have maintained her composure.[11]

Back at Fort Monroe, she won her power struggle with General Nelson Miles. This native of Massachusetts was in his late twenties, largely self-educated, and had worked as a clerk before the war. Portrayed by his biographer as a difficult, rough-hewn personality, he had achieved the rank of brigadier general of volunteers by 1865, and he would have a long military career. Secretary of War Edwin Stanton may have assigned Miles to guard Jefferson Davis because he was not a West Point graduate and would feel little sympathy for the prisoner. Miles believed for some reason that Varina Davis was a fire-breathing secessionist and a blue-blooded Virginian, and she hated him for authorizing the strip-search on the *Clyde*. They argued over the details of the prisoner's treatment, such as the lighting in Jefferson's cell, and whether she should have a military escort inside the fort, in the manner of the time. When she asked for lodging at the fort, Miles suggested she stay with local prostitutes. Another soldier arranged for her to stay in a casemate near the officers' wives, but she remembered the affront for decades. That summer John Craven, one of the prison doctors, and a ghostwriter published *The Prison Life of Jefferson Davis,* based partly on letters Varina supplied. Miles was portrayed as a callous man. After more controversies, Miles left the fort in 1866 for another assignment. General H. S. Burton, whom Varina liked much better, replaced him.[12]

At the same time, she did her duty to the different branches of her enormous family. She visited Caroline Leonard, Joseph Davis's daughter who resided in Norfolk with her second husband, and she asked friends to find jobs for the various Davis kinfolk. She made some short trips to Canada to see her children and to look after the Howells. Varina paid their bills and tried to help her brothers find employment, and regarding her sister Margaret, she asked her mother to "raise her self esteem." Varina's sister clearly needed guidance from somebody. When a journalist from a Chicago paper visited the Montreal household, Margaret brandished a blood-stained Union flag at him. Varina brought her back to Fort Monroe, while Margaret's infant son evidently stayed in Canada. Margaret seemed to calm down in her sister's presence, and Varina found her a comfort as they read novels together. She told Martha Phillips, "But for her companionship I cannot tell what I should do." She added, "You know it is absolutely necessary to have a woman to whom one may confide a 'woman's thoughts'" and who "will be responsive."[13]

As callers flocked to Fort Monroe to see Jefferson Davis, Varina had to resume her duties as a hostess. She welcomed three New York merchants who wanted to discuss commerce with her husband, a missionary who urged him to seek a pardon, and Franklin Pierce, who came to talk about possible terms for his release. Sometimes visitors wanted to talk to her too, and Charles O'Conor advised her to remember, "The eyes of the world will be upon you." Two Italian noblemen asked to meet her, and whenever she left the fort, her itinerary appeared in the press with accounts of how she was dressed (usually in black). Although she wore a heavy veil over her face as she traveled, whites recognized her and introduced themselves. Not everyone was civil, but she kept silent when insulted. When she visited friends in Baltimore, callers showed up at breakfast and came until ten o'clock at night. The good will from some members of the public, especially "the Richmond people," continued to surprise her.[14]

In the spring of 1867, as she campaigned for her husband's release from prison, Varina continued to perform tasks far beyond the domestic sphere and do them well. For two years President Johnson, his cabinet officers, members of the Supreme Court, and Republican congressmen had been unable to agree on what to do with the prisoner, who still had no trial date; they also differed on the larger question of the harm Davis's trial might do to the country and the particulars such as which judge should preside. Varina went to Baltimore to meet John Garrett, the railroad magnate she had known before the war, and together they consulted on the options—whether Jefferson might be paroled, freed on bail, or moved to another prison—as well as the likely opinion of Edwin Stanton, all of which Varina relayed to her husband. She asked Thomas Pratt, a former U.S. senator from Maryland, for his help, and she traveled to Washington again to ask other friends for their assistance. Even as she undertook these efforts, Varina assured her husband that she would not stay away from Fort Monroe an hour longer than necessary or spend any time on her own enjoyment.[15]

In the midst of this whirlwind of activities, her assumptions about gender did not change. Varina, like other white women who did unconventional things during the war, saw these actions as a temporary departure from her role as a wife, and she said not a word about her doubts in 1865 on the "inferior" sex. Now she made extravagant statements of deference to her husband, promising to obey his wishes in all their practical affairs. She acquiesced when he did not wish their children to visit him in prison, although she wanted to bring them to Fort Monroe. She was still not very introspective. She told a friend that when she ran into "a stone wall of hard realities," she just tried to get around it. Sometimes she felt the "sere and yellow leaf" of age upon her, paraphrasing *Macbeth,* and constant activity, she seemed to think, was the best way to fill her days. When there was nothing else to do, she took advantage of the fort's location to learn to swim.[16]

The tenacious efforts of Varina Davis and many other people brought results, and in May 1867 Jefferson was released from jail. Public hostility in the North toward him had decreased somewhat, and other Confederates had been let out of prison. Moderate Republicans began to say that the government should either try Davis or release him. Charles O'Conor obtained a writ for Jefferson's release, and on May 11 Varina accompanied her husband on a steamboat to Richmond, where on the dock there awaited a crowd, including a detachment of U.S. infantry in case there was any trouble. Thousands of people watched the Davises pass through the streets to the Spotswood Hotel. On May 13 Jefferson was brought before the U.S. Circuit Court and released on bail of one hundred thousand dollars paid by Horace Greeley and other prominent Northerners, with the expectation that the trial would take place in November. The Davises left for Canada, which they entered easily even though Jefferson had not taken the oath of allegiance to the United States and was a citizen of no country. After a joyous reunion in Montreal, the family moved into a plain house on Montagne (or Mountain) Street in a neighborhood of European immigrants and ex-slaves who had escaped from America before the war. Varina wryly noted that the Davises were "unsuccessful, ci-devant, threadbare great folks," and she was relieved that the neighbors were polite.[17]

About the war, she still wavered. She confided to William Preston, "It is a fearful thing to try an experiment with the civilized world for auditor, and spectator, judge, and jury." She was glad "the long agony" was over and that she had "relapsed" into her "normal obscurity," even if she was in "abnormal poverty." She thought it would be good for her husband to work for a living and observed that "the Confederacy is to him yet the dearest earthly object of contemplation," but, she said, she could not love it as he did. At the same time, she claimed to share Jefferson's disappointment with white Southerners who were "'reconstructed,'" and she believed that "Radicalism" now pervaded American politics. She did not mention and may not have read the books about the Davises that appeared after the war by such writers as Edward Pollard and Elizabeth Keckley.[18]

Instead she concentrated on the ceaseless, ongoing demands of her household. Varina continued to handle much of her husband's business correspondence, and when he thought about publishing a memoir, she started arranging his papers; when he discovered it was too painful to write the book, she put the papers aside. Because she knew a great deal about their money, Jefferson had to consult her about financial matters. Neither her mother nor her siblings could look after the children unaided, and the young Davises drove her husband wild, their voices sounding like trumpets in his ears, so she took care of the children too. Their offspring had lived in five cities in seven years (Washington, Montgomery, Richmond, Savannah, and Montreal), and they all knew that the family was famous, or infamous. When a Union veteran called on the household, probably out of curi-

Jefferson and Varina Davis, 1867. The weary couple in Montreal.
(Museum of the Confederacy, Richmond, Virginia)

osity, Maggie's admonition that he should help her father was re-ported in the London *Times*. They were fully aware of their poverty, Maggie lamenting her unstylish clothes, while Jeff Jr. declared that he had no desire to be a dandy anyway. Billy was partially deaf, probably due to a strep infection, which often causes childhood deafness. He could barely follow a normal conversation or write a letter by him-self, but he could talk, and he sometimes asked about James Limber. He, too, wanted his father to earn some money so they could be rich again.[19]

Varina's siblings left Montreal, three of her brothers drifting to New Orleans, where their tragicomic adventures continued. Joseph suffered a stroke, and after he recovered, began talking of moving to Mexico. Becket was apparently unemployed, and William, who had gone bankrupt in Montreal, now described himself as a "planter" al-though he did not own an acre of land, and his marriage was falling apart. Jeffy D. alone was prospering. He became a commercial sea-man and sailed all over the Atlantic, and, unique among his brothers, wrote regularly to the family. Jane Waller and her husband moved to Lynchburg, Virginia, where William practiced law, and Margaret Howell visited friends in Nova Scotia, the family maintaining its si-lence on her illegitimate child. Mrs. Howell died in the fall of 1867 and was buried in Montreal. Varina had mothered Mrs. Howell over much of the last decade, and before that had taken over much of her responsibilities for the Howell siblings, but she adored her mother to the end.[20]

The Davises moved again to Lennoxville, near Montreal, to a hotel where the fare was simple—the menu restricted to beef, beans, pud-ding, and pie—and the clientele picturesque, including some circus performers passing through town. The hotelier's wife recalled Mrs. Davis as a person with great conversational powers who was careful not to discuss the war, but Varina soon felt bored in the little town, lonely for her friends, and ashamed of her outdated wardrobe. She looked after Jefferson, who was emaciated and accident-prone; he fell down some stairs and broke his ribs. He followed the impeach-ment crisis in the United States with moderate interest, believing that things would go badly for him whether or not Andrew Johnson left office. Varina realized that Jefferson needed some kind of occupation, and she was worried about the family's finances. In the summer of 1868 the U.S. government, still unsure of what to do with Davis, postponed his trial again.[21]

JEFFERSON DECIDED to move to Great Britain to resuscitate his fortunes. Following his brother Joseph's advice, he took a job with a commission house. For her part, Varina was eager to start a new life abroad, and when the Davises sailed from Quebec in July 1868 for Liverpool, she felt a sense of "welcome" as the British Isles hove into view, because they were planning to live permanently in England. The London *Times* announced their arrival in Liverpool in advance, and an excited group of Britons and Confederate exiles greeted the ship on August 4. Jefferson Davis again had no trouble being admitted to the country, even though he was not an American citizen. The family moved to Liverpool's Adelphi Hotel, where they were besieged by callers, including such ex-Confederates as Wirt Adams, who came bearing greetings from Judah Benjamin, now an attorney in London. The Davises had so many visitors that they fled to the Welsh town of Llandudno, a tidy village overlooking Colwyn Bay.[22]

Mrs. Davis was acutely aware that her husband was a notorious public figure, and she wished to avoid any contretemps with expatriates from the northern United States. The Davises were celebrities of a singular kind, homeless, and the man of the family was in political limbo with legal problems that could conceivably result in another prison term in the United States. Yet a train of impostors appeared on both sides of the Atlantic claiming to have worked for them, and the Davises attracted newspaper coverage wherever they went. People recognized Jefferson in public, and many stopped to stare at him. Occasionally they recognized Varina. Europeans who had supported the Union cause or did not care about the war's outcome seem to have ignored them.[23]

Members of the British aristocracy, then at the zenith of their wealth and political power, rushed to embrace the Davises. Even though the government had not extended diplomatic recognition to the South, most aristocrats had supported the Confederacy as a bulwark of tradition. Charles, 19th Earl of Shrewsbury, who met them in America in 1851 and was a Conservative member of Parliament, journeyed to Llandudno to invite them to his estate. The Davises also heard from Lord Alexander Beresford-Hope, who had helped organize the Southern Independence Association to lobby for British recognition of the Confederacy. He too was a member of Parliament, and although the Beresford-Hope title was new, created earlier in the century, the family was very rich, and his wife, Lady Mildred Hope, the daughter of a marquis, told Varina that she would do anything to help the Davises. Within days of their arrival, she invited them to stay at their London home.[24]

That fall Varina set foot in the great metropolis for the first time. Both she and her husband began to feel more cheerful in the cauldron of human activity that was London. "Immensity was the great fact" about the city, according to Henry James. Home to more than three million people, London was undergoing phenomenal growth, many of its traffic-thronged streets lined with palatial clubs and colossal hotels, and the entire city was engaged in a stupendous range of activities. Jefferson was primarily concerned with making contacts for his new business venture, and Wirt Adams told him that friendships with what Adams bluntly called the "ruling class" could only help. He urged Davis to exert his "powers of pleasing," which he possessed "in so eminent a degree" when he saw "fit to use them." While Varina stayed in the city, Jefferson traveled the country to raise funds for his commission house. In December 1868, when Jefferson returned to London, Andrew Johnson issued an amnesty to all ex-Confederates, including Davis, and in February 1869 the U.S. attorney general dropped plans to bring him to trial. The way seemed open for the Davises to settle permanently in the Old World.[25]

Somehow they still had enough money. Friends such as Norman Walker and C. J. McRae had probably stashed some of their money in England during the war, and in 1868 the Davises had invested with a firm in Liverpool. They accepted gifts from Englishmen such as James Spence, a Confederate sympathizer who paid the tuition when their boys enrolled in private schools. The family moved to a flat on Upper Gloucester Place in the West End, and Margaret Howell arrived from Canada, apparently without her son, while Mary Ahern, an Irish American nurse, moved in to care for Winnie. The Davises could even afford to take a holiday at the seaside. But Varina lamented the fact that the family was "poor," and because she could not afford new clothes she did not want to go into society. In truth they had assumed a middle-class standard of living after being wealthy for a long time.[26]

The Davises visited Paris in the winter of 1868–69 with a view toward settling there. They now believed that the Continent would be cheaper than Britain, and the City of Light, with a population approaching two million, held many attractions. Baron Haussmann had almost finished his handiwork, and splendid public buildings graced the boulevards, although the French had enjoyed few political freedoms under Napoleon III's regime. Some four thousand Americans lived there, including the former Confederate minister John Slidell, whose daughter had married into the Erlanger family. The Davises enrolled their daughter Maggie in the Convent of the Assumption in Auteuil, 16th Arrondissement, and they seriously considered buying a house. Swarms of callers bustled forward to see them at Dudley Mann's residence on the Boulevard de Madeleine, both of the Davises now serving as symbols of the Confederate cause. When Varina had a moment alone with Dudley Mann, she did imitations of the ex-Confederates, although she did them offstage, unlike in Richmond.[27]

The war was never far from her mind. When the Davises visited the Louvre, Varina admired Jacques-Louis David's famous work of the 1790s, *The Oath of the Horatii*. The painting, which pioneered the neoclassical style, is celebrated for its spatial design, skillful lighting, and monumental human forms, but she seems to have been most taken by the subject matter, women separated by war. David took his theme from Titus-Levy's account of the contest between ancient Rome and the city of Alba, which was determined by personal combat between the Horatii brothers and the Curiatii brothers. The men, who are related by marriage, reach for their swords as the women and children collapse into tears. The painting reminded Jefferson of his wife's devotion and her ability to "heighten" his "happiness" and "soothe" his "misery." He also had the war on his mind. He refused an invitation to meet Napoleon III and the Empress Eugenie because, he said, the emperor had been insincere in his dealings with the Confederate government.[28]

Ultimately the Davises chose not to live in Paris, a result of their differing objections to the city. In May 1869 an election was carried out amid great violence, and Varina sensed that the days of the Second Empire were numbered—France's defeat in the Franco-Prussian War would force Napoleon out in 1870—but Jefferson had other concerns. He admitted that Paris offered bountiful opportunities for "intellectual cultivation," yet he thought the atmosphere was too decadent, and he disapproved of the nude statues in public places. So the couple returned to England, their arrival reported in the international press. In London the Davises saw Judah Benjamin, who was happily absorbed in his life in Britain. After granting Jefferson one lengthy talk about the American Civil War, Varina said, he did not want to discuss it again.[29]

Back in England, Mrs. Davis did not see much of her husband. He traveled on the Continent for several weeks, his itinerary published throughout the English-speaking world, and again he had no trouble traveling although he was a citizen of no country. When he returned to Britain, he visited Stratford-on-Avon, where one of his walking sticks went to a museum; Abbotsford, where Sir Walter Scott lived; and Inverlochy Castle, where Davis shot grouse with Lord Abinger. His letters to his wife were loving. He said his heart belonged to her, and he seemed to feel guilty when he scarcely saw their children. If Varina had been hoping for the companionate marriage he seemed to promise in his prison letters, she concealed her disappointment. She wrote to him faithfully during his travels and looked after him when he was at home, remarking to a friend that a good wife did her duty by helping her husband.[30]

The British aristocracy's courtship of the Davises reached its apogee in the spring and summer of 1869. The Earl of Shrewsbury and the Beresford-Hopes, who had become particularly fond of the couple, sent them invitations, and the Duke of Northumberland, holder of one of the country's oldest titles, asked them to dinner. Lord Abinger arranged for them to attend a service at the royal chapel at St. James's Palace, and in May 1869 Varina spent a day with Princess Mary of Cambridge, a first cousin of Queen Victoria and the wife of the German prince Francis of Teck, possibly at Mary's residence at Kensington Palace. The Tecks, as they were known, were highly sociable, but they must have had the informal consent of the monarch, possibly because Varina had met the Prince of Wales in 1860 or because the Queen, unlike her deceased husband, had a few flickers of Confederate sympathy in 1861. The American ambassador, Reverdy Johnson, lodged no protest, and Davis herself wrote nothing about it.[31]

Varina's response to other members of the British nobility was decidedly mixed. She described some of them, such as the royal physician Sir Henry Holland, as cordial, and the stuffy Lord Campbell, the 8th Duke of Argyll, as someone who improved upon further acquaintance. When she visited Stoneleigh in Warwickshire, home of Lord William Henry Leigh and Lady Caroline Leigh, the luxury of the place dwarfed that of the Hurricane, Brierfield, or any place she had ever lived. The magnificent house contained first editions of Shakespeare and paintings by Rembrandt, and she remembered its beauty for the rest of her days. She enjoyed talking to Lady Leigh, and the two women corresponded for decades. But the sheer wealth of the British elite intimidated her, as it has intimidated other Americans, and she felt uncomfortable associating with "such rich people." Moreover, she, like other Americans, found some of the nobles arrogant. She was shocked by the illness and want among working-class Londoners, although she had no comment on politics in Gladstone's England.[32]

She would have been happy nonetheless to live in Britain permanently if that was what her husband wanted to do. She once called

England the "Isle of fair delights" because it was the home of so many writers, from Byron to Gibbon. She found London stimulating, and in her letters she burst into some good-natured puns, such as this one to her niece: "My muse gets on her Pegasus for a doggerel ride—but I have made her dismount least you should deride her." She read the British press avidly, and she appreciated the kindness of the staff at William's academy when he fell ill. She responded deeply to the country's history. In 1869 she and her husband toured Westminster Abbey, where time seemed to vanish. She saw the places where Edward the Confessor and other monarchs were laid to rest, and she relished the eight-hundred-year-old coronation robes, the narrow staircases with the worn stones, and the Jerusalem Chamber. Her visit to the Tower of London affected her profoundly, as she saw the places where the "little strangled Princes" died, especially the inscriptions that the condemned had left on the dungeon walls, "rude mementoes of great names." About Mary Queen of Scots, whose biography she found so affecting in 1862, she remarked that her life was "woeful" and Darnley's indifference to her very sad.[33]

Her husband's efforts to raise money for his commission house were not going well, although most of London's financial institutions had been officially nonpartisan during the war and the great houses were open to outsiders with good investment ideas. The influential London *Times,* which stoutly insisted that the Confederate President was not dressed as a woman when captured, remained favorable toward him. But Davis was frequently sick and could do little work, and he had critics, including the American Unionist and one-time Mississippian Robert J. Walker, who published a wartime pamphlet to discourage the British from lending money to the Confederacy. Walker, whose wife had been Varina's friend in Washington, alleged that in the 1830s Davis supported repudiation of bonds held by Mississippi's banks, some of which were owned by British banks. Walker succeeded in making Davis look irresponsible, even though Davis had not begun his political career in the 1830s and Walker had himself supported repudiation. Judah Benjamin warned Davis to keep silent because the British public would not understand such a complicated issue from thirty years earlier, but Jefferson wrote a long indignant letter to the *Standard* anyway. Several Englishmen then contacted him directly to ask for their money back.[34]

By the summer of 1869, Jefferson had given up hope on the commission house. Even with powerful friends in the aristocracy in a city awash with money, he could not make a good living. The repudiation controversy hurt him, and he may have struck Englishmen as too sickly for the business world, too cantankerous, or too backward-looking, as suggested by his habit of distributing photographs of what he said was his attire at the capture in 1865. He had begun to find London dull, and he was homesick for the South. He decided to accept a job with the Baltimore office of the Carolina Life Insurance Company. The salary was adequate, and Jefferson thought the position "consistent with self respect." In September 1869 he left the country, planning to send for his wife and children in England. Calling Jefferson her "best beloved," Varina again took up the responsibilities of parenting their children alone.[35]

9

TOPIC OF THE DAY

 VARINA DAVIS'S CELEBRITY did not diminish after her husband left England. A stranger approached her about Mississippi's bonds and hinted that she should give him some money, but she refused. There were friendlier encounters. One of the city's Confederate exiles, Osmun Latrobe, took her to the theater, and she saw Lord and Lady Campbell. She enjoyed an outing to the Crystal Palace, the exhibition hall that was the pride of Victorian Britain. She accepted other invitations out of a sense of obligation, going reluctantly to dinner with Mr. and Mrs. James Arthur Fremantle, an English couple who were Confederate sympathizers. She had many callers at her London flat, including a couple she had known in Canada, the Rawsons, who had several silly disputes in Davis's presence about such matters as Mrs. Rawson's attire. Varina wrote a funny account of the drawing-room drama in her next letter to her husband.[1]

She thought his position with the insurance company in Baltimore offered the best prospect for what she again called a real home at last, but Jefferson was already changing his mind. After traveling through the Mississippi River Valley, he told Varina that because he had been identified with what he called the "South West," it would help his sons if they lived there. In the fall he decided to take a job with the insurance company in that region. He informed her that she needed to make a decision about her "own residence," adding the somewhat contradictory observation, "Your wishes must exercise an important influence on my action." Jefferson thought Varina probably would not like his decision but would accept it once she understood its advantages. The insurance company's board of directors appointed him company president, with an office in Memphis and a salary of twelve thousand dollars a year, a good income for a man who had been unemployed most of the time since 1865. He accepted on the spot.[2]

In November 1869, he wrote to his wife about the question of where she would live. In a letter dated the 23rd, he observed that Memphis would probably not be agreeable to her, but his new job gave him the means to enable her to "live elsewhere" until circumstances provided them with "a less restrained choice," possibly in about a year when the company moved its headquarters to Baltimore. In case she misunderstood this contorted language, he said she could remain in England with the children, or live in Baltimore with the children, or leave their sons in Baltimore and join him with their daughters in Memphis. He added that this change of plan would benefit the children. In fact, it was bereft of all logic. If he wanted his sons to benefit from his association with the Southwest, it made no sense to propose that they live in England or Baltimore, with or without their mother. If he was concerned about all of his offspring, it was even stranger to propose that they should continue to live apart from him. He could have simply asked his wife and children to join him right away, but he did not. While he was in prison, he said he wanted to be with his offspring as much as possible after he was released, yet he had seen little of them in England and he did not seem to miss them very much now.[3]

Jefferson Davis appeared to be more concerned with something else, his public image. He still saw himself as a public figure, and he somehow believed that his wife had forgotten who he was. In his letter of November 23 he reminded her of the sovereign fact that he was the former President of the Confederacy and what he called the "Representative of an oppressed people." Others did remember, he admonished her, and he was more significant than a businessman, soldier, planter, senator, or cabinet secretary. In Memphis he would receive more attention as the head of the insurance company than he would in Baltimore as a mere agent working for the same company. He had already "compounded with" his "pride" for his family, implying that this job was not quite what he deserved. He hoped they could "reason together" on the issue. But something other than reason seemed to be at work. In the same letter, he told his wife he had dreamed of her sitting beside him darning his socks and asking him what he expected to do without her assistance.[4]

The rapturous public welcome he received from white Southerners may also have turned his head. When he arrived in New Orleans in November 1869, an admirer actually kissed his signature on a hotel register, and the regional press still called him "the President" or "the Ex-President." Even though Memphis voted for the Unionist John Bell in 1860, Davis received such a rousing welcome at his Memphis hotel that it reminded him of the pandemonium after his release from prison in 1867. Some of the town's white citizens offered him a house to live in, and a group of them escorted him by train to Mardi Gras in 1870. Davis often wore Confederate gray, and he liked to see other people wearing that color. He "lived for the fame of our people," he said, and he deplored the current political situation, including the relatively mild Reconstruction policies of President Ulysses Grant.[5]

Jefferson Davis had another reason to settle in Memphis: Virginia Clay lived there. *Née* Virginia Tunstall in 1825, she had spent most of her youth in Alabama and in 1843 married Clement Clay Jr., a rich slaveowner who was elected to the United States Senate a decade later. In Washington she was admired for her wit, and in Richmond, where her husband served in the Confederate Senate, she had cut quite a figure in society. Her performance as Mrs. Malaprop in Sheridan's play *The Rivals,* with both of the Davises in the audience, won enthusiastic applause. Mary Chesnut noted that Mrs. Clay's sense of humor, like Varina's, was sharp. Virginia, who had no surviving children, kept her looks into middle age. Attractive rather than beautiful, she had an aquiline nose, a pale complexion, and pale eyes, and she had a girlish manner, earning the nickname "the virgin" while she lived in Richmond. By contrast, neither of the Davises was aging well. Varina had evidently been fitted for dentures in 1867 after having some of her teeth pulled, and in 1869 she had begun wearing reading glasses. Jefferson was as thin as a rail, with a stooped posture and a bad eye that glistened horribly at times.[6]

At the war's end, the two families were thrown together when

Virginia Clay. Jefferson Davis fell in love with her.
(Rare Book, Manuscript, and Special
Collections Library, Duke University,
Durham, North Carolina)

Clement Clay Jr. returned from an espionage mission to Canada and surrendered to military authorities in Georgia. The husbands went to prison at Fort Monroe, and Virginia relayed messages between Varina and Jefferson when she visited her own husband in prison. After his release, Clement Clay began practicing law in Memphis. The couple's residence on College Street in 1870 was within walking distance of the Carolina Insurance Company's office on Madison Street. Although they were near neighbors, Jefferson began writing to Virginia, and his missives have an urgency and intensity that his letters to other women lack, whether they were fond messages to favorite relatives, such as his niece Mary Stamps, or flirtatious letters to journalist Anna Carroll before the war. He enjoyed seeing Virginia because of their shared memories of Fort Monroe, he wrote, "and—and—," leaving the sentence unfinished. He began calling her "dearest Ginia" and exclaimed that a letter from her gladdened his heart "made sick by hope deferred." He wanted to tell her "many things," for he needed "an indulgent confessor," and he would strive to see her wherever she might be.[7]

In London, Varina began to wilt from the uncertainty. She felt embarrassed around friends who had homes of their own, as she did not. That December her mind roamed back to holidays in Natchez, gossamer memories of her family and Judge Winchester in the happy times, and then, turning to the present, she wrote to her spouse about the question of where they would live. She dreaded returning to America, thinking that their children, especially their sons, could have better lives in Europe. She knew that she did not have the "power" to decide their future, but she thought white Southerners would disappoint Jefferson with their expediency—what kind she did not say—and said that although she had tried to love them for his sake she did not share his "expectations." This was quite a set of admissions from the former First Lady, explaining again, if further explanation were needed, much of her difficulty in Richmond. Now she prayed that God would keep her husband safe, and would do "all for you which in these long years I have blindly & madly tried to do." She asked him when she and the children were supposed to return to the

States so she could budget her money, pleading, "Don't be offended at this request." His communication of November 23, in which he informed her that she would probably not want to live in Memphis with him, reached her in mid-December. She realized that the time had come to submit to his wishes, and she did. She asked him to choose where she and the children should live; whatever decision he made would be acceptable to her. In her last letter of the year, composed at the end of December, she thanked him for thinking of her and sending a Christmas gift, a photograph of himself.[8]

She tended as always to her other family duties, including those regarding her wayward sister Margaret. In February 1870, Carl de Wechmar Stoess, a successful merchant from Liverpool, told Varina he had fallen in love with Margaret. A widower in his late forties who already had a son of his own, he came from a titled Alsatian family. He did not object to Margaret's illegitimate son or her age, twenty-eight, which made her a spinster by nineteenth-century standards. He was savvy enough to understand that Varina had to be consulted, and he asked permission from both the Davises to marry his intended. Margaret proclaimed that she was very happy to be engaged, and Varina thought Carl was a man of good character, so she consented. Afterward Jefferson gave his consent in a redundant sort of way. Varina then discussed finances with Carl, traditionally a male responsibility. Margaret had no dowry, and Varina drove a hard bargain for her sister, insisting that the groom take out a large life insurance policy and pay his wife a regular allowance. She hoped that Jefferson would come over in the spring to attend the wedding, but he demurred, saying he could not afford it.[9]

The ceremony took place in April 1870 at St. Peter's Church in London, and the guest list included some of their titled friends, such as Lady Abinger. From Memphis, Jefferson coldly informed Varina that she would have to "bear the embarrassment of giving Maggie away" herself, because neither he nor any of the Howell brothers would attend, so she did. Her sister's match prompted Varina to think about her own marriage. She believed Margaret was not deeply in love and would be "mistress of herself at all times," which was all to the good, Varina wrote to her spouse. She also thought her sister would have realistic expectations of marriage, telling her husband, "Having married young I suppose I idealised more than she does." Jefferson responded that the implicit comparison was "not very flattering" to him but that he would "let it pass." He added that he had always told his sister-in-law to postpone marriage as long as possible.[10]

This exchange, as bitter as those from the 1840s when they quarreled over Joseph's will, suggests that both spouses had their regrets and resentments. When L. Q. C. Lamar of Mississippi, the future Supreme Court Justice, asked Jefferson that winter if Varina was not "the most intellectual woman I had ever seen," he responded that he thought of them as two persons combined into one, managing to deflect and absorb the compliment at the same time. On their anniversary, February 26, Jefferson sent his love and assured her that he wanted to provide for her as best he could, but his letters to her became shorter, chillier, and more surgical, and hers to him more bewildered. She felt that the trials of the last seven years, beginning with Joe's death in 1864, had taken such a toll that another heavy blow from the fates would drive her mad. By April 1870 she had not received a letter from him in more than a month, and she found his silence embarrassing. When her London friends asked if she had heard from her husband, she had to answer no, and they "look strangely at me & say oh."[11]

IN MEMPHIS, Jefferson's attentions to Virginia Clay began to win her over. At first she expressed sympathy for him, tinged with pity, telling her husband in January 1870 that the "Poor fellow" seemed "hopeless" about his money problems, but in April Virginia confided to Jefferson that it was a great blessing to have a friend with his "noble loving heart." She also thanked him for sending her flowers to "heal the pangs of disappointed love." His feelings for her grew stronger, the language in his letters going beyond nineteenth-century customs of polite correspondence. During a visit to New Orleans that spring, he found himself thinking that Virginia would enjoy this or that scene, and the day after Varina wrote from London to express her humiliation at his long silence, he wrote to Mrs. Clay wanting a "long confidential talk" because, he explained, he had to share his "innermost thoughts." He asked Virginia to visit him, pleading, "I must see you," and although he sent greetings to her husband, he wrote, "There is much I would hear and something I would say."[12]

His long-distance skirmish with his wife continued into the summer of 1870 with no resolution, as Jefferson remained in Memphis and Varina stayed in London. He told others that he was preparing a home for his family in Tennessee, but he did not buy a house and had no definite plans for their return. Telling Varina that her letters contained "wounding comment and extraordinary misconception," he asked her to write him a letter free from criticism of any kind. In the first six months of the year, he sent eight letters to Varina and eleven to Virginia Clay. On his birthday, June 3, he wrote to Varina to show that he was thinking of her and said that spending time with their children would draw her mind away from "sad reflections." It does not seem to have occurred to him that parenting four children alone in another country might prompt such reflections. Furthermore, his conduct violated her understanding of how women and men should relate to each other in marriage, and therefore also violated Varina's understanding of feminine identity. She begged him to write more frequently, saying that he could not understand the "agony" of a woman's suspense, and she was starving for the "little attentions" of love that meant so much to women. In fact, she felt she was becoming "unsexed."[13]

This plea did not seem to register with Jefferson Davis. Instead he declared to Virginia Clay that no one cared for her more than he did, and he mused that although "the evening of life" had not given him "mystical love," it had taught him "the value of true love" such as his "precious Clays feel and inspire." He proposed that the Clays travel to Europe with him, but they did not make that trip. Again he tried to see Virginia, saying that he booked rooms for her on *The Belle of St. Louis* when it docked at Memphis, and he hoped to have a chance to tell her "all which is left unsaid." Whether or not they met on the steamboat or said what had been left unsaid, the Clays chose to head north for a trip to Minnesota. Jefferson sent one more message to Virginia with his "love to Clay" and an "inexhaustible quantity of the same" to her.[14]

So Mrs. Davis passed another season in Britain without her husband, waiting. Somehow she managed to pay the bills, probably by accepting cash from relatives or friends, since English law prohibited married women from keeping bank accounts. For two months she took care of a motherless girl, the daughter of a Southern expatriate. The girl's ungrateful father, Louis DeRosset, complained that Mrs. Davis was tactless and her children badly behaved, while his sister, Mrs. Gaston Meares, who had known Varina before the war, called her kindhearted and, in view of her fame, "free from all sorts of affectation." After Sir Edward Bulwer-Lytton coaxed Varina out to a dinner party, she found him agreeable but spoiled, and she politely turned down an invitation to his estate, Knebworth, because she had to look after her children. She stayed in the Gloucester Terrace flat for days at a time, keeping company with Winnie, whose chatter fascinated her so much that she took notes on the girl's "table talk." The nights were harder, when, she told her husband, "I devour myself" with anxiety.[15]

At the end of the summer of 1870, after almost a year apart from his wife and children, Jefferson prepared to return to England. Just before he left, he tried again to see Virginia Clay. Starting with an awkward joke that she would be a presidential candidate when "woman's rights" became the law of the land, he said he would be grieved to part from her. Even though he said, "I suppose Mrs. Davis and the children will return with me," he also wrote that they had no firm plans, a comment that would have stunned his family, because they were expecting to return with him to the States. Jefferson told Virginia that she and his other friends had created an "oasis" in his "desert existence," and during the journey across the Atlantic, he wrote to her again to express the hope that his wife would stay in Baltimore, where his sons would go to school, and that he could go straight to the Clays' Alabama home. He closed by evoking what he called his spiritual connection with Virginia. "While I write it seems to me that you are with me," he confided, and "I have several times since we parted awoke in the act of answering you."[16]

His unsuspecting wife in London scrambled to pack the household goods for yet another move. After Jefferson arrived, the Davises received another cascade of invitations and calls from friends, acquaintances, and expatriates. But he soon left to go sightseeing in Glasgow, Belfast, and Dublin, where he had to decline an invitation to meet the Irish nationalist Lady Francesca Wilde and her husband Sir William Wilde. (Jefferson knew Lady Wilde's brother, John Elgee, an attorney in Louisiana.) Then the Davises learned that Joseph E. Davis died on September 18 in Mississippi. Jefferson was deeply grieved, not least because he wanted his sons to benefit from the example of what he called his brother's fine character, and he described Joseph as his "greatest benefactor."[17]

In the fall of 1870, the family left England, their departure for New York reported in the London *Times*. Varina wanted to stay in the Old World. When the ship docked at Queenstown, Ireland, on the first leg of the journey, she disembarked so she could touch the green earth of the Emerald Isle, and when the family settled in Memphis, living at a hotel for the next year, she thought the city looked small indeed after London. Founded in 1819, Memphis was a market town of some forty thousand residents, and because the town surrendered to Union forces in 1862, it sustained little damage during the war. After 1865 it prospered as a cotton depot, but the streets were dirty and the town was home to numerous opium dens and houses of prostitution. Some of the avenues were lined with so many abandoned buildings that parts of Memphis looked like an ancient ruin.[18]

As another winter turned into spring, Jefferson's feelings for Virginia Clay did not change. After she visited Alabama in early 1871, he complained that she did not write to him often enough, and he hoped that they could meet in New Orleans. Again he pondered the "consolations which most compensate for lost joys and withered hopes." How much Varina Davis knew or suspected is impossible to say, but

Clement Clay appeared to know nothing and see nothing. He had an office and a residence in Memphis, but he spent months alone on an Alabama farm while his wife traveled the region. He missed her, and he knew that she blamed him for their lack of money. They both felt their poverty keenly. Clement once had to borrow money from none other than Jefferson Davis, which debt he repaid as soon as possible.[19]

Jefferson traveled a lot, going on business to Raleigh, Columbia, and Augusta, where he received what he called "manifestations of good will" from the white public. His storied charm was on display in Augusta when a matron introduced him to her son who was named after him. His remark that Yankees were the meanest people on earth jolted her, but he complimented mother and son so graciously that she felt quite overcome. Echoing what many white women said, she declared that he was better looking than his photographs and withal had the air of a gentleman. His family was visiting Baltimore, where Varina wrote him several loving letters, while he kept traveling for his insurance company. As Jefferson took a train through Alabama, he wrote to Virginia Clay that he wished she had accompanied him and he felt comforted by something Virginia had told him, that she always knew what he was thinking. As he grew older his desire for her "cheering companionship" increased, he said. Although he did not want to complain, he thought his fate seemed "harder than that of others."[20]

<hr />

IF THERE IS ANYTHING more poignant than a neglected wife, it is one who has been humiliated in the national press. In July 1871, Jefferson took a train from Memphis to the University of the South in Sewanee, Tennessee, to attend a graduation ceremony; afterward he planned to go to Baltimore to see his family. On July 15 a Republican newspaper, the *Louisville Commercial,* broke the story that Jefferson Davis had a sexual encounter on the train with a woman other than his wife. According to this report, Davis gave this woman "constant attention" during the journey, and after the couple retired for the evening on July 11, someone, probably another passenger, noticed that two people were in Davis's sleeping car. The conductor arrived with a supervisor, and they supposedly found the couple in an intimate embrace. When Davis was informed that this behavior was not allowed, he replied that he had paid for the berth and could do as he pleased, but after threats from train officials the woman left at the next stop, Chattanooga. Jefferson traveled on to Baltimore and arrived just before the story burst into the headlines.[21]

Almost every major newspaper in the country reprinted the Louisville story, with much speculation about the woman's identity. She was white, and the *New York Times* called her "the wife of another man" who boarded at a Memphis hotel, while the *Albany Evening Journal* identified her as an actress, Nellie Bowers, with whom Davis had allegedly been corresponding. Gossip in Memphis indicated, however, that the lady was Virginia Clay. The press claimed that their relationship had been the subject of conjecture in the Mississippi River Valley, and soon it was discussed everywhere, the "topic of the day." From the Northern press came a chorus of jeers. The *New York Herald* claimed that Davis's taste for pretty ladies was well known in Memphis and gleefully punned that the man should be given a "wide berth."[22]

En route from Baltimore to Memphis, Jefferson Davis composed a carefully worded denial dated July 21, the day he returned to his Tennessee home with his family. Published first in the Memphis *Avalanche,* the statement declared that a Radical newspaper had attacked his character—"in connection," he wrote, "with that of a lady who, it is falsely stated, was traveling under my charge." He deemed it due to himself and to his "personal friends" to deny the story, which was the product of "malice" and "utterly false." Again, newspapers all over the country published his statement, including papers in Natchez, Varina's hometown, Baltimore, where she was staying that summer, and Memphis, her place of residence, where hundreds of copies of the *Louisville Commercial* were sold. Newspapers in the South cried that the story was a calumny on a man they compared to Saint Paul, William Pitt, and George Washington, or condemned it as a thinly veiled political attack, while others dismissed the allegation because it was published in the *Louisville Commercial,* which was known for sensational stories. Most Northern papers accepted the story as true, and most of them found Davis's explanation inadequate, one noting that the conductor was a Confederate veteran who stood by his story even though his job had been threatened. The *Albany Evening Journal* issued a mock defense of Davis, because a man who dressed in petticoats in 1865 would not insult a lady. One political foe of long standing, an ex-Whig from Mississippi, found the story hard to believe.[23]

We have to ask, could the story be true? One newspaper observed that Jefferson Davis could not have done something so reckless, because he was acutely aware of his position as the former Confederate President and, the paper added rather lamely, so strong-willed that he would not do anything he did not want to do. Contrary to this newspaper's assertion, Davis often lacked good judgment, and his denial was not ironclad, the most glaring omission being that the lady in question may have been traveling under someone else's charge, or on her own. Nor did he sue the paper for libel, as the *New York Herald* caustically advised him to do. So yes, it is at least possible. And who was the woman in question? Nellie Bowers? Virginia Clay? Or yet another woman? Or did the reference to an "actress" mean a prostitute, per common slang of the time? Bowers left no personal papers, and Clay neglected to mention the incident in her letters, and although she kept a diary, the volumes for 1870 and 1871 are missing. Jefferson's correspondence points to Virginia, but there is no way to know for certain what happened on the Memphis train.[24]

What Varina Davis thought of all this is unknown, for she said nothing in writing, then and for the rest of her life. She kept silent, just as she did during the war when the newspapers alleged that her husband fathered children out of wedlock. In 1871 she must have read the newspaper story if her husband did not tell her himself, and we will never know what they may have said in private. She had no comment for journalists and neither did anyone in her family or his, or the spouses of the women who may have been involved, Clement Clay and Mr. Bowers. Jefferson referred to it indirectly once, when he told Clement later in 1871 that the federal government was probably paying "slanderers" to follow him. Yet Varina knew that public figures cheated on their wives, if only from the Sickles-Key scandal in Washington, and she knew couples who lived apart in de facto divorces, such as Mr. and Mrs. Judah Benjamin. She apparently had not strayed in twenty-eight years of married life, and despite all of the time she spent apart from her husband—much of it at his insistence—there are no letters in her hand to another man like those her husband wrote to Virginia Clay. Despite Varina's celebrity, there had never been a breath of scandal about her conduct.[25]

If the possibility of betrayal was too much for Varina Davis to face, she could easily have rationalized the story as untrue. The press had made mistakes before. Impostors claiming to have worked for the Davises still surfaced in the newspapers, and a reporter declared in 1868 that the family planned to settle in Canada after they had already moved to England. Newspapers published tales that may or may not have been true about the marital problems of other public figures, such as former president Andrew Johnson. When a Cincinnati journalist later ridiculed the Howell family as obscure, Varina denounced stories willfully fabricated by reporters. Many times she witnessed the excitement that Jefferson's public appearances could generate. As the Davises journeyed together by train in Mississippi on another occasion, he kissed some pretty girls who approached him to say hello, and Varina told an onlooker that he had to kiss lots of ugly women, too. Or if she suspected that the story was true, she may have drawn upon her capacity to accept painful situations or perhaps wall them off, a capacity that had perforce been developed since 1861.[26]

She did not mention the possibility of a divorce, but if it crossed her mind, her private calculus would have differed little from what it had been in the 1840s: divorce had a terrible stigma, she had no money of her own, and she could not rely on her own family for help, because her father was dead and her brothers were hardly able to support themselves. Now, unlike in the 1840s, she had four children to raise, and her husband was an international political figure, so a divorce would have been front-page news on both sides of the Atlantic. Furthermore, Tennessee permitted divorce on a few specific grounds, such as habitual drunkenness, but not for attempting adultery, if that is what happened on the Memphis train. For all these reasons, or for reasons known only to her own heart, Varina chose to remain married to Jefferson. In September 1871 she went to Richmond to recover some of their furniture from the war years (she found one chair) and wrote an affectionate letter addressed to "My dear Husband" at White Sulphur Springs, inquiring about his health.[27]

Jefferson Davis's feelings for Virginia Clay were still alive, however, and he said in October 1871 that he felt more anxious than ever to see her. He told Virginia, "To both your questions I answer yes," responding to queries that are not recorded but can easily be imagined, for he added in the next breath, "I wish to come to you in this season of gorgeous colors and do love you not little but long." So it seems that Jefferson had fallen in love with her, maybe deeply in love, by the fall of 1871, if not earlier; it bears repeating that he did not write these kinds of letters to anyone else. In the most ruthlessly objective sense, Virginia probably would have made a better wife for him. She had a more conventional personality than Varina and was more likely to conform to his wishes. She was not as well read as Varina, and the voice in her letters is banal. Maybe most important, Virginia was a true believer in secession and the Confederate cause. Jefferson told Virginia in November 1871 that she was one of the few people with whom he could share his "most secret thoughts." He hoped to join her in Alabama and travel on to Sewanee or Nashville. If only they lived closer to each other, he said.[28]

The depth of Virginia Clay's feelings is more difficult to gauge. In her letters she is not quite as fervent as Jefferson is with her, and in her memoir, published in the twentieth century, she did not mention a romance, of course, but called him a man with a "rich and sonorous" voice who despite his haughty manners was "informal and frank" with friends in private. Later Virginia said that a photograph of her husband and Davis did not do justice to either of these handsome men. But that is all she said, and it is impossible to tell if she was deeply in love with Jefferson. After the train incident in 1871, she and Varina eventually crossed paths in Memphis. That winter she called on Mrs. Davis at their house on Court Street and had what Jefferson described as a "pleasant" visit. By his account, Virginia offered to give his wife some material for a quilt she was working on; Varina, with either virtuoso self-control or utter self-deception, politely thanked her for it. He also expressed the hope that Virginia would stay at the Davis home as their guest sometime, an idea that his wife did not comment on in writing.[29]

Life in Memphis ultimately returned to something like normality, by Davis standards. Jefferson worked at his office on Madison Street, as the Carolina Insurance Company continued to use his name prominently in their advertisements. Varina disliked the Court Street house for its cramped rooms and small yard, but she had a piano and the children could ramble through a leafy park down the street. The

Court Street. The Davis home in Memphis. (University of Memphis Libraries)

Episcopal church the family attended, St. Lazarus, was a few blocks away. The neighborhood was full of exuberant children who were not afraid to play a practical joke on the former Confederate President. One evening as he walked to a party at another residence, they pinned a paper tail to his coat and howled with laughter as he sauntered by.[30]

Into the new year, 1872, Jefferson kept traveling through the region, mainly for his insurance company and sometimes to visit relatives and friends. (He insisted that his wife follow antebellum custom and travel only with an escort.) He told Virginia Clay he felt "sad, and weak, and perplexed," and in September he fumed that his wife would not leave Memphis. In fact, Varina was not well. She missed England, according to her husband, and she was unhappy. But his thoughts centered on Virginia as he left Memphis for Baltimore in the fall. She saw him off, and he wrote, "The hours dragged wearily after you left me at the station, for the contrast with your sweet home was a strong one." Alone in his sleeping compartment, he wished they had a "fairy Godmother to fulfill all wishes and banish regrets for what might have been." A few weeks later, he sent his love to his wife, telling her that she had earned it by "many claims" and "long possession." He might best be described as deeply conflicted about the women in his life.[31]

In the Davis household, disaster was about to befall another of the sons, Billy. Like other partially deaf children, he was observant, and he enjoyed watching his father work in the office, handing over a pen as needed. In Jefferson's words, he was a "grave little gentleman." In the fall of 1872 the boy came down with diphtheria, an infection of the respiratory tract; in the era before penicillin, the victim typically suffocated as a membrane formed at the top of the throat. Billy died on October 16, at age ten, and was buried in Memphis's Elmwood Cemetery, as Varina stood by in silent despair and her husband's face blanched with agony. The boy's death was reported in the national press, and many people sent their condolences, but Varina did not hear from her sister Margaret, which wounded her to the core. She recalled this time in her life as one of intense mourning for Billy and her "narrowing circle of boys." After a trip to Canada the next year with her daughter Winnie, she gradually began to feel better.[32]

Alas, she would soon be called on to forgive another failure by her husband. By 1873 the Carolina Insurance Company was in dire financial straits, and in July the board of directors sold it to another corporation, whereupon Jefferson resigned. He lost his investment of fifteen thousand dollars' worth of stock, but, he informed his wife, that he had kept his self-respect. She put the most charitable interpretation on the situation, arguing that Jefferson had discovered too late that the company was badly managed and said it was a "comforting memory to him that he had lost heavily by the failure." That summer he told Varina that they might have to go wherever he could find some kind of employment, and he seemed unsure about what to do next, so much so that his neighbor Elizabeth Meriwether offered to help him financially. He declined her offer and thought instead of writing a book on the war or opening a farm in Kentucky. When some Texans offered him a tract of land and livestock, he refused, thinking the gift too generous, so the family stayed in Memphis.[33]

The Panic of 1873, which hit the country in September, made it even harder for Jefferson to find a job, so in 1874 he went abroad seeking work, while Varina remained behind with the children. He could find no prospects in England because of what he deemed Yankee influences, but it was probably just as important that he was six years older than he was during his visit in 1868, with another business failure behind him. Dudley Mann's suggestion that he settle in France and raise horses he did not take seriously. Even though he wanted to provide for his family, his ego was an impediment in his job search. He told Varina, "I cannot run round begging for employment" and, again, that he was unwilling to "go round soliciting employment." He was still conscious of the "dignity" conferred on him as the Confederate President, which did not allow him to ask outright for a job. He had not held office in nine years.[34]

While he was in England, his thoughts often returned to his wife. For the time being he put aside his feelings for Mrs. Clay, telling Virginia in 1873 that they had both learned what he called "the lesson of doing what we may, not what we would." On his wedding anniversary in 1874, which he spent with the de Wechmar Stoess family, he wrote a long letter to Varina. Thinking back on their courtship, he declared that they belonged to each other before they exchanged their wedding vows. They had fallen so deeply in love when they met, he said, that nothing could destroy the bonds between them. In another letter he apologized because she had to deal with her troubles alone, and, having enjoyed her tender care for so long, he wanted to bear some of her burdens. He longed to have her advice and confessed that he felt lost without her. In June he returned to the States, still unemployed.[35]

The Davises moved to another house on Court Street, free from the memories of Billy's death, and Varina came to like Memphis better, enjoying its friendly people. One of her neighbors described her as a highly competent housekeeper who set a fine table, and a visitor said she was an affable hostess who could put guests at ease. The surviving Davis children were growing up. Maggie, now in her late teens, was old enough to host a party by herself, and Jeff Jr. was "all aglow" because he was elected an officer in the local militia. Winnie was still Varina's favorite, however, and the bond between them only strengthened. The girl loved books just as her mother did, and when Varina read aloud to her from *The Tempest,* Winnie delighted her mother with her precocious literary criticism. The girl found the meeting of Miranda and Ferdinand, who fall instantly in love, to be unconvincing, but believed that the speeches by Ariel, the spirit in thrall to Prospero, represented Shakespeare's art at its best.[36]

10

CROWD OF SORROWS

 IN 1874, MRS. DAVIS began working for a salary for the first time, taking in sewing from local families in Memphis. She earned a small income, twenty or so dollars per piece of clothing. Before the war, she had sold an article to a magazine, and in 1862 and 1865 she had offered to take a job, and now she assured her husband that it did not "distress" her to work. It probably did not distress her more than anything else that had happened recently. She sympathized with war widows who had to support themselves, and she quietly asked other people to help them out. Varina must have enjoyed working, for in the 1880s she told a friend that working for a salary could be a "blessing in disguise." Regarding their own money, the Davises reverted to antebellum custom whereby Jefferson handled most of the finances, even though he did not have a job. He hated Northerners so much that he tried to avoid investments with any kind of "Yankee association," not the wisest economic strategy. Surviving records show that he owned about seven to eight thousand dollars' worth of business stock and land, a fraction of his antebellum fortune, and he found it dispiriting to hear from friends who could afford to live well.[1]

In the mid-1870s, Varina chose to put some of her energies into reform activities beyond the household. Some of them were rather traditional activities, such as collecting coal with church members to distribute to the poor, while other activities resembled some of her charitable work in wartime Richmond, with a few careful departures into the public sphere. With another matron she wrote a fund-raising letter for the St. Lazarus Church, and they sent it to Episcopalians all over the country with both of their names on it. For the first time, she joined a women's organization, the Woman's Christian Association (WCA), a national society founded in the late 1860s by white women to aid the poor. Women's clubs were springing up all over the South, and Memphis saw an outpouring of reform activity in the 1870s by the town's white middle-class women. In 1875 Elizabeth F. Johnson, daughter of a state legislator, formed the Memphis chapter of the WCA, which dispensed aid to needy families and unwed mothers. Varina Davis became the secretary for the local chapter and remained an officer until 1881, although she never explained this venture into reform.[2]

Nor did she discuss national politics in her correspondence. The animosity toward the North in her letters of 1865 had disappeared, maybe because she never felt it deeply in the first place. She scarcely mentioned state or local politics either, except to register her disgust as she watched an intoxicated neighbor stumble to the polls on election day in 1874. She became friendly with the town's most visible activist, Elizabeth Meriwether, one of the few white women in the region to criticize slavery publicly before the war and the publisher in 1872 of a short-lived newspaper on reform, the *Tablet*, to which Varina Davis subscribed. Interested in a host of issues, including equal pay for female teachers, Elizabeth attempted to vote in the national election in 1876. The two women were on friendly terms, although they politely disagreed about Elizabeth's lack of religious faith—she was a nominal Methodist—and Varina did not endorse woman suffrage.[3]

As for race, Davis continued to follow her old pattern of relating to individual black people. In 1875 she wrote a brief unsolicited recommendation for a black woman, Mrs. Robert Church, to be the organist for an African American congregation in Memphis. One autumn day, when Davis happened to be visiting the rector's office to consult him on some kind of church business, she wrote a short letter praising Mrs. Church's musical ability and calling her a person of "excellent" reputation. Why the rector allowed her to do this, and how Davis made the acquaintance of this member of the town's most prominent black family, remain a mystery. Two, perhaps three, servants worked in Varina's own household, but their race cannot be deciphered from her letters. Her other comments on race, few and far between, show she had not become an egalitarian, for she ridiculed a white Southern politician for appealing to black voters.[4]

Jefferson Davis, still unable to find a job, turned to another source of income, land that once belonged to his dead brother. Joseph left most of his estate to his grandchildren Joseph Mitchell and Lise Mitchell, with some land to other relatives and cash gifts to Jefferson's children. Although Joseph named Jefferson as an executor, he left nothing to his younger brother and sister-in-law Varina. After the war, Joseph had regained possession of Brierfield and the Hurricane and sold both plantations to three black men in the Montgomery family for three hundred thousand dollars, payable over ten years. The Montgomerys produced some good cotton crops, but by the early 1870s they fell behind in the payments. Jefferson thought his brother's decision to sell the property to them was a mistake, and in 1873 he began to consider a lawsuit to recover Brierfield. This led to some unpleasant conversations with his relatives, such as his niece Caroline Leonard, who screamed at him on the street in Vicksburg. In 1874 he filed suit in Chancery Court in Mississippi. He argued that Brierfield was part of his inheritance from his father and Joseph had always treated the land as if it were his. Still holding to the values of the Old South, Jefferson dreamed of setting up his children in adjoining plantations on the land one day.[5]

A hard fight ensued. Jefferson's grandniece Lise Mitchell Hamer became his chief antagonist, and she was determined to carry out what she believed to be her grandfather's wishes. Lise had fled with her grandfather when he became a war refugee and after 1865 lived with him instead of her father. She married only after Joseph's death and moved to Florence, Alabama, with her husband, William Hamer.

She and her allies argued that Jefferson's claim was unfair, especially in light of how much Joseph had helped his brother when he was young. Some family members sided with Lise, others with Jefferson, while others tried to avoid being sucked into the fray, but thirty members of the white family became parties to the suit before it was over. The antagonists collected documents and depositions from family members, friends, overseers, and former slaves. (Ben Montgomery actually wanted Jefferson to win because he feared he could not finish making payments on Brierfield.) Jefferson became deeply involved in the case, giving his attorney detailed instructions on what to ask witnesses.[6]

Jefferson told his wife that the "truth" would triumph, but the truth was not simple. Joseph had it both ways with his fraudulent dealings, maintaining legal ownership of Brierfield but allowing Jefferson to use the plantation and keep its profits, and now that the old man was gone, his legatees had to deal with the fundamental question of who owned the land. Lise focused on the fact that Joseph owned the plantation and could do with it as he wished, and Jefferson concentrated on the fact that Joseph let him act as if the land were his. Or as Jefferson put it, the "spirit" of Joseph's will should be carried out. This was the reverse of his position in the 1840s, when Jefferson argued that his brother's wishes had to be accepted regardless of who was excluded from the estate, and it contradicted his passing remark in 1865 that his brother was the "owner" of Brierfield. He decided not to follow the advice he gave a niece in 1870 in the midst of a property dispute with relatives: submit even if it meant suffering wrongdoing.[7]

He asked Varina not to revisit "old wounds" about her quarrels with her brother-in-law, as individuals testified that Joseph did not want her or anyone in the Howell family to inherit the property. Ten years later, Varina told Mary Chesnut, who had similar legal woes, that it was a "shame" that a "cranky old creature" could reach from beyond the grave to control his descendants. She believed that the "miseries" old men inflicted by their wills would be universally condemned—"the world would not hold the tirades"—if women did the same to men. But in 1875 Varina did as her husband asked. When he wanted her to track down documents to help make his case, she did so, and her response to their attorneys' questions about the property was written in crystalline prose. In October 1875 she gave two days of further testimony on the byzantine relationships in the Davis clan to a notary public at the Memphis residence. She described her relations with her brother-in-law as of "varying character," but she supported her husband's argument that most people assumed that Brierfield was his property, even if Joseph did not give him the title. She sidestepped the fact that her husband had not tried to protect her interests in the 1840s when Joseph sought to keep Brierfield out of her hands.[8]

Jefferson appreciated her testimony, however, and said so in his inimitable fashion. When he read her statements for the attorneys, he exclaimed that in happier times she could have been a writer. That was within the realm of possibility, of course—she published an article in the 1850s, she could write good prose, she had the writer's iconoclastic temperament, hundreds of American women had already published books, and Harriet Beecher Stowe's novel *Uncle Tom's Cabin* reached a worldwide readership before the war. Jefferson clung instead to the values of another era. Nor did he appear to understand the gulf between what he said about gender and how he and his wife conducted their lives. In a speech at the Texas State Fair in 1875, he praised white Southern women for supporting the Confederacy and proclaimed that women were nobler than men, made of finer stuff, and suited only for the home.[9]

SAD TIDINGS came that fall about Jeffy D., Varina's youngest brother. He was probably the best of her brothers, good-natured and affectionate in letters to his "darling old Fat Sis," and he helped his brother William find work in California. Jeffy D., a captain in the merchant marine, resided in San Francisco when he was not at sea. He had a reputation as a ladies man, although he had not married and did not seem interested in doing so. A natural-born sailor who was as strong as an ox, he had already achieved some renown for helping rescue a ship stalled off the coast. In 1875 he commanded a steamer that plied the waters from Seattle to San Francisco. He had told his sister it was a dangerous route, and in November he drowned. Another boat rammed his vessel, and after he evacuated the passengers he was swept into the icy water and disappeared. When she learned the news, Varina was so overcome she could scarcely summon her faculties to write a letter, which was exactly how she had felt after her son's death in 1864. Other sailors praised Jeffy D. as a brave man, and for years Varina cherished that praise. In 1875 the Davises did most of their grieving separately. Jefferson came home briefly and was away from Memphis for most of the calendar year, traveling on business to Montgomery, New Orleans, and Vicksburg.[10]

A sunburst of happy news came that winter: their oldest daughter, Maggie, became engaged to Addison Hayes Jr. Varina wanted her daughters to marry for love, and this was a love match. Maggie had grown up to be a pretty woman with soulful eyes, a mass of dark hair, and a taste for beautiful clothes. Addison, a Tennessee native, had served in the Confederate army and settled in Memphis after the war to work in a bank. Varina, who liked him from the first, thought he would make a good husband for Maggie, and Jefferson reluctantly accepted that another "authority," as he put it, would stand between him and his daughter. Varina persuaded a friend, Minor Meriwether, to help her buy a house in town for the young couple. How she came up with the money is unknown; most likely this was her income as a seamstress. Jefferson wanted to help pay for it, but could not because one of his debtors failed to repay a loan. Saying that he hated to see "this masculine duty" imposed upon his wife, he asked her to explain his financial woes to Meriwether. Maggie wed Addison in January 1876 in St. Lazarus Church, where according to the *New York Times* a large crowd attended. Soon afterward Jefferson landed a job. In January 1876 he was elected president of the American branch of the Mississippi Valley Society, which was founded to promote trade between England and the Americas, with a salary of approximately six thousand dollars a year.[11]

Misfortunes did not come singly, however, for in January 1876 Varina's youngest sister, Jane Waller, died of puerperal fever. Her family had settled in Wheeling, West Virginia, where William Waller edited a newspaper and Jane devoted herself to her children, Elizabeth and William, in their modest house near the banks of the Ohio River. After giving birth to a stillborn child, she died on January 6, at age thirty, from the illness that nearly killed Varina in 1857. Most of the obituaries mentioned Jane's famous in-laws, one of them announcing "Death of a Sister of Mrs. Jefferson Davis."[12]

Jane's demise, coming on the heels of Jeffy D.'s death, proved to be too much for Varina, and by the spring of 1876 she was on the verge of an emotional collapse. Her unhappiness had been building for some time. In 1874 she wrote to John Garrett that the "South West" seemed to be her "doom" and that she wished she could live in a more interesting place, such as Baltimore, and watch the "race" of life roll by. In 1875, after a friend told Varina she had put flowers on Samuel Davis's grave in Georgetown, the message set off a chain of memories of all of her deceased children and how much she missed them. That fall she told Dudley Mann that life seemed "very dark." She pulled herself together for the Bowmar deposition and after the first of the year for Maggie's wedding, but after that she scarcely left the house for weeks at a time. She stopped writing letters and went to bed. Later she told her friend Minna Blair that her "sorrows" had "crowded thick" upon her.[13]

She may have realized something else, which she did not tell Minna Blair—that her husband was still enamored of Virginia Clay. By the mid-1870s the Clays had moved to Alabama, but Jefferson tried to meet Virginia as he traversed the region, and he still confided in her, saying that few of his heart's desires had been fulfilled. He wrote to her more often than she wrote to him, and although he sent his love to Clement, he sent "much, very much" to Mrs. Clay. When he felt low one day in 1875, he thought that Virginia would lift him out of "this slough of despond." After his wife refused to leave Memphis that summer, he plaintively asked Virginia again about her travel plans, and she in turn complained of being trapped with those who had no hold on her heart. Her girlish manner was unchanged. When she met the governor, he complimented her profusely, which "covered my face with *blushes & filled* my eyes with tears," she told Jefferson.[14]

If Varina Davis realized that her husband had feelings for Clay, that may have been enough to shut her down. Or maybe she did not know. Perhaps she broke from the accumulated grief of so many deaths, too much time in the doomy Southwest, too many masculine duties taken on without her husband's assistance, or too much time alone while Jefferson perambulated the region. She was now well into middle age, and she may have been going through a difficult menopause. Whatever the cause of the crisis, her phenomenal resilience had finally run out. Her husband, who had relied on her strength so many times, did not know what to do. From New Orleans he proposed that she visit the seashore, or take a trip, or rent rooms near their sister-in-law Minnie Howell. He returned to Memphis, where he promised again to bear her burdens, but a month later he left for New Orleans to speak to a veterans' group. He wrote affectionate letters to her, yet he stayed in New Orleans through the spring, observing that his presence in Memphis would do nothing except help her pass the "weary hours." Someone sent Varina a present, but when she thanked Jefferson for it, he had to admit that it was not from him. In April he made a short visit to Memphis before going back to New Orleans to work for the Mississippi Valley Society.[15]

The medical wisdom of the day prescribed foreign travel for people undergoing an emotional crisis, and Varina's needs dovetailed with Jefferson's new job, so in May 1876 the Davises went to Britain, where he planned to do some work for the Society. They took Winnie with them. The London *Times* announced their arrival in Liverpool, just as it had in 1868. Varina was glad to see the country again, with the hedgerows decked out in pink flowers, and the family settled in London next to the flat they once occupied at Gloucester Place. Invitations arrived from the Earl of Shrewsbury, the Countess of Shrewsbury, and the attaché of the Japanese legation, writing on behalf of his country's minister to England.[16]

But Varina spent much of her time in seclusion. Her husband paid her "unremitting attention," she recalled, and he believed that she had a "nervous disease" of some kind. She was also in physical pain, the cause undetermined. At the last of the year Jefferson said that his wife had suffered "more than humans generally suffer and live." She could no longer take care of Winnie, so the Davises placed her in a boarding school in Karlsruhe on the Rhine River in Baden. Varina's brother-in-law Carl de Wechmar Stoess may have recommended the school, or maybe Julia Tyler, who had two children studying in Karlsruhe. Although a friend described it as a dreary place, with granite buildings and severe public squares, the school's curriculum was rigorous and the students hailed from elite Continental families. Winnie was a smart girl. At age ten she read Sir Walter Scott's *The Talisman,* which she discussed with her mother, and memorized Longfellow's "Wreck of the Hesperus," heavy weather for a young student. She struck other people as a miniature adult, but sending her to Karlsruhe nonetheless seems like a strange decision. When the Davis children enrolled in school in Canada, Britain, or France, at least one of their parents was in the country much of the time. Boarding school may have been the best option they could come up with in light of Varina's illness.[17]

When Jefferson returned to America in November 1876, Varina stayed in London, too sick to leave her doctor. Malie Brodhead's family in Pennsylvania sent her four thousand dollars, which was apparently her chief means of support. Varina's doctor suggested that she avoid "painful excitement," which described much of her life since 1861, and he advised her to rest. Later Varina confided to Minna Blair that for a year and a half she could hardly write a coherent sentence. The deaths in 1876 of Francis Preston Blair and in 1877 of Malie Brodhead did little to boost her spirits. She went through a cycle of improvements and relapses. When she felt well enough, she visited Winnie at Karlsruhe and her sister and brother-in-law in Liverpool. Jefferson sent her some warm letters, and in his message on their wedding anniversary in 1877, he said that they had been united through many joys and sorrows. He hoped that she was no longer in pain and added that she had less need of him than he had of her, "so far as nursing is involved."[18]

The Davis finances took another tumble in 1877, for Jefferson was again out of a job. The Mississippi Valley Society apparently collapsed, and yet another project of Jefferson's, a bank, did not work out, so he turned back to the idea of writing a memoir. This book had to make money, because Jefferson had received only a few paychecks from the Society. An acquaintance, Confederate veteran William T. Walthall, agreed to help Davis with the manuscript. Jefferson needed a place to write, and he thought he could not manage by himself much longer. He had made some honest efforts to support himself and his family, but he could not seem to adjust to the postwar world. In 1876 he felt like a "waif" and feared that he might be homeless in his old age.[19]

☙

ENTER SARAH DORSEY. Jefferson visited her estate, Beauvoir, on the Mississippi coast in December 1876, and in early 1877 he resolved to write his book there. Sarah would figure in the Davises' lives for years to come. She was born in Natchez in 1829 and inherited a fortune from her father, planter Thomas Ellis. As a girl she had been crowned May Queen, just as Varina Howell had been, and both girls attended Madame Grelaud's school in Philadelphia. Sarah's marriage to Samuel Dorsey was childless, so she filled her time by reading at their Louisiana plantation. When the war broke out, Sarah fervently supported the Confederacy, and after the conflict the Dorseys moved to Beauvoir, where Samuel died. The widow was not pretty, with bulging eyes and a long nose, but she was lively and energetic, and she had done what Jefferson thought his wife might have done, become a writer. She published a novel about the war, *Lucia Dare,* and an essay on Henry Watkins Allen, Louisiana's wartime governor. She was thrilled to host Jefferson Davis at Beauvoir. The Mississippi landscape was flat, sparsely settled, and thickly wooded, but the large airy

Sarah Dorsey. She took in Jefferson Davis when he was homeless.
(Beauvoir)

house, true to its name, was beautiful to see, with a long veranda that looked out on the ocean.[20]

Jefferson Davis and Sarah Dorsey were not exactly alone at Beauvoir, because one of Dorsey's cousins already lived there and a stream of visitors came and went. But Jefferson had moved to the estate without consulting his wife, who was sick and under a doctor's care in another country. Other famous couples in difficult marriages, such as Mr. and Mrs. William T. Sherman, lived apart in the postwar era, but this was not a separation so much as an abandonment. Varina had seen Sarah Dorsey only a few times since they were schoolmates in Philadelphia, and they were not good friends, Jefferson's insistence to the contrary. Sarah did not seem to care that he was married to someone else, and Jefferson's judgment seems to have utterly deserted him. As he began his book, Dorsey worked as his secretary for several hours a day. He had other assistants: William Walthall, who had a house nearby; Minnie Howell, William Howell's estranged wife and Jefferson's sister-in-law, who moved in next door; and one of Minnie's daughters, who found the old man irascible.[21]

In England, Varina Davis learned about her husband's residence at Beauvoir from a newspaper article. Her immediate reaction went unrecorded, but in the spring of 1877 Jefferson began trying to persuade her to join this unusual ménage, and Sarah Dorsey extended an invitation through Jefferson asking Varina to be her "guest." He described his hostess as "constantly attentive" to him. Jefferson told his daughter Maggie that he would leave Beauvoir if his wife wanted it, but then he equivocated, telling Varina he would reside wherever she wished, and, he stipulated, wherever he was able to live. When she did not reply, Jefferson passed along Sarah Dorsey's hope that Mrs. Davis would move in permanently with them at Beauvoir. He could not travel to England because an investment partner had gone bankrupt, so he decided Varina should remain abroad until the fall.[22]

So she stayed in Britain for another summer. Her health began to improve, and she visited the baths at Buxton and took carriage rides through the teeming streets of London. By the fall of 1877 her energy, and some measure of her dignity, had revived. In her letters she began raising objections about going to Beauvoir, such as the tropical climate, but the sticking point was Sarah Dorsey. Davis, like most wives of her generation, did not wish to live with her husband as a guest in another woman's home. To make her views absolutely clear, she added, "Nothing on earth would pain me like living in that kind of community in her house," meaning, with a large collection of Dorsey's relatives and guests. She did not want to be under any obligation to Dorsey, although she said, with the utmost graciousness, that she appreciated Sarah's kindness to her husband. When acquaintances asked her what part of her husband's book Dorsey was writing, she felt "aggravated nearly to death."[23]

Here matters stood when she returned in October 1877 to America after almost a year and a half abroad. Her husband asked Burton Harrison to meet her in New York, explaining that he could not afford it, and after Varina went to Memphis, she stayed there. Jefferson came to Memphis to induce her to move to Beauvoir, but she would not go. Maggie Hayes, who disliked what she called Dorsey's "mannish" demeanor, invited her mother to stay with her. Varina agreed, although she realized that she could not stay indefinitely. She told her friend Constance Cary Harrison that "in the course of human events" she would visit her husband's "earthly paradise" and she would probably have to live there, and that, paraphrasing St. Paul, "when we are old we are girded up and taken where we would not be." But she dreaded the isolation of the Gulf Coast. Friends acted on her like steel on flame, she explained, while Jefferson enjoyed the solitude. So, "behold we are a tie," she told Harrison, "and neither achieves the desired end."[24]

The Davis correspondence churned on, much as it had in 1848 or 1869 when they had disagreed on the cardinal question of where they would live. From her Memphis beachhead, Varina was willing to help with Jefferson's book, sending materials through the mail, but she would not go to Beauvoir, not yet. She spent time with Maggie's family and visited her friends, while Jefferson stayed at Beauvoir. He did not spend his wedding anniversary in February 1878 with his wife because he was too busy, he said, and in the spring of 1878 Dorsey volunteered to go to Memphis to recruit Mrs. Davis, which was more than Varina could stomach. There was only one favor she asked of him, begged of him, she said, and that was not to let Sarah visit her. She would try to bear their separation as she had for the last six months, she said, "as best I can." Then she made a thinly veiled comment about her sister-in-law Minnie Howell, whose husband William had gone to California. "It is very bitter to have to play the role of deserted Wife, and the pity of outsiders stings like scorpions," but at least Minnie knew that her husband did not "willingly" leave her.[25]

Deaf to this entreaty, Jefferson kept working on his book. His progress was slow. He had lost many of his papers over the decades, and he had difficulty recovering items from people who owned them as war souvenirs. Yet he was "pleasantly situated," he told friends, and he explained that his wife lived in Memphis because she was caring for their daughter. Later Varina took pains to say that Sarah Dorsey worked with her husband at "stated hours during the day," as if Dorsey were merely a part-time secretary, and Jefferson called Sarah his "hostess," but actually they had become fast friends. They worked closely together, as she wrote letters for him and read over the manuscript. She asked him to look after her business affairs, and Jefferson borrowed money from her. He increasingly involved her in family concerns, sharing with her letters from relatives and photographs of his children.[26]

This situation, so odd and so titillating, became the subject of gossip all over the region. Dorsey's own family was aghast. Her stepfather, Confederate veteran Charles Dahlgren, detested Jefferson Davis ever since they had disagreed about military strategy during the war, but he believed that there was no impropriety between the two, simply that Dorsey did not care about appearances. Her half-brother Mortimer Dahlgren left Beauvoir because he thought Davis was taking over the management of the place. Dorsey tended to idolize older men who resembled her father, and she revered Davis, but if she felt something more for him, he probably did not reciprocate, because, as time would prove, he still cared for Virginia Clay. Jefferson needed a place to live, and he wanted someone to help him with his book. Sarah Dorsey provided what he needed.[27]

The situation looked even more improper when Sarah Dorsey composed her will in 1878 and gave Davis her entire estate. She also named him as the sole executor. After disinheriting all of her family members, she rebuked white Southerners everywhere for their ingratitude toward the man she believed to be the "noblest in existence." Moreover, she declared that all of the property was to go to his daughter Winnie Davis if he predeceased her. Then Dorsey gave Jefferson power of attorney over all of her legal and financial business. His presence at Beauvoir was a "joy" and a "privilege," she exclaimed, and she would do anything to contribute to his happiness. She entertained hopes that Davis would consider her house his home for the rest of his life.[28]

In Memphis, Varina's resistance was wearing down. Her husband had presented her with a *fait accompli;* the writing was on the wall. In May 1878 she capitulated, just as she had when the Davises disagreed in 1848 and 1869 on where they would live, and she went to Beauvoir. The visit started badly. Varina expected to have some time alone with her husband, and when Sarah would not leave them alone the two women had a sharp exchange, either at the railroad station or in the house, and Varina ran into the woods, overcome with hurt and embarrassment. After Sarah apologized, Varina returned and later charmed the guests at a dinner party. Then Mrs. Davis agreed to move to Beauvoir, as her husband wanted, and live in the main house with him and Sarah Dorsey. At least the Davises had their own bedroom. Varina would misrepresent the sequence of events by implying that she stayed in Britain until April 1878, visited her daughter briefly in Memphis, and then moved to Beauvoir, where she implied her husband was living by himself, but in fact she had been in the America since October 1877 and Sarah Dorsey resided at Beauvoir for much of the summer and fall of 1878.[29]

Jefferson still felt something for his wife, saying in 1877 that he cherished the memory of the day he married this "gifted, accomplished girl." He also praised her as a wonderful mother. But when his wishes conflicted with hers, he expected her to submit. Even though he had not been able to provide a stable home for his family as a man of the Old South was expected to do, he still acted as a man of that society acted, taking Varina's subordination for granted. What is more, his ego, shattered by the Confederacy's failure, had rebounded to leviathan proportions as he assumed a new role as symbol of the "Lost Cause," as the Southern effort came to be called. He seemed to enjoy his fame more as he grew older. In a speech in Marshall, Texas, he thanked the white Southern public for not forgetting him, and they did not forget. When he attended a county fair in Missouri, the crowd applauded him, and during a visit to Alabama, strangers handed him bunches of flowers. Some whites still addressed him as "the President," and he received multigenerational fan mail praising him as a great man. He seemed to expect his wife to defer to him as members of the public did. So they remained at Beauvoir—Varina, Sarah, and the unabashed Jefferson.[30]

As this ménage continued its uneasy existence, tragedy struck again at the star-crossed Davis children, this time at Jeff Jr. He had enrolled at Virginia Military Institute but ranked near the bottom of his class, and in 1875 he was dismissed. After he returned to Memphis he received some tough advice from his father, who said he must look after his mother and sisters one day, and, furthermore, that his son should reach even "higher distinction" than he thought he himself had achieved. But Jeff Jr. did not have much drive. A teasing, affable young man, he had a *zelig*-like quality, adopting local idioms wherever he lived, trying to fit in, and he liked the outdoors, especially sailing and fishing. He could not hold a job very long, and he ended up working at his brother-in-law's bank. He was devoted to both parents and desperately wanted to please his father, prizing every one of his letters. Jefferson thought there was much good in his namesake, but called him "an *uneducated* boy" and thought he would never understand his son.[31]

Jeff Jr. was in Memphis in 1878 at the outbreak of one of the century's worst yellow fever epidemics. At the summer's end, government offices shut down, businesses closed, and thousands fled the city as wagons full of corpses rumbled through the streets. Jeff Jr. called the epidemic terrible to behold, but he did not leave, arguing that Addison might fall ill, and when they finally left the city in October, Jeff got sick, not Addison. They stopped at a railroad station outside Memphis, so William Walthall went there to care for him. Varina had an intuition that Jeff would die, but she thought her duty lay with her husband, and she hesitated until it was too late to reach her son. In mid-October, Jeff came down with the dreaded "black vomit" of blood as his internal organs broke down. He wished aloud that he had done more good in his life, and he asked for his parents and for Robert Brown, the African American who had worked for the Davises in Savannah. He succumbed on the anniversary of his brother Billy's death, October 16, and was buried next to him in Elmwood Cemetery. In the country at large some twenty thousand people died from yellow fever, five thousand of them in Memphis. Jeff died just before the onset of frost on October 18, which ended the epidemic.[32]

When Varina received the telegram at Beauvoir, she crawled into bed, undone with grief and guilt. The narrowing circle of boys had closed. Until the end of her life Varina regretted that she had not been with Jeff when he died, and she missed her "manly witty good son," the last of the "four bright strong sons," the one she expected to rely on in her old age. In the fall of 1878 Jefferson wrote some letters for his wife, one of the few times in their marriage he did so, and he too was filled with grief. Their son's death was reported in the national press, and Varina received condolences from family and friends all over the country, including Ellen Barnes McGuiness and her husband in Baltimore. But the Davises did much of their grieving separately. In November, Varina visited a relative for several weeks, while Jefferson remained at Beauvoir.[33]

No one in the trio seemed very comfortable at Beauvoir, and all of them traveled a good deal. In the new year, 1879, Sarah Dorsey went to New Orleans to meet an attorney, Jefferson to Vicksburg and Brierfield on business, and Varina to Memphis for several months to see daughter Maggie, who had a new daughter named Varina Howell

Davis Hayes. When he was at Beauvoir, Jefferson continued to be close to Sarah. He called her his "beloved friend," which is probably the best way to describe the relationship on his side, a close platonic friendship. Their finances soon became hopelessly entangled. He continued to borrow money from her, even as he insisted on paying rent at Beauvoir, and in 1879 he decided for some reason to buy the place for fifty-five hundred dollars, paid in installments, even though she had already left the property to him and he had a general idea of the will's contents, contrary to what was said later. Perhaps this was his idea of a chivalrous gesture, or just another instance of his bad judgment. In any case, as Varina observed, Sarah Dorsey's "deference to his wishes" had "endeared" her to Jefferson.[34]

11

FASCINATING FAILURES

AFTER SAYING LITTLE about the war for most of the 1870s, Varina Davis broke her silence in a letter to her husband in 1878. Again she spoke in the unorthodox voice. In February 1878, after Robert M. T. Hunter quarreled with Jefferson Davis over what had happened at the Hampton Roads peace conference in 1865, she reminded her spouse that even though she was a woman and was supposed to have no political opinions, she had said privately that she believed the Confederacy was doomed. Both Hunter and Robert E. Lee kept silent near the end about their desires for peace, which she thought was a "sorry spectacle." If she had been in a position to stop the war, she "would have interposed" her "own body" between the soldiers of the two armies and "preached a peace crusade" even if her life "had paid for it." Her husband had at least been consistent, she averred, believing in the Confederate cause until the very end. She suggested that he refrain from answering Hunter, observing, "You have not been a conciliatory man in your manners always," and added that she gave him this advice only because she loved him. She avoided saying the obvious, that many soldiers died after Hampton Roads because her husband was determined to fight when almost everyone else knew it was over.[1]

In the spring of 1879, she spoke further about public issues when the Davises met a journalist while traveling by steamboat down the Mississippi. After the writer interviewed Jefferson—who declared

that he had kind feelings for Northerners and did not want to re-
vive slavery, but strongly doubted that blacks should be educated or
trusted with the vote—the journalist, a Bostonian, talked at length
with Varina. They discussed the new ideas about evolution, including
works by Charles Darwin and Thomas Huxley, and although she was
not convinced by evolutionary theory, she was familiar with the debate. She reminisced about antebellum Washington—no details provided—and then shifted to current politics. She was in favor of education for black Southerners, speaking about it "far more hopefully"
than her husband. Expressing her "very decided opinion" that black
people were increasing in knowledge and self-reliance, she believed
that their progress was the result of the education that they had thus
far received. African Americans needed the tools of education, she
thought, to protect themselves from hostile white people. Then she
gave several examples among blacks of her acquaintance who had
benefited from schooling.[2]

If Varina Davis had more moderate views than her husband, she
was not egalitarian by modern standards. She told the journalist that
she felt no nostalgia for slavery because house slaves were a "burden
to the housekeeper," and she thought that free people did better
work. Nor were her ideas on social class among whites egalitarian,
for she believed strongly in "blood." When the journalist mentioned
another matron's project to save fallen women, she dismissed it as a
hopeless task, even though she was still an officer for the Woman's
Christian Association and her sister Margaret had fallen from the
straight and narrow. The Boston writer nevertheless deemed her "in-
tellectually . . . a very superior woman" and declared that she understood the questions of the day "far better than the average of the male
sex." Jefferson made no public response to her interview, and he may
not have understood the implications of some of her comments, for
he asserted in a speech in Mississippi a few months later that he had
yet to meet a white Southern woman who was "reconstructed."[3]

Sarah Dorsey became very ill in the spring of 1879, probably with
breast cancer. When she was bedridden in a hotel in New Orleans,
Jefferson was summoned to her side, and he was with her when she

died on July 4 at age fifty. He told his wife that he was grateful for Dorsey's generosity, but to others he effusively praised her religious faith, her forgiving nature, her patience, and what he called her service to humanity, and he asked someone to write an obituary as a "labor of love." Then he oversaw the distribution of her heirlooms to relatives and friends and burned most of her papers as she had requested.[4]

When Dorsey's outraged relatives learned the contents of Sarah's will, they quickly took action. Her half-brother Mortimer Dahlgren, living in St. Louis, attacked Jefferson Davis in the press for cheating him out of his legacy and alleged that Davis had taken over at Beauvoir by sheer force of will. Davis had such a bad temper, Dahlgren said, that he once kicked a black servant and threatened to strike another. In December 1879 Dorsey's kinfolk filed papers in the U.S. Circuit Court, and, led by Sarah's brother Stephen Ellis, they declared themselves to be her legal heirs. Davis, they alleged, had exercised "undue influence" upon Dorsey, who was unbalanced. Perceiving Jefferson Davis as a martyr for the South, she let herself be guided by what she thought were his wishes. This man of "domineering will," they alleged, had a "morbid feeling" that he suffered for ungrateful white Southerners, and he persuaded Dorsey it was her duty to reward his services to the Confederate cause. Last of all, they denied that Dorsey had ever been close friends with Varina Davis, which Jefferson had adduced as another reason for Dorsey giving him the property.[5]

Jefferson Davis and his legal counsel simply bypassed the facts of the complaint by arguing that the Circuit Court did not have jurisdiction, and in 1880 the court dismissed the suit. The Ellises appealed to the United States Supreme Court, but in 1883 they lost, and Davis kept the entire estate, which was worth about fifty thousand dollars. Afterward the Dorsey kinfolk claimed parts of the estate, and Jefferson won most of those suits or settled them out of court. If anyone noticed that Davis reversed the position he took during the Bowmar lawsuit—that blood ties counted more than the intentions of the deceased—no one in the family said so in writing.[6]

While this fight wound to its conclusion, the lawsuit over Joseph

Davis's will was resolved. In April 1878 the Mississippi Supreme Court decided in Jefferson's favor, and in 1881, after more legal maneuvers, Jefferson purchased Brierfield at auction, as Lise Hamer and her brother bought the Hurricane. Ben Montgomery died in 1877, and most of his family moved away. When Jefferson wrote his own testament in 1879, he left Brierfield to his wife. He called it the place "on which we lived and toiled together for many years," and he mused that the best days of his married life had been spent there. So he gave this property, the source of so much conflict, to his wife as long-standing custom dictated, but his iron will was evident, for he directed that after his wife's death the property should go to his two daughters only, and he did not allow his wife to choose how to dispose of the property after his death.[7]

SO THE DAVISES RESIDED at Beauvoir, alone together, for ten years. Jefferson loved the place, but to Varina this was always another woman's house, for Sarah Dorsey's silver was in the kitchen and Samuel Dorsey's portrait hung on the wall. But the building itself was lovely, as she had to admit, and the grounds were perfumed with roses every spring. She had a vegetable garden, a flower garden, a dairy, a carriage, and a sewing machine. To run the household, she hired about half a dozen servants, typically white women who worked indoors and black men who worked outdoors. The house did not have electricity, although the rest of the South was becoming more involved in the national market economy and was undergoing some measure of industrialization. The Davises may not have even had a working stove. When Varina contributed some recipes to a cookbook in 1885, she described preparing welsh rarebit in a fireplace.[8]

With her trademark ability to get things done, she stepped in to help her husband finish his memoir. The project was delayed by his grief for Sarah Dorsey, and when he returned to work, Varina and one of the Davis nephews sorted the papers to put them in order for William Tenney, an editor from Appleton's whom the publisher sent to Beauvoir to see the book through. Jefferson dictated much of the manuscript to Varina and several other assistants, including William M. Browne and W. T. Walthall. Even though typewriters were in wide usage then, they all worked by hand. Mrs. Davis put everything aside to labor on the book, and she said the work became "very heavy" as it drew to a close.[9]

Varina found it excruciating to relive the war. The conflict was going to be transformed into "a splendid but heartbreaking record of cherished hopes," she told Winnie. Brave men died in the "hopeless" struggle, and "this tremendous record," she dryly observed, her husband was telling the world. The phenomenal loss of life still haunted her. "The graves give up their dead," she shuddered, and "stalk before

Beauvoir. The house Sarah Dorsey left to Jefferson Davis.
(University of Memphis Libraries)

us all gory, and downcast." Then, perhaps taken aback by this visceral language in a letter to her teenage daughter, she retreated and said the Confederate army was a brave army fighting for their rights. She continued helping her husband with the book, and she wrote the final passage at four o'clock in the morning one day in the spring of 1880 after eight hours of taking his dictation. With a last flourish of illogic, he declared that secession was impractical but right, although now that the Union was reunited, secession should not be attempted again. He paused, and when she asked him to continue, he smiled and said he was done.[10]

With this book, *The Rise and Fall of the Confederate Government,* Jefferson Davis reiterated his political creed, unchanged since 1861: The Constitution protected the right to own slaves; slaves were private property; and the South fought for states' rights, which he called the foundation of the Union. The North violated the principles of the Constitution, and its army committed acts of savagery, Davis insisted. He denied any role in the Lincoln assassination, although he said he could not pretend to mourn for his enemy. He said little about his family and made only a few references to Varina, whom he blamed for his capture because when she threw her arms around him, he said, the opportunity to escape was "lost." The book was nevertheless dedicated to the "Women of the Confederacy," who, Jefferson said, had shown "zealous faith" in the cause. In 1881 both volumes appeared to praise from friends, attacks from Union veterans, and generally poor reviews for the tedious narrative. Walthall claimed that he had actually written most of volume 1, while Jefferson blamed Walthall because portions of the manuscript were never printed. A few white Southerners also criticized the book, but the controversy did not feed sales. Jefferson tried hard to make money from his investments, writing dogged letters about an ice machine and other projects, but nothing worked out. Sarah Dorsey's estate continued to be the greatest windfall from his tenure as head of the Confederacy.[11]

In the 1880s, the Davis marriage stabilized after years of intermittent conflict and nearly constant geographic mobility. An armistice was reached because, as usual, Varina accommodated her husband's wishes. Jefferson once singled out fidelity to fallen men as a hallmark of the female gender, and his wife certainly embodied that virtue. She cared for him when he fell sick, as she had so many times; she wrote many of his letters for him; and she sympathized with his financial worries. Jefferson had moments of self-pity, when he said he had suffered more than most men, and his neighbors in Mississippi had the impression that he leaned on Varina's physical and emotional strength more than ever. But his personal magnetism was undiminished, and his charm could still work its magic. He insisted on dressing formally for dinner when he dined alone with Varina, out of respect, he said, for her. When he visited Montreal in 1881 to register the copyright for his book, he plucked some grass from Mrs. Howell's grave and sent it to Varina with the tender remark that their loved ones were widely scattered. Yet he took her devotion for granted, informing an acquaintance that he had no secretary, saying so in a letter, one of many, he dictated to his wife.[12]

The Davis finances also stabilized. The income from the Dorsey properties was about twenty-five hundred dollars a year, and Brier-field, still plagued by floods, produced about sixty bales of cotton a year, much less than the 350 to 450 bales before the war, and a good deal less than the what other planters reaped in the 1880s. Jefferson still fretted about money, and in his worst moments he predicted complete ruin, but the Davises never went under. In 1881 his account with his New Orleans cotton factor contained thirteen thousand dollars, a considerable sum for the time. Varina had some money of her own, perhaps her seamstress money or a legacy given to her by Malie Brodhead's family after Malie died in 1877, plus the grand sum of eight dollars from a lawsuit filed by the Kempes over her grandfather's land in Virginia. She purchased some land from her nephew Joseph R. Davis and quietly gave money to an unnamed friend who needed it. She also sent meals to a neighbor who drank so much that he could not remember to eat.[13]

In 1881, Winnie Davis joined the Beauvoir household after her long sojourn abroad. Varina had hoped her daughter would avoid the habits of "idleness" that her other children had acquired from their haphazard schooling, and Winnie received an excellent education at Karlsruhe. In the summers she visited Brussels, Glasgow, and London, and the great museums in those cities. Dudley Mann said that Winnie conducted herself like a monarch's daughter, which he meant as a compliment. Her teachers assured Jefferson that she was learning self-control, which both her parents wanted, and that she had made friends at school. But Winnie, like her brother Jeff, craved her father's approval. She sent her sketches to him and asked him to remember that he taught her to draw. From schoolgirl gossip, Winnie heard about the Davis lawsuits, and she missed her family very much. This prompted a rush of guilty assurances from Varina, who worried that Winnie stayed abroad too long, and she promised that when the girl came home they would read together, walk by the ocean, and talk about everything. Jefferson told his wife year after year that she would be allowed to visit Winnie, but they did not have enough money until the summer of 1881, when they returned to Karlsruhe to collect their daughter.[14]

The family spent a leisurely holiday in Paris, where Winnie rounded off her education by immersing herself in the city's art world. Mother and daughter replenished their wardrobes—Varina still loved fashion, although she usually dressed in black—and the family saw Judah Benjamin, working hard at his legal career. Until his death three years later, Benjamin remained free from the war-obsession that consumed Jefferson Davis. The Davises took in all of sights, and at the Luxembourg Gardens Jefferson thought one of the statues resembled his niece Mary Stamps. When he described the scene to Mary, he admitted that although Paris was beautiful he missed the warm weather at home, and he asked her to forgive a "barbarian's want of culture." His wife, by contrast, experienced this visit as a heavenly interlude. She thrilled to see the city's glorious works of art, and she yearned to create something that would live after her, a longing she had felt on previous visits, she said. From her hotel window on the Avenue

Friedland, she savored what she called "the clatter, the rattle, the vo-ciferation, and agglomeration" on the streets. She found it a "great wrench" to leave Paris, just as she had felt on leaving Washington in 1861. The Davises' return to Mississippi was reported in the interna-tional press.[15]

Varina's hapless brothers did not live out the decade, dying one af-ter another in 1881, 1882, and 1884. They had ceased writing to her regularly by the mid-1870s, which hurt her very much, she said, after the sacrifices she made for them when she was younger, but she kept helping them to the end. Her brother Joseph died first. He supported himself by working as a gardener in Louisiana in the 1870s and turned up occasionally to visit relatives. Then he disappeared for some years before contacting Varina, in poor health and nearly penni-less, and she arranged to wire him some money. In 1881 Joseph died in Waterproof, Louisiana, of causes unknown. Becket worked as a manual laborer in Louisiana and Mississippi, still unmarried, poor, and in mediocre health. He died of a fever in 1882. An obituary de-scribed him as quiet, like his father.[16]

William Howell, the last to go, said that his life had gone so badly since the war that he wished he had died in it. His wife, Minnie Leacock Howell, had been granted a divorce, and he had not seen his children in years. He never made much money out west, and in 1884 he was bedridden in the county hospital in San Francisco. There he wrote a feverish letter to his "darling and dearest old sister" to say that he was making her his confessor and had made peace with God. He promised that his love would watch over her from the next world, and a few days later he died. One of his California friends assured Varina that her letters had meant much to William over the years. She grieved for all of her brothers, overlooking their faults, and be-cause they had lost touch with each other, when one of them died it sometimes fell to her to inform the remaining brothers of the death.[17]

She met her duties to the rest of the family as well. She forgave Margaret de Wechmar Stoess for her silence after her son Billy's death and invited her to visit in the winter of 1880–81, referring to her sister, who was nearing forty, as a "child." Her cousins from the Howell and Kempe clans asked Varina to visit New Orleans, and other kinfolk from the many branches of the family came to Beauvoir, such as her aunts Jane Kempe and Frances Sprague, now very old. Friends arrived from all phases of her life, including George Denison from Canada, who stayed a week and spent much of his time talking to her on the veranda, and the Meriwethers who came down from Memphis. All of this provided stimulation of a kind.[18]

Yet the isolation of Beauvoir bothered her from the first year, and it chafed even more after her enchanting Paris visit in 1881. As one of her kinfolk understood, Varina was a "woman of the world" who had been taken away to this country estate. Boredom, bone deep, afflicted her sorely. Sometimes Varina felt as if she were "weltering" in boredom, as if she were "buried alive." Solitude was appropriate for owls, not human beings, she thought, and she needed a quorum of good friends nearby in order to be happy. There were no good friends nearby, and Biloxi, the nearest town, was a sleepy village some ten miles away. In the torpor of rural life, she said, "everything that ever hurt me in my life comes up," and she longed for her old friends, she confessed to Minna Blair. She told Mary Chesnut in South Carolina that she wanted to "sit down beside" her and "pour out" what she felt. At other times Varina Davis felt as if she were waiting for something, anything, to happen.[19]

"Life here is so uneventful that there is nothing to write about," Jefferson once remarked of Beauvoir. He knew his wife was unhappy from the start of her residence there, but he asked her to make the best of it. She did, or tried to, as the months passed, turning to reading for solace as she had in the past. The house had a fine selection of books, and her friends sent her titles. She subscribed to magazines and newspapers from all over the country, such as the *New York World*. Literary references fill her letters, from classics such as *El Cid* to the works of once-popular poets, such as Joanna Baillie's *Metrical Legends*. Sometimes Varina communicated in literary code to her women friends. She said that life had become "a journey up the 'Hill Difficulty,'" and she could not see "the 'Delectable City,'" the promised land in *Pilgrim's Progress*. Therefore she had become "discouraged."[20]

❦

HER HUSBAND was still a public figure and highly conscious of himself as such. The Confederacy proved to have a long afterlife, and an acquaintance said Jefferson Davis belonged to the white Southern people, as indeed he did. He maintained in private that the North, especially the Republican Party, despised him, and his onetime hope that he could defuse this hostility by serving as a "scapegoat" for his region had not been fulfilled. In any case, he had no regrets, and he could still arouse controversy in the national press. After a speech in 1886 in Montgomery, Alabama, in which he described the Confederate cause as an honorable defense of constitutional liberties, the *Chicago Tribune* described him as a "senile old Rebel," and he was castigated at a public meeting in Albany, New York, for reviving the spirit of disunion. The *New York Times* exclaimed that Davis had learned nothing since 1861.[21]

Not surprisingly, Jefferson took a dim view of the reconciliation between white Southerners and white Northerners, as they chose to put aside many of their differences over the war. The process, which began in the 1870s among a few whites in both regions, gained momentum in the next decade. Veterans from both armies began to publish their memoirs, filled with nostalgic views of the war, and they held the first joint reunions, celebrating the valor of men in both armies. (The other features of regional reconciliation, the abandonment of any effort to create racial equality and the suppression of the black contribution to the Union effort, Jefferson did support.) He made a few temperate comments, once advising white Southerners to let go of their ill will for the North, but most of the time Davis was unrepentant. The war remained his obsession. He read the volumes of the federal government's *Official Records of the War of the Rebellion* and the pro-Confederate *Southern Historical Society Papers* as they appeared, noting errors he thought he detected, and when Confederate veter-

237

ans published articles he believed inaccurate, Davis sent emissaries to the authors to correct them. His hard-edged utterances about the war embarrassed some white Southerners, and at least one former Confederate officer asked him to cease, but he did not.[22]

Many white Southerners nonetheless worshipped the aging man now called the "Prince" of the Confederacy. To condense drastically the cultural trends of the 1880s, white Southerners who had opposed the war or reluctantly supported it fell silent or were silenced; the myth of the unanimous South was being created. Those who once blamed Jefferson Davis for losing the war forgave him and turned him into a martyr for the Lost Cause. At the same time they convinced themselves that Confederates had fought for a worthy cause— states' rights, they insisted, not slavery—and that the antebellum South was an Eden, a utopia, a perfect society. This was a comforting delusion, similar to those created by other defeated countries, and it distracted everyone from the hard fact that white men lost the war and thereby failed to protect the white family, including white women. Now much of that fervor was focused on Jefferson Davis. Robert E. Lee died in 1870, and although white Southerners venerated his memory, Davis was the Confederacy's only President, and he was alive. Strangers began showing up at his door unannounced to pay their respects. The parade of visitors, some arriving by foot and some by carriage, rarely stopped for long. The house at Beauvoir became a tourist attraction.[23]

For Varina Davis, this meant that her duties as hostess went on and on. She resurrected that persona, practiced with considerable success in Washington and less success in Richmond. In the spring of 1884 she entertained reporters from Illinois, the widow of a Confederate officer, two friends from Chicago, and a married couple from New York, hurriedly cleaning the house after each group left. Two North Carolinians appeared out of the blue to give their salutes, admitting that it was a little presumptuous, and on another day five Northerners suddenly arrived. They began peppering Varina with questions such as how long she had been married, whereupon she asked them to leave. Sometimes the numbers of guests approached the numbers she hosted at receptions in Washington, Montgomery, and Richmond, except that most of these visitors came with no advance notice. When a religious revival was held nearby, a "legion" of people tramped over to see Jefferson Davis, Varina related, all of them polite, but a legion nonetheless. One of her nieces thought Varina wearied of the strangers gawking at the house, and Mrs. Davis was amused and at times exasperated by the Confederate acolytes. Three decades of being a politician's wife had left her with no desire for "personal éclat," Varina said. She disliked the attention of "masses of people," which she compared in a private letter to a "monster," but she did her duty.[24]

Her labors as her husband's secretary only increased over the course of the decade, and she did more work than she had ever done in Washington, Montgomery, or Richmond, where Jefferson had a staff to assist him. The Davises did not have a telephone, which spread slowly through rural America after being patented in 1876, so they communicated by letter, or rather, she communicated by letter, writing most of his correspondence, sometimes in multiple drafts. As the letters poured in on what might be called the epiphenomena of the Confederacy—queries about pensions, requests for autographs, photographs, and loans—she answered them. She wrote the replies to more substantial queries, such as whether Jefferson Davis had stolen part of the Confederate treasury at the war's end. When Southerners sent Jefferson an assortment of presents, such as napkin rings, she wrote the thank-you letters. She began signing his autograph for him, and she became quite good at it.[25]

Some of her contemporaries perceived Varina Davis as a historical figure in her own right. White Southerners who knew of her wartime doubts about the Confederacy either forgot, kept silent, or forgave her, and she had outlived some of her Richmond critics, such as Josiah Gorgas and Stephen Mallory. Now she made some of the expected remarks in her correspondence, and guests who came to Beauvoir encountered a model hostess, obliging and self-effacing. White Southerners sometimes asked for her photograph, and a few of them named their daughters after her. Her fame also meant that she received her share of unsolicited advice. One former Confederate general took the liberty of telling her which flag should be buried in Jefferson's coffin when he died. She still appeared occasionally in satirical articles in the Northern press. A journalist in Astabula, Ohio, thought she was not as "guilty" as her husband, even though she lent him a dress at the capture in 1865.[26]

❦

IN HER OWN LETTERS, Varina's unresolved ambivalence about the war surfaced. She dissembled, referring to the Confederate struggle as "our struggle," and sometimes she told outright lies. To a journalist, she stated that contrary to newspaper reports she had always supported the Confederacy. She contradicted her statements from the postwar years as well. After one of her cousins extolled the "Lost Cause," she replied that she loved it too, "having made such sacrifices for it," which is at odds with her comment in 1867 that she could not love the Confederacy as her husband did. Then she added that she could not bear to relive the war and all the sorrow it brought in its wake. She made gnomic comments to her friend Mary Chesnut. After urging Chesnut to publish her wartime diary, she confided that she was "tired" of recent Confederate histories because "they do not want to tell the truth or to hear it," focusing on the individual "achievements" of each author. Which individuals, which truths, or which achievements, she did not say, but then she concluded that since the public seemed to like these books, she should not criticize them; Chesnut died a year later without publishing her diary. Davis made other cryptic statements in a letter to a namesake. She referred to her "association" with the Confederate cause as "accidental" and said that only a "true-hearted Confederate" would name a child for her after the "glamour of success had faded out of our lives."[27]

In any case, she did not despise Northerners as did many white Southerners. A Baltimore journalist who visited Beauvoir reported that she was proud of her husband's fame while "censuring" no one, and that she was still grateful to John Garrett for helping her family after the war. In her letters she sometimes disparaged individuals, such as a Yankee reporter who tried to interrogate her for gossip about the Confederate leadership, comparing him to "vermin," but she remained on cordial terms with longtime friends such as Minna Blair, to whom she sent heartfelt condolences when Montgomery died in 1883. She had always been fond of Montgomery, she told the widow, and praised his "loyal" character. Davis still corresponded with her Northern kinfolk, including her cousin Daniel Agnew, a member of the Pennsylvania supreme court since 1863 and chief justice since 1873. They agreed, as Agnew liked to say, that blood was thicker than water.[28]

Varina Davis developed an improbable friendship with a Yankee reformer, Frances Willard. They met in Memphis, probably in the 1870s when Willard was touring the country speaking on behalf of temperance. Thirteen years younger than Davis, she came from a Midwestern Republican family. After becoming president of the Woman's Christian Temperance Union (WCTU) in 1879, she advocated temperance as a means to protect the family, even though she did not marry and was wholly dedicated to her career. Willard had lost her youthful commitment to racial equality, and in her speeches in the 1880s as she tried to increase the WCTU membership in the South, she emphasized the shared experience of whites in both regions. Unable to persuade First Lady Lucy Hayes to endorse the cause, Willard converted a few women from the old planter class. Sallie Chapin of Charleston, an ex-Confederate who had published a temperance novel, became one of Willard's good friends in the organization.[29]

Willard and Davis met again in 1881 during the reformer's tour of the South, when Davis was visiting Memphis. The WCTU was the country's largest women's organization, and by the end of the decade it would have two hundred thousand members. In Memphis, Willard and Davis had a long talk about reform, because Davis was at that time secretary of the local chapter of the Woman's Christian Association. Willard later described Davis as "gifted" and one of the most "radiant" conversationalists she had ever met. The two women seemed to like each other. Willard, who made friends easily, was trim, grey-haired, blue-eyed, always soignée, with polite manners. Furthermore, both women were well read and both were famous, although they were of course different kinds of public figures. They probably sought different ends from the friendship: Davis enjoyed talking to educated women, and Willard realized that an endorsement from Davis could help the temperance cause.[30]

Through the rest of the decade, Willard tried to enlist Davis in the temperance movement. Varina was certainly interested in the issue. In 1882 she wished Frances "Godspeed" in her "noble work" and hoped that their "two faiths—in God, and in our own sex"—would bring them together soon. Davis closed by saying she would pray for Willard's "holy" work. The word "holy" suggests that she probably meant temperance, rather than suffrage, which the WCTU had officially endorsed in 1881. Varina had seen some hard drinking among her neighbors, although her own husband was not a heavy drinker by nineteenth-century standards. Frances made a point of meeting Winnie Davis when she was in New Orleans in 1882, and she praised Varina by name in *How to Win: A Book for Girls,* an advice book for young women. In Willard's book, published in 1886, she complimented Varina's graceful conversation and good health, and in another title, *Woman and Temperance,* she praised Davis's work in Memphis for the Woman's Christian Association. Davis did not become an active member of the WCTU, but Willard would not give up.[31]

In 1882, Varina Davis had one of the most unlikely social encounters of her life when Oscar Wilde visited Beauvoir. The writer was in the midst of his American tour, where he created a sensation as the apostle of the aesthetic movement. He had already given some eighty lectures when he reached the Deep South in June. His gregarious manners and family connections through his uncle John Elgee made a good impression, and Pierre Beauregard, the former Confederate general, gave Wilde a tour of New Orleans. The Davises asked Wilde to visit Beauvoir, possibly to return a courtesy, because Wilde's parents had invited Jefferson to their Dublin home years before, and the writer accepted. He told the press he admired the ex–Confederate President.[32]

Oscar Wilde. One of many callers at Beauvoir. (Billy Rose Theater Collection,
The New York Public Library for the Performing Arts,
Astor, Lenox, and Tilden Foundations)

7So Mrs. Davis hosted Oscar Wilde's one-day visit to Beauvoir on June 27, 1882, an enjoyable day of talk about books with a witty young man and an Irishman, no less. For all of his gathering fame, Wilde was yet another visitor like many she had hosted over the years, and she could talk to him, or anyone else, about books. He tried to be agreeable, comparing the Irish struggle for independence to the Confederate struggle for self-government. The next day he left to continue his lecture tour, and he told the newspapers that the Davises had a lovely home and Jefferson Davis a strong personality. In one of the most blatant acts of puffery ever committed by a writer, he described Davis's memoir as a "masterpiece." His honest opinions, which he shared with Julia Ward Howe, author of the "Battle Hymn of the Republic," were more piercing. His tour of the "passionate, ruined South" revealed a people absorbed in the past and falling ever farther behind the North, especially in the life of the mind. Of his meeting with Varina Davis he made no comment, but about Jefferson Davis he could only say, "How fascinating all failures are!"[33]

THE GIRDLED TREE

AFTER HER RETURN FROM EUROPE, Winnie Davis led a quiet life at Beauvoir. She was devoted to both her parents, and as one observer noted, she seemed to be trying to fill the places of her deceased brothers. A favorite in the Davis clan and described as "lovable" by her friends, she was set apart by her education, probably the only person in Mississippi who could write her initials in Sanskrit. Winnie read as widely as her mother did, and when Varina rearranged the Beauvoir library, she explained the new system to Winnie and included some imaginary exchanges between the authors, Macaulay in dialogue with the Girondists. Winnie was in fact more cerebral than either of her parents. One day when her mother was talking to her about fashion, Winnie interrupted to discuss the suffering of the Irish people and then segued to the labor question in the United States.[1]

Winnie's relationship with her only surviving sibling, Maggie, was more complicated. The sisters exchanged gifts and warm letters, and Winnie was godmother to Maggie's son Jefferson, born in 1884, yet the nine-year difference in their ages and Winnie's long absence in Karlsruhe meant that the sisters had little in common. Undercurrents of jealousy percolated between them, which their mother tried to smooth over. As can sometimes happen in families with two children, Maggie became her father's favorite, and Winnie, her mother's; the parents typically lauded Maggie for her good looks and Winnie for her brains. Maggie learned how to run a household, Winnie did not. As Varina liked to boast, Maggie was a fine mother to her four children, and the Hayes grandchildren gave her great pleasure. After Addison began to have health problems, however, the Hayes family moved to Colorado Springs in the mid-1880s, leaving Winnie in possession of her parents, as it were. The primal bond between Winnie and her mother grew stronger. In 1886 Varina told her, "You are all I have," and the *Ladies Home Journal* later quoted her as calling Winnie the "best and dearest of daughters." Winnie said that her mother always understood her, and she thought the Beauvoir household could not function without her mother.[2]

Winnie became a public figure in her own right, which was perhaps inevitable for Jefferson Davis's youngest child. Southern whites were curious about her, and Winnie started traveling with her father on speaking engagements. A tour they made in 1886 through the Deep South brought her fully into the spotlight. They went to Montgomery at the mayor's invitation so Jefferson could dedicate a Confederate monument, and cheering crowds greeted the train along the way. When the party arrived on April 27, several thousand people were waiting as cannons boomed, a band played, and fireworks exploded. At the hotel, they met more hurrahs from another surging crowd. The next day Winnie sat beside her father as he made his speech, and together they placed a Confederate battle flag in the cornerstone. The crowd's enthusiasm beggared description, but it was only the beginning.[3]

As Jefferson Davis proceeded on his tour with his daughter, the crowds grew larger and more delirious. White Southerners seemed to realize that he might not live much longer, and this could be the last chance to see him. The Davis train was festooned with bunting carrying the unsubtle slogan "He Was Manacled for Us," and in LaGrange, Georgia, residents scattered petals before their carriage. In Atlanta the governor and former Confederate general John B. Gordon introduced Winnie to a roaring crowd as the "daughter of the Confederacy." Jefferson Davis repeated the title in Macon, Georgia, when he introduced her to another cheering audience. In Savannah, where Jefferson arrived to speak to the local artillery company, another throng filled the streets. Henry Grady, usually a tough-minded journalist, proclaimed that everyone "fell in love" with Winnie Davis, and he asked for her photograph for the *Atlanta Constitution*. On the way home Jefferson made an extemporaneous speech at a railroad station, proclaiming that he was sorry for only one thing, that the South lost the war. For father and daughter, it was a perfervid, exciting, and exhausting trip. They staggered back to Beauvoir, he sick with bronchitis and she with the measles, and Varina nursed both of them back to health.[4]

Winnie Davis was now famous, and white Southerners began writing to ask for her autograph and her photograph. She was invited to join a host of honorary societies, including one named for her and founded for the "intellectual and social improvement" of young women in Eufaula, Alabama. Dozens of white Southerners named their daughters after her, and she wrote thank-you letters to the parents and kept a list of the girls' addresses. People started traveling to Beauvoir to meet her, rather than her father, and when she visited Richmond in 1887 the ex-Confederate elites in the capital embraced her, as they had not embraced her mother, and the following year the Ladies Confederate Memorial Association invited her to join. At age twenty-four she was listed in an encyclopedia called *Prominent Men and Women of the Day*. Soon she was appearing at events all over the region, entirely at ease in the public eye. John Gordon's sobriquet stuck, and whites all over the region hailed her as the "Daughter of the Confederacy."[5]

The title was factually correct, since Winnie was born in Richmond in 1864, but she did not remember the war and actually knew little of the South. In many respects she was scarcely an American, having spent almost half her life abroad before she returned to the States in 1881. In Karlsruhe she kept a scrapbook with numerous mementoes from such figures as Bismarck and Moltke, and a few images from her native country, including a Confederate flag. She was fluent in German and French, and her accent when she spoke English was mittel-European. Sometimes Winnie had to look up words such as *gingham* in the dictionary, and she made mistakes in usage, as if she were trying to translate German noun constructions into English. She is best described as a transatlantic figure—unlike her mother, an American who was drawn to European culture, or her father, who felt homesick in the Luxembourg Gardens.[6]

But she did have some of the right qualities for her highly specialized role. She was anointed partly because Maggie Hayes had left the South, and because she was more pliant than her sister and more anxious to please her parents. Although she was not beautiful by the standards of the late nineteenth century, having her mother's olive complexion and her father's sharp features, she was tall and slender with lustrous eyes. Ever since she was a girl, Winnie struck people as both young and old, and she was self-possessed for a woman in her twenties. At least one of her contemporaries found her a little affected, but white Southerners seemed to want an archetype to represent womanhood as they understood it, and she became that archetype, propelled forward by their expectations. She had no history with the public, as her mother did, and her fealty to the Confederacy delighted the older generation, especially veterans, while her sophisticated manner seemed to inspire young women. To her contemporaries, she represented both the Old South and the New. Perhaps she helped both generations convince themselves that something good had come out of the Confederacy.[7]

Soon Winnie became famous in the country at large. In 1886 she traveled to Syracuse to visit her mother's friends, the Emorys, and she was nervous about the reception she might receive in the North. Syracuse was a hilly town that had prospered from the salt trade and still possessed a frontier briskness. The city was proud of its reformer tradition, including a vital branch of the abolitionist movement, but Winnie received a cordial welcome from people who had known the Davises before the war or did not care about the conflict or who her parents might be. Callers flocked to meet Winnie, and journalists reported her every move as she attended the opera, went to a dance, and took a sleigh ride. One of her Yankee cousins, John Meredith Read, a Republican who had served as a brigadier general in the

United States Army and retired in Paris, deemed her an "honor" to the entire family. Winnie played her part, as expected. At a dinner party in Syracuse, she entertained guests with tales of plantation life, a subject she knew nothing about from personal experience. She received admiring mail from friends of the Emorys, such as Admiral James Jouette of the U.S. Navy and Manton Marble, a Democrat and former owner of the *New York World,* who began sending her books.[8]

Her subsequent trip to the North in 1888 to visit the Emorys and the Pulitzers sealed her fame. Charles Dudley Warner, editor of *Harper's Magazine,* approvingly pronounced her free from war-related "bitterness," and an anonymous Southerner declared that her willingness to travel through the North was an inspiration. To cap it off, a few Northerners named their daughters after her. A printer in St. Louis made seventy-five thousand copies of her image, and it sold throughout the country. At some time in the 1880s she met President Grover Cleveland, the first Democratic president since the war, who chanced to be in Richmond while she was in town, and they had a brief friendly conversation.[9]

Meeting the President was nice, but Winnie's friendship with Joseph and Kate Pulitzer would prove to be a godsend to the Davis women. Winnie met the couple in the late 1870s or early 1880s, in either Europe or the United States. Kate was a blood relation, the daughter of Judge William Worthington Davis of Washington D.C., Jefferson's first cousin, and Varina knew Kate's mother Catherine before the war. Joseph grew up near Budapest and served in the Union army at the war's end, but his political views were those of a moderate Democrat and he had many eclectic friendships. He became one of the country's most powerful journalists after he purchased the *New York World* in 1883. Tall, gaunt, redheaded, and nearsighted, he was moody, sometimes overbearing, and insatiably curious about almost everything. His wife, Kate, had a sunnier temperament and was also a great beauty. The Pulitzers asked Winnie to be godmother to one of their children, and they invited her to travel with them to New England and later to Europe. The couple met Jefferson and Varina by the mid-1880s, possibly in Paris in 1881, and although they liked him well enough, they became good friends with Varina. Kate described her as a "superior woman," and Joseph, who relished the pleasures of fine conversation, discovered that Varina was an excellent talker. Their friendship continued through the mails and a visit to Beauvoir in 1888. Varina read the *New York World* avidly, and the paper ran an article extolling her as a woman who could still preside over a state dinner.[10]

Varina enjoyed Joseph Pulitzer's intelligence, optimism, and tornado-force energy, and she admired what she called his efforts to help humankind with journalism. "In the Roman Catholic phrase," she told him, "I pray for your intentions." They were both moderate Democrats by the standards of the day, and she occasionally talked to him about politics, giving him her assessment of a speech by Grover Cleveland. Her acquaintance with the political elite from days gone by—she was twenty-one years his senior—fascinated the journalist in him. As she ruminated about the prospect of war over Alsace-Lorraine, she recalled a scene in Paris, probably from 1870, in which a member of the French diplomatic corps tearfully described the provinces as his wronged sisters. Elements of self-interest were at play on both sides of this friendship, but Davis and Pulitzer did like each other. Varina came to confide in him, telling of her dislike of Beauvoir's isolation, her daydreams about seeing Europe again, and her philosophy that emotional pain opened one's heart to the sufferings of others and made all of humanity "kin" to each other. She felt that she, like Gil Blas, the figure from Alain-René Lesage's eighteenth-century novel, had "sworn eternal friendship" with him.[11]

On the whole, Varina approved of her daughter's increasingly high profile in the nation at large. She worried at first that Winnie might encounter hostility from people who hated Jefferson Davis, but she did not want her child to vegetate at Beauvoir, where Winnie's "very old" father (Varina's description) dwelled on the past, weighed down by what Varina called the "Shadow of the Confederacy." Their home on the Mississippi Coast was as isolated from the world as the Isle of Elba, Varina said, and she did not want Winnie to spend all of her time with "*curious* strangers, unreasoning devotees, and two discouraged failing old people." She believed, moreover, that Winnie needed to take her place with her own generation, which was different from hers or her husband's, and meet people her own age. Jefferson grumbled about the prospect of his daughter taking holidays in the North, but Varina persuaded him to let her go.[12]

Many mothers believe their favorite daughter to be brilliant, and Varina was no exception. She encouraged Winnie's ambitions as a writer, just as she had approved of the careers of acquaintances who published books, bravely setting out in a cockleshell on the literary sea, as she described it. Varina asked Charles Dudley Warner, who had already helped other women from the South break into print, if he would help her daughter find a publisher. He quickly agreed, starting a correspondence with Winnie and sending her deluxe editions of his own books. Winnie also corresponded with Grace King and mailed her publications to the New Orleans writer, who wished her success in her "career."[13]

Winnie did want a career, one of the many paradoxes of her young life, and she was openly ambitious in a way that had been unacceptable for Varina's generation. She published under her own name, unlike some older women; she actively sought publishing opportunities, sending poems and articles to the newspapers; and she wrote for pay, five dollars a column. When her articles appeared, she sent copies to relatives and friends, and she enjoyed praise for her work. Nor was she afraid to disagree with people, including men, about books. Aspiring writers in both the North and the South began to perceive her as an influential figure and told her about their work. In Mississippi, women asked her to attend readings of their work, and she joined an all-female literary club in New Orleans. From across the ocean, the Confederate expatriate Dudley Mann made her his literary executor, an impractical gesture that nonetheless symbolized her growing prominence as a writer.[14]

Winnie had some literary talent, and her publications covered a wide—one might even say eccentric—range of topics. Her first article, published in 1888 in the prestigious *North American Review* and reprinted in various newspapers, concerned myths about serpents in the ancient world. (One reader had to ask, "Where on earth did you find all these snakes?") Her next project was an essay on the Irish nationalist Robert Emmet, which her parents had published privately. She received a great deal of mail from her readers, and a few letters from people who disapproved of her literary aspirations, such as the Georgian who sniffed that she could push her way forward if she wished.[15]

AS WINNIE LAUNCHED her writing career, Frances Willard persisted in her efforts to win the Davises' support for the temperance cause. Frances asked Winnie for both of their photographs, and both of the Davis women corresponded with her. Varina felt "sympathy" for the organization's efforts, as her husband did not, and she met a local official of the WCTU in New Orleans. She called Willard's book, *How to Win: A Book for Girls,* a "boon to every woman and girl." In 1887 she invited Frances to visit Beauvoir because Varina wanted to consult with her, one woman to another, about Winnie's future. She also looked forward to "a few unrestrained hours" of talk on all subjects. Winnie attended at least one temperance gathering in New Orleans, but mother and daughter declined with ornate excuses to become active members of the WCTU. Varina explained that she had to look after her aging husband, and when Sallie Chapin asked her to head a local WCTU chapter, she added that she was not in good health herself. Other wives of ex-Confederates became active members of the WCTU, but the Davis women would not. Jefferson's opposition to legal prohibition was probably reason enough to keep them from joining.[16]

Yet Varina's opinion on temperance became a public issue in 1887 when Texas voted on a state referendum on prohibition. In the hard-fought campaign, Texans traded charges about Yankee interference and violations of democratic rights, even though the Confederate government and the Southern states had passed their own temperance laws during the war. Jefferson spoke out publicly against the referendum, even as John Reagan, the former Confederate Postmaster

General, disagreed with his old boss, as did several clergymen. Then Sallie Chapin, the WCTU activist, handed Jefferson a temperance badge at a campground to give to his wife, and the press picked up the story, implying that Jefferson supported temperance, so he had to explain that his wife sympathized with the cause but he did not. She wrote that letter for him, and in another letter she said that his views reflected his understanding of states' rights, glossing over their diverging opinions. When the referendum in Texas lost, many credited Jefferson Davis with aiding its defeat, and twenty years passed before the prohibition movement tried another measure. When he said that he also opposed local option, she wrote that letter too.[17]

Frances Willard, undiscouraged, kept trying to persuade Varina Davis to support the temperance cause. In her memoir of 1889 Willard called Davis one of the best talkers she had ever met and a woman of "cosmopolitan culture and broad progressive views" who was proud of her New England tutor, George Winchester. On the issue of woman suffrage, a goal of the WCTU since 1881, Varina Davis had said nothing in public since reading Elizabeth Meriwether's newspaper, the *Tablet,* in 1872, but in 1888 the suffragist Susan B. Anthony contacted Varina Davis about the issue. Anthony had been an abolitionist and a firm Unionist, but in her suffrage work she, like her friend Willard, sought allies wherever she could find them, including famous writers such as Harriet Beecher Stowe, who declined to endorse suffrage publicly, and ex-Confederates or Confederate sympathizers, some of whom did support it. Mississippi had no woman suffrage organization before 1890, but Anthony asked Davis to attend a meeting of the National Woman Suffrage Association that would "bring together the women of all sections of our country," or to write a letter of support, or, if that was not possible, to contribute some money. Davis apparently did not reply.[18]

In her correspondence about the war, Varina still spoke with two voices, uttering polite fictions that had never been true, referring to the place where she served as Confederate First Lady as "dear old Virginia" where she was "so happy." She wrote to Jubal Early, the former Confederate general who was obsessed with proving that the

Confederate cause was a just one. He was just as devoted to proving that Robert E. Lee was a great man and U.S. Grant a "butcher."
Early, a crabby bachelor with a squeaky, high-pitched voice, a some-
time-lawyer who worked for the corrupt Louisiana state lottery, also
served as president of the Southern Historical Society. Varina thanked
him for sending the Davises a bolt of Confederate gray cloth, and
when a Cincinnati newspaper published an article disparaging the
Howell family, she told Jubal the article was a "Yankee trick," neglect-
ing to say that many of her relatives were Northerners. She criticized
some public figures who turned like a "Kaleidoscope," going from
"blue to gray & then become half & half." In fact, she herself turned
like a kaleidoscope, depending on whom she was addressing, an ability practiced for years now and in full flower at Beauvoir.[19]

The other voice, worldly and more realistic, appeared sotto voce
in her letters. She sent Joseph Pulitzer a medal struck to honor soldiers who died for the Confederacy, making the observation that to
die "in the full fruition of life and indeed of triumphal expectation—
is much, but to live is more." In the same letter, she estimated that
Grover Cleveland was not in the same league with what she called
"the Giants I knew of old, Calhoun, Clay, Webster, Adams, Dallas,
Marcy, and Cass," five of whom were of course Northerners—Daniel
Webster, John Quincy Adams, George M. Dallas, William L. Marcy,
and Lewis Cass—albeit from different generations with a range of
political views. She praised William Corcoran, another Washington
friend, who was so anguished by the Civil War that he left the country, for his "honorable" life.[20]

She maintained her friendly contacts with Northerners beyond
Joseph Pulitzer and Frances Willard, and these relationships did not
necessarily coincide with her husband's friendships. She corresponded
with her cousins Daniel Agnew and John Meredith Read, who like
Agnew believed that blood is thicker than water, and when they
shared genealogical information about the family, she told Read she
was glad to be the granddaughter of Richard Howell "of Revolutionary memory." She still wrote to Margaretta Hetzel, who had smuggled a letter to her in 1863 from Washington, and in 1886 she said

that Hetzel "always will be very dear to me." When she recalled life in Washington, she remembered the conviviality and the sense of possibility. After reminiscing about the capital in the 1850s, she told a friend considering a job offer in the diplomatic corps, "Do go because the outfit is good." She missed that life. In 1883 she informed the Blairs that she had hoped to grow old with them and other friends from her "beloved circle" in Washington.[21]

The few times she accompanied Jefferson on his public appearances in the South, Varina nonetheless played her part. She and both daughters went with him to Macon, Georgia, in 1887 to a reunion of Confederate veterans. As he stood on a porch to review a parade, supported on each side by his women, some excited veterans broke ranks and rushed toward the old man. Varina and Winnie stepped in front of him and warded them off, shaking hands with the soldiers and deftly turning them aside. When the veterans gave some tattered battle flags to Jefferson, he buried his face in one and wept. The women also embraced the flags, and one of them—in some news stories it was Winnie, in others, Varina—kissed a flag. When the family returned to Beauvoir, Jefferson was sick, and as usual Varina took care of him. She told Joseph Pulitzer that it had been "gratifying" to see the affection of the veterans who "nearly broke my heart."[22]

As she had done in the past, Varina handled the correspondence that rained in upon them. Typically she wrote the letters and he signed them: fan letters, historical queries, and family missives. All this writing Varina considered her duty, and unlike the wives of other famous men—Vera Nabokov comes to mind—she rarely complained. She dealt with the "constant" influx of company, and because the Davises still had no telephone they were at the mercy of all visitors. Some were welcome, such as William and Lizzie Waller, the widower and daughter of her sister Jane, or one of the Davis kinsmen, Hugh, with whom Varina liked to play backgammon, but many were strangers, including a party of three hundred people who came by train to meet Mr. Davis. Varina told her granddaughter, "I dread them," but she put palmettos and flowers around the house to dress it up a bit for the occasion. She performed the role of hostess, practiced for years now, with consummate skill. A reporter described her as both "domestic" and "cultivated" and one of the best conversationalists he had ever met. Usually attired in black, she wore her white hair in a coil at the nape of her neck, and she was "gone to smash—grown very fleshy," as she described herself to a friend.[23]

IN THE LATE 1880s, Jefferson Davis finally had to relinquish whatever hopes he had for Virginia Clay. They had exchanged a few letters since the 1870s, but after Clement Clay died in 1882, Jefferson contacted her in Huntsville, Alabama, because he wanted to talk about the past, "so much of which belongs exclusively to us two." In her businesslike reply she discussed her plans to write a book on her husband, so Jefferson sent her some material and added, "I greatly desire to see you." Then he wrote again, recollecting the talks he had with the Clays around the fireplace at their home, and he asked her to write, sending his "devotion to whatever will promote your happiness." In another letter, marked *strictly private,* he told his "beloved Ginie" that he longed to see her and "hear so many things." She replied that she would value his contributions toward the book. He tried to persuade her to come to Beauvoir, warning that he had aged since they had seen each other last. But he hoped for a visit or at least a letter.[24]

Thus the correspondence with Virginia Clay unfolded, proper letters Varina wrote at Jefferson's dictation in her robust script interleaved with longing letters he wrote himself in his small tight handwriting. In the dictated letters, Jefferson provided leads for Clay's research, drawing upon Varina's knowledge of the press, and he offered to write a chapter of Virginia's book, which was in fact never completed. In another letter, dictated to Varina, he feebly joked that Virginia would enjoy a trip to England more if his wife accompanied her, since she knew the country well and loved Europe. What Mrs. Davis felt as she penned these words, no one can know. In a letter he wrote himself, Jefferson told Virginia that their lives had taken a "succession of tangents" and wondered why their paths had not been "concurrent" instead. He then asked "Dearest Ginie" if she had forgotten him. He saw her briefly in 1886 in Montgomery, where she sat next to him at a public ceremony, but her letters to him were breezy and polite, that is all. She sent her best wishes and congratulated him on Winnie's growing fame.[25]

Five years after this tortured correspondence began, Jefferson Davis learned that Virginia Clay was engaged to David Clopton, a widower from Georgia who had been her childhood sweetheart. Clopton had served in the U.S. Congress, then the Confederate Congress, and after the war he became a judge in Alabama. Virginia's bewitching manners had not faded with time, and Clopton's daughter claimed that her father had fallen under Clay's spell. When Clay wrote to Davis to tell him of her engagement in 1887, it struck him like a thunderbolt. He responded immediately to "Dearest Ginie," gasping that he would congratulate her if he could, but then stopped and wrote a lowercase letter *x,* leaving the sentence unfinished. He said that he admired Clopton and deemed him "worthy of the best fortune, but," then scratched another lowercase *x,* leaving that sentence incomplete. (He did this at least once before in the grip of strong emotion: When asked to give the death date of his son Joe, he wrote, "Pardon me I cannot. xxx.") Jefferson thanked Virginia for telling him and said it was "worthy of the tender love which has so long united us." He was "not glad, which is not possible." Then he blurted out, "The years have been to me full of disappointments and for the future I must as cheerfully as is practicable go on to add new links to the long chain which it is my fate to drag." He exclaimed, "God bless you, best beloved," and after apologizing for his poor handwriting, saying that this was the first letter he had written in weeks, he cried, "Kiss me loved." Virginia Clay evidently did not reply. She married David Clopton in 1887, and after he died in 1892, she remained a widow until her death in 1915.[26]

So Jefferson Davis still loved Virginia Clay. She appeared to be his fantasy, his siren, the woman he thought he should have married, the one who supported wholeheartedly the great effort of his life—the Confederacy—and was all the more desirable perhaps because she was unobtainable. His wife must have been the "long chain" he had to drag about. But Varina's love, on which he had relied so many times, did mean something to him. During one of the many donnybrooks about the war, an Indiana soldier alleged that Varina Davis had given him a bouquet after the capture in 1865, and when a Confederate veteran challenged the man to a duel over the allegation——interpreting the gesture as a romantic one by Mrs. Davis——Jefferson wrote a public letter in 1884 stating that in a "life of extensive social intercourse, she has never required such defence," yet if she had, she would have called on her husband to defend her name. There is no word on the outcome of the duel, but Jefferson was probably correct about his wife's fidelity. Yet again he played his part as a gentleman of the Old South, showing the chivalrous grace that coexisted with his iron will. Throughout the 1880s Jefferson sent Varina loving messages when he was away from home and assured her of his "long, long devotion." But he was unable to think for very long about Varina's feelings, and his affection for Virginia Clay had lasted since 1871.[27]

Varina realized that her husband did not love her as she loved him, and she said so in 1889 to one of her Mississippi neighbors, William Morgan. A thoughtful man in late middle age, Morgan was liked by both of the Davises, but why Varina confided in him is unknown, as is the reason for the exact timing of the revelation. Possibly she had witnessed a profound reaction from her husband when someone asked him in 1889 if he would like to have a letter by his first wife, Knox Taylor Davis; his brief reply, which he wrote himself, was yes. For whatever reason, she was candid with Morgan as she had never been with anyone else, telling him in a letter that she did not like the prospect of his daughter Belle marrying a widower. A young woman should not marry a "burnt out vessel" whose "successful" love, the love of his soul, had been ended by death.

Then she confessed, "I gave the best & all of my life to a girdled tree," referring to the agricultural practice of cutting bark off a tree to deaden the limbs and reduce leaf cover. Her husband was "live oak," she said, "good for any purpose except for blossom & fruit," and she wanted Belle Morgan to have nothing less than "the whole of a

Jefferson Davis in old age. (Collection of The New-York Historical Society)

man's heart." Then she asked Morgan to burn the letter, but he did not. So Varina knew that Jefferson did not love her as much as he loved Knox Taylor, yet she did not seem to think that he felt anything for Virginia Clay, which may reveal how much she misunderstood her husband. In an essay written near the end of his life, Jefferson stated on page 1 that it had been his misfortune to have lost his wife early in their marriage. He meant Knox Taylor. He mentioned Varina Davis in the last paragraph, giving the wrong date, 1844, for their marriage. Maybe this was just an error by an old man, but even so, his second wife knew she did not have his whole heart.[28]

Jefferson Davis nonetheless remained at the center of Varina's life, her chief responsibility and her chief patient. He still came down with mysterious fevers, and his weight dropped to a hundred and forty pounds. He was a less-than-lighthearted companion, for after the war he never told a joke again, she said. Their satisfying sex life was probably over too. Jefferson told his wife in Paris in 1881 that he regretted that he could not "like the Eagle" "renew my youth" and be restored. He promised Varina he would see a doctor she found for him, but thought they should "'accept the situation' in this the natural and inevitable decay of all earthly things, and by cheerfully yielding to the law, mitigate its decree." The situation sounds like impotence. He was in his early seventies, and his wife was fifty-five. She told one of her women friends that "it is in the evening of life that a discrepancy of age tells in married relations." But she felt obligated to remain at Beauvoir and care for her husband, explaining to a friend, "I must, as you know, stay where duty calls me."[29]

Their daughter Winnie was still single in her early twenties, a *rara avis* on the marriage market if ever there was one. The daughter of a notorious public figure who had been involved in two lawsuits and various other scandals, she was also much better educated than women of her time, in the South or the North. But she was ethereal, vaguely foreign, and famous, and she attracted flirtatious letters from suitors of varying degrees of ardor, such as an Italian diplomat who thought highly indeed of Miss Davis. There was gossip about an engagement to a cousin in the Farrar family, but Winnie fell in love with

Alfred Wilkinson Jr. during her visit to Syracuse in 1886. Varina Davis said she wanted her daughters to marry for love, and Winnie was in love.[30]

Wilkinson had much to recommend him, save his birthplace, New York. He was born in 1858, one of seven children of Alfred and Charlotte May Wilkinson. His paternal grandfather, a lawyer, was one of the founders of the city of Syracuse, and his mother's father, Samuel May, was a leading abolitionist. Alfred Sr., who did not serve in the war, inherited a fortune from his parents and had done so well as a banker that he had a seat on the New York Stock Exchange. Wilkinson *père* grew more conservative as he aged, and he joined the Democratic Party, becoming a close friend of Governor Samuel Tilden. Alfred Jr. had a privileged upbringing. He attended Harvard University, where his classmates included Teddy Roosevelt and Albert Bushnell Hart. Upon graduation in 1880, he returned to Syracuse to study law while working as a cashier at Wilkinson Brothers, the bank run by his father and his uncle.[31]

The bank failed in 1884, and the public discovered that the Wilkinson brothers had been speculating with the bank's assets and had accumulated debts of hundreds of thousands of dollars. The New York press covered the story, a classic Gilded Age scandal, and the brothers were deluged with lawsuits from depositors, creditors, and other banks, because the Wilkinsons had lied about their assets to obtain loans from other institutions. Feigning a poor knowledge of the bank's records and showing no remorse, they appealed two judgments against them to the New York supreme court and lost both times. Syracuse was astounded to learn that these pillars of the community had committed such acts, but the brothers did not go to prison, possibly because of their political connections. Alfred Wilkinson Sr. died in the summer of 1886, and his mansion on James Street was sold at auction to his son for three hundred dollars, so the widow and daughters were not evicted. No one accused Alfred Jr. of misconduct, and he does not seem to have known what his elders were doing.[32]

When Winnie Davis arrived in Syracuse in the fall of 1886, she must have heard about the "Wilkinson failure," as it was called, and she must have known something about the family's abolitionist background. Maybe she did not care after she met Alfred. He was handsome, well mannered, companionable, and probably one of the best-educated men she had met in society. As he squired her around town, they fell in love. Sometime in 1887 or 1888, he proposed. Winnie accepted pending her parents' approval, but she postponed telling them for months, afraid they would not consent, and she did not tell her sister either. Alfred's mother, described by Varina as apolitical, approved of the match. Jefferson Davis's daughter wanted to marry the grandson of an abolitionist, suggesting that the title "Daughter of the Confederacy" was an assumed identity after all, a role she merely inhabited, at least when it came to this important matter of the heart. In the spring of 1889, when Alfred came to Mississippi to ask for the parents' permission, Winnie said she could never love anyone else but would give him up if her parents insisted on it.[33]

Varina met him first, because her husband happened to be away from Beauvoir. Alfred made an excellent impression. This "well born Yankee," as she called him, was six feet tall, refined, energetic, and very much in love with her daughter. She knew that the white Southern public would object, but she thought that her family "had given all to the Confederacy" and so that she should not have to sacrifice the happiness of her "ewe lamb." Jefferson's wishes were paramount, however, and when Varina broke the news to him upon his return, he responded, "Death would be preferable." In case his meaning was unclear, he added, "I will never consent." But he agreed to see Wilkinson, and after he met the young man, liked him well enough. Then Varina had a candid talk with Alfred, just the two of them, about money; why she took on this traditionally masculine role, usually the father's responsibility, is not clear. Varina admitted that Winnie did not know how to sew or run a household and had no dowry because the Davises were in debt, but Alfred did not mind, since he had a flourishing legal practice. He reminded Varina that he was too young to care about the war and called himself a "States' Rights Democrat."

His statement that he could not help being born in the North was ir-
refutable.[34]

Alfred hoped that he would eventually obtain Jefferson's consent,
and Winnie, elated at the prospect, was like someone let out of
prison, according to her mother. A few months later Jefferson re-
lented, to everyone's astonishment, and a wedding date was set for
sometime the following winter. Varina dreaded losing her daughter,
because she would then be "alone," and she hoped the wedding was a
"long way off," but she approved of the match because Alfred's "heart
& habits" were "good" and his practice brought in five to six thousand
dollars a year, a substantial income for the time. The two families did
not announce the engagement publicly, and when Winnie became ill
in the fall of 1889, she went abroad with the Pulitzers to recover. Alfred had the good sense to mail his future mother-in-law a packet of
books and newspapers, and he assured her that he could support
Winnie in comfort. That would be very important to Varina.[35]

13

DELECTABLE CITY

THE WEDDING PLANS, which were sure to be controversial because Wilkinson was a Northerner, ground to a halt when Jefferson Davis died in 1889. In November he had contracted a cold while visiting Brierfield, and after the overseer notified Varina, she had him taken to the home of friends in New Orleans. There she nursed him with the assistance of a doctor. A few weeks later, Jefferson took a turn for the worse, and in his last hours he wanted Varina close by. If she left his side for a moment, he asked for her, and when she tried to give him some medicine, he whispered, "Pray excuse me," the iron-willed gentleman to the end. He passed away on December 6 of acute bronchitis, probably aged eighty-one. His wife had nursed him through worse illnesses, and she had not expected him to die. She broke down and wept, kissing him before the body was taken to lie in state at city hall. Winnie was in Paris and Maggie on her way to New Orleans when they learned of his death.[1]

Across the South, bells tolled, buildings were draped in black, schools closed, and resolutions were passed in honor of Jefferson Davis. Thousands of people viewed his body at city hall. White Southern papers praised Davis as the region's "beloved chief" who had led a blameless life. Most African American papers ignored his passing, and the white Northern press gave the deceased some respectful notices along with a few barbs, such as the comment by the *New York Times*

that Davis, the embodiment of the old planter class, had failed as a war leader. Friends gave their encomia. From Paris, Kate Pulitzer described him as generous in spirit, not the intolerant man the public usually saw, and from London, Mr. Grey, soon to be Lord Stamford, called him a courteous man who nonetheless despised the North. A few ex-Confederates puzzled over Davis's character. One man, quoted anonymously, said that Davis was so certain of his opinion that he did not listen to anyone who differed with him, never forgot a friend, and never forgave an enemy.[2]

The widow, long accustomed to doing her duty, collected herself and did her duty. In the days before the burial in New Orleans, she received callers and issued a statement thanking citizens from "all parts of the United States" for their condolences. On December 11, she went to Metairie Cemetery for the funeral—a long procession with orations and prayers—and afterward she wrote the letters acknowledging messages of sympathy. She then distributed her spouse's mementos, giving Fred McGuinness, the husband of Ellen Barnes, one of her husband's walking canes. Maggie and her husband returned to Colorado, and Winnie, still sick, remained abroad with the Pulitzers. As Varina acknowledged earlier that year, her husband never loved her as much as he loved his first wife, but she grieved for the love of her youth and the father of her children, and her grief was sincere.[3]

Her financial situation, specifically the idea of a government pension, immediately became a public issue. Jefferson evidently did not have a life insurance policy, and although he left Brierfield to her— the will was published in the *New York Times*—he gave Beauvoir to Winnie, some of the Dorsey properties to Sarah's kinfolk, and most of the rest of the estate to Maggie. Other white men of the postwar era appointed their wives as executors, but Jefferson selected his son-in-law Addison Hayes and his friend Jacob Payne, so when Varina needed money she had to ask them for advances from Brierfield's income. President John Tyler's widow, Julia, who died in 1889, had received a federal pension of five thousand dollars a year even though her husband had renounced his American citizenship, the only ex-president to do so. One national magazine, *Frank Leslie's Illustrated Weekly,* urged Davis to seek a federal pension, believing that the husband's sins should not be visited upon the widow, but she did not apply for one, even for his service in the Mexican War. A few Southern newspapers called for a pension to be paid by the ex-Confederate states, but nothing came of it, and Davis might not have accepted a pension if it came with a residency requirement. When Mississippi's governor asked people to contribute money for the family's support, she wrote a public letter in 1890 stating that she did not want "charity" and was writing a book about her husband. Jefferson had asked her to do it, and she was one of the first politician's widows to write such a book, and the only First Lady to do so up to that time. She reeled off the chapters, and the book appeared in the fall of 1890. She was hoping to live off the sales.[4]

As we might expect, a memoir written quickly in a state of fresh grief is deeply flawed. Almost a thousand pages long, this big wobbly book is replete with quotes from government documents and other writers, including her husband, whose memoir, speeches, and private writings consume entire chapters. Approximately half of the book consists of verbatim quotes from other authors. It contains some glaring typographical errors, such as the wrong death date for her son Billy, and the narrative is disjointed, with events discussed out of sequence. The prose style rarely equals that of her correspondence. The reader encounters long sections of eye-glazing boredom interspersed with passages that spring to life, typically when Davis discusses her friends, her travels, or antebellum Washington. She did not write an exposé like some famous widows, such as Mrs. Paul Tillich, nor did she maintain total silence, as did Mrs. James Joyce. Nor does the book reflect Varina Davis's experience accurately, and in that respect it resembles memoirs by other public figures, from Libbie Custer to Emma Goldman.[5]

In Davis's discussion of her husband, she indulged in much sentimentality and misrepresentation, a few scorching criticisms, and some telling silences. Her purpose, Davis wrote, was to vindicate her husband and the Southern cause. She called him a representative

Southerner, a patriot, and an outstanding public servant who believed in the Constitution. He could have been President of the United States if he had been willing to abandon "his own people," and he became the Confederate President only because the office sought him. But mixed with the panegyrics is her startling observation that this political man did not know the "arts of the politician" and would not have practiced them if he did know them. He believed so deeply in his convictions that he could not understand how opponents held different views, and, she added, sometimes he talked to her that way at home. He had a talent for "governing" people, she said, but he was most comfortable with soldiers, children, and slaves. Her treatment of the marriage is full of inaccuracies, such as how long she and her spouse lived apart during the quarrel over Joseph Davis's will, how long she was in England with their children in 1869–1870, or how long she was there alone in 1876–1877, all those separations telescoped down. She concluded that her husband was an able man of the finest character. On other matters—the "holocausts of herself," the wartime allegations of adultery against her husband, the train incident in 1871, the "girdled tree"—she kept mute.[6]

About the secession crisis, the same pattern of sentiment, misrepresentation, unorthodoxy, and silence prevails. On slavery, she recalled the "affectionate" relations between masters and slaves, and she claimed that the Constitution guaranteed the right to own slaves. The Confederacy had to be created, she said, to protect the rights of the South. Then she abruptly disclosed her theory, formulated before the war, that the conflict could have been avoided if Northerners had been educated in the South and Southerners in the North, revealing how much the regions had in common and moderating "extreme" political opinions, which is of course the kind of education she had. One of the book's loveliest images conveys her nostalgia for Washington: the Baches had rose geraniums in their drawing room, which created "a flickering green and gray light" on the windows, and years later the fragrance evoked with Proustian clarity "the old joy" of seeing her friends. She also provided new details about the secession crisis. During the journey to Montgomery in 1861, when young men told her they were eager to fight for the South, she found it depressing. But she said nothing about her oscillating opinions in the secession winter or her letter to her mother in June 1861, when she said she would "run with the rest."[7]

On the war, she was no more consistent. Most of these chapters read like Lost Cause ideology, drenched in sentimentality, and she dedicated the book to the soldiers of the Confederacy. She fully supported the war effort, as did most white Southerners, she claimed. Her husband was a great head of state who bore no responsibility for any of the Confederacy's problems. In Jefferson's disputes with Joseph E. Johnston and others, he was right and they were wrong. Despite the "utter ruin" the war brought, she concluded, she was proud of her husband. Beneath the Confederate pieties, *inter alia,* another voice can be heard. She informed the reader that she left her husband's inaugural in 1862 overcome with fear. Again, she provided new information about the conflict. In 1862 John Taylor Wood brought to the Confederate White House a bloodsoaked flag won by the Navy, which sent her to her room "sick of war" and "sorrowful" over the dead in both regions. But she did not mention her semi-secret correspondence with Northern friends and relatives, the William Jackson interviews, the fact that she nursed Union prisoners in Richmond, her comments in 1865 about the "inferior?" sex, or white Southerners "unwhipped of justice."[8]

With the book completed, she had to decide where she and Winnie were going to live. In Varina's eyes, Beauvoir was still Sarah Dorsey's house, and strangers kept appearing unannounced at the property. Someone burglarized the house when she was away, and she did not feel safe. Nor did she want to live at hot, swampy Brierfield, remarking in 1887 of the plantation, "Where our treasure is there is not my heart also," and she thought it nearly impossible to make money from planting. Varina ruled out living in Colorado with Maggie's family because she thought the high altitude unhealthy. She made a foray to New York in January 1890 to meet publishers, and by the fall she and her daughter took a suite in a local hotel, their arrival covered in the national press. She was in her sixties, not the ideal age for starting over in a new city more than a thousand miles away in another part of the country, but she considered it a "great boon" to be alive. As she told Maggie, she was "free, brown & 64" and could do as she wished. This sardonic reference to her olive complexion, one of the few in her writings, suggests that she did not accept the Confederate view of her appearance.[9]

DAVIS HAD compelling practical reasons to move to New York. She thought the rents were cheap, and among the several thousand white Southerners who had moved there since 1865, some of them, such as her husband's secretary Burton Harrison, had done well. Just as significant, New York appealed to Varina's imagination. She had always enjoyed the city more than the country, and *fin de siècle* New York was alluring after ten years at Beauvoir. Much like Paris in 1881, it was full of clatter and vociferation, her delectable city. The population reached 1.5 million in 1890, and Gotham was a true world capital, a beacon for iconoclasts, cultural exiles, and immigrants of all kinds, spectacularly multiethnic and multiracial, the nerve center of the publishing world, filled with boundless ferment in the arts and growth in almost every economic activity, and studded with magnificent buildings, bridges, skyscrapers, and museums. She had been born into a world where fires were started with flint, she told Maggie, and she lived to see telegraphs, sewing machines, and telephones. Travel, so dangerous in the steamboat era, was now easy and within the reach of many people. The world had made great strides, she declared, and she was not yet tired of living. She resided in New York for sixteen years, her longest residence in any one place since her girlhood in Natchez.[10]

The Davises lived in several large apartment-hotels in what is now the theater district. Varina described her neighbors as persons of "good standing" from all parts of the United States, including a Livingston, and, she noted with no apparent irony, a McClellan (probably the general's son, then a journalist). Varina and her daughter eventually settled at 123 West Forty-fourth Street at the Gerard Hotel, which was thirteen stories tall with more than 150 rooms. From her apartment Varina could hear carriages go by on opening night at the opera. She went to the theater, and she shopped at Macy's. She stayed up late, slept late, and read a great deal. Just as she had in Washington before the war, or in Paris in 1881, she liked to sit at the window and watch the city go by.[11]

Varina adapted easily to New York, just as she had to antebellum Washington, Richmond again being the exception. She began exchanging social calls right away with individuals from all regions, including Libbie Custer, whom she and Winnie called on at a Fifth Avenue Hotel. It is not clear who initiated the visit or what they discussed, but the friendship did not flourish, since Custer told a reporter afterward that Winnie was spoiled. For the most part, however, Northern society accepted both of the Davis women. While they visited Narragansett Pier in Rhode Island, a General Draper and his wife invited them to dinner with two United States senators and a cabinet officer. At the Gerard, Varina saw relatives, friends, and acquaintances who sent calling cards to her suite or had the hotel staff yell their names into the "speaking tube" on the ground floor. Visitors encountered a woman who was "large all around," as one described her. She had rheumatism, which sometimes necessitated a cane or a wheelchair, but aside from occasional chest pains her physical health was good. In fact, she had convinced herself that the extra weight—her photographs suggest she was forty to fifty pounds overweight—was the secret to her longevity. She dressed in simple, tailored attire and always in black. She was still a great conversationalist, according to Preston Johnston.[12]

After Jefferson's death, Varina had the authority to approve or disapprove of her daughter's engagement to Alfred Wilkinson. In the spring of 1890, Fred pursued his betrothed to Italy to press his case, and in April the engagement was made public. Winnie bought her trousseau in Paris, and because Victorian custom required a year of mourning after a parent's death, the wedding was set for late 1890. The Northern press either gave the engagement perfunctory notice or described it as a fitting symbol of regional reconciliation. A Syracuse newspaper declared that the marriage would end all animosities between the regions. The Pulitzers fully supported the match, thinking it a splendid symbol of peace between South and North.[13]

The reaction from most white Southerners was ferocious, heightened perhaps by Jefferson Davis's recent death. His daughter had become an archetype, and white people thought the perfect match for her would be a marriage to, say, a son of Robert E. Lee, as one man would have her know. A friend had warned Winnie that she would break the heart of every white Southern man if she married a Yankee, but the storm of opposition seems to have surprised the Davises. Furious letters arrived at Beauvoir and Syracuse, including one from a Confederate veteran threatening to kill Wilkinson if he married Winnie Davis. Varina followed the newspaper coverage closely and wrote a public letter defending the match. Wilkinson was not an abolitionist but a supporter of states' rights, she explained, and the citizens of Syracuse had been kind to Winnie. Furthermore, Jefferson Davis had liked the young man. She related that the white Southern public's affection for her daughter was a "rich inheritance" and that neither she nor Winnie wanted to lose it. Mother and daughter were discovering anew how vigilant that public could be. Winnie returned from Europe in June 1890, and both of them, and Wilkinson, seemed paralyzed by the public furor.[14]

One of Wilkinson's most determined enemies was Jubal Early, who objected to Alfred's abolitionist grandfather and charged the Davises with concealing this information from him, which Varina denied. She tried to mollify him by promising to discuss the subject of the engagement with him, but the old man would not be placated. Early and his close friends, Confederate veterans obsessed with the past, had fervently hoped that Jefferson Davis would not ask for a pardon on his deathbed (he did not), and they tended to have a proprietary attitude toward the famous Southern widows. One of Early's comrades, ex-Confederate general Lunsford Lomax, a college president in Virginia, said in April 1890 that he was sorry indeed to learn that Winnie Davis was engaged to a New Yorker. Feeling no compunction about interfering in her private life, he prodded Early, "Can't you break it off."[15]

Jubal Early most likely did not need much prodding. Some white men, described in the newspapers only as "Mississippians," began inquiries in Syracuse that summer about Wilkinson's background, while other unidentified persons contacted residents for more details about the bank failure, which they obtained. Then Wilkinson's house, the only sizable asset he had left, burned down. The newspapers reported that a servant might have accidentally started the fire, but other possibilities present themselves: a Confederate interloper—possibly sent by Jubal Early or maybe a volunteer—or a creditor who felt cheated by Alfred's father and uncle.[16]

The fire turned out to be an apt metaphor for the engagement. In August 1890, the Davises postponed the wedding, and in October the match was broken off. Wilkinson confirmed that it was over, and the story again blasted across the national press, treated with puzzlement in the North, disappointment in Syracuse, and satisfaction in most white Southern papers. Wilkinson was still smitten but reported that his fiancée ended the engagement for unspecified reasons, and, he said, a gentleman had to accept a lady's decision in such circumstances. Neither Varina nor Winnie would divulge those reasons to journalists. Other people speculated that Winnie turned Alfred down because she wanted to keep her father's name.[17]

The truth was more prosaic. Varina Davis was worried about Alfred's lack of money, and the possessive mother could not let her daughter go. Wilkinson's friends said that questions about his finances and especially the destruction of his house ended the engagement, and the ghastly parallels to William Burr Howell's bankruptcy may have been too much for Varina to bear. Her daughter would have married a man without a home, and Varina evidently did not have enough money to help them buy a house, as she helped Maggie and Addison in the 1870s. Yet other powerful motives were at work. Varina said in 1890 that only one person, Winnie, needed her now, but she needed Winnie just as much. Her daughter complied with her wishes, Varina once remarked, and this time Winnie did as her mother wanted. Alfred, whom friends portrayed as despondent, returned to his legal practice, which prospered, and he never saw Winnie again. In 1889 Alfred had predicted that their lives would be ruined if they were not allowed to follow their hearts and marry. He never married, and neither did Winnie.[18]

Varina's next task, selecting the final resting place for her husband, proved controversial for other reasons. An unseemly competition for the body began right after Jefferson's death, with almost every Southern state making its bid. Although she said she wanted to take a full year to think about it, Mississippi governor Robert Lowry, a former Confederate general, almost demanded the corpse in a brusque letter. A group of Virginians came to New York in 1891 to do some tactful lobbying, and after thinking it over, she chose Richmond. As she explained in a public letter in 1891, the coastline near Beauvoir, where Mississippi wanted to bury her husband, was eroding, and most of the Southern veterans who wrote to her preferred Richmond. In private she said her husband was very fond of Virginia. One Mississippi newspaper described her public letter as "pathetic," and some of her in-laws said that Jefferson wanted to be buried in Mississippi. The controversy rankled for a long time, and she was glad when the "grating and weary debate" was over.[19]

IN NEW YORK, Varina soon realized that she had to earn some money. Although she hired canvassers to travel the South to sell her memoir, she could not live off the book's proceeds, and Brierfield's sporadic income would not support her and Winnie. Beauvoir, which she deemed a "white elephant," she tried to rent with little success. In 1891 she and her daughters regained ownership of Tunisberg, the Howell residence that had been confiscated by the federal government during the war, but that too brought in little income. Varina received some financial help from her son-in-law, and Winnie had a small income from her father's estate, but it was not enough. The idea developed that she and Winnie lived in luxury, but they did not. In 1891

Varina pegged her income at less than a thousand dollars a year, requiring her to watch every cent so she would not be "dependent" on anyone outside the family. She had grown up in a world where no respectable white woman worked for a salary, and many Southerners still believed that they should not do so. William F. Howell's father-in-law disinherited his granddaughter, Varina's niece, because she wrote fiction for pay, and only a tiny percentage of white women in the Mississippi Delta worked outside the home in the early twentieth century.[20]

Varina decided to write for a living anyway. The Davis women sought work with the Southern newspapers, but in vain, so Varina began cultivating opportunities in the Northeast, again asking Charles Dudley Warner for his help. Within a year of Jefferson's death, New York publications began contacting Varina to review books, and an arrangement she made with Joseph Pulitzer's *New York World* became her main source of income. The city's preeminent newspaper and one of the most powerful in the country, the *World* was the first muckraking paper, both popular and notorious for its sensational news coverage, and by the late 1890s it had a daily circulation of 1.5 million readers. On women's issues, the paper took a middle path between traditional and progressive views, celebrating women's roles as wives and mothers, opposing woman suffrage, but calling for equal pay for women who worked outside the home.[21]

The agreement may have been Pulitzer's idea, since he already had said he admired Davis's literary flair, and he made similar arrangements for other friends. He paid Varina an annual stipend of twelve hundred dollars, and she communicated directly with him about ideas for articles. The paper did not use all of her copy but printed occasional articles, such as her account of a Christmas in Richmond in 1864, with an emphasis on making do with little, and her profile of ex-Confederate Fitzhugh Lee, whom she praised for serving in Havana in 1898, underscoring his descent from heroes of the Revolutionary War. She also wrote about seventy advice columns on etiquette, which were later published as a book. The prose was pretty good, not as sharp as in her letters, but other writers recognized that

Davis's contacts in the publishing world, especially with Pulitzer, could benefit them. Men and women began asking her for help, and Davis usually obliged.[22]

For the rest of her life she worried, not quite rationally, about money. By the mid-1890s, the debts owed by her husband's estate had been paid. She tried to avoid borrowing from his executors against

Joseph Pulitzer. Varina Davis's mentor in New York. (Library of Congress)

future earnings and kept her checkbook with meticulous care. She sometimes described herself as poor, measuring her resources against antebellum standards, but she was not poor. She liked to take cabs, and she had a maid, Irishwoman Margaret Connelly, for many years. Her summers she spent at Northern resorts such as Narragansett Pier or Bar Harbor. She had enough money to help other people, and she could be openhanded with female kinfolk. She sent regular gifts of cash to her impoverished niece Nannie Smith, and, after they moved to British Columbia, her sister Margaret and niece Christine Stoess, and she mailed money, food, and clothing to her niece Caroline Leonard, Joseph Davis's daughter, who was confined to a mental institution in Virginia and shunned by the rest of the family.[23]

Varina Davis remained a public figure, and white Southerners expected a lot from her. She could not cut the Gordian knot of the war. A constituency of white Southerners had been more or less imposed on her, and she was willing to do what she saw as her duty to that public, up to a point. She called herself "Varina Jefferson Davis" or "Varina Jefferson-Davis," and, contrary to Joseph Davis's anxieties years before, she never considered marrying again. In her articles she often said what was expected, describing Mrs. Stonewall Jackson in the *Ladies' Home Journal* as a selfless woman married to a heroic man. She joined the expected organizations. The United Daughters of the Confederacy, founded in 1894, named her their "Honorary President General." The UDC chapter in New York City was founded in 1897 by several other white women—although they apparently had her blessing—and a UDC chapter in Galveston was named for Davis. She seemed pleased when the Confederate Memorial Literary Society invited her to serve as an officer, and she went to at least one meeting, and when a museum opened in the Confederate White House, she attended the ceremony with her daughter Maggie. She apparently made these public appearances for free, although sometimes her travel expenses were paid. Her status as Jefferson's widow was enough for most whites, who either forgot, overlooked, or did not know about her war-related heresies. She was a living link to the great conflict, and people wanted to see her.[24]

She adopted her public persona at these ceremonies, which had all the spontaneity of a kabuki play: she was expected to smile, bow, and wave, but not speak to the crowd, and she did as expected, when, for example, a hundred or so Confederate veterans met in New York's Scottish Rite Hall. The UDC chapter in St. Louis said they could raise ten thousand dollars if she appeared at their meeting, so she agreed to go, although she said she would rather give them the ten thousand than make the trip to the Midwest. When her husband's body was re-interred in Richmond in 1893, she negotiated the complex business of who should be invited to the event and then endured the long elab-orate ceremony; feeling overcome by memories, she left town as rap-idly as possible. In her role as custodian of historical artifacts, she do-nated items to museums, expositions, and historical societies when asked. She replied when authors such as Pierce Butler requested in-formation about Judah Benjamin or William Dodd asked for informa-tion about Brierfield. (Dodd discarded most of her material, includ-ing the fact that she disagreed with her husband's ideas "very often" but understood his motives, and Dodd gave the wrong birthplace for her—Vicksburg—when he published a biography of Jefferson in 1907.) Varina defended her husband's wartime record, no matter what she really thought. She lauded his determination to fight to the very end in 1865 and criticized those who said he should have ended the war earlier, even though she had begun longing for peace well be-fore the fighting stopped.[25]

But there were some things she would not do. She would not allow anyone to use her name or Winnie's for fund-raising without per-mission, and she corrected false stories in the press, such as the tale that she did not want Mortimer Dahlgren, her husband's foe in the Dorsey suit, to obtain a government appointment. She wrote a public letter wishing him every success and wondering "who takes it upon himself to speak for me." She avoided summertime events in the South because she found the weather debilitating, and she would not accept every invitation to every veterans' reunion or every reception by the women's auxiliary, and she knew how to put people off, gra-ciously and indefinitely. She did not feel comfortable at these events, telling a friend that she dreaded going to a Confederate fund-raiser, and she found the "nervous tension" of appearing in public more difficult as she grew older.[26]

Nor would she give up her Northern relatives and friends. In fact, she cherished these ties. She made sure that Winnie met some of the Howell cousins in New York and Washington, D.C., and when Varina was in the nation's capital she visited her old friends without fanfare. When Northern relatives asked for genealogical information about the Howells, she replied and sent regards to "all" her kinfolk. When her Northern friends traveled to the South, she wrote letters of introduction for them. She corresponded with the descendants of Michigan Senator Lewis Cass, whom she knew before the war, and she and Winnie had them as their guests in Rhode Island one summer. She joined organizations far afield from the UDC. In 1892 she became an officer of the United States Daughters of 1812, for descendants of veterans of that war, and in 1898 the Daughters of the American Revolution invited her to join. To complete the symbolism, she was invited to visit Mount Vernon. She donated some objects to the house, including the Martha Washington quilt she received during the war, saying that she had always been interested in Pamela Cunningham's efforts to restore the house.[27]

Most important of all, and most perplexing for many white Southerners, she would not leave New York, stronghold of the North. The majority of white Northerners probably conceded her the right to live there, while black Americans for a host of reasons did not seem to care, but the white Southern public did care, and the skirmish went on for the rest of her days. Even now, some whites referred to Ulysses Grant and other Yankees as "foreigners," and they saw Davis's Northern residence as a defection, much as they perceived the Northern residence of Burton Harrison and the Republican allegiances of James Longstreet and John Singleton Mosby as defections. After Davis's devotion to her husband in his old age, and the panegyrics in her memoir, whites expected she would live, and die, in Dixie. Other famous widows, such as Mrs. Robert E. Lee and Mrs. Stonewall Jackson, spent their widowhoods in the South. In 1891 a veterans' group in Mississippi ventured the hope that Davis would come back to the South, and the newspapers reported that she planned to move back, but she did not. A Birmingham paper criticized Varina and Winnie Davis so severely for "abandoning" the South that the New York Times leapt to their defense, stating that they had the right to live where they wished.[28]

Varina went to the South every year or so to visit relatives and friends, but, as she patiently explained, the literary work was in New York, the cost of living was lower in New York, the New York climate was healthier, and she and Winnie felt unsafe at the isolated house on the beach in Mississippi. But the truth was, even if money, the climate, and safety were not at issue, she preferred the great city in the North. When the Richmond City Council proposed in 1891 to give her a residence for the rest of her life, she declined, even though she could have done her writing there, Richmond's climate was milder than that of the Gulf Coast, and it would presumably be safer than a house in rural Mississippi. At the heart of her decision to live in New York was an embrace of urban life at its most cosmopolitan, as well as an attempt to gain some control over her fame and her role as the Confederate First Lady. In New York, she was just one of many famous people, much like she had been in Washington before the war.[29]

Just as perplexing to white Southerners, Davis had a friendly meeting in 1893 with another famous widow, Julia Dent Grant. In June, Varina went to Cranston's Hotel on the Hudson River to enjoy the cool weather, and Mrs. Grant, who often summered at the hotel, happened to be there when Davis arrived. Grant said she had long wanted to make Davis's acquaintance and sought her out, knocking on her door.

"I am Mrs. Grant," she announced when Davis opened the door.

"I am very glad to meet you," Davis replied and extended her hand.

Davis must have been surprised, but she recovered quickly, and she, like Grant, followed proper etiquette to the last scintilla. They expressed great pleasure at making each other's acquaintance, thanked each other most cordially for the opportunity, and offered their individual hopes that they would see each other again. Over the next few days they met several times, taking an afternoon drive together and talking amiably on the hotel veranda. No one knows exactly what they discussed, but the sight of these widows having a friendly chat thrilled the other guests. One witness declared that they constituted the perfect symbol for the end of sectional rancor, in part because they met at a hotel near West Point Military Academy, which both of their husbands attended. Afterward, Grant said that Mrs. Davis was a bit stout but a "noble looking lady." She already liked Davis, she told a reporter, and she hoped that they would become friends.[30]

Much of the white Northern public was happy to agree. Varina Davis received a letter of congratulations from a Union veteran, and the *New York Times* proclaimed on page 1 that "Celebrated Women Meet" and a day later added that their acquaintance "Promises to Ripen into Warm Friendship." The two women did become friends. They lived about twenty blocks apart in Manhattan—Grant resided on Sixty-sixth Street—and when they took a drive together, that too was in the newspapers. They compared travel plans, and when Davis and Grant both happened to be at Narragansett Pier in 1893 and again in 1894, they had lunch. Winnie and her mother also developed a warm relationship with Julia's daughter Nellie Sartoris. A friend exaggerated when he said that Mrs. Davis and Mrs. Grant were like sisters, and Davis did not go to the dedication of Ulysses Grant's tomb in New York in 1897, possibly because General Nelson Miles, once of Fort Monroe, attended. But the two widows maintained a friendly correspondence into the new century.[31]

At first glance, this friendship seems to be one of the most unlikely in Davis's long predilection for them. Yet Grant and Davis had a good deal in common, and both had been public figures for a long time. Grant came from a slaveowning family in Missouri and possessed four bondsmen at the time of emancipation; after the war, she insisted they had all been contented. She drafted an autobiography, but never published it, and even though she enjoyed being First Lady, she too had been controversial for her faux pas, her alleged meddling in policy, her supposed influence over her husband, her attendance at cabinet meetings, and her physical appearance, including a crossed eye. Furthermore, the widows had mutual friends, such as Lizzie Blair Lee, and they both had sociable temperaments. When Varina was in Washington in 1866, Ulysses Grant sent a message offering to help her, and although they did not meet, she appreciated the courtesy. The widows shared something else, the intensity of the war experience and its profound effect on the memory. Grant told a reporter in 1893 that the war seemed so long ago that it was like a dream, yet she

Julia Grant. Widow of Ulysses Grant and friend of Varina Davis in New York. (Library of Congress)

remembered certain moments as keenly as if they happened yesterday, and Davis told a friend in 1894 that it seemed like a "troubled dream" when she lived in the Confederate White House.[32]

Varina Davis's public friendship with Julia Grant reflected views that she had held for years, such as her assertion in a private letter in the fall of 1865 that the existing government structure gave ample scope to advocates of states' rights, and in her memoir that Northerners and Southerners had more in common than they knew. These ideas were now at the heart of the reconciliation process underway in the nation at large. She had the right background for such a role because of her family ties, her education, and her temperament, and she was more comfortable playing this role than she had ever been as Confederate First Lady. Another requirement for the role was an ability to overlook the fact that slavery was the cause of the war, and, like most of their white contemporaries, Davis and Grant ignored the nation's failure to achieve racial equality after the war. At the same time there is no evidence that the two women ever had probing conversations about history, politics, or anything potentially embarrassing, such as Julia Grant's tour of the Confederate White House in 1865 after the Davises left town. Both women chose to overlook certain needling comments in print: Varina, who read his memoir, U. S. Grant's view that Jefferson was no military genius and his desire to escape at capture was understandable no matter how he was dressed, and Julia, the implication in Varina's memoir that General Grant had triumphed because of persistence rather than strategic skill. But Davis sincerely wanted whites in both regions to make peace, and she genuinely liked Julia Grant. Her friendship with Ulysses Grant's widow probably would have been impossible while Jefferson Davis walked the earth.[33]

14

LIKE MARTHA

 IN THE EARLY 1890S, Varina Davis again departed from the expected script in her thoughts on a key issue of the day, woman suffrage. In that decade, a woman suffrage movement emerged among white Southerners, led by moderate to conservative reformers from elite backgrounds. In an article in the *Atlanta Constitution* in 1893, Davis declared that antebellum women had been "sequestered" in the domestic sphere at the insistence of men, a practice that had perhaps been "erroneous." This tentative observation is the closest any First Lady came to endorsing woman suffrage in the nineteenth century; Varina's friend Julia Grant privately supported it without saying so in public. We might conclude that if it was "erroneous" to bar women from public life in the antebellum era, the error might be corrected in the 1890s, but Davis never took that step. Then she reversed field in a public letter the same year, saying that she opposed "women performing, as well as interfering with public functions."[1]

The matter did not end there, however, for Davis took a step toward suffrage in another newspaper article written soon afterward at the editor's request. She argued that the sexes were intellectual equals and women had the duty to teach their children about the Constitution—endorsing, about a century after its inception, the concept of "Republican motherhood"—but she feared that politics

283

would introduce "discord" into the home. Few subjects, she thought, created discord so "grave" as political differences. Her own domestic duties had been so "numerous and arduous" that she could scarcely meet them all, and she did not want any more responsibilities. Nor was she sure if women should take on male duties such as serving in the military. Yet she admitted that women were being taxed without representation, which was "an infringement of their rights," and she knew that some women had to make their way in the world without a male protector. This side of the issue she had pondered, she said, without reaching a conclusion. Then she ended with the observation that a woman's primary "duty" was in the home, and these were only the opinions of an "old-fashioned woman." Her belief in states' rights may also have inhibited her from supporting a federal amendment enfranchising women. New York women did not obtain the suffrage in her lifetime, and she apparently never joined any suffrage organization. Nor was she active in the New York chapter of the WCTU. Her friend Frances Willard spent most of the 1890s in England, and although they exchanged the occasional letter they evidently did not meet again before Willard's death in 1898.[2]

When the Spanish-American War broke out in April 1898, Davis hovered in the middle of the political spectrum of the day, telling a friend that she had hoped the Civil War, which she called "disastrous," would be the last one she would see. Eleven of her relatives served— all of them evidently survived—but she did not quite celebrate the fact that the sons of Confederate and Union soldiers fought a common foe, as many of her contemporaries did. She detested war itself and wanted "this awful war" to end quickly. Yet she as a citizen "of the United States" would feel "miserable" if America lost. In a magazine article, she declared that every "citizen of the Union" should be willing to fight for his country, and she called herself an "anti-imperialist" and "anti-expansionist" on the acquisition of the Philippines. (She also supported the Boers against the British in South Africa). She believed that white Americans might grant political rights to black Filipinos but would probably not allow social equality, which she did not believe in herself. Referring to the American Civil War, she asked,

"Have we not already sacrificed enough blood and enough money for the Negro race?"[3]

In a subsequent interview with a journalist she repeated these ideas, which many white Americans shared, and then turned sharply in another direction. She observed that almost everyone was a "half breed" of one kind or another and they were smarter than so-called full-bloods. Here was another startling communication from Jefferson Davis's widow, perhaps an oblique reference to the obsession with racial purity that swept the United States and the Western world at the century's end. Different kinds of prejudice flourish or fade in different environments, and her residence in New York may have prompted her to question the racial views she had taken for granted for most of her life. In any case, she was more moderate in this respect than Libbie Custer, sixteen years her junior, who believed that Mexicans were little better than animals, or Carey Thomas, president of Bryn Mawr College since 1894 and thirty-one years younger than Davis, who had a pathological hatred of Jews and people of color that grew worse as she aged. Davis's ideas on "half breeds" would seem to contradict or undermine her rhetorical question about the "Negro," but again she did not follow through on the implications.[4]

Her dispute with Nelson Miles resurfaced in the national press in 1898. He became commander of the American army in 1895, and he always felt that the press had portrayed his conduct at Fort Monroe unfairly. He may have been thinking of running for national office. For whatever reason, he reopened the issue in 1898 by claiming that Varina Davis had thanked him for treating her husband well at the Fort, and for the better part of seven years they exchanged testy public statements on the issue. She had not forgotten his attempt to lodge her with prostitutes, and in private she called him an unprincipled man. In 1905 she finally challenged him to document his statement, and he published the first two sentences of her note dated May 23, 1865. In the full text, Davis had thanked him for answering her questions about Jefferson's health, a somewhat different matter. Miles called for reconciliation and fell silent. He might believe she was a coward, Davis said, but she would not run from a fight.[5]

As the Miles controversy indicates, Varina's fame was undiminished. Images of her face appeared in the national press, so she was recognized in public. Correspondents saved her letters as historical documents—one recipient writing *"Preserve. From Mrs. Jefferson Davis"* on a missive from her—and everyday objects, such as two pitchers she gave a Washington neighbor in the 1840s, became historical artifacts. She and Winnie both appeared in a biographical dictionary of leading American women. She joined other prominent women in a successful campaign for the release of one Evangelina Cisneros, who was arrested in Spain for supporting Cuban independence. After so many years in the public eye, Varina became adroit at dealing with the press. She contacted the newspapers if she wanted to publicize something, as she did when she was too sick to attend a Confederate gathering in Shreveport. But in New York she usually went about her day unaccosted, and no Beauvoir-style crowds turned up at her door.[6]

Davis received what she called an "avalanche" of letters every year, and even with Winnie's help she could barely keep up with the volume. Most of the replies she wrote by hand, and sometimes she wrote all day long. She gave letters of introduction to friends seeking jobs in New York and responded to strangers who asked for her husband's autograph. She had to tell one collector that she, not her husband, had signed a letter in his possession. Because some of her husband's obituaries had indicated that Jefferson was still married to Sarah Knox Taylor, one writer asked her for Zachary Taylor's autograph, and she had to explain she was not the President's daughter. She tried to reclaim belongings that turned up in private hands as souvenirs, writing without success to the owners of some vases sold from the Richmond household in 1865. She received annoying mail, such as the letter from the Union veteran who asked what her husband was wearing at the capture, and unnerving mail, such as the letter from the Confederate veteran who asserted that William Seward had hired assassins to kill her husband during the war. To these messages, she apparently did not reply.[7]

Regarding her inner life, she tried to focus on the present and not look back, because, she told her Richmond friend Anne Grant, most people's lives were "swallowed up by time and the world knows them no more." She still had a sense of humor. Her size inspired a train conductor to trundle her and her wheelchair into an elevator, as she wryly told a friend, with the other heavy luggage. She tried to count her blessings, observing, "I have more than I deserve I expect." She attended the local Episcopal church, St. Stephens, and told Anne Grant that she turned to prayer and willpower to endure difficult experiences. Over the years, she had gained a little self-knowledge. She admitted that she became troubled about things like the biblical Martha, and although she wished she could act the better part of Mary, serene and unruffled, she could not. Her life had been "stormy," she observed, but her sorrows eased as she grew older, as the scriptures promised.[8]

Within two years of her husband's death, Varina had recovered from her grief, she confided to Anne Grant, and her friendships, especially with women, loomed larger than ever in her emotional life. She described her friendships as "sacred," and she liked to visit face-to-face, telling Anne Grant that she was "hungry for a long talk" with her, a "heart to heart talk," and "You will know how I feel." She told Henrietta Cohen she would like to see her "dear face" and closed with "the love of nearly thirty years." Her letters to Margaret Sprague Winchester, Constance Cary Harrison, and others were imbued with deep affection, and she was good at the kindnesses that are the stuff of friendship. When one of the Cohens fell ill while visiting New York, Davis called a doctor for her, and her condolence letters to her friends are models of sympathetic affection.[9]

HER DAUGHTER WINNIE led a busy life in the great metropolis. She worked hard at her writing, earning three to four hundred dollars a year, and she published two moderately good novels with Harper & Publishers. Both are concerned with thwarted love, and unlike some other titles published in the 1890s by white Southern women, depict Northerners in a sympathetic fashion. In *The Veiled Doctor,* a small-town doctor, supposedly based on one of her Pennsylvania relatives—not the protagonist in Nathaniel Hawthorne's story—is disfigured, puts a veil over his face, then discovers that his wife loves him after all. In *A Romance of Summer Seas,* a couple marries, despite an interfering chaperone, to live happily ever after in New England. The books earned some respectful notices from other writers and warm praise from Varina, who seemed blind to the possibility that she was the model for the chaperone. Winnie published a variety of articles, including one in the *New York Herald,* in which she called her father a man of excellent character. In the *Ladies' Home Journal* she protested the foreign education of American girls, particularly the struggle to relearn English, the ignorance of American history, and what she called the absence of wholesome contact with men. She placed other articles in magazines and literary journals, on such topics as Shakespeare's plays, German life, and the Christmas holiday, some of the pieces anonymous and some of them signed.[10]

Suitors may have crossed Winnie's path, but she did not fall in love again. She took an active part in New York society and met other writers, such as Poultney Bigelow, a Harper's author and friend of Mark Twain. She held a variety of honorary appointments, being a manager at the World's Columbian Exposition in 1890, and the next year was crowned queen of Mardi Gras in New Orleans. Hers was in some ways an exotic life. In 1898 she traveled with Kate Pulitzer to the Middle East, and Senator John Sherman, brother of the deceased Union general, wrote an open letter asking diplomats to extend courtesies to "Miss Winnie Davis of Mississippi." But Winnie felt lonely inside her celebrity, saying she had few close friends, and she had grown used to letting her mother make plans for both of them. Varina said rather plaintively that Winnie had not met anyone else she wished to marry, and Winnie called herself a "bachelor" because no one would have her. One of her neighbors believed that she never stopped pining for Alfred Wilkinson.[11]

Winnie had the love of the white Southern public, who rewarded her break with Wilkinson with its devotion. White Southerners did not seem to care that she lived in New York, maybe because they assumed her mother chose for both of them. Winnie received gifts, tributes, invitations, and requests for her picture, and yet more couples named their daughters after her. She appeared in the South at Confederate benefits, sometimes filling in for her mother. She too was expected to smile and say nothing, and she came home from such events sore from shaking so many hands. Again her peers lauded her composure, and she in turn wanted to be "acceptable" to her father's friends. At a Confederate reunion in Houston, Francis Lubbock, who had been at the capture in 1865, told the assembly that he had carried

Winnie Davis. The so-called Daughter of the Confederacy.
(Collection of The New-York Historical Society)

the infant Winnie in his arms, and as she embraced him, grizzled old soldiers wept. Maggie Hayes sometimes felt excluded by all the attention lavished on her sister, but it was hard to duplicate Winnie's bond with the neo-Confederate public.[12]

In 1898 Winnie gave her life, in a sense, for the Lost Cause. Mother and daughter moved to Narragansett Pier to spend the summer writing, and in July Winnie left for Atlanta to appear before a veterans' group in place of her mother, who was sick. After riding in an open carriage through a downpour, Winnie came back to Rhode Island very ill. The diagnosis was gastritis, but she expected to recover, promising her mother that her last novel would make money for them both. Varina felt increasingly guilty as she nursed her daughter, crying that never again would she send her child on such a "useless" errand. She needed Winnie too much to "sacrifice" her to give a crowd the fleeting pleasure of seeing her daughter, and she exclaimed, "I reproach myself bitterly." Her anxiety turned to fear, then terror, as Winnie's condition deteriorated. At summer's end, the hotel emptied out, and because Winnie was too sick to be moved, doctors arrived to treat her, but she grew thinner, weaker, and more feverish, until she died on September 18 at age thirty-three.[13]

Kate Pulitzer came right away to comfort the devastated mother, as did Maggie Hayes from Colorado and a host of relatives from the New York area. Varina received an outpouring of sympathy from kinfolk from all over the country and friends from all periods of her life, including Julia Grant and her daughter Nellie. Hundreds of acquaintances such as Adolph Ochs, publisher of the *New York Times,* the novelist Thomas Nelson Page, and Virginia Governor Hoge Tyler sent messages, as did Virginia Clay-Clopton, now a widow, to whom Varina sent a polite reply. From Syracuse, the Emorys telegraphed their sympathies, but Varina evidently did not hear from Alfred Wilkinson.[14]

Winnie's funeral in Richmond was a public spectacle. A multitude waited at the train station for Varina's arrival, and the wake at St. Paul's Church was jammed with people. Thousands more, including a brace of Varina's kinsmen and friends, attended the burial on September 23 as Winnie was laid to rest in Hollywood Cemetery next to her father and brothers. The casket was opened at the grave so her mother and sister could kiss her goodbye. The UDC and Confederate veterans eulogized Winnie as the ideal Southern woman, even as Pulitzer's *New York World* called her the ideal American woman, although neither description quite fits. The fact that her father was the Confederate President determined the course of her life and in some respects ruined it.[15]

Varina returned to New York with her surviving daughter, who stayed six weeks and tried to comfort her in what the mother called her "utter loneliness." In the 1890s she lost other relatives—her aunts Frances Sprague and Jane Kempe, her nephew Joseph R. Davis, and her brothers-in-law Carl de Wechmar Stoess and William Waller— but Winnie's death was of course much harder. If someone mentioned Winnie's name in her presence, Varina broke into tears, and on the anniversary of Winnie's death in 1899, she said they had meant everything to each other. She also observed that she had seen much of the "seamy side of life," much "suffering," and many "tragedies," none of which she described. She encouraged a friend to write Winnie's biography, but the book was never completed, and Varina decided she was not "heroic" enough to write it herself. She was happy to see her daughter honored, however, and she encouraged a group of Georgians who planned to construct a building called Winnie Davis Hall. She also paid for a window dedicated to her in an Episcopal church in Narragansett Pier where they both worshipped.[16]

⚜

AFTER WINNIE'S DEATH, Varina continued to meet some of the expectations of the white Southern public. She contributed money to a veterans' organization, and in 1902 she agreed to sell Beauvoir to the Mississippi chapter of the Sons of Confederate Veterans for ten thousand dollars, although the transaction took several years to complete because the parties could not agree on how much land should be sold with the house. She wrote an affectionate eulogy for her nephew, Confederate veteran John Taylor Wood, who died in Nova Scotia in

1904. Although she once referred to her husband's book as the *Decline and Fall of the Confederate Government,* confusing it in a Freudian slip with Gibbon's book on the Roman Empire, she insisted that all of Jefferson's sacrifices for the Confederacy had not been in vain. She became tetchy about what she called the "cult" surrounding Robert E. Lee, who, she said, knew little of politics. Regarding Jefferson Davis's role in the sectional crisis, she thought that, "unlike my dear radical husband, and his beloved equally radical friends, to whom I lay claim an inheritance, I believe much is achieved by compromises." What those radicals had done, and what compromises she might have made, she did not discuss. She thanked a young white Southerner for complimenting her husband, whom she called a "hero" for sacrificing the "happiness and prosperity of his family" for the states' rights cause, leaving unanswered the obvious question, was it worth it.[17]

Varina heard a new flurry of exhortations to move to the South, and she thought briefly about spending her winters in New Orleans, but her doctor advised against it. Some white Southerners expected her to return anyway. Her kinsman Edgar Farrar, a prominent lawyer in the Deep South, was "very critical" of her living in New York and said she lost "prestige" because of it, and her Richmond housekeeper Mary O'Melia never forgave Davis for moving to New York. The Yankee press observed that she "alienated" white Southerners because of her long Northern residence, especially after her refusal to live in a Virginia residence free of charge. She had a few defenders, such as Anna Farrar, granddaughter of her cousin Anna Girault Farrar, who thought Varina was a "human being with personal rights," among them the right to achieve some happiness and financial security.[18]

As we might expect, Davis had an increasingly contentious relationship with the Confederate organizations in Richmond. The staff at Hollywood Cemetery informed her in November 1898 that there might not be room for her in the Davis plot, though the matter was later resolved, probably at a committee meeting the next year. Then the Richmond "ladies" disagreed with her ideas about the design of a statue for Winnie's grave and a church tablet for her sons, one of many such disputes over public monuments in this era. This too was resolved to the mother's satisfaction, and in 1899 Varina went to the dedication in Richmond, which entailed another massive crowd, another procession, more odes and prayers. She felt obliged to go, she told Anne Grant, so she passed some wretched days in town revisiting the deaths of her children, and she attended a UDC reception with Maggie Hayes at one of the premiere hotels. The UDC's Richmond chapter paid Varina's hotel bill, although she offered to pay it herself, and then leaked the story to the press that one of the meals cost sixteen dollars. Davis told Anne Grant that she was already "unhappy enough from causes no one could avert," attending yet another graveside ceremony, but said nothing in public. Instead she paid the bill and told Grant she would never go anywhere again as a guest of the UDC. The next time she went to Richmond, she told Grant, she would arrive feet first.[19]

Behind this petty, vindictive behavior by the UDC were serious political differences about the war and its meaning. Most UDC members were middle-class and upper-middle-class women, and most were deeply conservative—more conservative, ironically, than the former First Lady—and nourishing a deep hatred of Yankees. Most were wholly dedicated to the organization, raising funds, running museums, celebrating Confederate Memorial Day, and urging members to read only those books that praised the Confederacy. The group, which had some fourteen thousand members by 1898, also experienced the infighting common to sectarian organizations; the United Confederate Veterans were similarly divided over reconciliation. Some members of the UDC tolerated the reconciliation process, while others opposed it, one white lady deriding reconciliation as the idea that "there is no North or South, but one nation." "No true Southerner" could believe this, she declared, and those "WHO DO should be ostracized" by the UDC. In 1901 a UDC officer said that Northerners should not be allowed to teach in the South's public schools. The militant, anti-reconciliation wing seemed to be more powerful in the organization, and they had Varina Davis in their crosshairs. They embraced the Lost Cause as a secular religion and could scarcely abide anyone who departed from its tenets. The authoritarian tendencies in Lost Cause culture seem to have grown stronger in the 1890s, when free speech in the South about public issues such as lynching disappeared. Mrs. Davis's Northern residence was almost more than these white women of Richmond could bear. The antipathy was mutual, although Davis expressed it only privately to Anne Grant. The idea of being buried apart from her family was "revolting," complaining about a hotel bill was "vulgar," and one of the Mrs. Randolphs of Richmond was "too high and mighty" for her, perhaps too much like the white ladies from thirty years ago.[20]

Davis had to deal with other controversies about her days in Richmond—the war, always the war—after she allegedly told a reporter from the *New Voice* in 1899 that secession was treason and sectionalism had disappeared. John Reagan, the former Confederate postmaster general, wrote to the paper from Texas, insisting she had been misquoted, and he wrote to Davis too. She denied the comments on treason but not those on sectionalism, and he conceded that whatever she said, she must have been sincere. Reagan liked her and had already tried to help her financially, an offer she tactfully declined, but he must have realized long before that she was unreliable on some Confederate questions. Because the original of the *New Voice* article has disappeared, it is impossible to know what she said, though her statements to a journalist from the London *Times* are just as ambivalent. During the secession crisis, she told him, she felt like a creature in a whirlpool, "helpless and drawing every moment nearer to the vortex." She thought the "birthright of our people," which she did not define, was worth fighting for, but from the beginning she believed the war was lost.[21]

She had to correct false accounts of her own life from such persons as John S. Wise, a New York attorney who was also a Confederate veteran and the son of former Virginia governor Henry Wise. John's memoir of 1899, *End of an Era*, contained many factual errors about the Davis family. Varina declined the opportunity to review the book, but wrote a private letter to the author instead. She objected to his statement that her sisters had been at a Richmond wedding, which neither one attended, what he said about their appearance, which was dead wrong, as well as his portrayal of her as a "well fed" mare who was a "better horse" than her husband and so powerful she could obtain promotions for Confederate soldiers. Her husband would not "submit to domination" by anyone, Varina noted, and she did not believe that extra pounds detracted from a woman's charms. The author blithely admitted fabricating the material on the Howell sisters but said he only meant to compliment Varina's good health by comparing her to a horse. Wise did not intend to imply that she dominated her husband, he said, and wanted to keep her good opinion. He closed with his best regards.[22]

Many people asked her to write a memoir of her own life, but she gently declined, saying that the prospect was too daunting. Autobiography is nonetheless seeded through her columns from the *New York World*, published in a single volume in 1900 as *Etiquette for All Occasions*. In answer to questions from readers such as "Young Housekeeper," she gave advice on how to make introductions during social calls and what refreshments to serve at a wedding. On the subject of marriage, her two voices, the traditional and the unorthodox, are evident. She thought marriage was a "life mortgage" and a wife had to make most of the accommodations. She also observed that there should be "plain dealing and true partnership" between spouses, especially about money. She thought it was remarkable that couples with "contending tastes, habits and education" stayed together, probably an unconscious paraphrase of her husband's letter from 1848 on her "habits, education, combativeness." Resorting to literary code, she depicted the bride's departure from home to live with her husband, whose compliments are replaced by "fault-finding," and she quoted Alfred Lord Tennyson's "The Lady of Shalott" to illustrate how the "web of her life" became unraveled and "floated wide" as the young bride "felt all the horror of the loss." In this poem from 1832, a princess in Camelot is imprisoned, cursed, and dies, destroyed by love. In a private letter to her cousin Margaret Winchester, Davis quoted the same poem, saying that she would like to visit her hometown and "pick up the threads which have so long 'floated wide' in the web" of her life.[23]

In her other columns, her ideas on gender went far beyond the rigid ideas of the Old South. She thought it wrong to ridicule a man as effeminate because he liked art or a woman as masculine because she liked to go riding, and she hoped that "the New Woman" would halt the custom of the sexes separating after a meal, when the men, "lords of creation" and "smiling sybarites," withdrew to talk among themselves and smoke cigars. She believed that the "New Woman" would "sweep aside" other forms of "barbarism" that might be masked by "gallantry." When it came to gender *and* race, the unorthodox voice also emerged. In one column, she translated and quoted with approval an article from *Le Figaro* that suggested that the woman of the future might be best represented by the American woman, because of, Davis said, "the intermingling of many races," and the "pursuit of outdoor sports." Few would quarrel with her advocacy of outdoor exercise, but the comment on race suggests that she envisioned a multiracial society of what she might have called "half breeds." But Davis did not take the next step and spell out the ramifications of her comment about the "intermingling" of the races—that segregation was wrong as well as pointless, and that lynching, which was often linked to the fear of interracial sex, was reprehensible.[24]

In her private correspondence, Davis followed her old habit of keeping up relationships with a few black people of her acquaintance. The Montgomerys stayed in touch with her, probably from a combination of sincere regard and enlightened self-interest. When she asked Isaiah to make a public statement denying the report that her husband kept bloodhounds to track runaway slaves, he agreed. The family wrote to her about their business ventures and their activities in the Negro Business League, which Isaiah co-founded with Booker T. Washington. They were longtime Republicans, but she congratulated one of them when he gave a speech at a political convention. She also corresponded with James Jones, who had worked for the Davises in Raleigh and Richmond. After the war, he too was an active Republican. When he asked for a recommendation so he could keep his job in the stationery room of the U.S. Senate, she wrote one, and she visited him when she was in Washington in 1900. These black men were probably her only regular contacts in the Republican Party.[25]

All this helps explain her polite greeting to Booker T. Washington when they met by chance in the spring of 1901. It was a quintessential New York moment. Robert Erskine Ely, whose acquaintance she had made, introduced her to the Russian anarchist Prince Kropotkin, who was staying at the Gerard during a lecture tour. Kropotkin, a sparkling conversationalist, was much sought after during his American travels, and as they talked in the hotel parlor, Washington, who gave a speech at Madison Square Garden in March, was announced in the hotel lobby. He wanted to meet the Prince, and Davis "expressed a desire" to meet Washington, so they were all introduced, and the three of them conversed "politely" on topics unknown. Washington had become famous following his Atlanta Compromise speech in 1895, with its conservative message of self-help for blacks, and he too was a public figure, accustomed to talking to persons of all political views. Perhaps Kropotkin, Davis, and Washington talked about memoirs, since all three had authored one; perhaps they talked about politics; perhaps they talked about the weather.[26]

In any case, Davis made a spontaneous decision in favor of civility, much as she did after her chance encounter with Julia Grant in 1893, although this conversation could be said to have been even more daring. Talking with a black man in this way implied social equality, which is why most white Southerners never forgave Theodore Roosevelt for inviting Washington to dinner at the White House in October 1901. Most black and white papers ignored her meeting with Washington, but it also probably would have been impossible while Jefferson Davis was alive. She may not have been willing to talk to W. E. B. Du Bois or William Monroe Trotter—assuming that they would have been willing to talk to her—and this single conversation did not turn into a friendship as her meeting with Grant did. Five years later, in a private letter, she swerved back toward orthodoxy. In 1906 she was offended when Washington seemed to imply that more money should be spent to educate working-class whites, possibly referring to his suggestion that boys of both races should get the best available education. She sarcastically called him Roosevelt's "ultimate friend," although she had met Washington on civil terms not too different from the president's dinner; what is more, a friendly meeting between a white woman and a black man could be said to be even more daring, in the context of the time. Davis then opined in 1906 that whites were "superior" to blacks, making no reference this time to "half breeds."[27]

❦

IN THE SPRING OF 1901, about the same time she met Booker T. Washington, she published an extraordinary article on Ulysses Grant in the *New York World* at the paper's request. The title, "The Humanity of Grant," summarizes her argument—that he was a decent person and a "great man" who did not lord his victory over white Southerners—as she refuted the argument that he was a "butcher." Because she had never met the general, she asked Julia Grant for anecdotes from domestic life and incorporated them into her essay. The article was partly a response to Owen Wister's mildly critical biography of Grant published in 1900, but in her essay Davis developed other ideas as well. She celebrated the decline in the "bitter prejudices" of sectionalism, which had been modified by social contacts, intermarriage, and education. Although she called herself a "Confederate," she said that advocates of states' rights simply had to make a greater effort to maintain those rights within the existing government, which God "in His wisdom allowed to prevail." She made similar comments in private in 1862, saying that if the South lost the war it would be because God decreed it, and again in 1865 when she told Mary Chesnut that states' rights advocates could easily make their case inside the Union. But now she declared her views in stronger language in a newspaper with a readership of 1.5 million people. Her true opinions, it seems, had emerged in public at last.[28]

Her friendship with the widow Grant lasted until Julia's death in 1902. Davis sympathized with Julia Grant when another newspaper article criticized the Union general, and in a letter to Julia she said both of their spouses had "unselfishly" served their own people. She advised Grant to ask another Union officer to respond and signed the letter, "with the sympathy of one who has suffered in a like way, I am affectionately your friend." After Julia Grant died, Davis could not attend the funeral because of illness but wrote to convey her "great respect and sincere affection" for Mrs. Grant. In an interview in 1905, after both the Grants were dead, she defended the Union general as someone who was magnanimous in victory, which her husband had specifically denied in a letter to Jubal Early in 1888. Like widows of famous politicians before and since, she expressed a number of opinions that diverged from those of her late husband.[29]

In her public appearances in New York, she tried to strike a balance. Within the first six months of the year 1900, she attended the annual meeting of the Confederate Veterans' Camp of New York and the annual meeting of the Sons of the American Revolution, both held at the Waldorf-Astoria. As usual she said nothing but was applauded at both events. In her private letters, the predominant theme is reconciliation. She apprised a correspondent that she was not a New Jersey native, as some people believed, and although her Southern birth was a "dear heritage," her Northern relatives were "by no means subjects of indifference" to her. She was proud that the "Howells of New Jersey" fought for their country, meaning the United States. She had a revealing exchange with Mary Mitchell White, a Northerner by birth and distantly related to her through the Davis family. The two women had words at a New York reception after Davis objected to the tune "Marching through Georgia." White apologized, and in her reply Davis observed that people in both regions would naturally champion their own views of the war. But now, she wrote, "you are ours, and we are yours" and "I, being a half breed Yankee on one side and Confederate the other, can understand both sides." This time she obviously meant a *cultural* half-breed, rather than a racial half-breed.[30]

Her skirmishes with the neo-Confederate establishment continued. In 1902 she disagreed with "the ladies" of Richmond about the design of another monument, this time an arch, and said the press gave her "an old fashioned setting down" and repeated some unflattering words "the ladies were said to have uttered" about her. Again, she said nothing in public but told friends, "Of course these things hurt me greatly." The issues of where she lived and how she supported herself persisted. When she was traveling through the South in 1902, someone told her that the "ladies" had declared that the widow Davis was supported by the "bounty of the South." Therefore, this person informed her, Varina should act like a "lady" and live where white Southerners thought she should live, somewhere, anywhere, in the former Confederacy. The astonished Davis wrote a statement for the UDC in which she objected to the "mandatory" tone adopted toward her, never dreaming that while she gave away family mementos that the public would somehow conclude that she was its "beneficiary." She worked for a living, she wrote, and earned about twelve hundred dollars a year, even though white Southerners often asked her for money because they thought she was rich. Her letter was read aloud at a UDC meeting, probably in Mississippi, and most of those present discovered for the first time that Davis supported herself. With some satisfaction, Varina Davis told her son-in-law that "there is life in the old woman yet."[31]

In her correspondence she explained, yet again, why she lived in the North: she had to work, and she did not want to accept charity, which she thought "degrading." She told an acquaintance that the Confederacy had cost the Davis family its fortune, which she had learned to accept, but that it was much harder to accept the loss of Winnie, who died after a public appearance for Confederate veterans. She found criticisms from white Southerners "unjust" yet hoped they would understand her point of view. By her reckoning, she had done a lot to fulfill her duty as the widow, but the fund-raisers, public appearances, donations to museums, and prolific correspondence seemed to go for naught. After years of living in Gotham, she was sick of the controversy about her Northern residence and tired of the demands of the neo-Confederate public. Now that Winnie was dead, the unorthodox voice grew stronger. In 1905 she said that the "Confederates" had "abused" her because she lived in the North, and she no longer cared what anyone thought. At age seventy-nine, she remarked, she looked on high for approval.[32]

In her last years, she shrugged off another set of old ideas about the propriety of women working outside the home. In 1899 she lobbied a museum director in New Orleans to hire Margaret Davis, the widow of her nephew Joseph R., as an assistant because she was a woman of "unremitting industry" trying to raise two children on her own. If a married woman had a career, Davis now approved. She was delighted to become friends with Ruth Burgess, wife of John Burgess, a Tennessee Unionist who served in the federal army and later became a dean at Columbia University; according to Varina, Ruth "made of herself a professional artist." In 1905 she told a niece who worked as a seamstress that although it was hard to "stand alone," she admired her "independence of spirit." These statements are most likely the result of supporting herself in New York for over a decade.[33]

Davis still worried about money, feeling uncomfortable around what she called "rich people." She kept writing, working quickly like a journalist, composing one story in about an hour. She had other financial resources beyond her salary. She sold some land in Mississippi for several thousand dollars, and because Winnie left almost everything to her mother in her will, Varina had a small income from a plantation in Louisiana, thanks to Sarah Dorsey, who had left it to Jefferson, who had left it to Winnie, who had left it to her. She refused to accept charity, returning a check from a Georgia chapter of the UDC because she would rather not take "gratuities." At the same time, she gave cash to her sister Margaret de Wechmar Stoess and niece Christine Stoess, two of her Howell nieces, and her niece by marriage Margaret Davis. Varina called them her "dependents," and she sent them money to the end of her life. She also gave money to onetime supplicants such as Beckie Hooks, sister of a white servant from Beauvoir who appeared in New York to ask Davis for help, and individuals who did not ask for her help, such as a friend who had recently moved to New York. Davis decided to have the woman's kitchen outfitted with appliances and charged it to her own account at Wanamaker's.[34]

Davis's fame persisted to the end of her life. At her grandniece's wedding in New York, the guests clustered around her and someone spilled a glass of water in her lap, but she kept smiling and greeting everyone, her public persona in place. In New Orleans in 1902, a reception was held in her honor at the St. Charles Hotel, and during the visit one of the Davis kinswomen said that Varina could be "most gracious" and was "much admired and complimented" but sneered that she had grown used to the attention. The Davises as usual misunderstood. Varina confided to friends during the same visit that she had "blundered" many times over the last forty years and did not deserve to be "honored" for what she had "endured." Journalists still wanted to interview her. She talked to Horace White, the veteran reporter from Illinois, for four hours off the record on subjects unknown, prompting White's cryptic remark, "If Mr. Lincoln could only have had such a wife!" In conversation with Randall Blackshaw, she said nothing about the war, although she was happy to talk about personalities she had known, such as Fanny Kemble, whom she described as large, florid, and eloquent. She told a correspondent that she knew a great deal of "unwritten" history but dreaded controversy too much to write it down. The "true history" would die with her, she said.[35]

The mail poured in, fifteen to eighteen letters a day, the missives falling upon her "in showers 'like the leaves in Vallombrosa,'" she said, quoting Milton. She loved hearing from relatives and friends, but much of her mail was from strangers and much of it pertained, even now, to the war. She tried to answer most of the letters herself, including queries about the Confederate White House. (Did it have a secret room? No.) When an old friend from Washington, the historian Frederick Bancroft, tried to locate a manuscript by Dudley Mann, she asked the Baroness Erlanger to assist him. She still received hate mail, such as the missive postmarked Detroit from a man who said her husband should have been hanged and she should return to Mississippi to make her "rebel yell." On the second point, he agreed with the firebrands in the UDC. She received worse messages, she said, all of which she apparently destroyed.[36]

She kept to her New York habits, staying up late, sleeping late, taking a daily drive, and receiving callers in the afternoon. She read newspapers, magazines, and many books on popular fiction, biography, science fiction, and exploration, such as Henry Landor's account of Tibet. She was also intensely social for a person her age. At the Gerard she made new friends, who sent bouquets to her room when she returned from out of town and again on her birthdays. When Frederike Quitman Smith, the daughter of neighbors from Mississippi, came to visit, they talked until one in the morning and the next day drove through Central Park. Relatives from out of town arrived, including her niece Lizzie Waller from Savannah, her grandson Jefferson Hayes, an undergraduate at Princeton, and the growing battalion of nieces, nephews, grandnieces, grandnephews, and cousins who lived in the New York area. Mary Bateson, granddaughter of Varina's niece Mary Stamps, lunched with her on Sundays, and Anna Farrar, an art student, visited often. Anna found Davis's humor "rich and quick" and described her as more complex than Jefferson, more faulty, and more down-to-earth.[37]

Davis traveled frequently, spending her holidays in Atlantic City, where she enjoyed rolling down the boardwalk in a wheelchair as the "humans various" went by like figures in the *Divine Comedy*. Once, to her great delight, she met Mrs. Hamilton Fish and her daughter. She also sojourned at Lake Erie and all over New England, where her "democratic" manners sometimes disarmed people not favorably disposed toward Jefferson Davis's widow. With friends she occasionally reflected on her life, which had been "checkered," she said, with some "stirring" times, which was something of an understatement. Varina still shied away from profound contemplation. She observed that "constant occupation about tangible things" was the best way to deal with loss, and when she thought of her griefs, she tried characteristically to interest herself in the "outer world."[38]

In 1905, her health started to fail. She had trouble with her eye-

Four generations of Davis women, 1905: Varina Davis, her great-granddaughter, granddaughter (left), and daughter. (Museum of the Confederacy, Richmond, Virginia)

sight, and she began losing sensation in her extremities, probably because she was taking doses of nitroglycerin and strychnine, then common treatment for heart disease. In 1906 she moved from the Gerard to the Hotel Majestic at Seventy-second Street and Central Park West. In October 1906, when she was eighty years old, she returned from a holiday in the Adirondack Mountains with a cold, which turned into pneumonia. She had already lived twice as long as the average life expectancy for women in her generation, and she had outlived all but one of her children, Maggie, and all but one of her siblings, Margaret. She did not have the life she wanted, which would have been a permanent residence in Washington, as she told Minna Blair in 1883, and she did not fulfill her desire to create some lasting work of art, as she stated in Paris in 1881, but she had always derived satisfaction from performing her duty to the family. She had told a kinsman a decade before that her faith helped overcome her fear of death, and now she was ready to die. Maggie Hayes arrived in New York with two of the grandchildren, and she was at her bedside along with Davis's grandniece Mary Bateson, her cousin Kate Pulitzer, her pastor, and a doctor. Davis expired on October 16, 1906, the anniversary of the deaths of her sons William and Jeff in 1872 and 1878. In her last hours she talked about the war—maybe a few words of "true history"—but no one recorded what she said.[39]

15

AT PEACE

BECAUSE VARINA DAVIS died well after the nation had embarked upon the reconciliation process, she received much more tribute than Mary Todd Lincoln, who died in 1882. White newspapers all over the United States carried the wire story from the Associated Press, as did a few black papers. The London *Times* also noted her passing. Many of the obituaries agreed on one idea, that she was a gifted conversationalist, but her unorthodox behavior provoked some surprising commentary. Mrs. John Logan, whose husband had excoriated Jefferson Davis throughout the post-war era, praised what she called Varina Davis's Spartan qualities, and Corporal James Tanner, the former commander of the Grand Army of the Republic who met her in 1896, described Davis as a "lady" who embodied the best of American domestic life. The Richmond chapter of the UDC sent a floral arrangement but issued a cool statement expressing sorrow over the death of Jefferson Davis's widow and Winnie Davis's mother. They declared that Mrs. Davis had "meant much" to the organization because she was "associated" with the war.[1]

Most of the press coverage divided along regional lines, however, in what newspapers chose to praise, report, or ignore. Northern papers lauded her friendship with Julia Grant, which most papers in Dixie overlooked, while the *New York Times* emphasized the fact that Davis had grieved for the dead in both armies during the war, another theme most Southern papers neglected. Only the *Washington Post*

mentioned Davis's remark that her years in the nation's capital were the happiest of her life, and her habit, when she was in the city after the war, of stopping to gaze at the house on I Street where the family had lived in the 1850s. Most Southern journals praised her as a perfect Confederate patriot, which was not accurate, and her marriage as a perfect romance, which was not true. The *Confederate Veteran* observed with more honesty that "many thousands" of white Southerners never accepted her decision to reside in New York, but defended her right to make a living there. Some people had long memories. The *Richmond Evening Journal* recalled that the Confederate First Lady talked fondly about life in Washington at her wartime receptions. The *Richmond Times-Dispatch* may have come closest to the mark when it observed that Davis had become a "stranger to Dixie" in her last years but was nonetheless "loyal" to her husband. Of such contrasts, irony laid upon irony, her life was made.[2]

Her will, composed in 1901, reflects these ironies. She gave most of her estate to her daughter Maggie, with cash bequests to her sister Margaret, four of her nieces, her maid Margaret Connelly, Winnie's nurse Mary Ahern, and her doctor, inserting the droll remark that the South was her home and New York a "resort" where she lived because of the climate. Her frugality had produced results, for she died out of debt. Her life insurance policy was worth ten thousand dollars, and the estates she inherited from her husband and daughter were probably worth at least that much, but there was no inventory of the estate. In a separate letter she distributed mementos—her books, her piano, her jewelry, and a tortoise shell fan—among thirty-two people. The recipients included Margaret McLean, her Northern friend in Richmond, her cousin Margaret Winchester in Natchez, and her friend Ruth Burgess in New York. She also asked the Hayes family to pay the costs for two friends, New Yorkers of limited means named Margaret Shields and Rose Hanratty, to go to her funeral. She wanted her "countrymen and countrywomen" to attend the burial and show "respect" for the deceased.[3]

The burial was another public spectacle. After a memorial service at the Hotel Majestic for family and close friends, a military escort from the U.S. army arranged by Julia Grant's son General Frederick Grant accompanied the casket to Richmond. An ecumenical service took place at St. Paul's Church, and then some fifty thousand people watched the cortege pass through town to Hollywood Cemetery, where Varina Davis was buried on October 19 in the family plot. A throng of relatives and friends, including Kate Pulitzer, attended the ceremony. President Roosevelt telegraphed his condolences and sent a wreath, and the white newspapers made much of the fact that James Jones, now an alderman in Raleigh, came to the funeral, although some of them reported the wrong name, calling him James Brown or James Johnson. Davis's tombstone inscription, probably selected by her daughter, read "At Peace."[4]

But the friction between Davis and her times was not yet over. The unorthodox voice emerged one last time from beyond the grave as she responded to her critics in the old Confederacy. In 1894 she had written a letter and given it to her Mississippi neighbor Judge Allen M. Kimbrough, a calm, level-headed attorney who had handled some legal business for her. Davis knew the Kimbroughs' daughter Mary, who studied in New York in the 1890s and later married Upton Sinclair, and Varina was fond of the entire family. During one of Davis's visits to Mississippi, the judge's wife, Mary Southworth Kimbrough, showed her news clippings attacking her Northern residence, and Varina drafted a letter in response. She instructed Judge Kimbrough to make it public after her death, and in 1905 she reminded him to publish it because it "justifies" her actions.[5]

So in November 1906, Mrs. Kimbrough read the letter aloud at a UDC meeting in Gulfport, Mississippi. According to one newspaper, Varina Davis condemned Mississippians in "extremely harsh" language for criticizing her decision to live in New York, and the letter caused a "sensation." An officer suggested that Kimbrough be censured for reading the letter, which did not happen, but the convention voted to keep its contents secret, after which the hopeless Mrs. Randolph announced that she still did not accept Davis's reasons for living in the North. The letter was never published, although a partial draft from October 1894, one page in length, survives in the Library of Con-

Varina Davis. The pensive widow.
(Courtesy of Mississippi Department
of Archives and History)

gress. In it Davis states that the "abuse" heaped on her was "unreasonable," including a newspaper article in Greenwood, Mississippi, describing her as "too stupid and spiteful" to write a book. She planned to address what she called three counts in the "indictment" against her: that she buried her husband in Virginia, she had not praised Mississippi adequately in her memoir, and she lived in the North. Her husband had told her she would have to decide where he would be buried, she said, and the publisher made her cut material from the book. There the letter breaks off, the remainder lost or destroyed, but press reports indicate that the final version repeated one last time her oft-stated reasons for moving to New York.[6]

The national press made much of the "post-mortem" letter, as it came to be called, with the *Washington Post* relating that Mrs. Davis used "severe" language to explain why she resided in the North. The *Atlanta Constitution* called her criticisms "tart" and said Davis was trying to "vindicate herself." Many white Southerners blamed Kimbrough for making the letter public, as did Maggie Hayes. She claimed that the Kimbroughs had goaded her mother into writing the letter, and that she had tried to persuade Mary to destroy it, but Maggie felt compelled to explain again in the *Confederate Veteran* why her mother and sister moved to New York—they were afraid to live at Beauvoir, they wanted literary careers, and Varina disliked the climate of the Deep South. Her mother "loved and honored the South," Maggie insisted, but had the right to live where she wished.[7]

After this last controversy, Varina Davis faded swiftly from the nation's memory. If Mary Todd Lincoln is remembered as the First Lady who went to an insane asylum, Davis is scarcely remembered at all; the town of Varina, Virginia, commonly thought to be named for her, was founded in the 1600s. She was forgotten in large part because she did not conform to the stereotypes of her time or our own. Her ambivalence about the Confederacy troubled white Southerners, and her life in New York violated the norms of the Lost Cause culture, for she became friends with Mrs. Ulysses Grant, had a civil conversation with Booker T. Washington, said in print that God had allowed the Union to prevail, died in a hotel on Central Park, and reproached the white Southern public from the grave. And most Southerners did not know that she had visited Union prisoners in Richmond, or the extent of her wartime correspondence with Northerners, or her thoughts on the war in her private letters during and after the conflict.

Since we know what she did and what she said in those letters, how do we assess her life? By almost every measure—including her education in Philadelphia, her relatives in the North, and her years in Washington—Davis was poorly prepared to be the Confederate First Lady. Her physical appearance, her wide reading, and her wit did not help, and of course her doubts about the Confederate cause worked against her. Her anti-war comments are probably more authentic than her pro-war comments, considering when she made those statements and to whom, and keeping in view the lifelong pressures on her to support the Southern cause. Her years in Richmond were the worst of her life, and after the war, the Confederacy was a burden and a blight, but it also gave her the opportunity to start over in New York as a widow. There she assumed a more congenial public role advocating reconciliation, and she rejoined metropolitan culture. Because she was famous, her long effort to come to terms with the war was a public struggle. The criticism she received from white Southerners only highlights how conformist the Lost Cause culture became, perhaps as conformist as the Confederacy itself.

She followed a long trajectory from Natchez to New York, which she was able to survive because her personality was practical and adaptable, but these traits coexisted with a Hamlet-like indecision on the political and cultural issues of her time. Her unwillingness to follow through on many of her own observations, her feints and retreats, her silences artful and otherwise, are understandable for a woman of her generation. The unexamined life might not be worth living, but her life might have been unbearable if she had examined it too closely, for she made many sacrifices for a cause she did not fully support and for a husband who did not fully return her love. In her old age she resolved some of the dilemmas dating from her childhood about region, riches, gender, and race. She left the South and supported herself, and in doing so she went far beyond conventional ideas on gender, although she did not endorse woman suffrage. She made some unexpected comments about race but never transcended the ideas of her youth. She made one significant breakthrough, however, and mustered the intellectual courage to say it in a newspaper in 1901, concluding that the right side won the Civil War.

NOTES

A NOTE ON SOURCES

ACKNOWLEDGMENTS

INDEX

Abbreviations

AL	William Stanley Hoole Special Collections Library, University of Alabama, Tuscaloosa
BR	Beauvoir, the Jefferson Davis Home & Presidential Library
DU	William R. Perkins Library, Duke University, Durham, North Carolina
GHS	Georgia Historical Society, Savannah, Georgia
HL	The Huntington Library, San Marino, California
IU	Lilly Library, Indiana University, Bloomington
JD	Jefferson Davis
JD Papers	*Papers of Jefferson Davis,* 11 vols. (Houston: Rice University, 1971–)
JED	Joseph E. Davis
Johnston Papers	A. S. Johnston and W. P. Johnston Papers, Mrs. Mason Barrett Collection, Tulane Libraries, Tulane University, New Orleans
LC	Library of Congress, Washington, D.C.
MBC	Mary Boykin Chesnut
MC	Museum of the Confederacy, Richmond, Virginia
Memoir	Varina Davis, *Jefferson Davis, Ex-President of the Confederate States of America: A Memoir, by His Wife,* 2 vols. (New York: Belford Co., 1890)
MS	Archives of the State of Mississippi, Jackson
NA	National Archives, Washington, D.C.
OR	*The War of the Rebellion: A Compilation of the Official Records of the Union and Confederate Armies* (Washington, D.C.: Government Printing Office, 1897)
RU	Rice University, Houston
TL	Tulane Libraries, Tulane University, New Orleans
TU	Special Collections, Transylvania University Library, Lexington, Kentucky
UGA	The Hargrett Rare Book and Manuscript Library, University of Georgia, Athens
UM	Ned R. McWherter Library, University of Memphis, Memphis, Tennessee
UNC	Southern Historical Collection, Wilson Library, University of North Carolina at Chapel Hill
USC	South Caroliniana Library, University of South Carolina, Columbia
UVA	Alderman Library, University of Virginia, Charlottesville
VC	Virginia Clay
VHD	Varina Howell Davis
VHS	Virginia Historical Society, Richmond
WD	Varina Anne ("Winnie") Davis

NOTES

INTRODUCTION

1. VHD to Rosa Johnston, 13 Aug. 1862, Johnston Papers; VHD to JD, 12 June 1862, JD Papers, AL; Paula Backschneider, *Reflections on Biography* (New York: Oxford University Press, 1999), 100, 122; Agnes Strickland, *Life of Mary Queen of Scots,* 2 vols. (repr., London: George Bell and Sons, 1893); Una Pope-Hennessy, *Agnes Strickland, Biographer of the Queens of England, 1796–1874* (London: Chatto and Windus, 1940).

2. "Mrs. Davis Dies of Pneumonia," *New York World,* 17 Oct. 1906, p. 9, WHC Vertical Files, MC.

3. Elizabeth Blair Lee, *Wartime Washington: The Civil War Letters of Elizabeth Blair Lee,* ed. Virginia Jeans Laas, foreword by Dudley T. Cornish (Urbana: University of Illinois Press, 1991), 110; JD to VHD, 9 Dec. 1884, JD Papers, AL.

4. "Mr. Yancey's Speech," *New York Herald,* 23 Feb. 1861, p. 2; W. E. B. Du Bois, "Jefferson Davis as a Representative of Civilization," in *W. E. B. Du Bois: Writings* (New York: Library of America Series, 1986), 811–814; JD to Ben King, 23 June 1885, BR; "Will" to "Kate" [Polk], 30 July 1864, Leonidas Polk Papers, University of the South–Sewanee.

5. Lee, *Wartime Washington,* 47–50. On women, see Drew Gilpin Faust, *Mothers of Invention: Women of the Slaveholding South in the American Civil War* (Chapel Hill: University of North Carolina Press, 1996); LeeAnn Whites, *The Civil War as a Crisis in Gender: Augusta, Georgia, 1860–1890* (Athens: University of Georgia Press, 1995); George C. Rable, *Civil Wars: Women and the Crisis of Southern Nationalism* (Urbana: University of Illinois Press, 1989).

6. Edward L. Ayers, *In the Presence of Mine Enemies: War in the Heart of America, 1859–1863* (New York: W. W. Norton, 2003), xix–xx; David Williams, Teresa Crisp Williams, and David Carlson, *Plain Folk in a Rich Man's War: Class and Dissent in Confederate Georgia* (Gainesville: University Press of Florida, 2002); Daniel Sutherland, ed., *Guerillas, Unionists, and Violence on the Confederate Home Front* (Fayetteville:

University of Arkansas Press, 1999); Noel C. Fisher, *War at Every Door: Partisan Politics and Guerilla Violence in East Tennessee, 1860–1869* (Chapel Hill: University of North Carolina Press, 1997); Stephen V. Ash, *When the Yankees Came: Conflict and Chaos in the Occupied South, 1861–1865* (Chapel Hill: University of North Carolina Press, 1995), 108–130; Richard Nelson Current, *Lincoln's Loyalists: Union Soldiers from the Confederacy* (Boston: Northeastern University Press, 1992); Daniel Crofts, *Reluctant Confederates: Upper South Unionists in the Secession Crisis* (Chapel Hill: University of North Carolina Press, 1989); Philip Paludan, *Victims: A True Story of the Civil War* (Knoxville: University of Tennessee Press, 1981); Paul D. Escott, *After Secession: Jefferson Davis and the Failure of Confederate Nationalism* (Baton Rouge: Louisiana State University Press, 1978); James L. Roark, *Masters without Slaves: Southern Planters in the Civil War and Reconstruction* (New York: W. W. Norton, 1977), 55–58; Carl N. Degler, *The Other South: Southern Dissenters in the Nineteenth Century* (New York: Harper and Row, 1974). Cf. Gary Gallagher, *The Confederate War* (Cambridge, Mass.: Harvard University Press, 1997), and James M. McPherson, *Battle Cry of Freedom: The Civil War Era* (New York: Oxford University Press, 1988), who argue that the majority of Southern whites strongly supported the Confederacy.

7. *Memoir,* 1:222; Jean H. Baker, *Mary Todd Lincoln: A Biography* (New York: W. W. Norton, 1987), 136–141, 226, 238–239, 241; Henry Kyd Douglas, *I Rode with Stonewall* (Chapel Hill: University of North Carolina Press, 1940), 272.

8. William Howard Russell, *My Diary North and South,* ed. and with an introduction by Fletcher Pratt (New York: Harper and Bros., 1954), 46, 32–33; John W. Burgess, *Reminiscences of an American Scholar: The Beginnings of Columbia University,* with a foreword by Nicholas Murray Butler (New York: Columbia University Press, 1934), 292; Carl Sferrazza Anthony, *First Ladies: The Saga of the Presidents' Wives and Their Power 1789–1961* (New York: William Morrow, 1990), 164, 172–174; Lee, *Wartime Washington,* 61; Betty Boyd Caroli, *First Ladies,* expanded ed. (New York: Oxford University, 1995), 71; Wendy Hamand Venet, *Neither Ballots nor Bullets: Women Abolitionists and the Civil War* (Charlottesville: University Press of Virginia, 1991), 123, 76; Baker, *Mary Todd Lincoln,* 198, 222, 224, 326–330.

9. Charles Reagan Wilson, *Baptized in Blood: The Religion of the Lost Cause, 1865–1920* (Athens: University of Georgia Press, 1980), 1; Leo Braudy, *The Frenzy of Renown: Fame and Its History* (New York: Oxford University Press, 1986), 5.

10. William C. Davis, *Jefferson Davis: The Man and His Hour* (New York: HarperCollins, 1991); William J. Cooper Jr., *Jefferson Davis, American* (New York: Alfred A. Knopf, 2000).

1. HALF BREED

1. VHD to Varina H. D. Hayes, 15 June 1895, VHD to Jefferson Hayes-Davis, 20 May 1894, JD and Family Papers, MS; VHD to Anne Grant, 21 Oct. n.d. [1896], JD Family Coll., MC; VHD, "Self life sketch," n.p., n.d. [mid-1890s], JD Papers, AL.

2. VHD to Anne Grant, 25 Apr. 1898, JD Family Coll., MC; "Aunt Bettie" to Lise Hamer, 20 Mar. 1899, Mitchell Family Papers, TL; Anna Farrar Goldsborough, "Notes on Varina Howell Davis," 15, JD Assoc., RU.

3. VHD to James G. Holmes, 26 Mar. 1896, A. J. Eastwood Library, Limestone College; VHD to "Dear Sir," 11 Apr. 1896, JD Family Coll., MC; VHD to Anne E. Snyder, 9 May 1897, Autograph File: D, Houghton Library, Harvard Univ.; VHD to "Dear Ladies," 1 May 1899, Mount Vernon Ladies Assoc.; VHD to JD, 7 Sept. 1871, JD Papers, AL; VHD to Amy Thin Bowie, 22 Sept. 1899, JD and Family Papers, MS; VHD to Henry T. Louthan, 20 Nov. 1898, Henry T. Louthan Papers, VHS; VHD to Addison Hayes, n.d. May 1905, JD and Family Papers, MS; *JD Papers,* 2:121–122n.

4. VHD, "Self life sketch," n.p., JD Papers, AL.

5. VHD to Mary Mitchell White, 19 Feb. 1905, in Mary Mitchell White, "Interludes," JD Assoc., RU; VHD to William B. Howell, 14 Nov. 1858, JD Papers, AL; VHD to Varina D. Howell, 1 Oct. 1905, BR.

6. Gilbert Cope, *Genealogy of the Sharpless Family, Descended from John and Jane Sharpless, Settlers near Chester, Pennsylvania* (Philadelphia: Published for the Family, Under the Auspices of the Bi-Centennial Committee, 1887), 324, 204–205; Deed, Stephen Ayars to Ebenezer Howell, 8 Dec. 1768, Secretary of State's Office, Deeds, Surveys, and Commissions, c. 1650–1856, New Jersey State Archives; Tax Ratable for Ebenezer Howell, Sept. 1779, New Jersey General Assembly, Stoe Creek Township, Cumberland County, New Jersey State Archives; Will of Ebenezer Howell, 13 Oct. 1785, Secretary of State's Office, Wills and Inventories, New Jersey State Archives; VHD to General Read, n.d., JD Family Coll., MC.

7. Paul A. Stellhorn and Michael J. Birkner, eds., *The Governors of New Jersey, 1664–1974: Biographical Essays* (Trenton: New Jersey Historical Commission, 1982), 84; John T. Cunningham, *This Is New Jersey,* rev. ed. (New Brunswick: Rutgers University Press, 1968), 174; VHD to William E. Dodd, 16 June 1905, William E. Dodd Papers, LC; Richard Howell to George Read, 10 July 1776, Edwin A. Ely Coll., New Jersey Historical Society; Daniel Agnew, "A Biographical Sketch of Governor Richard Howell of New Jersey," *Pennsylvania Magazine of History and Biography* 22 (n.d. 1898): 221–230; Daniel Agnew to VHD, 19 Oct. 1880, JD Family Coll., MC; John Meredith Read to VHD, 26 Mar. 1888, JD Family Coll., MC.

8. Rudolph J. Pasler and Margaret C. Pasler, *The New Jersey Federalists* (Rutherford, N.J.: Fairleigh Dickinson University Press, 1975), 52, 61–62, 67 n. 10; Richard Howell, General Order, 29 Sept. 1794, William Leddell Papers, New Jersey Historical Society; Franklin Ellis, *History of Monmouth County, New Jersey* (1885; repr., Cottonport, La.: Shrewsbury Historical Society, 1974), 646; George Washington, *The Papers of George Washington, Presidential Series,* ed. W. W. Abbot, Dorothy Twohig, Philander D. Chase, and Beverly Runge (Charlottesville: University Press of Virginia, 1987), 2:108–109; George Washington, *The Diaries of George Washington,* eds. Donald Jackson and Dorothy Twohig (Charlottesville: University Press of Virginia, 1979), 6:193; Stellhorn and Birkner, *New Jersey Governors,* 85; Edward Raymond Turner, "Women's Suffrage in New Jersey, 1790–1807," *Smith College Studies in History* 1 (July 1916): 169–170.

9. Obituary for Richard Howell, 4 May 1802, *The Federalist & New Jersey State Gazette,* New Jersey State Archives; Richard Howell to Israel Shreve, 5 Oct. 1778, Israel Shreve Papers, Rutgers Univ. Libraries, New Brunswick; Larry R. Gerlach, ed., *New*

Jersey in the American Revolution, 1763–1783: A Documentary History (Trenton: New Jersey Historical Commission, 1975), 140; Christine I. De Wechmar Stoess, comp. Lorraine Chapman, "Episodes in the Life of Margaret Graham Howell," 8, 11, JD Assoc., RU; A. N. Cole to JD, 3 Apr. 1888, JD Family Coll., MC.

10. Charles Burr Todd, *A General History of the Burr Family in America, with a Genealogical Record from 1570 to 1878* (New York: E. Wells Sackett and Bro., 1878), 369, 373; VHD to Lydia C. M. Purnell, 10 Apr. 1881, typescript, JD Assoc., RU; Cope, *Genealogy of the Sharpless Family,* 325–326; Stoess, "Episodes," 13, JD Assoc., RU; Pasler and Pasler, *New Jersey Federalists,* 210; Will of Keziah Burr Howell, 13 May 1813, Office of the Register of Wills, Court of Common Pleas, County of Allegheny, Penn.; William B. Howell to Robert J. Walker, 20 July 1846, Robert J. Walker Papers, LC; Daniel Agnew to VHD, 19 Oct. 1880, JD Family Coll., MC; William B. Howell to VHD, 11 Aug. 1857, JD Papers, LC; VHD to William B. Howell, 14 Nov. 1858, JD Papers, AL; Genealogy of Richard Howell and Descendants, Howell Family Papers, HL; VHD to Mrs. Owen, 23 Feb. 1901, JD Family Coll., MC; Sarah Agnew to Joseph B. Howell, 22 Feb. 1861, Howell Family Papers, HL; Cope, *Genealogy of the Sharpless Family,* 325–326, 533–534; tombstone of William B. Howell, Oakwood Cemetery, Montgomery, Ala., author's visit, 1995; Federal Census of 1850, New Jersey, Mercer County, n.p. William's sister Maria died unmarried, and his brother Charles died in 1822. Aaron Burr was Keziah Burr Howell's cousin; see *Memoir,* 1:553.

11. Daniel Agnew to VHD, 19 Oct. 1880, JD Family Coll., MC; VHD to Thomas Scharfe, 22 May 1889, JD Papers, DU; "Genealogy & Notes," Howell Family Papers, HL; VHD to Lydia C. M. Purnell, 10 Apr. 1881, typescript, JD Assoc., RU; VHD to Col. Marchant, 8 June 1889, Varina Howell Davis Letters, VHS; VHD to "My very dear friends," 7 Mar. 1906, Kimbrough Family Papers, Mississippi State Univ.

12. VHD to General Read, n.d., JD Family Coll., MC; Abel Bowen, *The Naval Monument, Containing Official and Other Accounts of All the Battles Fought between the Navies of the United States and Great Britain during the Late War,* rev. ed. (Boston: George Clark, 1840), 153–154, 160, 163, Ohio Historical Society; VHD to Richard F. Reed, 3 June 1898, copy at JD Assoc., RU; William B. Howell to A. Dallas, 1 Aug. 1815, Record Group 94, NA; John Hebron Moore, *The Emergence of the Cotton Kingdom in the Old Southwest: Mississippi, 1770–1860* (Baton Rouge: Louisiana State University Press, 1988), 188; VHD to Lydia C. M. Purnell, 10 Apr. 1881, typescript, JD Assoc., RU.

13. Charles Sackett Sydnor, *Slavery in Mississippi* (Gloucester, Mass.: Peter Smith, 1965), vii, 5 n. 11; D. Clayton James, *Antebellum Natchez* (Baton Rouge: Louisiana State University Press, 1968), 1–76, 136–161; Michael Wayne, *The Reshaping of Plantation Society: The Natchez District, 1860–1880* (Baton Rouge: Louisiana State University Press, 1983), 1–15.

14. Tombstones, Natchez City Cemetery, author's visit, 1995; James, *Antebellum Natchez,* 164; Leo E. Turitz and Evelyn Turitz, *Jews in Early Mississippi* (Jackson: University Press of Mississippi, 1983), 11–18; James, *Antebellum Natchez,* 236 n. 30, 163,

265; Joseph Holt Ingraham, *The South-West, by a Yankee,* 2 vols. (New York: Harper and Bro., 1835), 2:35, 45–48.

15. James, *Antebellum Natchez,* 81, 144, 161n, 170; Deed Book N, p. 129, Deed Book O, p. 315, Chancery Court, Natchez, Adams County Courthouse; *JD Papers,* 2:124 n. 8.

16. Goldsborough, "Notes on Varina Howell Davis," 13–14, JD Assoc., RU; Edward Maclysaght, *The Surnames of Ireland,* 6th ed. (Dublin: Irish Academic Press, 1785), 175; A. Campbell, "A Historical Reminiscence," *Natchez Courier,* 7 July 1837, JD and Family Papers, MS; Deeds, K, 1758–1768, Book 217, p. 133, Book 247, p. 214, Registry of Deeds, Dublin; Register 1740, Registry 1784, Registry of Plate, Degrees and Censures, Manuscripts Room, Trinity College Dublin; T. C. De Leon, *Belles, Beaux and Brains of the 60's* (New York: G. W. Dillingham Co., 1909), 68; VHD to General Read, n.d., JD Family Coll., MC; Martha Eheart King, "James Kempe," *Virginia Genealogist* (Jan.–Mar. 1977): 3–6; Henry S. Foote, *Casket of Reminiscences* (Washington, D.C.: Chronicle Publishing Co., 1874), 178–179; *Louisiana Portraits,* comp. Mrs. Thomas N. C. Bruns (n.p.: National Society of the Colonial Dames of America in the State of Louisiana, 1975), 147.

17. James Balfour Paul, ed., *The Scots Peerage* (Edinburgh: David Douglas, 1909), 4:142–165; Christening Record of George Graham, Port of Monteith, Frame 96, 388/1, 31 Aug. 1742, New Register House, General Register House, Edinburgh; W. Innes Addison, *The Matriculation Albums of the University of Glasgow from 1728 to 1858* (Glasgow: James Maclehouse and Sons, 1913), 58; Class Lists of Alexander Monro, 1750–1765, Student 121, 1761, Student 84, 1762–1763, Special Colls., Univ. of Edinburgh; King, "James Kempe," 5–7; Federal Census of 1810, Prince William County, Virginia, n.p.; VHD to "My very dearly beloved old Friend," 26 Apr. 1890, JD Papers, AL.

18. Foote, *Casket of Reminiscences,* 179; Jane Kempe to "My Dear Nannie," 6 Jan. 1876, Richardson and Farrar Papers, UNC; King, "James Kempe," 7–9; Thomas B. Kempe vs. James Kempe et al., File 11, Chancery Court, Public notice by clerk of court, 6 Jan. 1873, J. S. Adams to E. E. Meredith, 20 Jan. 1881, Office of the Circuit Court, Prince William County, Va.; Company Muster Roll, Hinds' Battalion, James Kempe, 1813–1815, NA.

19. Land Deed, Deed Book A-4/326s, 19 Feb. 1810, David and Frances Pannel to James Kempe, Clerk's Office, Seventh Judicial District Court, Concordia Parish, La.; VHD to Mrs. Owen, 23 Feb. 1901, JD Family Coll., MC; Tax Records, State of Mississippi, Adams County, 1825, Estate of James Kempe, p. 5; VHD, "Self life sketch," n.p., JD Papers, AL; Deed Book 3-G, p. 478, Chancery Court, Natchez, Adams County Courthouse; Roger W. Shugg, *Origins of Class Struggle in Louisiana: A Social History of White Farmers and Laborers during Slavery and after, 1840–1875* (Baton Rouge: Louisiana State University Press, 1938), 6–7; *Memoir,* 1:552; Tax Records, State of Mississippi, Adams County, 1823, Estate of James Kempe, p. 6; VHD to Mrs. Nevitt F. Baker, 16 Mar. 1899, typescript, JD Assoc., RU.

20. VHD to Mrs. Nevitt F. Baker, 16 Mar. 1899, typescript, JD Assoc., RU; James Kempe to unnamed person, 9 Jan. 1815, James Kempe Letter, UNC; James

Kempe, Hinds' Battalion Cavalry, War of 1812, Compiled Military Service Records, Record Group 94, Records of the Adjutant General's Office, 1780s–1917, NA; VHD to General Read, n.d. [post 1865], JD Family Coll., MC; Stoess, "Episodes," 15, JD Assoc., RU; M. P. Stringer to VHD, 1 June 1863, JD Family Coll., MC; Goldsborough, "Notes on Varina Howell Davis," 14, JD Assoc., RU; Francis Girault to "Ann," 12 Feb. 1815, Girault Family Papers, MS; James, *Antebellum Natchez*, 150; *Marriages and Deaths from Mississippi Newspapers*, vol. 2: *1801–1850*, comp. Betty Couch Wiltshire (n.p., Heritage Books, n.d.), 118; Marriage Contract between Sturges Sprague and Frances E. Kempe, Deed Book N, pp. 268–271, Chancery Court, Natchez, Adams County Courthouse; VHD to William Hunter, 23 Apr. 1887, JD Papers, DU.

21. James Kempe's Estate, Probate Record, A/246, 1813–1824, pp. 246–251, Concordia Parish Courthouse, La.; Orphan's Court Minutes, Book 5, Sept. 1827, p. 80, Chancery Court, Natchez, Adams County Courthouse; VHD to Varina D. Bonney, 6 June 1884, Subject File, Varina Howell Davis, MS; VHD to Mrs. Owen, 23 Feb. 1901, JD Family Coll., MC; William B. Howell to Joseph B. Howell, 7 Dec. 1857, Howell Family Papers, HL; Maria L. Chotard to Eliza Chotard, 10 Nov. 1822, Maria Louisa Chotard Marshall and Family Papers, Hill Memorial Library, Louisiana State Univ.; "The Davis Family," *New York Times*, 11 Oct. 1866, p. 2; VHD, "Self life sketch," n.p., JD Papers, AL; Obituary of Varina Banks, [Natchez] *Mississippi Republican*, 1 Sept. 1824; William B. Howell to Joseph B. Howell, 1 July 1858, Howell Family Papers, HL.

22. Diary of John Nevitt, 7 Mar. 1831, UNC; Joseph A. Arrigo, *The Grace and Grandeur of Natchez Homes* (Stillwater, Minn.: Voyageur Press, 1994), 24–25; Deed Book AA, pp. 460–461, Chancery Court, Natchez, Adams County Courthouse; Statement of Significance, The Briars, National Register of Historic Places, Historic Natchez Foundation; Notice of sale, P. R. Nichols, *Daily Courier* (Natchez), 21 Nov. 1852, p. 2.

23. Deed Book V, pp. 472–473, Deed Book W, p. 494, Deed Book X, pp. 13–14, 82–83, Deed Book Y, pp. 232, 347–348, Chancery Court, Natchez, Adams County Courthouse; William Johnson, *William Johnson's Natchez: The Ante-Bellum Diary of a Free Negro*, ed. William Ransom Hogan and Edwin Adams Davis, with a new introduction by William L. Andrews (Baton Rouge: Louisiana State University Press, 1979), 126–127, 134, 216; Estate of James Kempe Decd., Auction, 31 Dec. 1831, B/467–468, Office of the Seventh Judicial District, Court of Concordia Parish, La.; Arrigo, *Natchez Homes*, 48–49.

24. Tax Records, State of Mississippi, Adams County, 1836, William B. Howell, p. 5; VHD to Mrs. E. M. Durham, 16 Mar. 1906, Davis Family Papers, Historic New Orleans Coll.; Diary of John Nevitt, 26 Jan. 1832, UNC; Johnson, *William Johnson's Natchez*, 263.

25. Margaret Howell to William F. Howell, 17–22 June 1850, Leacock Coll., BR; JD to W. D. Northend, 28 Aug. 1883, Montague Coll. of Historical Autographs, New York Public Library; VHD to Margaret S. Winchester, 25 Mar. 1895, Varina Davis Letter, MS; VHD to Josiah Winchester, 9 Aug. 1906, copy to the author cour-

tesy of Jayne Eannarino; VHD to Addison Hayes, n.d. May 1905, JD and Family Papers, MS; Federal Census of 1850, Louisiana, New Orleans, right bank, family 450; VHD to her parents, 14 June 1850, JD Papers, AL.

26. James, *Antebellum Natchez,* 235–236; VHD to William Hunter, 23 Apr. 1887, JD Papers, DU; VHD to Margaret Howell, 16 n.d. [Jan. 1859], JD Papers, AL; VHD to C. C. Harrison, 5 Apr. 1880, Harrison Family Papers, UVA; Margaret Howell to VHD, 25 Nov. 1847, George Winchester to Margaret Howell, n.d. [1836], postscript by William B. Howell, JD Papers, AL; VHD to Joseph Pulitzer, 10 Dec. 1887, Joseph Pulitzer Papers, Rare Book and Manuscript Library, Columbia Univ.; Hannah More, *The Works of Hannah More, Volume 4, Containing Hints towards Forming the Character of a Young Princess* (London: Henry G. Bohn, 1805, 1853), 11–12, 264–283; VHD to Glenna M. L. Davies, 21 Nov. 1904, Glenna Montague Latimer Davies Papers, VHS; VHD to James Redpath, 1 Oct. 1888, JD Papers, MS; Margaret Howell to JD, 14 July 1859, JD Papers, AL; Joseph and Varina Howell to Margaret Howell, 1 July 1838, JD and Family Papers, MS.

27. *Biographical Sketches of the Members of the Class of 1816, Yale College* (New Haven: T. J. Stafford, 1867), 68; *JD Papers,* 2:123 n. 6; Johnson, *William Johnson's Natchez,* 491; James, *Antebellum Natchez,* 281, 283; Deed Book W, pp. 35–37, 159, Chancery Court, Adams County Courthouse; Stoess, "Episodes," 18–19, JD Assoc., RU; George Winchester to Margaret Howell, n.d. [1836], postscript by William B. Howell, JD Papers, AL; [George Lewis Prentiss], *A Memoir of S. S. Prentiss, Edited by His Brother,* 2 vols. (New York: Charles Scribner, 1855), 1:353; Henry S. Foote, *The Bench and Bar of the South and Southwest* (St. Louis: Soule, Thomas and Wentworth, 1876), 109; tombstone for George Winchester, plot 2, Natchez Cemetery, author's visit, 1995.

28. *Memoir,* 1:188–189, 209; Daniel Walker Howe, *The Political Culture of the American Whigs* (Chicago: University of Chicago Press, 1979), 299–301; James, *Antebellum Natchez,* 249; VHD to Margaret Howell, n.d. 1850, Varina and Joseph Howell to Margaret Howell, 17 Apr. 1836, VHD to Margaret Howell, n.d. [Jan. 1848], JD Papers, AL.

29. VHD to Addison Hayes, 7 Oct. 1896, JD and Family Papers, MS; Lucy Leigh Bowie, "Madame Grelaud's French School," *Maryland Historical Magazine* 39 (June 1944): 141–148; Nelly Custis Lewis, *George Washington's Beautiful Nelly: The Letters of Eleanor Parke Custis Lewis to Elizabeth Bordley Gibson 1794–1851,* ed. Patricia Brady (Columbia: University of South Carolina Press, 1991), 79 n. 7, 82; Federal Census of 1830, Pennsylvania, Philadelphia, p. 126; Carl Sferrazza Anthony, *First Ladies: The Saga of the Presidents' Wives and Their Powers, 1789–1961* (New York: William Morrow, 1990), 116.

30. VHD to Jefferson Hayes-Davis, 20 May 1894, JD and Family Papers, MS; VHD to James G. Holmes, 29 Mar. 1906, A. J. Eastwood Library, Limestone College; William B. Howell to Joseph B. Howell, 1 July 1858, Howell Family Papers, HL; VHD to Margaret Howell, 2 June 1850, JD Papers, AL; Diary of Mary Savage Conner, 2 May 1839, Historic Natchez Foundation; Louisa Quitman to John Quitman, 2 May 1843, Quitman Family Papers, UNC; Bertram Wyatt-Brown, *The House*

of Percy: Honor, Melancholy, and Imagination in a Southern Family (New York: Oxford University Press, 1994), 119–123; Mahala Roach to Thomas R. Roach, 22 Aug. 1897, The Roach Letter, MS.

31. VHD to Margaret Howell, 15 Nov. 1848, VHD to her parents, 3 Aug. 1850, VHD to Margaret Howell, n.d. May 1857, JD Papers, AL; Mary E. M. White, ed., *Etiquette for All Occasions* (Allston Station, Mass.: n.p., 1900), 82–83; *Memoir,* 2:811; VHD to [Martha Phillips], n.d. 1865, Philip Phillips Papers, LC.

32. VHD to her parents, 28 Oct. 1851, VHD to Margaret Howell, 3 Mar. 1854, JD Papers, AL; W. H. Sparks, *The Memories of Fifty Years,* 3rd ed. (Philadelphia: Claxton, Remsen and Haffelfinger, 1872), 364; Johnson, *William Johnson's Natchez,* 238; Joan E. Cashin, *A Family Venture: Men and Women on the Southern Frontier* (New York: Oxford University Press, 1991), 85–86; James, *Antebellum Natchez,* 185, 202.

33. Deed Book AA, pp. 355–358, 366, 400, 460–461, Deed Book CC, p. 173, Chancery Court, Natchez, Adams County Courthouse; tombstone inscription for Sturges Sprague, Natchez City Cemetery, author's visit, 1995; Johnson, *William Johnson's Natchez,* 265–266; JD to J. William Jones, 26 Jan. 1882, JD Papers, DU; Deed Book DD, pp. 47–48, Chancery Court, Natchez, Adams County Courthouse; Tax Records, State of Mississippi, Adams County, 1840, Mrs. F. Sprague, p. 11; Federal Census of 1850, Louisiana, Tensas Parish, n.p.; Joseph Karl Menn, *The Large Slaveholders of Louisiana, 1860* (New Orleans: Pelican, 1964), 405–406; William B. Howell to Joseph B. Howell, 30 Nov. 1849, Howell Family Papers, HL.

34. VHD to Varina D. Howell, 1 Oct. 1905, BR; VHD to "Lizzie," n.d. [16 Sept. 1894], Lewis Cass Papers, William L. Clements Library, Univ. of Michigan; VHD to Joseph Pulitzer, 10 Dec. 1887, Pulitzer Papers, Rare Book and Manuscript Library, Columbia Univ.; Tax Records, State of Mississippi, Adams County, 1839, William B. Howell, p. 6; VHD to Margaret Howell, 13 Dec. 1847, Joseph Howell to Margaret Howell, 21 Nov. 1845, VHD to Margaret Howell, 9 Feb. 1852, VHD to JD, 3 Dec. 1869, JD Papers, AL; Joseph D. Howell to VHD, 29 June 1859, JD Papers, LC; VHD to Margaret Howell, 31 Jan. 1857, JD Papers, AL; VHD to M. B. Morgan, 21 June 1896, BR.

35. Joan E. Cashin, ed., *Our Common Affairs: Texts from Women in the Old South* (Baltimore: Johns Hopkins University Press, 1996), 2–3, 14–15; Eliza Ripley, *Social Life in Old New Orleans* (1912; repr., New York: Arno Press, 1975), 154.

36. Federal Census of 1840, Louisiana, Concordia Parish, n.p.; Report of the Trustees of the Troy Female Seminary, 1 Feb. 1839, Archives of Emma Willard School, Troy, New York; Menn, *Large Slaveholders of Louisiana,* 204–205; Robert Dabney Calhoun, *A History of Concordia Parish, 1768–1931* (New Orleans: n.p., 1932), 96; Johnson, *William Johnson's Natchez,* 319, 344–347, 351; Merritt M. Robinson, *Reports of Cases Argued and Determined in the Supreme Court of Louisiana,* 12 vols. (n.p.: E. Johns and Co., 1841–1846), 2:316–321, 2:360–362, 3:201–206, 4:113–115, 4:396–400; Margaret Howell to VHD, 22 Feb. 1852, William Burr Howell and Family Papers, MS; VHD to Margaret Howell, 15 Nov. 1848, JD Papers, AL; VHD to Mr. and Mrs. Kimbrough, 23 Apr. 1902, A. McC. Kimbrough and Family Papers, MS.

37. VHD to Mrs. Owen, 23 Feb. 1901, JD Family Coll., MC; VHD to Mr. Guion, 27 Dec. 1889, Guion Family Papers, UNC; Kenneth Silverman, *Edgar A. Poe: Mourning and Never-Ending Remembrance* (New York: HarperCollins, 1991), 141; Bowie, "Madame Grelaud's French School," 141–148; VHD to "My dear Mary," n.d. [1892–1893], Pegram-Johnson-McIntosh Family Papers, VHS; VHD to General Reed, n.d. [after 1865], JD Family Coll., MC; VHD to Margaret Howell, n.d. spring 1852, JD Papers, AL; VHD to Mary E. P. Anderson, 17 Apr. 1895, Pegram-Johnson-McIntosh Papers, VHS; VHD to Richard F. Reed, 3 June 1898, copy at JD Assoc., RU.

38. Stoess, "Episodes," 18, JD Assoc., RU; Christie Anne Farnham, *The Education of the Southern Belle: Higher Education and Student Socialization in the Antebellum South* (New York: New York University Press, 1994), 59–60.

39. Jane Turner Censer, *North Carolina Planters and Their Children, 1800–1860* (Baton Rouge: Louisiana State University Press, 1984), 91–93; Orville Vernon Burton, *In My Father's House Are Many Mansions: Family and Community in Edgefield, South Carolina* (Chapel Hill: University of North Carolina Press, 1985), 118–119; VHD to Anne Grant, 12 July 1894, JD Family Coll., MC; VHD to Margaret Howell, 14 Nov. 1845, Old Court House Museum, Vicksburg; VHD to Margaret Howell, n.d. [Jan. 1848], JD Papers, AL.

40. Cashin, *Our Common Affairs,* 1–41; VHD to Francis Preston Blair, 22 July 1865, Blair and Lee Papers, Rare Books and Special Colls., Princeton Univ. Library.

41. Johnson, *William Johnson's Natchez,* 260; VHD to JD, 23 Feb. 1866, VHD to William B. Howell, 11 Apr. 1845, VHD to Margaret Howell, 13 Dec. 1847, JD Papers, AL.

42. Johnson, eds., *William Johnson's Natchez,* 333 n. 7, 334 n. 9; James, *Antebellum Natchez,* 127.

43. William Wells Brown, *My Southern Home, or, the South and Its People* (1880; repr., New York: Negro Universities Press, 1969), 218; Mary Boykin Chesnut, *Mary Chesnut's Civil War,* ed. C. Vann Woodward (New Haven: Yale University Press, 1981), 29, 31, 262; Cashin, *Our Common Affairs,* 12–26; Judith Lorber, *Paradoxes of Gender* (New Haven: Yale University Press, 1994), 35.

44. Pasler and Pasler, *New Jersey Federalists,* 25; William Gillette, *Jersey Blue: Civil War Politics in New Jersey, 1854–1865* (New Brunswick: Rutgers University Press, 1995), 6; Winthrop D. Jordan, *White over Black: American Attitudes toward the Negro, 1550–1812* (Chapel Hill: Institute of Early American History and Culture at Williamsburg and University of North Carolina Press, 1968), 345; Federal Census of 1830, New Jersey, Hunterdon County, p. 353; Will of Ebenezer Howell, 13 Oct. 1785, Secretary of State's Offices, Wills and Inventories, New Jersey State Archives; Federal Census of 1840, Mississippi, Adams County, p. 22; Federal Census of 1830, Pennsylvania, Philadelphia, p. 126; Gary B. Nash, *Forging Freedom: The Formation of Philadelphia's Black Community, 1720–1840* (Cambridge, Mass.: Harvard University Press, 1988), 277.

45. Deed Book AA, p. 355, Chancery Court, Natchez, Adams County Courthouse; VHD to Josie F. Cappleman, 12 May 1904, catalog of Cohasco, p. 23, photo-

copy in author's possession; M. P. Stringer to VHD, 1 June 1863, JD Family Coll., MC; VHD to Margaret Howell, 26 Nov. 1847, JD Papers, AL; Sydnor, *Slavery in Mississippi,* 83–85; James, *Antebellum Natchez,* 179–180; M. G. Jones, *Hannah More* (Cambridge: Cambridge University Press, 1952), 82–91; Charles Dickens, *American Notes,* introduction by Christopher Hitchens (New York: Modern Library, 1996), 300–320.

46. Susan-Mary Grant, *North over South: Northern Nationalism and American Identity in the Antebellum Era* (Lawrence: University Press of Kansas, 2000), 1–18, 61–80; Eric H. Walther, *The Fire-Eaters* (Baton Rouge: Louisiana State University Press, 1992), 8–56, 121–136.

47. VHD to Margaret Howell, 14 Nov. 1845, Old Court House Museum, Vicksburg.

48. VHD to JD, 23 Feb. 1866, JD Papers, AL; *Memoir,* 1:187–188.

2. THIS MR. DAVIS

1. Deposition of E. C. Laughlin, 248, 251, Jefferson Davis v. J. H. D. Bowmar et al., MS; Ex-Slave Narrative, Interview with Jefferson Johnson, Tape 4778B, 1942, Mississippi, Motion Picture, Broadcasting, and Recorded Sound Division, LC; *JD Papers,* 2:57 n. 3; *Memoir,* 1:188, 475; William Wood, *Autobiography of William Wood,* 2 vols. (New York: J. S. Babcock, 1895), 1:458.

2. Anna Farrar Goldsborough, "Notes on Varina Howell Davis," 4, JD Assoc., RU; *JD Papers,* 1:8 n. 11, lxvii, lxxxii n 1; JD to Crafts J. Wright, 3 June 1878, JD Papers, TU; Janet Sharp Hermann, *Joseph E. Davis: Pioneer Patriarch* (Jackson: University Press of Mississippi, 1990), 16–17, 23–24.

3. *JD Papers,* 1:4–5; William C. Davis, *Jefferson Davis: The Man and His Hour* (New York: HarperCollins, 1991), 10–18; JD to E. G. Booth, 15 Aug. 1884, Hugh S. Cummings Papers, UVA; Janet Sharp Hermann, *The Pursuit of a Dream* (New York: Oxford University Press, 1981), 11; Deposition of William Stamps, 204, Davis v. Bowmar; Terms of Complaint, Original Bill, Chancery Court, Warren County, Mississippi, Davis v. Bowmar.

4. JD to G. T. McGehee, 16 Sept. 1888, Franklin L. Riley Papers, MS; JD, "Reminiscences," n.d. [c. 1881], n.p., JD Papers, TL, Louisiana Historical Assoc.; W. C. Davis, *Jefferson Davis,* 25–38, 39–52.

5. George P. Rawick, ed., *The American Slave: A Composite Autobiography* (Westport, Conn.: Greenwood Press, 1977), suppl. ser. 1, vol. 8, Mississippi, pt. 3, p. 994, Florida Hewitt; JD to Thomas C Reynolds, 12 Nov. 1882, Thomas F. Madigan's Autograph Bulletin, at JD Assoc., RU; Holman Hamilton, *Zachary Taylor: Soldier of the Republic* (Indianapolis: Bobbs-Merrill, 1941), 101–108; W. C. Davis, *Jefferson Davis,* 48, 52–54, 61–75; *JD Papers,* 1:345–348, 406–409.

6. Deposition of Hagar Allen, 416–417, 422, Davis v. Bowmar; Lucy Bradford Mitchell to Lise Mitchell, 20 Jan. 1899, Mitchell Family Papers, TL; JD, "Reminiscences," n.d. [c. 1881], JD Papers, TL, Louisiana Historical Assoc.; *Memoir,* 1:171–172, 187–188.

7. Elizabeth Meriwether to Minor Meriwether, 19 Nov. 1869, Meriwether Fam-

ily Papers, West Tennessee Historical Society, at UM; Goldsborough, "Notes on Varina Howell Davis," 11, JD Assoc., RU; Bertram Wyatt-Brown, *Southern Honor: Ethics and Behavior in the Old South* (New York: Oxford University Press, 1982), 149–174, 327–361; Joan E. Cashin, *A Family Venture: Men and Women on the Southern Frontier* (New York: Oxford University Press, 1991), 102–108; VHD to JD, 8 Feb. 1866, JD Papers, AL; *Memoir,* 2:918, 1:475, 1:191.

8. *JD Papers,* 2:52–53.

9. Hermann, *Joseph E. Davis,* 50, 70, 77–78; Rawick, *American Slave,* suppl. ser. 1, vol. 9, Mississippi, pt. 4, p. 1540, Isaiah Montgomery; Personal Tax Rolls, Warren County, Mississippi, 1848, p. 48, 1842, p. 11, MS; *Memoir,* 1:192–194; Wood, *Autobiography,* 1:457; Mahala Roach to Thomas R. Roach, 22 Aug. 1897, The Roach Letter, MS; VHD to William E. Dodd, 8 Mar. 1905, William E. Dodd Papers, LC.

10. Wood, *Autobiography,* 1:456–457; Reuben Davis, *Recollections of Mississippi and Mississippians* (Boston: Houghton Mifflin and Co., 1889), 79; *Memoir,* 1:171–172; VHD to William E. Dodd, 8 Mar. 1905, Dodd Papers, LC; Deposition of Mary E. Stamps, 175, Davis v. Bowmar; Rawick, *American Slave,* suppl. ser. 1, vol. 8, Mississippi, pt. 3, p. 995, Florida Hewitt; Mahala Roach to Thomas R. Roach, 22 Aug. 1897, The Roach Letter, MS; Hermann, *Joseph E. Davis,* 43, 57, 48; Rawick, *American Slave,* suppl. ser. 1, vol. 9, Mississippi, pt. 4, p. 1538, Isaiah Montgomery; *JD Papers,* 1:303; VHD to Margaret Howell, 13 Dec. 1847, VHD to Margaret Howell, 9 Feb. 1852, JD Papers, AL.

11. VHD to JD, 13 Nov. 1865, 8 Feb. 1866, n.d. Oct. 1865, 2 Feb. 1866, 7 Nov. 1865, JD Papers, AL; Goldsborough, "Notes on Varina Howell Davis," 1, JD Assoc., RU; VHD to JD, 7 Dec. 1865, RG 94, Letters Received, Adjutant General's Office, Main Series, File 1401 A 1865, NA; JD to VHD, 26 Feb. 1877, JD Papers, AL; VHD to the Smith family, n.d. [c. 1890], copy at JD Assoc., RU; Deposition of Varina Davis, 346, Davis v. Bowmar; *Memoir,* 1:163.

12. *Memoir,* 1:197–198; *JD Papers,* 2:127, xxxiv–xxxv, 705; W. C. Davis, *Jefferson Davis,* 101–107.

13. *JD Papers,* 3:456; D. Clayton James, *Antebellum Natchez* (Baton Rouge: Louisiana State University Press, 1968), 249; Joan D. Hedrick, *Harriet Beecher Stowe: A Life* (New York: Oxford University Press, 1994), 96, 99; *Memoir,* 1:199–200, 164; VHD to Philip H. Ward, n.d. [1892–1898], Frederick C. Schang Manuscript Coll., Rare Book and Manuscript Library, Columbia University; "Second Edition: Jeff Davis Is Dead," *Chicago Tribune,* 6 Dec. 1889, p. 1; author's telephone interview with Marka Stewart, 4 Aug. 1993.

14. *JD Papers,* 3:53; *Memoir,* 1:202–204; Rawick, *American Slave,* suppl., ser. 1, vol. 8, Mississippi, pt. 3, p. 1339, James Lucas; VHD to Margaret Howell, 5 Sept. 1845, JD Papers, AL; *JD Papers,* 2:244; VHD to Margaret Howell, 14 Nov. 1845, Old Court House Museum, Vicksburg; VHD and JD to the Howells, 11 Dec. 1845, JD and Family Papers, MS; VHD to Margaret Howell, 9 Mar. 1845, JD Papers, AL.

15. VHD to Margaret Howell, 5 Sept. 1845, JD Papers, AL; Christopher Morris, *Becoming Southern: The Evolution of a Way of Life, Warren County and Vicksburg, Mississippi, 1770–1860* (New York: Oxford University Press, 1995), 68; Eliza Davis to Mary D.

Mitchell, 15 Sept. 1845, Mitchell Journal and Letters, TL, copy at UNC; VHD to Lucinda D. Stamps, 17 Sept. 1845, JD Family Coll., MC; VHD to Margaret Howell, 5 Sept. 1845, n.d. July 1845, 17 [Nov.?] 1847, 26 Nov. 1847, VHD to her parents, 1 Jan. 1848, JD Papers, AL; Rawick, *American Slave,* suppl. ser. 1, vol. 8, Mississippi, pt. 3, p. 1332, James Lucas; Orland Kay Armstrong, *Old Massa's People: The Old Slaves Tell Their Story* (Indianapolis: Bobbs-Merrill, 1931), 40–41.

16. VHD to her parents, 4–5 Jan. 1847, VHD to Margaret Howell, 31 Jan. 1848, 9 Mar. 1845, 26 Nov. 1847, JD Papers, AL; *JD Papers,* 2:714–715; VHD to Margaret Howell, n.d. [Jan. 1848], 12 Nov. 1847, JD Papers, AL.

17. VHD to Margaret Howell, n.d. July 1845, 5 Sept. 1845, 21 Nov. 1858, JD Papers, AL; Andrea Tone, ed., *Controlling Reproduction: An American History* (Wilmington, Del.: Scholarly Resources Books, 1997), 23; Mahala Roach to Thomas R. Roach, 22 Aug. 1897, The Roach Letter, MS; VHD to Margaret Howell, 2 Aug. [1848], JD Papers, AL; Charles D. Meigs to VHD, 8 Dec. 1848, JD Papers, TU; Mahala Roach, "Christmas Days," 3, Roach and Eggleston Papers, UNC; VHD to JD, 7 Nov. 1865, JD Papers, AL.

18. VHD to Margaret Howell, 9 Mar. 1845, n.d. July 1845, JD Papers, AL; VHD to Lucinda D. Stamps, 17 Sept. 1845, JD Family Coll., MC; Rawick, *American Slave,* suppl. ser. 1, vol. 8, Mississippi, pt. 3, p. 1338, James Lucas; Goldsborough, "Notes on Varina Howell Davis," 5, 8–9, 13–14, JD Assoc., RU; VHD to "My Dear Varina," 10 Oct. 1893, BR.

19. *JD Papers,* 1:273–274; Eliza Davis to Mary Davis Mitchell, 15 Sept. 1845, Mitchell Journal and Letters, TL, copy at UNC; *JD Papers,* 2:208; VHD to JD, 23 Mar. 1867, JD Family Coll., MC; VHD to "My Dear Varina," 10 Oct. 1893, BR; VHD to Joseph Pulitzer, 20 Sept. 1887, Joseph Pulitzer Papers, Rare Book and Manuscript Library, Columbia Univ.

20. VHD to Lucinda D. Stamps, 17 Sept. 1845, JD Family Coll., MC; *JD Papers,* 3:53, 8:221; *Memoir,* 1:208–213; Irving H. Bartlett, *John C. Calhoun: A Biography* (New York: W. W. Norton, 1993), 329–330; *JD Papers,* 2:375.

21. U.S. Department of Commerce, *Historical Statistics of the United States, Colonial Times to 1970,* pt. 1 (Washington, D.C.: Bureau of the Census, 1975), 26; Charles Dickens, *American Notes,* introduction by Christopher Hitchens (New York: Modern Library, 1996), 153–154; Mrs. Roger A. Pryor, *Reminiscences of Peace and War,* rev. ed (New York: Macmillan, 1905), 3–5; *Memoir,* 1:224–225, 244–245; *JD Papers,* 2:533.

22. James P. Shenton, *Robert John Walker: A Politician from Jackson to Lincoln* (New York: Columbia University Press, 1961), 9–10, 46; VHD to William E. Dodd, 10 Mar. 1905, Dodd Papers, LC; *Memoir,* 1:220, 260–263, 277–278, 259–260, 265, 281–282; Elizabeth Blair Lee, *Wartime Washington: The Civil War Letters of Elizabeth Blair Lee,* ed. Virginia Jeans Laas (Urbana: University of Illinois Press, 1991), 434; *JD Papers,* 2:533–534.

23. Margaret Bayard Smith, *The First Forty Years of Washington Society,* ed. Gaillard Hunt (New York: Charles Scribner's Sons, 1906), 147; Bartlett, *John C. Calhoun,* 61; William M. Meigs, *The Life of Charles Jared Ingersoll,* 2nd ed. (Philadelphia: J. B.

Lippincott, 1900), 312; *Memoir*, 1:222–224; Josiah Quincy, *Figures of the Past: From the Leaves of Old Journals* (Boston: Roberts Bros., 1883), 274–275; *JD Papers*, 2:421; Pryor, *Reminiscences*, 35; Virginia Clay-Clopton, *A Belle of the Fifties: Memoirs of Mrs. Clay of Alabama, Covering Social and Political Life in Washington and the South, 1853–66*, ed. Ada Sterling (New York: Doubleday, Page and Co., 1904), 74.

24. *JD Papers*, 2:641–642, 3:13–14; VHD to Mrs. R. H. Chilton, 29 Mar. 1847, JD Family Coll., MC.

25. Deposition of Varina Davis, 346–347, 364–366, 346, Deposition of John Perkins, 470, Deposition of Elizabeth P. White, 509, Deposition of E. G. Cook, 553, Davis v. Bowmar.

26. M. L. McMurran to "My dear Cousin," 17 Nov. 1846, Quitman Family Papers, UNC; Deposition of E. C. Laughlin, 248, Deposition of Varina Davis, 369, Davis v. Bowmar; Hermann, *Joseph E. Davis*, 45; Deposition of Mary E. Stamps, 175–176, Deposition of William Stamps, 212, Davis v. Bowmar.

27. *JD Papers*, 3:xxxii–xxxiii; JD to Mary Stamps, 7 Jan. 1870, Mary Stamps Papers, UNC; JD, "Reminiscences," n.d. [c. 1881], JD Papers, TL, Louisiana Historical Assoc.; *JD Papers*, 3:94–95; VHD to her parents, 4–5 Jan. 1847, JD Papers, AL; *JD Papers*, 3:119,121 n. 12.

28. Deposition of Varina Davis, 354, Davis v. Bowmar; Hermann, *Pursuit of a Dream*, 9; *JD Papers*, 2:129 n. 6; *JD Papers*, 3:238–241; VHD to Margaret Howell, n.d. [Jan. 1848], JD Papers, AL.

29. VHD to Anne Grant, 12 July 1894, JD Family Coll., MC; Cashin, *A Family Venture*, 79, 143, table 5; Deposition of David Laumaster, 486, Davis v. Bowmar; VHD to her parents, 4–5 Jan. 1847, JD Papers, AL; Deposition of Varina Davis, 356, Davis v. Bowmar.

30. Goldsborough, "Notes on Varina Howell Davis," 12, JD Assoc., RU; Henry S. Foote, *The Bench and Bar of the South and Southwest* (St. Louis: Soule, Thomas and Wentworth, 1876), 226; T. C. De Leon, *Belles, Beaux and Brains of the 60's* (New York: G. W. Dillingham Co., 1909), 77; Hermann, *Joseph E. Davis*, 16, 66, 47–48; *JD Papers*, 1:514 n. 25; Deposition of Mary E. Hamer, 436, Davis v. Bowmar; *JD Papers*, 2:65 n. 35; Julia Dent Grant, *The Personal Memoirs of Julia Dent Grant (Mrs. Ulysses S. Grant)*, ed. with notes and foreword by John Y. Simon, with introductions by Bruce Catton and Ralph G. Newman (New York: G. P. Putnam's Sons, 1975), 122, 143 n. 3.

31. Hermann, *Joseph E. Davis*, 47; Peter W. Bardaglio, *Reconstructing the Household: Families, Sex, and the Law in the Nineteenth-Century South* (Chapel Hill: University of North Carolina Press, 1996), 91–92; Eliza Davis to JD, 15 July 1859, JD Papers, AL.

32. Deposition of Varina Davis, 349–351, 358, 361, Davis v. Bowmar; *JD Papers*, 3:96 n. 11.

33. Joan E. Cashin, "According to His Wish and Desire: Female Kin and Female Slaves in Planter Wills," in *Women of the American South: A Multicultural Reader*, ed. Christie Ann Farnham (New York: New York University Press, 1997), 94–99; A. Hutchinson, comp., *Code of Mississippi* (Jackson.: Price and Fall, 1848), 623, 496–497.

34. *JD Papers*, 3:183, ed. note, 3:207; VHD to Margaret Howell, 26 Nov. 1847,

12 Nov. 1847, 13 Dec. 1847, JD Papers, AL; JD to VHD, 3–4 Jan. 1848, p. 66, Goodspeed's Catalog, copy at JD Assoc., RU; VHD to Margaret Howell, n.d. [Jan. 1848], JD Papers, AL.

35. JD to VHD, 18 Apr. 1848, E 187 Manuscripts, Massachusetts Historical Society.

36. Memoir of Temple Bodley, 20, Filson Historical Society.

37. VHD to her parents, 15 Sept. 1856, JD Papers, AL; VHD to MBC, 25 Mar. 1885, Williams-Chesnut-Manning Papers, USC; VHD to Austin Smith, 15 Apr. 1903, Mary Frederike Quitman Ogden Smith Papers, MS.

38. *JD Papers,* 3:xxxvi; VHD to Margaret Howell, 15 Nov. 1848, JD Papers, AL; Hutchinson, *Code of Mississippi,* 495–496; Jane Turner Censer, "'Smiling through Her Tears': Ante-Bellum Southern Women and Divorce," *American Journal of Legal History* 25 (1981): 34, 40; Personal Tax Rolls, Warren County, Mississippi, 1848, p. 10, MS; VHD to Mary C. Kimbrough, n.d. 1903, M. C. K. Sinclair Papers, IU; Mary E. M. White, ed., *Etiquette for All Occasions* (Boston: Allston Station, 1900), 91; Mary Craig Sinclair, *Southern Belle,* with a foreword by Upton Sinclair and an afterword by Peggy Whitman Prenshaw (1957; repr., Jackson: University Press of Mississippi and Banner Books, 1999), 55, 86.

39. Goldsborough, "Notes on Varina Howell Davis," 11, JD Assoc., RU; VHD to Margaret Howell, 24 [n.d.] 1849, JD Papers, AL; *JD Papers,* 4:7–8; Deposition of William Zeigler, 264, Davis v. Bowmar; JD to VHD, 14 Oct. 1849, Civil War and Underground Railroad Museum of Philadelphia; *JD Papers,* 4:62; E. H. Anderson to JD, n.d. May 1886, JD Family Coll., MC; *JD Papers,* 4:xxxii. On somewhat similar accommodations by white Southern women, see George C. Rable, *Civil Wars: Women and the Crisis of Southern Nationalism* (Urbana: University of Illinois Press, 1989), 8–12.

40. *JD Papers,* 2:535; William B. Howell to Robert J. Walker, 20 July 1846, Robert J. Walker Papers, LC; VHD to Margaret Howell, 15 Nov. 1848, 24 [n.d.] 1849, VHD to her parents, 1 Jan. 1848, JD Papers, AL.

41. VHD to her parents, 4–5 Jan. 1847, JD Papers, AL; Deposition of Varina Davis, 369, 367, Deposition of Florida Laughlin, 382, Davis v. Bowmar; Personal Tax Rolls, Warren County, Mississippi, 1848, p. 10, MS; VHD to Margaret Howell, 24 [n.d.] 1849, JD Papers, AL.

3. FLATTERED AND COURTED

1. *Memoir,* 1:409; VHD to Margaret Howell, 27 Dec. 1849–6 Jan. 1850, JD Papers, AL; Henry Adams, *The Education of Henry Adams: An Autobiography,* with a new introduction by D. W. Brogan (1918; repr., Boston: Houghton Mifflin, 1961), 45; Mrs. Roger A. Pryor, *Reminiscences of Peace and War,* rev. ed. (New York: Macmillan, 1905), 9–10; VHD to her parents, 3 Aug. 1850, 10 July 1850, JD Papers, AL; VHD to Mary Ann Cobb, 13 Jan. 1851, 22 Oct. 1868, Howell Cobb Papers, UGA; James P. Shenton, *Robert John Walker: A Politician from Jackson to Lincoln* (New York: Columbia University Press, 1961), x, 9–10; VHD to Margaret Howell, n.d. 1850, 26 Mar. 1854, JD Papers, AL; Allan Nevins, *Hamilton Fish: The Inner History of the Grant Admin-*

istration, rev. ed., 2 vols. (New York: Frederick Ungar Publishing Co., 1936, 1957), 1:17–19, 42–45.

2. *Memoir,* 1:414; VHD to her parents, 3 Aug. 1850, VHD to Margaret Howell, 18–20 May 1850, JD Papers, AL; *JD Papers,* 1:279 n. 20; VHD to her parents, 14 June 1850, VHD to Margaret Howell, n.d. 1850, JD Papers, AL.

3. Mrs. Franklin Elmore to Ellen Elmore, 8 May 1850, Franklin Elmore Papers, USC; *Memoir,* 2:919; Daniel Roche, *The Culture of Clothing: Dress and Fashion in the Ancien Regime,* trans. Jean Birrell (Cambridge: Cambridge University Press, 1996), 3; VHD to her parents, 14 June 1850, VHD to Margaret Howell, 27 Dec. 1849–6 Jan. 1850, 18–20 May 1850, JD Papers, AL; Rebecca Latimer Felton, *Country Life in Georgia in the Days of My Youth* (Atlanta: Index Printing Co., 1919), 63; *Memoir,* 1:459; VHD to Margaret Howell, 16 n.d. [Jan.] 1859, JD Papers, AL.

4. Reuben Davis, *Recollections of Mississippi and Mississippians* (Boston: Houghton Mifflin, 1889), 202, 291; Walt Whitman, *Complete Prose Works* (Boston: Small, Maynard and Co., 1881, 1907), 440; Betty Boyd Caroli, *First Ladies,* expanded ed. (New York: Oxford University Press, 1995), 48; Zachary Taylor, *Letters of Zachary Taylor,* ed. William K. Bixby (Rochester: n.p., 1908), ix; VHD to Margaret Howell, 18–20 May 1850, JD Papers, AL.

5. William C. Davis, *Jefferson Davis: The Man and His Hour* (New York: HarperCollins, 1991), 192–203; *JD Papers,* 4:79–87; *Memoir,* 1:447–448.

6. *JD Papers,* 4:62; VHD to William B. Howell, 13 Feb. 1857, JD Papers, AL; *Memoir,* 1:412–413; *JD Papers,* 2:173; VHD to her parents, 14 June 1850, JD Papers, AL.

7. VHD to her parents, 10 July 1850, JD Papers, AL; Taylor, *Letters,* x; Holman Hamilton, *Zachary Taylor: Soldier in the White House* (Indianapolis: Bobbs-Merrill, 1951), 264–265, 301, 383, 401; Robert W. Johannsen, *Stephen A. Douglas* (New York: Oxford University Press, 1973), 291, 293, 295–297; W. C. Davis, *Jefferson Davis,* 202–203; *JD Papers,* 4:123.

8. *JD Papers,* 4:120 n. 5; Federal Census for 1850, Free Schedule, Louisiana, New Orleans, right bank, household 450; Margaret Howell to William F. Howell, 17–22 June 1850, 14 May 1851, Leacock Coll., BR; Margaret Howell to VHD, n.d. 1859, 14 Feb. 1852, William Burr Howell and Family Papers, MS; VHD to Mrs. E. M. Durham, 28 Mar. 1902, Davis Family Papers, Historic New Orleans Coll.; Margaret Howell to VHD, 22 Feb. 1852, William Burr Howell and Family Papers, MS.

9. *JD Papers,* 4:119; VHD to her parents, 14 June 1850, VHD to Margaret Howell, 9 Feb. 1852, n.d. 1853, Margaret Howell to VHD, n.d. [1854], VHD to Margaret Howell, 2 June 1850, 26–30 July 1853, Joseph D. Howell to VHD, 14 Nov. 1853, JD Papers, AL; *JD Papers,* 4:120 n. 5; Margaret Howell to William B. Howell, 29 Oct. 1854, William B. Howell and Family Papers, MS; Abner Doubleday, *My Life in the Old Army: The Reminiscences of Abner Doubleday from the Collections of the New-York Historical Society,* ed. Joseph E. Chance (Fort Worth: Texas Christian University Press, 1998), 344–345, 167–168, 171–172; *JD Papers,* 5:151; VHD to Margaret Howell, 27 Jan. 1852, JD Papers, AL.

10. *JD Papers,* 4:132, xxxv–xxxvi; Deposition of William H. Zeigler, 260, Jeffer-

son Davis v. J. H. D. Bowmar et al., MS; *JD Papers,* 4:13, 181; Mary Carol Miller, *Lost Mansions of Mississippi* (Jackson: University Press of Mississippi, 1996), 41–42; Deposition of Varina Davis, 370, Davis v. Bowmar; VHD to Mrs. Ellyson, 3 Jan. 1895, JD Family Coll., MC; *JD Papers,* 9:301, 299; *JD Papers,* 4:237; *Memoir,* 1:227; VHD to Margaret Howell, 1 Mar. 1859, JD Papers, AL; VHD to Mary Ann Cobb, 13 Jan. 1851, Howell Cobb Papers, UGA.

11. W. C. Davis, *Jefferson Davis,* 215–217; *JD Papers,* 4:213–214; *Memoir,* 1:469; Robert E. May, *John A. Quitman, an Old South Crusader* (Baton Rouge: Louisiana State University Press, 1985), 264; VHD to her parents, 28 Oct. 1851, JD Papers, AL.

12. Deposition of James E. Dunham, 169, Davis v. Bowmar; Federal Census for 1850, Free Schedule, Mississippi, Warren County, p. 213; VHD to William E. Dodd, 16 June 1905, William E. Dodd Papers, LC; Charles Sackett Sydnor, *Slavery in Mississippi* (Gloucester, Mass.: Peter Smith, 1965), 155–156; *JD Papers,* 6:164 n. 5; Personal Tax Rolls, Warren County, Mississippi, 1856, p. 10, MS; Ex-Slave Narrative, Interview with Jefferson Johnson, Tape 4777B, 1942, Mississippi, Motion Picture, Broadcasting, and Recorded Sound Division, LC; Lord Shrewsbury to JD, 28 Aug. 1868, JD Family Coll., MC.

13. Joan E. Cashin, *A Family Venture: Men and Women on the Southern Frontier* (New York: Oxford University Press, 1991), 112–118; Sydnor, *Slavery in Mississippi,* 248; John Hebron Moore, *The Emergence of the Cotton Kingdom in the Old Southwest: Mississippi, 1770–1860* (Baton Rouge: Louisiana State University Press, 1988), 291–292; JD, "Reminiscences," [c. 1881], n.p., JD Papers, TL, Louisiana Historical Assoc.; VHD to William E. Dodd, 8 Mar. 1905, Dodd Papers, LC; *Reminiscences of General Basil W. Duke, C.S.A.* (Garden City, N.Y.: Doubleday, Page and Co., 1911), 232–233; George P. Rawick, ed., *The American Slave: A Composite Autobiography* (Westport, Conn.: Greenwood Press, 1977), suppl. ser. 1, vol. 8, Mississippi, pt. 3, p. 994, Florida Hewitt, suppl. ser. 1, vol. 2, Arkansas, Colorado, Minnesota, p. 72, Frank Loper; Interview with Jefferson Johnson, Tape 4778A, Tape 4778B, LC.

14. William J. Cooper Jr., *Jefferson Davis, American* (New York: Alfred A. Knopf, 2000), 231; Interview with Jefferson Johnson, Tape 4778A, Tape 4778B, LC; May, *John A. Quitman,* 134, Ronald L. F. Davis, *Good and Faithful Labor: From Slavery to Sharecropping in the Natchez District, 1860–1890* (Westport, Conn.: Greenwood Press, 1982), 35; Rawick, *American Slave,* suppl. ser. 1, vol. 8, Mississippi, pt. 3, p. 1158, George Johnson; JED to John Quitman, 9 Dec. 1852, Quitman Family Papers, UNC; Deposition of William Stamps, 209, Deposition of T. J. Coe, 271, Davis v. Bowmar; *JD Papers,* 5:117–118.

15. VHD to Margaret Howell, 9 Feb. 1852, 25 May 1852, 26 Mar. 1854, n.d. [summer] 1852, VHD to her parents, 28 Oct. 1851, JD to VHD, 23 Aug. 1857, JD Papers, AL; Rawick, *American Slave,* suppl. ser. 1, vol. 8, Mississippi, pt. 3, p. 1339, James Lucas; *Memoir,* 1:478–479.

16. *Memoir,* 1:474–475; VHD to Margaret Howell, 4 Mar. 1852, JD Papers, AL; *JD Papers,* 4:xxxviii–xxxix, 291–292; VHD to Margaret Howell, n.d. [summer 1852], JD Papers, AL; Margaret Howell to VHD, 28 June 1852, William B. Howell and Family Papers, MS.

17. VHD to Margaret Howell, 26 Nov. 1847, 4 Mar. 1852, JD Papers, AL; Reginald Horsman, *Josiah Nott of Mobile: Southerner, Physician, and Racial Theorist* (Baton Rouge: Louisiana State University Press, 1987), 170–221; Ivan Hannaford, *Race: The History of an Idea in the West* (Washington, D.C.: Woodrow Wilson Center Press, 1996), 260–276; *JD Papers,* 3:315.

18. Deposition of Varina Davis, 361–363, 385–386, 358, 375, Davis v. Bowmar; Margaret Howell to William B. Howell, 20 Aug. 1852, JD Papers, AL; *JD Papers,* 5:112–113; Deposition of John Perkins, 470, Davis v. Bowmar.

19. Roy Franklin Nichols, *Franklin Pierce: Young Hickory of the Granite Hills,* 2nd ed. (1931; repr., Philadelphia: University of Pennsylvania Press, 1958), 97, 13, 83–84, 257–258, 276, 381, 544–545; May, *John A. Quitman,* 271; *Memoir,* 1:533, 541, 543–544, 559; VHD to Margaret Howell, 3 Mar. 1854, JD Papers, AL.

20. Caroli, *First Ladies,* 53; Maggie Howell to Mrs. Howell, 29 Dec. 1856, JD Papers, AL; Carl Sferrazza Anthony, *First Ladies: The Saga of the Presidents' Wives and Their Powers, 1789–1961* (New York: William Morrow, 1990), 157–158; Nichols, *Franklin Pierce,* 75–76, 241–242, 313; *Memoir,* 1:539–540, 548.

21. U.S. Department of Commerce, *Historical Statistics of the United States, Colonial Times to 1970,* pt. 1 (Washington, D.C.: Bureau of the Census, 1975), 1084; *Memoir,* 1:547–548, 535, 564; VHD to Margaret Howell, n.d. 1854, 26 Mar. 1854, JD Papers, AL; JD, *The Rise and Fall of the Confederate Government,* 2 vols., foreword by Bell I. Wiley (New York: Thomas Yoseloff, 1958), 1:28; VHD to Margaret Howell, n.d. 1853, JD Papers, AL.

22. Mary E. M. White, ed., *Etiquette for All Occasions,* ed. (Boston: Allston Station, 1900), 161, 99, 95, 126–127; Margaret Howell to William B. Howell, 29 Oct. 1854, William B. Howell and Family Papers, MS; VHD to Margaret Howell, 26 Mar. 1854, JD Papers, AL; Catherine Allgor, *Parlor Politics: In Which the Ladies of Washington Help Build a City and a Government* (Charlottesville: University Press of Virginia, 2000), 54–79, 93–100; *Memoir,* 1:552–553; VHD to Margaret Howell, n.d. 1854, 16 [Jan.] 1859, JD Papers, AL.

23. *JD Papers,* 5:14; VHD to Margaret Howell, 26 Mar. 1854, 16 [Jan.] 1859, 29 [n.d.] 1854, JD Papers, AL; *Memoir,* 1:579–580, 556–557, 551, 549–550; Christine I. De Wechmar Stoess, comp. Lorraine Chapman, "Episodes in the Life of Margaret Graham Howell," 26, JD Assoc., RU; Maria Costantino, *Whistler* (New York: Barnes and Noble Books, 1997), 6; VHD to Margaret Howell, n.d. 1854, JD Papers, AL.

24. VHD, "Self life sketch," VHD to William B. Howell, 7 Sept. 1857, JD Papers, AL; May, *Quitman,* 298; VHD to William B. Howell, 13 Feb. 1857, VHD to unnamed person, n.d. [1857], JD Papers, AL; *JD Papers,* 5:197; *Memoir,* 1:544–546; VHD to Margaret Howell, 1 Mar. 1859, JD Papers, AL.

25. Elizabeth R. Varon, *We Mean to Be Counted: White Women and Politics in Antebellum Virginia* (Chapel Hill: University of North Carolina Press, 1998), 71–101; Rebecca Edwards, *Angels in the Machinery: Gender in American Party Politics from the Civil War to the Progressive Era* (New York: Oxford University Press, 1997), 3–27; *Memoir,* 1:459.

26. VHD to Margaret Howell, 26–30 July 1853, 3 Mar. 1854, JD Papers, AL;

Memoir, 1:534–535, 538–539, 542; *JD Papers,* 5:72–73, 17, 91–92, ix, xli; VHD to her parents, n.d. July 1854, JD Papers, AL.

27. Margaret Howell to William B. Howell, 7 Apr. 1855, William Burr Howell and Family Papers, MS; "The Davis Family," *New York Times,* 11 Oct. 1866, p. 2; *Memoir,* 1:559, 566; Stoess, "Episodes," 23–25, JD Assoc., RU; VHD to Margaret Howell, 21 Nov. 1858, JD Papers, AL; VHD to JD, 3 Apr. 1859, JD and Family Papers, MS.

28. VHD to her parents, n.d. July 1854, JD Papers, AL; Becket Howell to William B. Howell, 5 Sept. 1854, JD and Family Papers, MS; VHD to MH, 3 Mar. 1854, JD Papers, AL; JD to Joseph Howell, 5 Apr. 1853, Howell Family Papers, HL; Jeffy D. Howell to JD, 28 June 1868, JD Papers, AL; Stoess, "Episodes," 22, JD Assoc., RU; *Memoir,* 1:532; VHD to Margaret Howell, n.d. 1858, 15 Sept. 1858, VHD to William B. Howell, 7 Sept. 1857, JD Papers, AL.

29. Stoess, "Episodes," 23–24, JD Assoc., RU; VHD to Margaret Howell, 26–30 July 1853, 21 Nov. 1858, 15 Feb. 1859, VHD to William B. Howell, 1 Sept. 1859, JD Papers, AL; Confirmations, 12 Sept. 1858, Records from St. Mary's Hall, 1858–1859, Doane Academy, Burlington, New Jersey; William B. Howell to VHD, 11 Aug. 1857, JD Papers, LC.

30. Bill of Sale, 7 July 1848, Joseph B. Howell, VHD to Joseph B. Howell, 16 Nov. 1858, 12 Aug. 1850, A. L. Harris to Joseph B. Howell, 16 Oct. 1858, William B. Howell to Joseph B. Howell, 5 Nov. 1858, Margaret Howell to Joseph Howell, 4 June 1858, Howell Family Papers, HL; Stoess, "Episodes," 25, JD Assoc., RU; Letter Account Book of George Howell, Letters Received, Answered, 1858–1859, Josephine Howell, "Mementos of Friendship," 1859, JD to Joseph Howell, 5 Apr. 1853, Sarah Agnew to Joseph B. Howell, 22 Feb. 1861, Joseph B. Howell to Mary S. Howell, 20 Jan. 1854, Franklin Glaser to Joseph Howell, 25 Feb. 1861, Joseph B. Howell to Richard Glaser and Varina Davis, 11 Jan. 1861, Howell Family Papers, HL.

31. Margaret Howell to VHD, 27 Jan. 1852, William B. Howell and Family Papers, MS; Orland Kay Armstrong, *Old Massa's People: The Old Slaves Tell Their Story* (Indianapolis: Bobbs-Merrill, 1931), 40; *JD Papers,* 4:119–121; *JD Papers,* 5:10–11; *Memoir* 2:923; VHD to Mr. Blair, 6 June 1865, Blair Family Papers, LC; John M. Taylor, *William Henry Seward: Lincoln's Right Hand* (New York: HarperCollins, 1991), 90–91; Carl Schurz, *The Reminiscences of Carl Schurz,* 2 vols. (Garden City, N.Y.: Doubleday, Page and Co., 1913), 2:21; Virginia Clay-Clopton, *A Belle of the Fifties: Memoirs of Mrs. Clay of Alabama, Covering Social and Political Life in Washington and the South, 1853–66,* ed. Ada Sterling (New York: Doubleday, Page and Co., 1904), 68.

32. *Memoir,* 1:563–564, 575–576; Elizabeth Blair Lee, *Wartime Washington: The Civil War Letters of Elizabeth Blair Lee,* ed. Virginia Jeans Laas, foreword by Dudley T. Cornish (Urbana: University of Illinois Press, 1991), 76; W. C. Davis, *Jefferson Davis,* 75; *JD Papers,* 4:225; Interview with Jefferson Johnson, Tape 4778B, LC; *JD Papers,* 5:118; *JD Papers,* 6:172. William C. Davis, *Jefferson Davis,* 112, suggests that herpes may have caused Jefferson's blindness, but presumably Varina would have contracted the virus from him and lost her vision too.

33. Deposition of Varina Davis, 359, Davis v. Bowmar; VHD to Margaret Howell, 9 Feb. 1852, n.d. 1853, JD Papers, AL; W. Preston Johnston to Rosa Johnston, 4 May 1862, Johnston Papers, TL; VHD to Margaret Howell, 26 Mar. 1854, JD Papers, AL; *JD Papers,* 4:119–121; VHD to Margaret Howell, 29 [n.d.] 1854, JD Papers, AL.

34. *Memoir,* 1:534, 556–557, 571; VHD to Francis G. Lawley, 8 June 1898, Pierce Butler Papers, TL; *JD Papers,* 7:112 n. 13; VHD to Martha Phillips, 16 Apr. 1867, Philip Phillips Papers, LC; VHD to Margaret Howell, 7–14 May 1855, JD Papers, AL; *JD Papers,* 2:662 n. 3, 6:373 n. 9; Francis B. Heitman, *Historical Register and Dictionary of the United States Army* (Washington, D.C.: Government Printing Office, 1903), 1:527.

35. "Winnie Davis in Syracuse," unknown newspaper, [1880s], n.p., in George W. Jones to JD, 25 Nov. 1886, JD Family Coll., MC; Lizzie Blair Lee to S. P. Lee, 28 Apr. 1856, Blair and Lee Papers, Rare Books and Special Colls., Princeton Univ. Library; VHD to Margaret Howell, n.d. 1853, 7–14 May 1855, VHD to JD, 10 Apr. 1859, VHD to Margaret Howell, n.d. [May] 1857, VHD to William B. Howell, 1 Sept. 1859, JD Papers, AL.

36. Randall Blackshaw, "Mrs. Jefferson Davis: The Record of Two Conversations," *Putnam's Magazine* 1 (Dec. 1906): 363; VHD to Margaret Howell, 16 [Jan.] 1859, JD Papers, AL; *Memoir,* 1:414–415; "Mrs. Davis Passes Away," *Baltimore Sun,* 17 Oct. 1906, p. 1; *JD Papers,* 5:126; VHD to Margaret Howell, 1 Mar. 1859, JD Papers, AL; VHD to F. Philp, 2 July 1859, Huntington Ms. 21002, HL.

37. *Memoir,* 1:415; Maggie Howell to Mrs. Howell, 29 Dec. 1856, JD Papers, AL; Mary Kelley, "Reading Women/Women Reading: The Making of Learned Women in Antebellum America," *Journal of American History* 83 (Sept. 1996): 401–424; VHD to Jane Pierce, 25 May 1857, Varina Davis Subject File, MS; VHD to Jane Pierce, 9 Oct. 1859, Franklin Pierce Papers, LC; VHD to her parents, 15 Sept. 1856, JD Papers, AL; *JD Papers,* 4:173–175, 5:28, 123.

38. W. C. Davis, *Jefferson Davis,* 245; Philip Shriver Klein, *President James Buchanan: A Biography* (University Park, Penn.: Pennsylvania State University Press, 1962), 37, 55, 93, 102, 141–142, 193–194, 208–209, 215, 224, 245; Schurz, *Reminiscences,* 2:210–211; *Memoir,* 1:448, 531, 222–223; Pryor, *Reminiscences,* 56, 53; Charles B. Sedgwick to Dora Sedgwick, 15 Dec. 1859, Charles B. Sedgwick Papers, Syracuse Univ.; Caroli, *First Ladies,* 337–338; VHD to James Buchanan, 18 Mar. 1861, James Buchanan Papers, Historical Society of Pennsylvania; Clay-Clopton, *Belle of the Fifties,* 114.

39. VHD to Margaret Howell, 31 Jan. 1857, JD Papers, AL; *Memoir,* 1:570–571; William B. Howell to JD, 20 Jan. 1857, JD and Family Papers, MS.

40. *JD Papers,* 6:110 n. 4; VHD to William B. Howell, 13 Feb. 1857, JD Papers, AL; *JD Papers,* 5:112; VHD to her parents, 15 Sept. 1856, JD Papers, AL; Deposition of Varina Davis, 366–367, Davis v. Bowmar; "Local News," *Washington Daily Union,* 5 Mar. 1857, p. 3; VHD to Margaret Howell, n.d. [May] 1857, JD Papers, AL.

41. William B. Howell to VHD, 11 Aug. 1857, JD Papers, LC; Federal Census of 1860, Free Schedule, Louisiana, New Orleans, 11th Ward, p. 832; VHD to William

B. Howell, 7 Sept. 1857, JD Papers, AL; William B. Howell to Joseph B. Howell, 1 Sept. 1858, 2–3 May 1859, 7 Dec. 1857, Howell Family Papers, HL; Joseph Howell to William B. Howell, 8 Sept. 1858, William B. Howell and Family Papers, MS; *JD Papers,* 2:332–333 n. 18, 5:73 n. 2; VHD to William B. Howell, 14 Nov. 1858, VHD to her parents, 15 Sept. 1856, VHD to Margaret Howell, 19 [July] 1857, JD Papers, AL.

4. FIRST LADY

1. George Mifflin Dallas, *Diary of George Mifflin Dallas, while United States Minister to Russia 1837 to 1839, and to England 1856–1861,* ed. Susan Dallas (Philadelphia: J. B. Lippincott, 1892), 323; Mrs. Roger A. Pryor, *Reminiscences of Peace and War,* rev. ed. (New York: Macmillan, 1905), 74, 59; Virginia Clay-Clopton, *A Belle of the Fifties: Memoirs of Mrs. Clay of Alabama, Covering Social and Political Life in Washington and the South, 1853–66,* ed. Ada Sterling (New York: Doubleday, Page and Co., 1904), 87; Mary Logan, *Reminiscences of the Civil War and Reconstruction,* ed. George Washington Adams (Carbondale: Southern Illinois University Press, 1970), 17; JD to VHD, 27 July 1857, JD Papers, TU; VHD to Margaret Howell, 16 [n.d.] 1859, JD Papers, AL; VHD to Jane Pierce, [4 Apr.] 1858, Franklin Pierce Papers, LC.

2. Almira Hancock, *Reminiscences of Winfield Scott Hancock, by His Wife* (New York: Charles L. Webster and Co., 1887), 45–46; Pryor, *Reminiscences,* 81; Mary E. M. White, ed., *Etiquette for All Occasions* (Boston: Allston Station, 1900), 162; VHD to Margaret Howell, 16 [n.d.] 1859, JD Papers, AL; Elizabeth Blair Lee to S. P. Lee, 28 Mar. 1860, Blair and Lee Papers, Rare Books and Special Colls., Princeton Univ. Library; VHD to Margaret Howell, 21 Nov. 1858, JD Papers, AL; "Hon. Jefferson Davis," *Harper's,* 9 Jan. 1858, p. 1.

3. Timothy D. Johnson, *Winfield Scott: The Quest for Military Glory* (Lawrence: University Press of Kansas, 1998), 217–219, 2, 141–142; *Memoir,* 1:555; George T. Denison, *Soldiering in Canada: Recollections and Experiences* (Toronto: George N. Morang and Co., 1901), 72–74; Clay-Clopton, *Belle of the Fifties,* 134; "Local Intelligence," *Washington Union,* 10 Apr. 1858, p. 3.

4. VHD to Margaret Howell, 15 Feb. 1859, 1 Mar. 1859, JD Papers, AL; *JD Papers,* 6:xlix; *Memoir,* 1:584–586, 589–592; Christine I. De Wechmar Stoess, comp. Lorraine Chapman, "Episodes in the Life of Margaret Graham Howell," 26, JD Assoc., RU; VHD to Mrs. White, 16 Mar. 1884, JD Family Coll., MC; James P. Shenton, *Robert John Walker: A Politician from Jackson to Lincoln* (New York: Columbia University Press, 1961), 9–10.

5. *Memoir,* 1:593–594, 608; William B. Howell to Joseph B. Howell, 5 Nov. 1858, Howell Family Papers, HL; Elizabeth Blair Lee to S. P. Lee, 22 Oct. 1858, Blair and Lee Papers, Rare Books and Special Colls., Princeton Univ. Library.

6. VHD to Margaret Howell, 15 Sept. 1858, VHD to William B. Howell, 14 Nov. 1858, VHD to Margaret Howell, 21 Nov. 1858, JD Papers, AL; *JD Papers,* 6:60 n. 13; Richard Rankin, *Ambivalent Churchmen and Evangelical Churchwomen: The Religion of the Episcopal Elite in North Carolina, 1800–1860* (Columbia: University of South

Carolina Press, 1993), 79–80; VHD to Margaret Howell, 15 Feb. 1859, JD Papers, AL.

7. VHD to JD, 10 Apr. 1859, VHD to JD, 2 July 1859, JD Papers, AL; *JD Papers,* 6:xlvi–lii, 130; VHD to Margaret Howell, 1 Mar. 1859, VHD to William B. Howell, 7 Sept. 1857, VHD to Margaret Howell, 15 Sept. 1858, JD Papers, AL.

8. Ralph Korngold, *Thaddeus Stevens: A Being Darkly Wise and Rudely Great* (New York: Harcourt Brace, 1955), 62–63, 72–76; Johnson, *Winfield Scott,* 101, 222; Eli N. Evans, *Judah Benjamin: The Jewish Confederate* (New York: Free Press, 1988), 103–105; Mary Boykin Chesnut, *Mary Chesnut's Civil War,* ed. C. Vann Woodward (New Haven: Yale University Press, 1981), 414; W. Andy Holman to VHD, 17 Mar. 1890, JD Family Coll., MC; Theophilus Noel, *Autobiography and Reminiscences* (Chicago: Theo. Noel Company Print, 1904), 150; Robert J. Brugger, *Maryland: A Middle Temperament, 1634–1890* (Baltimore: Johns Hopkins University Press and the Maryland Historical Society, 1989), 262; JD to Anna E. Carroll, 22 Dec. 185[7], 26 Mar. 1860, Anna Ella Carroll Papers, H. Furlong Baldwin Library, Maryland Historical Society; *JD Papers,* 6:24 n. 2; VHD to Mrs. Howell Cobb, 13 Jan. 1851, Howell Cobb Papers, UGA.

9. VHD to Margaret Howell, 18–20 May 1850, n.d. 1850, VHD to JD, 2 July 1859, VHD to Margaret Howell, 1 Mar. 1859, JD Papers, AL; *JD Papers,* 6:244.

10. *JD Papers,* 6:243; VHD to Margaret Howell, 1 Mar. 1859, JD Papers, AL; Mrs. D. Giraud Wright, *A Southern Girl in '61: The War-Time Memories of a Confederate Senator's Daughter* (New York: Doubleday, Page and Co., 1905), 29; VHD to JD, 3 Apr. 1859, Jefferson Davis and Family Papers, MS; JD to Mrs. Howell, 28 Mar. 1859, JD Papers, AL; *Memoir,* 1:587; JD to William B. Howell, 17 July 1859, JD and Family Papers, MS; VHD to Margaret Howell, 21 Nov. 1858, VHD to JD, 2 July 1859, JD Papers, AL.

11. VHD to Margaret Howell, 25 Apr. 1859, VHD to JD, 10 Apr. 1859, JD Papers, AL; *JD Papers,* 4:402–416, 6:259 n. 3; Deposition of Varina Davis, 360, Jefferson Davis v. J. H. D. Bowmar et al., MS; VHD to Margaret Howell, n.d. [May], 1859, JD Papers, AL.

12. Deposition of Varina Davis, 367, Davis v. Bowmar; VHD to William B. Howell, 1 Sept. 1859, JD Papers, AL; *JD Papers,* 6:lii; Poem, in *Life in Letters: American Autograph Journal* (May 1939): n.p., misdated 1854, copy at JD Assoc., RU.

13. W. Preston Johnston to Rosa Johnston, 4 May 1862, Johnston Papers, TL; VHD to Margaret Howell, 1 Mar. 1859, JD Papers, AL; Grace Rogers Cooper, *The Sewing Machine: Its Invention and Development* (Washington, D.C.: Smithsonian Institution Press for the National Museum of History and Technology, 1976), 35–38; VHD to unnamed person [Margaret Howell], n.d. [late 1859], JD Papers, AL; *JD Papers,* 6:lii; Advertisements, Grover and Baker Noiseless Sewing Machine, *Harper's Weekly,* 29 Sept. 1860, p. 623, *Harper's Weekly,* 3 Nov. 1860, p. 703.

14. Clay-Clopton, *Belle of the Fifties,* 140–142; Pryor, *Reminiscences,* 98; "Mrs. Gen. Logan Writes on Mrs. Jefferson Davis," *Richmond Evening Journal,* 20 Oct. 1906, p. 6; VHD to Margaret Howell, 16 [n.d.] 1859, JD Papers, AL; Robert W.

Johannsen, *Stephen A. Douglas* (New York: Oxford University Press, 1973), 685–686; VHD to her parents, 15 Sept. 1856, JD Papers, AL; Elizabeth Blair Lee, *Wartime Washington: The Civil War Letters of Elizabeth Blair Lee,* ed. Virginia Jeans Laas, foreword by Dudley T. Cornish (Urbana: University of Illinois, 1991), 398; Lizzie Blair Lee to S. P. Lee, 5 Oct. 1860, Blair and Lee Papers, Rare Books and Special Colls., Princeton Univ. Library; VHD to Jane Pierce, 13 Oct. 1860, Subject File, Varina Howell Davis, MS.

15. William E. Parrish, *Frank Blair: Lincoln's Conservative* (Columbia: University of Missouri Press, 1998), 47, 62, 83, 112 n. 1; Elbert Smith, *Francis Preston Blair* (New York: Free Press, 1980), 42–46, 219, 262–263, 92–93, 192, 237, 240, 181–189, 3–5; *Memoir,* 1:224; Lee, *Wartime Washington,* 27, 223, 262.

16. Smith, *Francis Preston Blair,* 221–223; Lizzie Blair Lee to S. P. Lee, 7 Oct. 1851, 28 Mar. 1860, 26 Sept. 1860, Blair and Lee Family Papers, Rare Books and Special Colls., Princeton Univ. Library; JD to Mrs. Howell, 28 Mar. 1859, JD Papers, AL.

17. Chesnut, *Mary Chesnut's Civil War,* 800; VHD to Jane Pierce, 13 Oct. 1860, Subject File, Varina Howell Davis, MS; *JD Papers,* 6:liv–lv; VHD to Miss Hudson, 10 Oct. 1860, copy courtesy of Lee and Debbie Cravens; William C. Davis, *Breckinridge: Statesman, Soldier, Symbol* (Baton Rouge: Louisiana State University Press, 1974), 245.

18. *JD Papers,* 6:371–374.

19. *JD Papers,* 6:liv–lv; VHD to Dunning R. McNair, n.d. Dec. 1860, VHD to James Buchanan, 25 Dec. 1860, Buchanan Papers, Historical Society of Pennsylvania; James Buchanan, *Mr. Buchanan's Administration on the Eve of the Rebellion* (Salem, N.H.: Ayer Co., 1865, 1990), 184; JD to VHD, 3–4 Feb. 1866, JD Papers, TU; James Buchanan to VHD, 20 Jan. 1861, James Buchanan Papers, Historical Society of Pennsylvania; James Morris Morgan, *Recollections of a Rebel Reefer* (Boston: Houghton Mifflin, 1917), 221–222; VHD to unnamed person, 1 Jan. 1861, Mrs. Jefferson Davis Letters, State Historical Society of Iowa.

20. Lizzie Blair Lee to S. P. Lee, 5 Dec. 1860, n.d. [Dec. 1–2], 1860, Blair and Lee Family Papers, Rare Books and Special Colls., Princeton Univ. Library; Lee, *Wartime Washington,* 14, 79, 18.

21. Lizzie Blair Lee to S. P. Lee, 3–4 Dec. 1860, Blair and Lee Family Papers, Rare Books and Special Colls., Princeton Univ. Library; Memoirs of A. G. Brown, 55–59, J. F. H. Claiborne Papers, UNC; Gideon Welles, *Diary of Gideon Welles, Secretary of the Navy under Lincoln and Johnson,* ed. Howard K. Beale assisted by Alan W. Brownsword, 3 vols. (New York: W. W. Norton, 1960), 2:255–256; David Dixon Porter, *Incidents and Anecdotes of the Civil War* (New York: D. Appleton, 1885), 7–11; Frank Freidel, comp. and ed., *Union Pamphlets of the Civil War, 1861–1865,* 2 vols. (Cambridge, Mass.: Belknap Press of Harvard University Press, 1967), 2:620; "From Maryland," *New York Tribune,* 10 Apr. 1861, p. 6.

22. Elizabeth Keckley, *Behind the Scenes, Or, Thirty Years a Slave, and Four Years in the White House,* with an introduction by James Olney (New York: Oxford University Press, 1988), 65–73; Chesnut, *Mary Chesnut's Civil War,* 800, 40.

23. VHD to Jane Pierce, 13 Oct. 1860, Subject File, Varina Howell Davis, MS; VHD to her parents, 28 Oct. 1851, JD Papers, AL; Lee, *Wartime Washington,* 476.

24. VHD to Mary Ann Cobb, 6 Sept. 1867, Papers of Howell Cobb and Wife and Others, New-York Historical Society; *Memoir,* 2:211–215; *Memoir,* 1:420, 581–583; Robert C. Toll, *Blacking Up: The Minstrel Show in Nineteenth Century America* (New York: Oxford University Press, 1977), v, 31; Carl Sferrazza Anthony, *First Ladies: The Saga of the Presidents' Wives and Their Powers, 1789–1961* (New York: William Morrow, 1990), 145.

25. Anthony, *First Ladies,* 162; Roy Franklin Nichols, *Franklin Pierce: Young Hickory of the Granite Hills,* 2nd ed. (1931; repr., Philadelphia: University of Pennsylvania Press, 1958), 515–522; John M. Belohlavek, *George Mifflin Dallas: Jacksonian Patrician* (University Park: Pennsylvania State University Press, 1977), 174, 180–181; Shenton, *Robert John Walker,* 185–189; Royce Gordon Shingleton, *John Taylor Wood: Sea Ghost of the Confederacy* (Athens: University of Georgia, 1979), 10–19.

26. VHD to [Margaret Howell], n.d. [June] 1861, postscript by William B. Howell, JD Papers, AL; D. Clayton James, *Antebellum Natchez* (Baton Rouge: Louisiana State University Press, 1968), 291–292; Lewis Howell to Joseph B. Howell, 4 June 1865, James Agnew to Joseph B. Howell, 23 Aug. 1862, Sarah H. Agnew to Joseph B. Howell, 3 July–1 Aug. 1864, Howell Family Papers, HL; Joseph B. Howell to William B. Howell, 10 Dec. 1860, William B. Howell and Family Papers, MS; William B. Thomas to Joseph B. Howell, 30 May 1861, Franklin Glaser to Joseph B. Howell, 16 Nov. 1864, Memoranda Book by George F. Howell, 22 Apr. 1861, 6 Nov. 1861, 17 June 1864, A. L. Harris to Joseph B. Howell, 5 Oct. n.d. [1862], Howell Family Papers, HL; VHD to William E. Dodd, 16 June 1905, William E. Dodd Papers, LC; unnamed person to Joseph B. Howell, n.d. 1860–1861, Lewis Howell to Joseph B. Howell, 5 Feb. 1865, Howell Family Papers, HL.

27. Virginia Jeans Laas, "Elizabeth Blair Lee: Union Counterpart of Mary Boykin Chesnut," *Journal of Southern History* 50 (Aug. 1984): 398; Chesnut, *Mary Chesnut's Civil War,* 68, 101; John d'Entremont, *Southern Emancipator: Moncure Conway, the American Years, 1832–1865* (New York: Oxford University Press, 1987), 14–15, 152.

28. Drew Gilpin Faust, *Mothers of Invention: Women of the Slaveholding South in the American Civil War* (Chapel Hill: University of North Carolina Press, 1996), 13–18; VHD to JD, 2 July 1859, JD Papers, AL; "McArone," *Life and Adventures of Jeff Davis* (Hinsdale, N.H.: Hunter and Co., 1865), p. 25.

29. Welles, *Diary,* 2:273; L. S. Foster to his wife, 22 Dec. n.d. [1860, misdated 1859], Lafayette S. Foster Papers, Massachusetts Historical Society; M. E. Gwin to Mary Ann Cobb, 5 Jan. 1861, Howell Cobb Papers, UGA; Henry Watterson, *'Marse Henry': An Autobiography,* 2 vols. (New York: George H. Doran Co., 1919), 1:76; *Memoir,* 2:55; Anthony, *First Ladies,* 167; VHD to unnamed person, 1 Jan. 1861, Mrs. Jefferson Davis Letters, State Historical Society of Iowa; James M. McPherson, *Battle Cry of Freedom: The Civil War Era* (New York: Oxford University Press, 1988), 252–254.

30. Edward Cross to "Dear General," 14 Feb. 1858, Lytle Family Papers, Cin-

cinnati Historical Society Library; Lee, *Wartime Washington*, 37; Basil Wilson Duke, *Reminiscences of General Basil W. Duke, C.S.A.* (Garden City, N.Y.: Doubleday, Page and Co., 1911), 340; John H. Reagan, *Memoirs, with Special Reference to Secession and the Civil War*, ed. Walter Flavius McCaleb, intro. by George P. Garrison (New York: Neale Publishing Co., 1906), 252; Christopher J. Olsen, *Political Culture and Secession in Mississippi: Masculinity, Honor, and the Antiparty Tradition, 1830–1860* (New York: Oxford University Press, 2000), 49–50; JD, *The Rise and Fall of the Confederate Government*, foreword by Bell I. Wiley, 2 vols. (New York: Thomas Yoseloff, 1880, 1958), 1:205–206.

31. Steven A. Channing, *Crisis of Fear: Secession in South Carolina* (New York: W. W. Norton, 1970), 252–293; David Williams, Teresa Crisp Williams, and David Carlson, *Plain Folk in a Rich Man's War: Class and Dissent in Confederate Georgia* (Gainesville: University Press of Florida, 2002), 10–20; William C. Davis, *Jefferson Davis: The Man and the Hour* (New York: HarperCollins, 1991), 308; McPherson, *Battle Cry of Freedom*, 235; *Memoir*, 2:3n, 1:697–699; *JD Papers*, 7:xxxix, 18–23.

32. *JD Papers*, 7:35, 27; Keckley, *Behind the Scenes*, 89–90; Eugenia Phillips, "Memoirs," in *Memoirs of American Jews*, ed. Jacob Rader Marcus (Philadelphia: Jewish Society of America, 1955), 3:165; *Memoir*, 2:5; *JD Papers*, 2:377, 379; M. E. Gwin to Mary Ann Cobb, 5 Jan. 1861, Howell Cobb Papers, UGA; David Herbert Donald, *Lincoln* (New York: Simon and Schuster, 1995), 278–279.

33. William Terry Moore Reminiscences, n.p., Archives and Special Colls., Univ. of Mississippi; *Memoir*, 2:6–7, 11–12, 18–19, 34; VHD to James Buchanan, 18 Mar. 1861, James Buchanan Papers, Historical Society of Pennsylvania; *JD Papers*, 7:37; W. C. Davis, *Jefferson Davis*, 301–304; George P. Rawick, ed., *The American Slave: A Composite Autobiography* (Westport, Conn.: Greenwood Press, 1977), suppl. ser. 1, vol. 8, Mississippi, pt. 3, p. 1003, Florida Hewitt; Frank E. Everett Jr., *Brierfield: Plantation Home of Jefferson Davis* (Hattiesburg: University and College Press of Mississippi, 1971), 74; C. Vann Woodward and Elisabeth Muhlenfeld, *The Private Mary Chesnut: The Unpublished Civil War Diaries* (New York: Oxford University Press, 1984), 23.

34. Deposition of Varina Davis, 359–362, Davis v. Bowmar.

35. VHD to James Buchanan, 18 Mar. 1861, James Buchanan Papers, Historical Society of Pennsylvania; *JD Papers*, 7:54 n. 3; *Memoir*, 2:37; "From Fortress Monroe," *New York Times*, 2 July 1865, p. 2; William Warren Rogers Jr., *Confederate Home Front: Montgomery during the Civil War* (Tuscaloosa: University of Alabama Press, 1999), 1–8, 24–25.

36. "Mr. Yancey's Speech," *New York Herald*, 23 Feb. 1861, p. 2; W. T. Walthall to Mrs. W. T. Walthall, 14 Mar. 1861, W. T. Walthall Papers, MS; Reuben Davis, *Recollections of Mississippi and Mississippians* (Boston: Houghton Mifflin, 1889), 320; VHD to C. C. Clay, 10 May 1861, C. C. Clay Papers, DU; Diary of Anita Dwyer Withers, 20 June 1861, UNC; William Howard Russell, *My Diary North and South*, ed. and with an introduction by Fletcher Pratt (New York: Harper and Bros., 1954), 97; T. C. De Leon, *Belles, Beaux and Brains of the 60's* (New York: G. W. Dillingham Co., 1909), 48; "Mrs. Davis," *Charleston Mercury*, 11 Mar. 1861, p. 1; Chesnut, *Mary*

Chesnut's Civil War, 17; W. Preston Johnston to William Preston, 3 May 1861, Wickliffe-Preston Family Papers, Special Colls., Univ. of Kentucky.

37. VHD to C. C. Clay, 10 May 1861, Clay Papers, DU; Howell Cobb to his son, 5 Mar. 1861, Howell Cobb Papers, UGA; Chesnut, *Mary Chesnut's Civil War*, 60–61, 59 n. 5, 113, 109, 68, 101; "A Northern Woman in the Confederacy: From the Diary of Margaret S. McLean," *Harper's Weekly*, Feb. 1914, 442–443, 451; Keckley, *Behind the Scenes*, 73; DeLeon, *Belles, Beaux and Brains*, 50; Faust, *Mothers of Invention*, 201–202, 231; George C. Rable, *Civil Wars: Women and the Crisis of Southern Nationalism* (Urbana: University of Illinois Press, 1989), 47–49; Lee Ann Whites, *The Civil War as a Crisis in Gender: Augusta, Georgia, 1860–1890* (Athens: University of Georgia Press, 1995), 24, 105–106.

38. Philip Shriver Klein, *President James Buchanan: A Biography* (University Park: Pennsylvania State University Press, 1962), 391, 402; James Buchanan to VHD, 20 Jan. 1861, VHD to James Buchanan, 18 Mar. 1861, James Buchanan Papers, Historical Society of Pennsylvania.

5. NO MATTER WHAT DANGER THERE WAS

1. *JD Papers*, 7:xl; Elizabeth Blair Lee, *Wartime Washington: The Civil War Letters of Elizabeth Blair Lee*, ed. Virginia Jeans Laas, foreword by Dudley T. Cornish (Urbana: University of Illinois Press, 1991), 33; *JD Papers*, 7:63, 302; *Register of Officers of the Confederate States Navy, 1861–1865* (Washington, D.C.: Government Printing Office, 1931), 93, NA; *JD Papers*, 8:181 n. 12; Ralph W. Donnelly, *The History of the Confederate States Marine Corps* (Washington, D.C.: Author, 1976), 121.

2. "Graceful Letter from Our President's Wife," *Richmond Daily Dispatch*, 18 May 1861, p. 1; *JD Papers*, 7:170 n. 1, 73 n. 18; William Howard Russell, *My Diary North and South*, ed. and with an introduction by Fletcher Pratt (New York: Harper and Bros., 1954), 117–119, 98; VHD to C. C. Clay, 10 May 1861, C. C. Clay Papers, DU.

3. *JD Papers*, 7:183, lxi; H. A. Herbert, "Grandfather's Talks," 107–108, Hilary Abner Herbert Papers, UNC; Gregg D. Kimball, *American City, Southern Place: A Cultural History of Antebellum Richmond* (Athens: University of Georgia Press, 2000), 5, 14–36; *Memoir*, 2:75; "Serenade," *Southern Confederacy* (Atlanta), 8 June 1861, p. 1; "Fragrant Bouquet," *Richmond Daily Dispatch*, 21 June 1861, p. 2; VHD to [Margaret Howell], n.d. June 1861, postscript by William B. Howell, JD Papers, AL; Mary Boykin Chesnut, *Mary Chesnut's Civil War*, ed. C. Vann Woodward (New Haven: Yale University Press, 1981), 90.

4. VHD to [Margaret Howell], n.d. June 1861, postscript by William B. Howell, JD Papers, AL. Cf. William C. Davis, *Jefferson Davis: The Man and His Hour* (New York: HarperCollins, 1991), 428, and William J. Cooper Jr., *Jefferson Davis, American* (New York: Alfred A. Knopf, 2000), 372–373, 388–391, which emphasize Varina Davis's support for the Confederacy.

5. *JD Papers*, 7:258–259; John H. Reagan, *Memoirs, with Special Reference to Secession and the Civil War*, ed. Walter Flavius McCaleb, intro. by George P. Garrison (New York: Neale Publishing Co., 1906), 141; Chesnut, *Mary Chesnut's Civil War*, 105–106;

JD Papers, 7:258; "A Northern Woman in the Confederacy: From the Diary of Mrs. Eugene McLean," *Harper's Magazine*, Feb. 1914, p. 447; Lise Mitchell Journal, 27, Mitchell Journal and Letters, TL, copy at UNC; Diary of Anita Dwyer Withers, 20 July 1861, UNC.

6. *White House of the Confederacy: An Illustrated History* (Richmond: Cadmus Marketing, n.d.), 15, 57, 58, 87, 17; W. C. Davis, *Jefferson Davis*, 340; VHD to [Margaret Howell], n.d. June 1861, postscript by William B. Howell, JD Papers, AL; Viscount Wolseley, *The American Civil War: An English View* (Charlottesville: University Press of Virginia, 1964), 18; VHD to George Barksdale, 18 June 1903, Miscellaneous Manuscripts, Valentine Richmond History Center Museum; Kate Doyle to Mrs. Carey, 25 Apr. 1907, Virginia Room Accession Papers, MC; *Memoir*, 2:201–203; Lee, *Wartime Washington*, 228 n. 2.

7. T. C. De Leon, *Four Years in Rebel Capitals: An Inside View of Life in the Southern Confederacy, from Birth to Death* (Mobile: Gossip Printing Co., 1890), 153–155; Edward A. Pollard, *Life of Jefferson Davis, with a Secret History of the Southern Confederacy* (Philadelphia: National Pub. Co., 1869), 154; "The President's Reception," *Charleston Mercury*, 6 Jan. 1862, p. 1; David Herbert Donald, *Lincoln* (New York: Simon and Schuster, 1995), 335; Rembert W. Patrick, *Jefferson Davis and His Cabinet* (Baton Rouge: Louisiana State University Press, 1944), 331–332.

8. *Memoir*, 2:202–203; T. C. De Leon, *Belles, Beaux and Brains of the 60's* (New York: G. W. Dillingham Co., 1907, 1909), 59, 198–199; Virginia Clay-Clopton, *A Belle of the Fifties: Memoirs of Mrs. Clay of Alabama, Covering Social and Political Life in Washington and the South, 1853–66*, ed. Ada Sterling (New York: Doubleday, Page and Co. 1904), 174–175.

9. Sallie A. Putnam, *In Richmond during the Confederacy* (New York: Robert M. McBride Co., 1961), 38; Emma L. Bryan, "Reminiscences," 3, Early Papers, VHS; Chesnut, *Mary Chesnut's Civil War*, 127, 667, 504; Warren Akin, *Letters of Warren Akin, Confederate Congressman*, ed. Bell Irvin Wiley (Athens: University of Georgia Press, 1959), 20; *JD Papers*, 8:515; *White House of the Confederacy*, 38.

10. Recollections of Leeland Hathaway, 21, Leeland Hathaway Papers, UNC; Putnam, *In Richmond*, 38; Bell Irvin Wiley, *Confederate Women* (Westport, Conn.: Greenwood Press, 1975), 118; Pollard, *Life of Jefferson Davis*, 154; Varina Davis's clothing, MC; "Chronicle of the Rebellion," *Burlington Free Press* (Vermont), 18 May 1862, n.p.; John Q. Anderson, introduction to *Brokenburn: The Journal of Kate Stone, 1861–1868*, ed. John Q. Anderson (Baton Rouge: Louisiana State University Press, 1956), xviii; Putnam, *In Richmond*, 38; Elisabeth Muhlenfeld, *Mary Boykin Chesnut: A Biography*, foreword by C. Vann Woodward (Baton Rouge: Louisiana State University Press, 1981), 53; Thomas E. Schott, *Alexander H. Stephens of Georgia* (Baton Rouge: Louisiana State University Press, 1988), 20; T. Harry Williams, *P. G. T. Beauregard: Napoleon in Gray* (Baton Rouge: Louisiana State University Press, 1955), 51.

11. Henry Kyd Douglas, *I Rode with Stonewall* (Chapel Hill: University of North Carolina Press, 1940), 272; James Morris Morgan, *Recollections of a Rebel Reefer* (Boston: Houghton Mifflin, 1917), 221; "Mrs. Davis in Richmond," *Richmond Daily*

Dispatch, 30 May 1861, p. 2; Chesnut, *Mary Chesnut's Civil War,* 325, 137, 500–501, 748; "Jeff Davis's Coachman," *New York Tribune,* 24 May 1862, p. 8; Constance Cary Harrison, *Recollections Grave and Gay* (New York: Charles Scribner's Sons, 1911), 70.

12. Diary of Stephen R. Mallory, 23 June 1861, UNC; De Leon, *Belles, Beaux and Brains,* 67; Mrs. D. Girard Wright, *A Southern Girl in '61: The War-Times Memories of a Confederate Senator's Daughter* (New York: Doubleday, Page and Co., 1905), 56–57.

13. Mary Boykin Chesnut, *The Private Mary Chesnut: The Unpublished Civil War Diaries,* ed. C. Vann Woodward and Elisabeth Muhlenfeld (New York: Oxford University Press, 1984), 101–102; Memoir of Anna C. L. Logan, 42–43, copy at VHS; Diary of Stephen R. Mallory, 23 June 1861, UNC; W. W. Blackford, *War Years with Jeb Stuart* (Baton Rouge: Louisiana State University Press, 1993), 15–16; Chesnut, *Mary Chesnut's Civil War,* 136; Judith W. McGuire, *Diary of a Southern Refugee during the War* (1867; repr., New York: Arno Press, 1972), 96; Bryan, "Reminiscences," 1, Early Papers, VHS.

14. Claire Tomalin, *Jane Austen: A Life* (New York: Alfred A. Knopf, 1998), 134–135; James Fox, *Five Sisters: The Langhornes of Virginia* (New York: Simon and Schuster, 2000), 114–115; George Cary Eggleston, *A Rebel's Recollections* (New York: Hurd and Houghton, 1875), 47, 56–76; Daniel W. Crofts, *Reluctant Confederates: Upper South Unionists and the Secession Crisis* (Chapel Hill: University of North Carolina Press, 1989), 315; Elizabeth Van Lew, *A Yankee Spy in Richmond: The Civil War Diary of 'Crazy Bet' Van Lew,* ed. David D. Ryan (Mechanicsburg, Penn.: Stackpole Books, 1996), 32–33; Kimball, *American City, Southern Place,* 217, 234; Chesnut, *Mary Chesnut's Civil War,* 75, 361–363, 459; *JD Papers,* 9:124 n. 2; Patrick, *Davis and His Cabinet,* 58n, 304, 337.

15. Chesnut, *Mary Chesnut's Civil War,* 82, 134; Lee, *Wartime Washington,* 47–50, 232–233; Reagan, *Memoirs,* 132; John B. Jones, *A Rebel War Clerk's Diary,* ed. Earl Schenck Miers (New York: Sagamore Press, 1958), 55; Edwin C. Fishel, *The Secret War for the Union: The Untold Story of Military Intelligence in the Civil War* (Boston: Houghton Mifflin, 1996), 312; Charles A. Dana, *Recollections of the Civil War: With the Leaders at Washington and in the Field in the Sixties* (New York: D. Appleton and Co., 1898), 235–237; John H. Brinton, *Personal Memoirs of John H. Brinton, Major and Surgeon, U.S.V., 1861–1865* (New York: Neale Pub. Co., 1914), 65; Julia G. Tyler to Juliana M. Gardiner, 12 May 1863, Tyler Family Papers, Earl Gregg Swem Library, College of William and Mary.

16. Chesnut, *Private Mary Chesnut,* 99; Franklin Glaser to Joseph B. Howell, 25 Feb. 1861, 16 Nov. 1864, 26 Oct. 1861, Joseph B. Howell to Francis Southwick, 10 Oct. 1863, Letter Account Book of George Howell, Letters Recd., Answered, 1858–1866, Sarah H. Agnew to Joseph B. Howell, 4 July 1864, Howell Family Papers, HL.

17. Kimball, *American City, Southern Place,* 234; *JD Papers,* 9:284–285; Mark E. Neely Jr., *Southern Rights: Political Prisoners and the Myth of Confederate Constitutionalism* (Charlottesville: University Press of Virginia, 1999), 87–91, 112–113, 128–133; Thomas G. Dyer, *Secret Yankees: The Union Circle in Confederate Atlanta* (Baltimore:

Johns Hopkins University Press, 1999), 97–114, 271; William M. Robinson Jr., *Justice in Grey: A History of the Judicial System of the Confederate States of America* (Cambridge, Mass.: Harvard University Press, 1941), 292–293, 446–447; Jones, *Rebel War Clerk's Diary,* 47–48; Memoir of John G. Lange, 2 vols., 1:171, VHS; Jon L. Wakelyn, *Confederates against the Confederacy: Essays on Leadership and Loyalty* (Westport, Conn.: Praeger, 2002), 53–58.

18. W. C. Davis, *Jefferson Davis,* 317; Janet Sharp Hermann, *Joseph E. Davis: Pioneer Patriarch* (Jackson: University Press of Mississippi, 1990), 98; Jane Howell to William Howell, 17 July 1862, JD Family Coll., MC; Eliza Davis to "Dear Mattie," 10 Aug. 1861, Lise Mitchell Papers, TL; Pocket Diary of Edward Owen, 22 Aug. 1863, 24 Dec. 1863, MC; McGuire, *Southern Refugee,* 116; *White House of the Confederacy,* 83; Chesnut, *Mary Chesnut's Civil War,* 595.

19. VHD to [Margaret Howell], n.d. June 1861, postscript by William B. Howell, JD Papers, AL; Bryan, "Reminiscences," 2–3, Early Papers, VHS; VHD to C. C. Clay, 10 May 1861, Clay Papers, DU; Isabella Middleton Leland, ed., "Middleton Correspondence, 1861–1865," *South Carolina Historical Magazine* 63 (Apr. 1962): 65; Occasional Book of Miss Lizzie Rowland, Family Coll. Series / Kate Mason Rowland Coll., MC; Clay-Clopton, *Belle of the Fifties,* 170; "This Quilt," 8 Mar. 1862, Armistead Burt Papers, DU; VHD to "Dear Ladies," 1 May 1899, Mount Vernon Ladies Assoc.; "New Year's Day," *Richmond Daily Dispatch,* 2 Jan. 1862, p. 2.

20. *JD Papers,* 8:58n; Harrison, *Recollections Grave and Gay,* 70; *JD Papers,* 8:55; *Memoir,* 2:183; Betty Boyd Caroli, *First Ladies,* rev. ed. (New York: Oxford University Press, 1995), 9, 53; Jones, *Rebel War Clerk's Diary,* 68; James R. McLean to "My Dear Wife," 23 Feb. 1862, Eldridge Coll., HL.

21. Lee, *Wartime Washington,* 110, 232; "Mrs. Jefferson Davis Wants," *Delaware Democratic Standard* (Ohio), 19 Feb. 1863, n.p.; "Seizure of Boots for Jeff Davis and Night Gowns for Mrs. Jeff," *Chicago Tribune,* 3 Apr. 1863, p. 1; "Proclamation by the President," *Daily Constitutionalist,* 4 Mar. 1863, p. 1; *JD Papers,* 9:231–232.

22. Bryan, "Reminiscences," 3, Early Papers, VHS; Chesnut, *Mary Chesnut's Civil War,* 271 n. 5; Robert G. H. Kean, *Inside the Confederate Government: The Diary of Robert Garlick Kean, Head of the Bureau of War,* ed. Edward Younger (New York: Oxford University Press, 1957), 90; Rayna Green, "The Pocahontas Perplex: The Image of Indian Women in American Culture," in *Unequal Sisters: A Multicultural Reader in U.S. Women's History,* ed. Ellen Carol DuBois and Vicki L. Ruiz (New York: Routledge, 1990), 17–19; G. W. B. [Bagby] to Robert B. Rhett Jr., n.d. [1862], Robert B. Rhett Papers, USC; Isabella Middleton Leland, ed., "Middleton Correspondence, 1861–1865," *South Carolina Historical Magazine* 64 (Jan. 1963): 30.

23. Claudia T. Johnson, *Lady Bird Johnson: A White House Diary* (New York: Holt, Rinehart and Winston, 1970), 577, 622–623; Betty Ford, *The Times of My Life,* with Chris Chase (New York: Harper and Row / Reader's Digest Assoc., 1978), 207–208, 222, 261; Gail Collins, *Scorpion Tongues: Gossip, Celebrity, and American Politics* (New York: William Morrow, 1998), 6–7; Carl Sferrazza Anthony, *First Ladies: The Saga of the Presidents' Wives and Their Powers, 1789–1961* (New York: William Morrow,

1990); Caroli, *First Ladies;* Muhlenfeld, *Mary Boykin Chesnut,* 128; Eliza Ripley, *Social Life in Old New Orleans* (New York: Arno Press, 1975), 202; Joan E. Cashin, ed., *Our Common Affairs: Texts from Women in the Old South* (Baltimore: Johns Hopkins University Press, 1996), 245–247.

24. Caroli, *First Ladies,* 46; Mary E. M. White, ed., *Etiquette for All Occasions* (Boston: Allston Station, 1900), 101–102; Mary Soames, *Clementine Churchill,* rev. ed. (London: Doubleday, 2002), 96–97, 238–239, 336; Johnson, *White House Diary,* 15, 317–318, 639; Ford, *Times of My Life,* 222.

25. Chesnut, *Mary Chesnut's Civil War,* 61 n. 3, 15 n. 2, 91, 60–61, 25, 62, 76, 83, 467–468, 429, 17, 549; Muhlenfeld, *Mary Boykin Chesnut,* 53–54, 25–28, 123–126, 109–110, 99.

26. VHD to Francis G. Lawley, 8 June 1898, Pierce Butler Papers, TL; De Leon, *Belles, Beaux and Brains,* 92; Eli N. Evans, *Judah P. Benjamin: The Jewish Confederate* (New York: Free Press, 1988), 3–35, 83–112, 127–128, 135–136, 156.

27. VHD to Francis G. Lawley, 8 June 1898, Pierce Butler Papers, TL; VHD, "Women of the 60's: Letter by Mrs. Jefferson Davis," *Atlanta Constitution,* n.d. 1893, Scrapbook Coll., MC; Evans, *Judah P. Benjamin,* 17.

28. Leonard Dinnerstein, *Antisemitism in America* (New York: Oxford University Press, 1994), 177, 31–33; Chesnut, *Mary Chesnut's Civil War,* 288; Henry S. Foote, *Casket of Reminiscences* (Washington, D.C.: Chronicle Pub. Co., 1874), 237; De Leon, *Belles, Beaux and Brains,* 91; Evans, *Judah P. Benjamin,* 145; John W. Burgess, *Reminiscences of an American Scholar: The Beginnings of Columbia University,* with a foreword by Nicholas Murray Butler (New York: Columbia University Press, 1934), 291; VHD to Francis G. Lawley, 8 June 1898, Pierce Butler Papers, TL.

29. "Jeff Davis's Coachman," *New York Tribune,* 24 May 1862, p. 8; Thomas Hood, *Selected Poems of Thomas Hood,* ed. John Clubbe (Cambridge, Mass.: Harvard University Press, 1970), 71–73; VHD to MBC, 27 Apr. 1862, Chesnut-Miller-Manning Papers, USC; *JD Papers,* 8:222 n. 12, 220.

30. *JD Papers,* 8:53, 196, 197 n. 15, 204 n. 7, 519 n. 8; Hermann, *Joseph E. Davis,* 102, 120–121; Certificate of A. H. Arthur, 540, Jefferson Davis v. J. H. D. Bowmar et al., MS; George P. Rawick, ed., *The American Slave: A Composite Autobiography* (Westport, Conn.: Greenwood Press, 1977), suppl. ser. 1, vol. 9, Mississippi, pt. 4, pp. 1542–43, Isaiah Montgomery; *Memoir,* 2:266–267; VHD to Mr. Guion, 27 Dec. 1889, Guion Family Papers, UNC; VHD to "My Dear Sir," 16 Sept. 1901, Frank E. Stevens Papers, Abraham Lincoln Presidential Library, Springfield, Illinois; H. W. Burton to VHD, 18 Feb. 1890, JD Family Coll., MC; Jefferson Davis, Biographical Files, Costume Coll., Chicago Historical Society.

31. *JD Papers,* 7:352; "Some Clippings Sent by Mrs. Jefferson Davis," *Times Dispatch,* 19 Jan. 1896, n.p., Nannie Ellyson Crump Scrapbook, Scrapbook Coll., E 12, MC; *JD Papers,* 8:182 n. 19; JD to VHD, 26 Nov. 1865, JD Papers, TU; W. Preston Johnston to Rosa Johnston, 31 Oct. 1863, Johnston Papers, TL; B. Lewis Blackford to his mother, 1 Oct. 1862, Blackford Papers, UVA; JD to A. Y. P. Garnett, 9 Nov. 1863, Garnett Family Papers, VHS.

32. *Memoir*, 2:162–163, 919, 301–302; VHD to Rosa Johnston, 7 Aug. 1862, Johnston Papers, TL; *JD Papers*, 8:179; "Will" to "Kate," 30 July 1864, Leonidas Polk Papers, University of the South-Sewanee.

33. Helen M. Keary to "My Dear Mother and Fannie," 7–8 May 1862, in "Jeff Davis behind the Curtain," *New York Tribune*, 8 Aug. 1862, p. 2; *Memoir*, 2:268–269; *JD Papers*, 8:168n, 173 n. 2, 168–169, 253, 188; VHD to "My Dear Mr. Burgwyn," 14 Sept. 1903, W. H. S. Burgwyn Papers, North Carolina State Archives.

34. Untitled article, *Memphis Daily Appeal*, 30 May 1862, p. 1; *JD Papers*, 8:173 n. 2; Catherine Devereux Edmondston, *Journal of a Secesh Lady: The Diary of Catherine Ann Devereux Edmondston, 1860–1866*, ed. Beth G. Crabtree and James W. Patton (Raleigh: Division of Archives and History, Dept. of Cultural Resources, 1979), 176, 180; *White House of the Confederacy*, 51–52.

35. "From McDowell's Army," *New York Tribune*, 12 May 1862, p. 1; "Jefferson Davis's Coachman," *National Anti-Slavery Standard*, 24 May 1862, p. 3; "Jeff Davis's Coachman," *New York Tribune*, 24 May 1862, p. 8.

36. "Jeff Davis's Coachman," *New York Tribune*, 24 May 1862, p. 8; "Jeff Davis's Coachman," *Harper's Weekly*, 7 June 1862, 365.

6. HOLOCAUSTS OF HERSELF

1. "William A. Jackson," *National Anti-Slavery Standard*, 5 Mar. 1864, p. 2; R. J. M. Blackett, *Divided Hearts: Britain and the American Civil War* (Baton Rouge: Louisiana State University Press, 2001), 133; "Among the 'Celebrities,'" *Delaware Democratic Standard* (Ohio), 12 Mar. 1863, p. 1; Isabella Middleton Leland, ed., "Middleton Correspondence, 1861–1865," *South Carolina Historical Magazine* 63 (Apr. 1962): 66; *JD Papers*, 8:178–179; VHD to JD, 12 June 1862, JD and Family Papers, MS.

2. VHD to William F. Howell, 28 May 1862, JD Papers, AL; *JD Papers*, 8:200, 282; VHD to JD, 26 June 1862, JD and Family Papers, MS.

3. *JD Papers*, 8:205–206, 219–221, xlvi–xlvii, 243, 208, 278 n. 9, 282 n. 7; JD to VHD, 21 June 1862, JD Family Coll., MC; Mary Boykin Chesnut, *Mary Chesnut's Civil War*, ed. C. Vann Woodward (New Haven: Yale University Press, 1981), 411.

4. VHD to JD, 6 July 1862, VHD to JD, 5 June 1862, VHD to JD, 12 June 1862, JD and Family Papers, MS; *JD Papers*, 8:205.

5. *JD Papers*, 8:221, 3:53; VHD to Rosa Johnston, 7 Aug. 1862, Johnston Papers, TL; Francis W. Smith to Anna M. D. D. Smith, 24 July 1862, Smith Family Papers, VHS.

6. Helen Keary to "My Dear Mother and Fannie," 7–8 May 1862, in "Jeff Davis behind the Curtain," *New York Tribune*, 8 Aug. 1862, p. 2; *JD Papers*, 8:352, 253–254; *Memoir*, 2:270–274; Louise Barnett, *Touched by Fire: The Life, Death, and Mythic Afterlife of George Armstrong Custer* (New York: Henry Holt, 1996), 42; "Jeff Davis in Tribulation," *New York Times*, 15 May 1864, p. 6.

7. William Preston Johnston, "In Memoriam: Rosa Duncan Johnston," n.p., VHD to Rosa Johnston, 13 Aug. 1862, Johnston Papers, TL.

8. VHD to Rosa Johnston, 13 Aug. 1862, Johnston Papers, TL; Agnes Strickland, *Life of Mary Queen of Scots* (London: George Bell and Sons, 1844, 1893), 1:1, 51–52,

328–333, 459–460, 2:16, 331, 466; Jenny Wormald, *Mary Queen of Scots: A Study in Failure* (London: George Philip, 1988), 8–20, 187–189; Jayne Elizabeth Lewis, *Mary Queen of Scots: Romance and Nation* (London: Routledge, 1998), 10, 178–186

9. VHD to JD, 13 Aug. 1862, JD and Family Papers, MS; W. Preston Johnston to Rosa Johnston, 26 Aug. 1862, Johnston Papers, TL.

10. VHD to JD, 26 June 1862, 12 June 1862, JD and Family Papers, MS.

11. W. Preston Johnston to Rosa Johnston, 24 Oct. 1862, Johnston Papers, TL; B. Lewis Blackford to his mother, 1 Oct. 1862, Blackford Papers, UVA; Thomas Hawkins, *The Origin of the English Drama,* vol. 3 (Oxford: Clarendon Press, 1778); VHD to Angela Mallory, 2 Oct. 1862, Angela Mallory to VHD, [n.d. Oct.] 1862, Mallory Family Papers, Pensacola Historical Society; Josiah Gorgas, *The Journals of Josiah Gorgas, 1857–1878,* ed. Sarah Woolfolk Wiggins, foreword by Frank E. Vandiver (Tuscaloosa: University of Alabama Press, 1995), 54; Chesnut, *Mary Chesnut's Civil War,* 434.

12. Mary Denis Maher, *To Bind Up the Wounds: Catholic Sister Nurses in the U.S. Civil War* (New York: Greenwood Press, 1989), 114; Lizzie Cary Daniel, ed., *Confederate Scrap-Book* (Richmond: J. L. Hill Printing Co., 1893), 17–18; "Direct from Richmond," *New York Times,* 1 Sept. 1861, p. 2.

13. H. H. Cunningham, *Doctors in Gray: The Confederate Medical Service* (Baton Rouge: Louisiana State University Press, 1958), 53; *Memoir,* 2:210, 495, 618, 324; Emma L. Bryan, "Reminiscences," 3, Early Papers, VHS; Thomas Ellis to JD, 2 Nov. 1880, JD Family Coll., MC.

14. Margaret L. Rossiter, *Women in the Resistance* (New York: Praeger, 1986), 115, 197; Alistair Horne, *A Savage War of Peace: Algeria 1954–1962* (London: Macmillan, 1977), 401; Victoria E. Bynum, *Unruly Women: The Politics of Social and Sexual Control in the Old South* (Chapel Hill: University of North Carolina Press, 1992), 130–142; Noel C. Fisher, *War at Every Door: Partisan Politics and Guerilla Violence in East Tennessee, 1860–1869* (Chapel Hill: University of North Carolina Press, 1997), 74; Edwin C. Fishel, *The Secret War for the Union: The Untold Story of Military Intelligence in the Civil War* (Boston: Houghton Mifflin, 1996), 650 n. 95, 85–100, 131; Elizabeth R. Varon, *Southern Lady, Yankee Spy: The True Story of Elizabeth Van Lew, a Union Agent in the Heart of the Confederacy* (New York: Oxford University Press, 2003).

15. Varon, *Southern Lady, Yankee Spy,* 74; Allan Pinkerton, *The Spy of the Rebellion* (New York: G. W. Carleton and Co., 1886), 549–550; VHD to Miss Maury, 17 Apr. 1905, JD Family Coll., MC.

16. *JD Papers,* 8:xlviii, 548–550, 552–553, 557–558; VHD to W. Preston Johnston, 25 Dec. [1862, misdated 1863], Johnston Papers, TL; VHD to MBC, n.d. [Jan.–Feb.] 1863, Williams-Chesnut-Miller-Manning Papers, USC.

17. *JD Papers,* 2:125; Christine I. De Wechmar Stoess, comp. Lorraine Chapman, "Episodes in the Life of Margaret Graham Howell," 31–32, JD Assoc., RU; VHD to William F. Howell, 28 May 1862, JD Papers, AL; *JD Papers,* 9:xlii; W. Preston Johnston to Rosa Johnston, 18 Mar. 1863, Johnston Papers, TL; John B. Jones, *A Rebel War Clerk's Diary,* ed. Earl Schenck Miers (New York: Sagamore Press, 1958), 329; VHD to JD, 28 [Mar.] 1863, JD and Family Papers, MS; *JD Papers,* 9:127–129; VHD

to JD, n.d. Mar. 1863, in "The Late Rebel Leaders," *New York Herald,* 2 July 1865, p. 1.

18. VHD to JD, 28 [Mar.] 1863, JD and Family Papers, MS; William Miller Owen, *In Camp and Battle with the Washington Artillery of New Orleans,* with a new introduction by Nathaniel Cheairs Hughes Jr. (Baton Rouge: Louisiana State University Press, 1999), 204; *JD Papers,* 9:127–129; Robert Seager II, *And Tyler Too: A Biography of John and Julia Gardiner Tyler* (New York: McGraw-Hill, 1963), 4, 29, 123, 243–266, 466–467; Julia G. Tyler to Juliana M. Gardiner, 12 May 1863, Tyler Family Papers, Earl Gregg Swem Library, College of William and Mary.

19. VHD to JD, n.d. Mar. 1863, in "The Late Rebel Leaders," *New York Herald,* 2 July 1865, p. 1.

20. *JD Papers,* 9:xlii; VHD to JD, 28 [Mar.] 1863, JD and Family Papers, MS; Stoess, "Episodes," 32–33, JD Assoc., RU; W. Preston Johnston to Rosa Johnston, 21 Jan. 1863, Johnston Papers, TL; *JD Papers,* 8:181 n. 12, 554 n. 13; Bryan, "Reminiscences," 1, Early Papers, VHS; Seager, *And Tyler Too,* 466, 482; [Arthur James Lyon Fremantle], *The Fremantle Diary, Being the Journal of Lieutenant Colonel James Arthur Lyon Fremantle, Coldstream Guards, on His Three Months in the Southern States,* ed. Walter Lord, introduction by Maurice Ashley (London: Andre Deutsch, 1956), 164; William Alexander Gordon Memoirs, 148, Leyburn Library, Washington and Lee University; Memoir of Catherine Cochran, pt. 1, 23a, VHS.

21. *Memoir,* 2:529; Judith W. McGuire, *Diary of a Southern Refugee during the War* (New York: Arno Press, 1867, 1972), 197; Mrs. Roger A. Pryor, *Reminiscences of Peace and War,* rev. ed. (New York: Macmillan, 1905), 237; George Cary Eggleston, *A Rebel's Recollections* (New York: Hurd and Houghton, 1875), 103–104; W. Preston Johnston to Rosa Johnston, 5 Aug. 1863, Johnston Papers, TL; Campbell Brown, *Campbell Brown's Civil War, with Ewell and the Army of Northern Virginia,* ed. with an introduction by Terry L. Jones (Baton Rouge: Louisiana State University Press, 2001), 186; VHD, "Women of the 60's: Letter by Mrs. Jefferson Davis," *Atlanta Constitution,* n.d. 1893, MC; VHD to Mrs. Clopton, [n.d.] 1864, JD Family Coll., MC; "From Fortress Monroe," *New York Times,* 2 July 1865, p. 2.

22. Pryor, *Reminiscences,* 249; W. Preston Johnston to Rosa Johnston, 16 July 1863, Johnston Papers, TL; Anna Farrar Goldsborough, "Notes on Varina Howell Davis," 6, JD Assoc., RU; *JD Papers,* 9:235 n. 6; *JD Papers,* 6:373 n. 9; W. Preston Johnston to Rosa Johnston, 11 July 1863, Johnston Papers, TL; Alice Fahs, *The Imagined Civil War: Popular Literature of the North and South, 1861–1865* (Chapel Hill: University of North Carolina Press, 2001), 201–202.

23. Chesnut, *Mary Chesnut's Civil War,* 729, 60–61, 136; Lydia Johnston to Charlotte Wigfall, 19 Jan. 1863, Wigfall Family Papers, LC; Mrs. D. Girard Wright, *A Southern Girl in '61: The War-Time Memories of a Confederate Senator's Daughter* (New York: Doubleday, Page and Co., 1905), 90; *JD Papers,* 9:xli; Mary Boykin Chesnut, *The Private Mary Chesnut: The Unpublished Civil War Diaries,* ed. C. Vann Woodward and Elisabeth Muhlenfeld (New York: Oxford University Press, 1984), 89–90, 98, 102; Alvy King, *Louis T. Wigfall, Southern Fire-eater* (Baton Rouge: Louisiana State University Press, 1970), 37, 133, 141, 184; Lydia Johnston to L. Wigfall, 22 Jan. 1865,

Wigfall Family Papers, LC; Craig L. Symonds, *Joseph E. Johnston: A Civil War Biography* (New York: W. W. Norton, 1992), 383–386.

24. George C. Rable, *The Confederate Republic: A Revolution against Politics* (Chapel Hill: University of North Carolina Press, 1994); William C. Davis, *Jefferson Davis: The Man and His Hour* (New York: HarperCollins, 1991), 326, 342–343, 375–376, 388–389; Eggleston, *A Rebel's Recollections,* 222, 225, 105–106; Chesnut, *Mary Chesnut's Civil War,* 141; Mr. Lawley to VHD, 9 Mar. 1863, JD Family Coll., MC; Emory M. Thomas, *Robert E. Lee: A Biography* (New York: W. W. Norton, 1995), 220; *Memoir,* 2:206; *JD Papers,* 9:xli–xliii; Burton Harrison to JD, 24 May 1877, Burton Norvell Harrison Family Papers, LC.

25. "Caxton," "A Plea for the Soldier," *Richmond Daily Whig,* 30 Sept. 1861, p. 1; Ann K. Clarke to VHD, 25 Sept. n.d. [1861–1864], Charles C. Coffin Papers, New England Historic Genealogy Society; VHD to "My Dear Friend," n.d. [1862], Mrs. L. O'B. Branch Papers, vol. 2, pp. 46–48, North Carolina State Archives; *JD Papers,* 7:435; Kate Doyle to Mrs. Carey, 25 Apr. 1907, Virginia Room Accession Papers, MC; Mary J. Yerby to VHD, 5 Oct. 1863, RG 109, War Dept., Collection of Confederate Records, Citizens File, NA; Chesnut, *Mary Chesnut's Civil War,* 610–611; "Sympathy for the Distressed," *Richmond Daily Dispatch,* 18 July 1862, p. 1.

26. VHD to R. E. Lee, n.d. [1861], John Clopton Papers, DU; VHD to Mrs. Randolph, n.d. [1863], Eldridge Coll., HL; McGuire, *Southern Refugee,* 116; Robert H. Davis to VHD, 16 Sept. 1864, Jefferson D. Bradford to VHD, 22 Apr. 1862, JD Family Coll., MC; VHD to MBC, 27 Apr. 1862, Chesnut-Miller-Manning Papers, USC.

27. G. W. Bagby to Robert B. Rhett Jr., n.d. [1862], Robert Barnwell Rhett Papers, USC; Catherine Devereux Edmondston, *Journal of a Secesh Lady: The Diary of Catherine Ann Devereux Edmondston, 1860–1866,* ed. Beth G. Crabtree and James W. Patton (Raleigh: Division of Archives and History, Department of Cultural Resources, 1979), 256; Isabella Middleton Leland, ed., "Middleton Correspondence, 1861–1865," *South Carolina Historical Magazine* 64 (Jan. 1963): 30; Edward A. Pollard, *The Lost Cause: A New Southern History of the War of the Confederates* (New York: E. B. Treat and Co., 1867), 657; VHD to Josiah Gorgas, 5 July 1864, VIP File, Alabama Archives; VHD to C. C. Clay, 10 May 1861, C. C. Clay Papers, DU; VHD to JD, 7 Apr. 1865, Walter L. Fleming Coll., New York Public Library.

28. Gil Troy, *Affairs of State: The Rise and Rejection of the Presidential Couple since World War II* (New York: Free Press, 1997), 374; Henry S. Foote, *Casket of Reminiscences* (Washington, D.C.: Chronicle Pub. Co., 1874), 148–149; Edward A. Pollard, *Life of Jefferson Davis, with a Secret History of the Southern Confederacy* (Philadelphia: National Pub. Co., 1869), 155–156; "Changes in the Departments," *New York Times,* 30 Apr. 1865, p. 2.

29. G. F. Walker to Julia G. Tyler, 22 Dec. 1863, Tyler Family Papers, Earl Gregg Swem Library, College of William and Mary; Henri Garidel, *Exile in Richmond: The Confederate Journal of Henri Garidel,* ed. Michael Bedout Chesson and Leslie Jean Roberts (Charlottesville: University Press of Virginia, 2001), 104; "The Presidential Reception," *Richmond Daily Whig,* 2 Jan. 1864, p. 1; Chesnut, *Mary Chesnut's Civil War,*

532–533, 556–557; Elizabeth Blair Lee, *Wartime Washington: The Civil War Letters of Elizabeth Blair Lee*, ed. Virginia Jeans Laas, foreword by Dudley T. Cornish (Urbana: University of Illinois Press, 1991), 346.

30. *JD Papers*, 9:235, n. 11; "A Deserted Monarch," *New York Times*, 26 Jan. 1864, p. 4; Chesnut, *Mary Chesnut's Civil War*, 535, 545; *Memoir*, 2:217–218; "Villainous," *Richmond Daily Whig*, 22 Jan. 1864, p. 1; untitled article, *Richmond Examiner*, 21 Jan. 1864, p. 1, White House Vertical Files, Ser. 1, D-23, MC.

31. "Attempt to Burn Out Jeff Davis," *New York Herald*, 27 Jan. 1864, p. 4; "Latest from Richmond," *Chicago Tribune*, 29 Jan. 1864, p. 3; Gideon Welles, *Diary of Gideon Welles, Secretary of the Navy under Lincoln and Johnson*, ed. Howard K. Beale, assisted by Alan K. Brownsword (New York: W. W. Norton, 1960), 1:515; "A Deserted Monarch," *New York Times*, 26 Jan. 1864, p. 4. Apparently no one interviewed the runaway Betsey.

32. Untitled article, *Charleston Daily Courier*, 11 Feb. 1864, p. 1; "Reports from Richmond," *Daily Ohio State Journal*, 29 Jan. 1864, p. 1; "Another Nigger [*sic*] Loose," *Houston Daily Telegraph*, 17 Feb. 1864, p. 1; Chesnut, *Mary Chesnut's Civil War*, 535; Frances R. B. Spragins Raine, "Personal Recollections," 14, VHS.

33. Amy E. Murrell, "Union Father, Rebel Son: Families and the Question of Civil War Loyalty," in *The War Was You and Me: Civilians in the American Civil War*, ed. Joan E. Cashin (Princeton: Princeton University Press, 2002), 376–377, 389 n. 48; "Items of Interest," *Colored Tennessean* (Nashville), 31 Mar. 1866, p. 1.

34. General Index to Marriages, Elizabeth Co., Va., Book 1, p. 3, Library of Virginia; VHD to Mrs. Clopton, [n.d.] 1864, JD Family Coll., MC; *Memoir*, 2:750 n; "From Fortress Monroe," *New York Times*, 2 July 1865, p. 2.

35. *Memoir*, 2:198–199n, 642; Federal Census of 1860, Henrico County, Richmond, 138, 177; *White House of the Confederacy: An Illustrated History* (Richmond: Cadmus Marketing, n.d.), 54; Marie Tyler-McGraw and Gregg D. Kimball, *Bondage and Freedom: Antebellum Black Life in Richmond, Virginia* (Richmond: Valentine Museum and University of North Carolina Press, 1988), 35–48; Elizabeth Hyde Botume, *First Days amongst the Contrabands* (New York: Arno Press and the New York Times, 1968), 182–183.

36. Stephen W. Sears, *Controversies and Commanders: Dispatches from the Army of the Potomac* (Boston: Houghton Mifflin, 1999), 240, 242–246; David Herbert Donald, *Lincoln* (New York: Simon and Schuster, 1995), 489–490; Chesnut, *Mary Chesnut's Civil War*, 578; S. H. M. Byers, *What I Saw in Dixie: Or Sixteen Months in Rebel Prisons* (Dansville, N.Y.: Robbins and Poore, 1868), 27; William Alexander Gordon Memoirs, 155, Leyburn Library, Washington and Lee University; *Memoir*, 2:467–472; JD, *The Rise and Fall of the Confederate Government*, 2 vols., Foreword by Bell I. Wiley (1881; repr., New York: Thomas Yoseloff, 1958), 2:506–507.

37. Chesnut, *Mary Chesnut's Civil War*, 601–602; *Memoir*, 2:496–497; "A Sad Casualty," *New York Times*, 12 May 1864, p. 9; Constance Cary Harrison, *Recollections Grave and Gay* (New York: Charles Scribner's Sons, 1911), 182.

38. McGuire, *Southern Refugee*, 261–262; "President Davis' Sudden Bereavement,"

Charleston Mercury, 9 May 1864, p. 1; Chesnut, *Mary Chesnut's Civil War,* 609; VHD to Mrs. General Griffith, 8 May 1864, Old Court House Museum, Vicksburg; VHD to Margaret Howell, 22 May 1864, JD Family Coll., MC; Maria S. P. Marrow to "My dear friends," 16 May 1864, Marrow Family Papers, VHS; *Memoir,* 2:498.

39. VHD to Mr. Leonard, 25 Oct. 1889, Lewis A. Leonard Papers, Robert W. Woodruff Library, Emory University; VHD to JD, n.d. [1870], JD Papers, AL; Chesnut, *Mary Chesnut's Civil War,* 594; Garidel, *Exile in Richmond,* 136, 154; VHD to Mrs. General Griffith, 8 May 1864, Old Court House Museum, Vicksburg; Lester V. Berrey and Merlin Van Den Bark, *The American Thesaurus of Slang: A Complete Reference Book of Colloquial Speech* (New York: Thomas Y. Crowell, 1942), 8; VHD to Burton Harrison, 13 July 1864, Burton Norvell Harrison Family Papers, LC; Lee, *Wartime Washington,* 346; VHD to Margaret Howell, 22 May 1864, JD Family Coll., MC.

40. Chesnut, *Mary Chesnut's Civil War,* 663, 595, 566, 530; VHD to A. M. Kimbrough, 10 May 1902, A. McC. Kimbrough and Family Papers, MS; Virginia Clay-Clopton, *A Belle of the Fifties: Memoirs of Mrs. Clay of Alabama, Covering Social and Political Life in Washington and the South, 1853–1866* (New York: Doubleday, Page and Co., 1904), 226; *JD Papers,* 9:303, 402; VHD to Mrs. Richard Griffith, 8 May 1864, Old Court House Museum, Vicksburg.

41. VHD to Margaret Howell, 29 June 1863, Margaret Howell to Jeffy D. Howell, 4 Mar. 1864, JD Papers, AL; William N. Waller to William G. Waller, 15 Aug. n.d. [1864], Chamberlayne Family Papers, VHS; Chesnut, *Mary Chesnut's Civil War,* 527–528, 674–675, 663, 670; Robert D. Minor Journal, 201–202, Minor Family Papers, VHS.

42. Sallie A. Putnam, *In Richmond during the Confederacy* (New York: Robert M. McBride Co., 1961), 315, 303, 341, 320; Emory T. Thomas, *The Confederate State of Richmond: A Biography of the Capital* (Austin: University of Texas Press, 1971), 68; Byers, *What I Saw in Dixie,* 28; McGuire, *Southern Refugee,* 322; VHD, "Christmas in the Confederate White House," *New York World Sunday Magazine,* 13 Dec. 1896, pp. 25, 40, WHC Vertical Files, MC.

7. RUN WITH THE REST

1. Henri Garidel, *Exile in Richmond: The Confederate Journal of Henri Garidel,* ed. Michael Bedout Chesson and Leslie Jean Roberts (Charlottesville: University Press of Virginia, 2001), 271–274; Edgeworth and Sallie Bird, *The Granite Farm Letters: The Civil War Correspondence of Edgeworth and Sallie Bird,* ed. John Rozier, foreword by Theodore Rosengarten (Athens: University of Georgia Press, 1988), 233–235; David Herbert Donald, *Lincoln* (New York: Simon and Schuster, 1995), 533–535, 556; Elizabeth Blair Lee, *Wartime Washington: The Civil War Letters of Elizabeth Blair Lee,* ed. Virginia Jeans Laas, foreword by Dudley T. Cornish (Urbana: University of Illinois Press, 1991), 462 n. 1; Elbert B. Smith, *Francis Preston Blair* (New York: Free Press, 1980), 365–366.

2. Mary Boykin Chesnut, *Mary Chesnut's Civil War,* ed. C. Vann Woodward (New Haven: Yale University Press, 1981), 706; Virginia Jeans Laas, "Elizabeth Blair Lee:

Union Counterpart of Mary Boykin Chesnut," *Journal of Southern History* 50 (Aug. 1984): 391; *Memoir,* 2:471–472; Smith, *Francis Preston Blair,* 367; Lee, *Wartime Washington,* 463, 469–470.

3. William M. Robinson Jr., *Justice in Grey: A History of the Judicial System of the Confederate States of America* (Cambridge, Mass.: Harvard University Press, 1941), 202–203; *JD Papers,* 5:261; Lee, *Wartime Washington,* 82 n. 5, 113 n. 2; VHD to "My dear old Liz," n.d. [Jan. 1865], Blair Family Papers, LC.

4. VHD to "My dear old Liz," n.d. [Jan. 1865], Blair Family Papers, LC.

5. Donald, *Lincoln,* 557–561; Pierce Butler, *Judah P. Benjamin* (Philadelphia: George W. Jacobs and Co., 1906), 351.

6. Garidel, *Exile in Richmond,* 321, 331–332, 338; Memoirs of A. G. Brown, 63, J. F. H. Claiborne Papers, UNC; S. Cooper to "Maria," 1 Apr. 1865, Occasional Book of Lizzie Rowland, Family Coll. Series, Kate Mason Rowland Coll., MC; Memoir of John G. Lange, 1:186, VHS; Thomas E. Schott, *Alexander H. Stephens of Georgia* (Baton Rouge: Louisiana State University Press, 1988), 448–449; VHD to unnamed person [Gen. Preston], 1 Apr. 1865, JD Family Coll., MC; Isoline Moses to VHD, 5 Nov. 1891, JD Family Coll., MC; VHD to Editors of *Metropolitan Record and Vindicator,* 9 July 1865, Huntington Ms. 23250, HL.

7. Bell Irvin Wiley, *Confederate Women* (Westport, Conn.: Greenwood Press, 1975), 109–110; "The Diary of Thomas Conolly, M. P.: Virginia, Mar.–Apr. 1865," ed. Nelson D. Lankford, *Virginia Magazine of History and Biography* 95 (Jan. 1987): 87; *JD Papers,* 9:234 n. 6; *Official Register of the Volunteer Force of the United States Army for the Years 1861–1865,* part 2: New York and New Jersey (Washington, D.C.: Secretary of War, 1865), p. 710; "From Fortress Monroe," *New York Times,* 2 July 1865, p. 2, name misspelled "Bond."

8. Campbell Brown, *Campbell Brown's Civil War: With Ewell and the Army of Northern Virginia,* ed. with an introduction by Terry L. Jones (Baton Rouge: Louisiana State University Press, 2001), 82 n. 12; Daniel W. Crofts, *Reluctant Confederates: Upper South Unionists in the Secession Crisis* (Chapel Hill: University of North Carolina Press, 1989), 139, 256, 264; Thomas Moore, *The Poetical Works of Thomas Moore,* ed. A. D. Godley (London: Oxford University Press, 1924), 221; VHD to Alexander R. Boteler, 13 Mar. 1865, Eldridge Coll., HL.

9. VHD to unnamed person [General Preston], 1 Apr. 1865, JD Family Coll., MC; Drew Gilpin Faust, *Mothers of Invention: Women of the Slaveholding South in the American Civil War* (Chapel Hill: University of North Carolina, 1996), 231–232; George C. Rable, *Civil Wars: Women and the Crisis of Southern Nationalism* (Urbana: University of Illinois Press, 1989), 147, 227.

10. Mrs. Roger A. Pryor, *Reminiscences of Peace and War* (New York: Macmillan, 1905), 359; William C. Oates, *The War between the Union and the Confederacy and Its Lost Opportunities* (New York: Neale Publishing Co., 1905), 518; *Memoir,* 2:575; "From Fortress Monroe," *New York Times,* 2 July 1865, p. 2; VHD to Mr. Blair, 6 June 1865, Blair Family Papers, LC; VHD to JD, n.d. spring 1865, Walter L. Fleming Coll., New York Public Library; Arthur R. Henry Report, n.p., copy at VHS; Kate Doyle to Mrs. Carey, 25 Apr. 1907, Virginia Room Accession Papers, MC; W. H.

Crook, *Through Five Administrations: Reminiscences of Colonel William H. Crook, Body-Guard to President Lincoln,* comp. and ed. Margarita Spalding Gerry (New York: Harper and Bros., 1910), 55.

11. *Memoir,* 2:577–578; James Morris Morgan, *Recollections of a Rebel Reefer* (Boston: Houghton Mifflin, 1917), 220, 228, 231–232, MC; "From Fortress Monroe," p. 2; VHD to Mr. Blair, 6 June 1865, Blair Family Papers, LC; Kate Cumming, *A Journal of Hospital Life in the Confederate Army of Tennessee* (Louisville: John P. Morton and Co., 1866), 181.

12. Pryor, *Reminiscences,* 354; Judith W. McGuire, *Diary of a Southern Refugee during the War* (1867; repr., New York: Arno Press, 1972), 345–346; Memoir of John G. Lange, 1:190, VHS; David Dixon Porter, *Incidents and Anecdotes of the Civil War* (New York: D. Appleton and Co., 1885), 302; Kate Doyle to Mrs. Carey, 25 Apr. 1907, 6 May 1907, Virginia Room Accession Papers, MC; C. Acer-Doolight to unnamed person, 25 Mar. 1902, Virginia Room Accession Papers, MC; Biographical Files, card catalog, acc. no. 1922.49, Costume Coll., Chicago Historical Society; Louise Barnett, *Touched by Fire: The Life, Death, and Mythic Afterlife of George Armstrong Custer* (New York: Henry Holt, 1996), 45.

13. *JD Papers,* 11:513; Chesnut, *Mary Chesnut's Civil War,* 785, 800; VHD to JD, 13 Apr. 1865, JD Papers, AL; William Harwar Parker, *Recollections of a Naval Officer 1841–1865,* with an introduction and notes by Craig L. Symonds (Annapolis: Naval Institute Press, 1985), 346–347, 378–379; *Register of Officers of the Confederate States Navy 1861–1863* (Washington, D.C.: Government Printing Office, 1931), 93, NA; *Memoir,* 2:610.

14. *Memoir,* 2:611–612; George E. Stephens, *A Voice of Thunder: The Civil War Letters of George E. Stephens,* ed. Donald Yacovone (Urbana: University of Illinois Press, 1997), 82; Margaret Graves, "Some Facts and Thoughts of Ante-Bellum Days, [and] the Stirring Events of the War 61–65," Charles I. Graves Papers, UNC; Helen Trenholm to VHD, 19 Apr. n.d. [1865], JD Family Coll., MC; *JD Papers,* 11:545–546.

15. *JD Papers,* 11:545–546; *Memoir,* 2:614–615; Thomas Reed Turner, *Beware the People Weeping: Public Opinion and the Assassination of Abraham Lincoln* (Baton Rouge: Louisiana State University Press, 1982), 125–128; Diary of Annie G. Dudley, 21 May 1865, Huntington Ms. 58019, HL.

16. VHD to JD, n.d. [Apr.–May], 1865, JD Family Coll., MC; VHD to Mr. Blair, 6 June 1865, Blair Family Papers, LC; *Memoir,* 2:615–616; VHD to JD, n.d. 1865; "Intercepted Letters by Jefferson Davis in Flight," *New York Times Sunday Magazine,* 9 Nov. 1913, p. 7; Eliza Frances Andrews, *The War-Time Journal of a Georgia Girl, 1864–1865* (New York: D. Appleton and Co., 1908), 191–193.

17. Constance Cary Harrison, *Recollections Grave and Gay* (New York: Charles Scribner's Sons, 1911), 225; Parker, *Recollections of a Naval Officer,* 391; Andrews, *War-Time Journal,* 202, 206; *JD Papers,* 11:541–542; Eli N. Evans, *Judah P. Benjamin: The Jewish Confederate* (New York: Free Press, 1988), 309–312; *JD Papers,* 11:569–570.

18. *Memoir,* 2:617–619; "Mr. Davis' Capture" *Richmond Dispatch,* 11 Dec. 1889,

n.p.; Morgan, *Recollections of a Rebel Reefer,* 234, 236; "From Fortress Monroe," p. 2; Recollections of Leeland Hathaway, 1–2, Leeland Hathaway Papers, UNC; VHD to Mr. Blair, 6 June 1865, Blair Family Papers, LC.

19. Recollections of Leeland Hathaway, 3–4, 9, Leeland Hathaway Papers, UNC; *JD Papers,* 11:576; VHD to Mr. Blair, 6 June 1865, Blair Family Papers, LC; *Memoir,* 2:636–637; Christine I. De Wechmar Stoess, comp. Lorraine Chapman, "Episodes in the Life of Margaret Graham Howell," 39, JD Assoc., RU; *OR,* ser. 1, vol. 49, pt. 2, p. 743; "From Fortress Monroe," p. 2; *OR,* ser. 1, vol. 49, pt. 1, p. 377.

20. *Memoir,* 2:637–639; VHD to Mr. Blair, 6 June 1865, Blair Family Papers, LC; Royce Gordon Shingleton, *John Taylor Wood: Sea Ghost of the Confederacy* (Athens: University of Georgia Press, 1979), 161; *OR,* ser. 1, vol. 49, pt. 1, p. 378; Diary of William F. True, 10 May 1865, Huntington Ms. 38336, HL; "From Fortress Monroe," p. 2; JD, *The Rise and Fall of the Confederate Government,* 2 vols., foreword by Bell Wiley (1881; repr., New York: Thomas Yoseloff, 1958), 2:702; "Mr. Davis' Capture," *Richmond Dispatch,* 11 Dec. 1889, n.p.; James Harrison Wilson, *Under the Old Flag: Recollections of Military Operations in the War for the Union, the Spanish War, the Boxer Rebellion, Etc.* (New York: D. Appleton and Co., 1912), 2:330–331.

21. W. Preston Johnston to W. T. Walthall, 14 July 1877, *Southern Historical Society Papers* 5 (Jan.–June 1878): 120; Davis, *Rise and Fall,* 2:700–702; Wilson, *Under the Old Flag,* 329; Harrison, *Recollections Grave and Gay,* 225; Shingleton, *John Taylor Wood,* 161–162; VHD to Mr. Blair, 6 June 1865, Blair Family Papers, LC; *Memoir,* 2:641.

22. Hannah Pakula, *An Uncommon Woman: The Empress Frederick, Daughter of Queen Victoria, Wife of the Crown Prince of Prussia, Mother of Kaiser Wilhelm* (New York: Simon and Schuster, 1995), 46; "Grandmother Davis," Patriotic Covers, Portraits, Massachusetts Historical Society; John A. Fox Auction House, "The Capture of Jefferson Davis: A Documentary," William L. Clements Library, University of Michigan; *OR,* ser. 1, vol. 49, pt. 2, p. 743; "McArone," *Life and Adventures of Jeff Davis* (Hinsdale, N.H.: Hunter and Co., 1865); William L. Clements Library, University of Michigan; Recollections of Leeland Hathaway, 20, Leeland Hathaway Papers, UNC; Franz Wilhelm von Schilling to William von Schilling, 26 May 1865, Franz Wilhelm von Schilling Papers, VHS.

23. Nina Silber, *The Romance of Reunion: Northerners and the South, 1865–1900* (Chapel Hill: University of North Carolina, 1993), 30–36; "Who Is President of the Confederacy," *New York Times,* 17 May 1865, p. 4; Gaines M. Foster, *Ghosts of the Confederacy: Defeat, the Lost Cause, and the Emergence of the New South, 1865 to 1913* (New York: Oxford University Press, 1987), 26–28.

24. Recollections of Leeland Hathaway, 12–18, 36, 38–39, Leeland Hathaway Papers, UNC; Shingleton, *John Taylor Wood,* 164, 203; Biographical Files, card catalog, item 24, Costume Coll., Chicago Historical Society; George P. Rawick, ed., *The American Slave: A Composite Autobiography* (Westport, Conn.: Greenwood Press, 1977), suppl. ser. 1, vol. 3, Georgia, pt. 1, p. 5, Alice Battle; Virginia Clay-Clopton, *A Belle of the Fifties: Memoirs of Mrs. Clay of Alabama, Covering Social and Political Life in Washington and the South, 1853–66,* ed. Ada Sterling (New York: Doubleday, Page and

Co., 1904), 253, 256–257, 261; "Jeff Davis," *New York Herald,* 23 May 1865, p. 1; *Memoir,* 2:645 n; VHD to Mr. Scomp, 27 Feb. 1905, Harrodsburg Historical Society, Harrodsburg, Ky.; VHD to Mr. Blair, 6 June 1865, Blair Family Papers, LC.

25. *Memoir,* 2:704n, 641–642; W. Preston Johnston to Henry T. Louthan, 14 Mar. 1898, Henry T. Louthan Papers, VHS; VHD to H. T. Louthan, 10 May 1898, JD Papers, AL; VHD to Massa [Waller], 15 Feb. 1905, JD Papers, Robert W. Woodruff Library, Emory Univ.; JD to Walker Taylor, 31 Aug. 1889, C. Seymour Bullock Papers, UNC.

26. William A. Tidwell, *Come Retribution: The Confederate Secret Service and the Assassination of Lincoln,* with James O. Hall and David Winfred Gaddy (Jackson: University Press of Mississippi, 1989); Turner, *Beware the People Weeping,* 95; Donald, *Lincoln,* 587; William J. Cooper Jr., *Jefferson Davis, American* (New York: Alfred A. Knopf, 2000), 541–542, 558–559; VHD to Mr. Blair, 6 June 1865, Blair Family Papers, LC; VHD to Horace Greeley, 22 June 1865, JD Family Coll., MC; VHD to Massa [Waller], 15 Feb. 1905, JD Papers, Robert W. Woodruff Library, Emory Univ.

27. VHD to Mr. Blair, 6 June 1865, Blair Family Papers, LC; Clay-Clopton, *Belle of the Fifties,* 263, 261, 265.

28. VHD to Miles, 23 May 1865, Nelson Miles Papers, U.S. Army Military History Institute, Carlisle Barracks, Pennsylvania; *Memoir,* 2:709, 645n–646n; "From Fortress Monroe," p. 2; Elizabeth Hyde Botume, *First Days amongst the Contrabands* (New York: Arno Press and the New York Times, 1968), 182–190; Benjamin W. Thompson, "Recollections," 80, U.S. Army Military History Institute, Carlisle Barracks, Penn.; Diary of Virginia Clay, 15 May 1865, C. C. Clay Papers, DU.

29. Lizzie Cary Daniel, ed., *Confederate Scrap-Book* (Richmond: J. L. Hill Printing Co., 1893), 49; VHD to Francis Preston Blair, 5 July 1865, JD Family Coll., MC; Clay-Clopton, *Belle of the Fifties,* 276; VHD to Editors of *Metropolitan Record and Vindicator,* 9 July 1865, Huntington Ms. 23250, HL; VHD to Henry W. Birge, 15 June 1865, JD Family Coll., MC; *Memoir,* 2:714–715; Stoess, "Episodes," 42, 46–48, JD Assoc., RU; "Gen. Ripley," *Montreal Gazette,* 21 Sept. 1865, p. 1; VHD to Mr. Cohen, 3 Aug. 1865, JD Family Coll., MC; VHD to Mrs. Cohen, 17 Jan. 1894, Cohen-Phillips Papers, GHS; John M. Brannan to Frank Brannan, 20 July 1865, Miscellaneous Manuscripts of John M. Brannan, New-York Historical Society.

30. VHD to John Garrett, 8 Sept. 1865, Robert Garrett Family Papers, LC; Rawick, *American Slave,* suppl. 1, vol. 3, Georgia, pt. 1, p. 132, Augustus Burden; VHD to MBC, 20 Sept. 1865, Chesnut Letterbook, USC; VHD to Francis Preston Blair, 26 Sept. 1865, Andrew Johnson Papers, LC; VHD to Martha Phillips, 22 Aug. 1865, 17 Sept. 1865, Philip Phillips Papers, LC.

31. Robert Wooster, *Nelson A. Miles and the Twilight of the Frontier Army* (Lincoln: University of Nebraska Press, 1993), 40–41; VHD to Mr. Blair, 6 June 1865, Blair Family Papers, LC; Andrew Johnson, *The Papers of Andrew Johnson,* ed. Leroy P. Graf and Ralph W. Haskins (Knoxville: University of Tennessee Press, 1967–), 8:672; "The South Carolina Committee," *Harper's Weekly,* 28 Oct. 1865, p. 675; VHD to George Shea, 14 July 1865, JD Family Coll., MC.

32. Mrs. Montgomery Blair to VHD, 9 Sept. n.d. [1865], JD Family Coll., MC; G. V. Moody to Montgomery Blair, n.d. [July 1865], Blair Family Papers, LC; VHD to JD, 7 Nov. 1865, n.d. [Oct. 1865], 13 Nov. 1865, JD Papers, AL; *JD Papers*, 1:279.

33. VHD to George Shea, 14 July 1865, JD Family Coll., MC; Francis Preston Blair to VHD, 12 June 1865, JD Family Coll., MC; VHD to MBC, 20 Sept. 1865, Chesnut Letterbook, USC; VHD to John Garrett, 8 Sept. 1865, Robert Garrett Family Papers, LC; Robert J. Brugger, *Maryland: A Middle Temperament, 1634–1980* (Baltimore: Johns Hopkins University Press in association with the Maryland Historical Society, 1989), 292.

34. VHD to MBC, 20 Sept. 1865, Chesnut Letterbook, USC; VHD to Martha Phillips, 18 Aug. 1865, Philip Phillips Papers, LC; Nina Silber, *Daughters of the Union: Northern Women Fight the Civil War* (Cambridge, Mass.: Harvard University Press, 2005), 256–258; VHD to Mr. Blair, 6 June 1865, Blair Papers, LC; VHD to Francis Preston Blair, 5 July 1865, JD Family Coll., MC.

35. VHD to Martha Phillips, 17 Sept. 1865, Philip Phillips Papers, LC.

36. VHD to JD, n.d. Nov. 1865, JD Papers, AL; Leon F. Litwack, *Been in the Storm So Long: The Aftermath of Slavery* (New York: Alfred A. Knopf, 1980), 163; VHD to JD, 7 Nov. 1865, JD Papers, AL.

37. VHD to Lise Mitchell, 7 Dec. 1865, Lise Mitchell Papers, TL; VHD to JD, 14 Sept. 1865, 7 Nov. 1865, JD Papers, AL; General Index to Marriages, Elizabeth City County, Va., book 1, p. 3, Library of Virginia; *Wood's Baltimore City Directory, 1867–1868* (Baltimore: John W. Woods, n.d.), 383, George Peabody Library, Johns Hopkins University; VHD to JD, 4 May 1867, JD Family Coll., MC.

8. THREADBARE GREAT FOLKS

1. Nelson Miles to E. D. Townsend, 20 Aug. 1865, Nelson Miles Papers, U.S. Army Military History Institute, Carlisle Barracks, Pennsylvania; JD to VHD, 21 Aug. 1865, Davis Papers, TU; VHD to JD, 31 Aug. 1865, Andrew Johnson Papers, LC; VHD to MBC, 20 Sept. 1865, Chesnut Letterbook, USC; VHD to Francis Preston Blair, 23 June 1865, Blair and Lee Papers, Rare Books and Special Colls., Princeton Univ. Library; VHD to John Garrett, 8 Sept. 1865, Robert Garrett Family Papers, LC; Horace Greeley to VHD, 27 June 1865, JD Family Coll., MC; *Memoir*, 1:555–556.

2. Janet Sharp Hermann, *Pursuit of a Dream* (New York: Oxford University Press, 1981), 41–60; *JD Papers*, 8:519–520; Henry S. Foote, *Casket of Reminiscences* (Washington, D.C.: Chronicle Publishing Co., 1974), 150–151; VHD to Editors of *Metropolitan Vindicator and Record*, 9 July 1865, Huntington Ms. 23250, HL; Judah Benjamin to VHD, 1 Sept. 1865, [misdated 1869], JD Papers, TU; VHD to Mr. Cohen, 3 Aug. 1865, JD Family Coll., MC; "Letter from Mrs. Davis," *True Index* (Warrenton, Va.), 20 Jan. 1866, n.p.; John J. Pullen, *Comic Relief: The Life and Laughter of Artemus Ward, 1834–1867* (Hamden, Conn.: Archon Books, 1983), 132–133; VHD to JD, n.d. [Oct. 1865], JD Papers, AL; Receipt, 20 Nov. 1865, Received of Mrs. Varina Davis by E. Willis, Eola Willis Papers, South Carolina Historical Society; VHD to

Martha Phillips, 17 Sept. 1865, Philip Phillips Papers, LC; VHD to JD, 12 Apr. 1866, JD Papers, AL.

3. VHD to Martha Phillips, 17 Sept. 1865, Philip Phillips Papers, LC; Jeffy D. Howell to Joseph B. Howell, 18 Jan. 1866, Howell Family Papers, HL; Index to War of 1812 Pension Application Files, Hoo-Howe, Roll 47, M313, NA; VHD to JD, 7 Nov. 1865, JD Papers, AL; JD to VHD, 24–26 Jan. 1866, Jeffy D. Howell to VHD, 18 Dec. 1865, JD Papers, TU; VHD to Edward Willis, 5 June 1866, Willis Papers, South Carolina Historical Society; VHD to Martha Phillips, 22 Aug. 1865, Philip Phillips Papers, LC.

4. Certified Copy, Death Certificate for Philip Stoess, 3 Feb. 1942, age 75, 7 mos., 8 days, Washington State Dept of Vital Statistics, King County, Seattle; VHD to Martha Phillips, n.d. [Aug–Sept. 1865], Philip Phillips Papers, LC; "The Davis Family," New York Times, 11 Oct. 1866, p. 2; VHD to W. Preston Johnston, 11 Jan. 1866, Johnston Papers, TL; Maggie Davis to JD, 25 Mar. 1867, JD Papers, AL.

5. Elbert B. Smith, Francis Preston Blair (New York: Free Press, 1980), 385–386; VHD to MBC, 20 Sept. 1865, Chesnut Letterbook, USC; VHD to Armistead Burt, 3 Dec. 1865, Armistead Burt Papers, DU; E. M. Stanton to Nelson Miles, 14 July 1865, Nelson Miles to E. D. Townsend, 12 Dec. 1865, Nelson Miles Papers, U.S. Army Military History Institute, Carlisle Barracks, Penn.; JD to VHD, 20 Oct. 1865, 13–14 Mar. 1866, VHD to JD, 21–22 Nov. 1865, JD Papers, TU.

6. VHD to JD, 7 Nov. 1865, n.d. [Nov. 1865], 13 Nov. 1865, 22 Jan. 1866, n.d. [Oct. 1865], JD Papers, AL.

7. JD to VHD, 21–22 Nov. 1865, 26 Sept. 1865, 30 Dec. 1865–1 Jan. 1866, 3–4 Feb. 1866, JD to VHD, 15 Sept. 1865, JD Papers, TU; VHD to JD, 1 Oct. 1865, JD Papers, AL; JD to VHD, 20 Oct. 1865, 3–4 Feb. 1866, JD Papers, TU.

8. VHD to JD, 2 Feb. 1866, 23 Feb. 1866, JD Papers, AL; William Reed to VHD, 15 Feb. 1866, JD Family Coll., MC; Basil W. Duke, Reminiscences of General Basil W. Duke, C.S.A. (Garden City, NY: Doubleday, Page and Co., 1911), 344; VHD to JD, 18–22 Mar., 1866, JD Papers, AL; Memoir, 2:756.

9. E. D. Townsend to VHD, 26 Apr. 1866, Nelson Miles Papers, U.S. Army Military History Institute, Carlisle Barracks, Penn.; untitled article, Times (London), 9 May 1866, p. 14; Parole of Honor by VHD, Witnessed by J. A. Fessenden, 3 May 1866, Nelson Miles Papers, U.S. Army Military History Institute, Carlisle Barracks, Penn.; untitled article, Times (London), 18 May 1866, p. 11; JD to Maggie Davis, 23 May 1866, JD Papers, TU; "Jeff Davis—Reports about His Health—A Visit to Mrs. Davis," Daily National Intelligencer, 18 May 1866, p. 1; G. E. Cooper to Nelson Miles, 9 May 1866, Nelson Miles Papers, Carlisle.

10. "Jeff Davis—Reports about His Health—A Visit to Mrs. Davis," Daily National Intelligence, 18 May 1866, p. 1; VHD to Andrew Johnson, 19 May 1866, n.d. May 1866, Andrew Johnson Papers, LC; "Further Care for Jeff Davis' Health," New York Herald, 15 May 1866, p. 1; Nelson Miles to "General," 29 May 1866, Andrew Johnson to E. M. Stanton, 6 June 1866, J. K. Barnes to Edwin Stanton, 6 June 1866, Nelson Miles Papers, U.S. Army Military History Institute, Carlisle Barracks, Penn.;

Memoir, 2:757–766; VHD to J. U. Payne, 12 Apr. 1867, Charles Erasmus Fenner Papers, UNC; VHD to W. H. S. Burgwyn, 25 Feb. 1867, W. H. S. Burgwyn Papers, North Carolina State Archives; Elva Cooper to Mrs. Gittings, 26 n.d. [1866–1867], JD Family Coll., MC.

11. "Mrs. Davis in Washington," *New York Herald,* 26 May 1866, p. 5; JD to VHD, 21–23 Apr. 1866, JD Papers, TU; Hans L. Trefousse, *Andrew Johnson: A Biography* (New York: W. W. Norton, 1989), 260–264, 234–235, 245–247; *Memoir,* 2:769–771, 1:575; Elizabeth Blair Lee, *Wartime Washington: The Civil War Letters of Elizabeth Blair Lee,* ed. Virginia Jeans Laas, foreword by Dudley T. Cornish (Urbana: University of Illinois Press, 1991), 76, 50 n. 17; Lafayette Foster to his wife, 26 May 1866, Lafayette S. Foster Papers, Massachusetts Historical Society.

12. Peter R. DeMontravel, *A Hero to His Fighting Men: Nelson A. Miles, 1839–1925* (Kent, Ohio: Kent State University Press, 1998), 3–6, 59, 356, 331, 50; Chester D. Bradley, "Dr. Craven and the Prison Life of Jefferson Davis," *Virginia Magazine of History and Biography* 62 (Jan. 1954): 51, 55–56, 70; VHD to Lise Mitchell, 7 Dec. 1865, Mitchell Papers, TL; *Memoir,* 2:760–772; H. A. DuPont to "Sir," 21 May 1866, postscript, Henry A. DuPont Papers, Winterthur Manuscripts, Hagley Museum and Library; VHD to H. A. Scomp, 6 May 1904, Harrodsburg Historical Society, Harrodsburg, Ky.; VHD to [James M. Morgan], 30 June–1 July [1898], Varina Davis Letter, copy at VHS; William Hanchett, *Irish: Charles G. Halpine in Civil War America* (Syracuse: Syracuse University Press, 1970), 145; James Crossett et al. to Nelson Miles, 2 Sept. 1866, Nelson Miles Papers, U.S. Army Military Institute, Carlisle Barracks, Penn.; Robert Wooster, *Nelson A. Miles and the Twilight of the Frontier Army* (Lincoln: University of Nebraska Press, 1993) 44–46; VHD to Edward Willis, 12 Sept. 1866, Willis Papers, South Carolina Historical Society.

13. Untitled article, *New York Herald,* 19 May 1866, p. 1; VHD to Edward Willis, n.d. [late 1865], Willis Papers, South Carolina Historical Society; VHD to JD, 12 Dec. 1866, JD Papers, AL; VHD to Edward Willis, 15 Oct. 1866, Willis Papers, South Carolina Historical Society; VHD to Mrs. Howell, 18 Oct. 1866, JD Papers, AL; "The Davis Family," *New York Times,* 11 Oct. 1866, p. 2; VHD to Martha Phillips, 16 Apr. 1867, Philip Phillips Papers, LC.

14. "Jefferson Davis Visited," *Baltimore Sun,* 11 Mar. 1867, p. 2; "Pardon of Jefferson Davis," *Baltimore Sun,* 24 Apr. 1867, p. 1; "The Visit of Ex-President Pierce," *Baltimore Sun,* 11 May 1867, p. 1; Charles O'Conor to VHD, 18 Sept. 1866, Imprisonment and Trial File, MC; Burton Harrison to VHD, 16 Jan. 1867, JED to VHD, 1 Jan. 1867, JD Family Coll., MC; "Jeff Davis—Reports About His Health," p. 1; VHD to JD, 14 Aug. 1866, 17 Aug. 1866, 18 Mar. 1867, JD Papers, AL; VHD to Mr. Woodbridge, 7 Oct. 1866, JD Family Coll., MC.

15. William J. Cooper Jr., *Jefferson Davis, American* (New York: Alfred A. Knopf, 2000), 541–542, 558–564; *Memoir,* 2:776–780; VHD to JD, 23 Mar. 1867, JD Family Coll., MC; VHD to JD, 18 Mar. 1867, JD Papers, AL; "Return of Mrs. Jeff Davis," *Baltimore Sun,* 1 May 1867, p. 1.

16. George C. Rable, *Civil Wars: Women and the Crisis of Southern Nationalism* (Urbana: University of Illinois Press, 1989), 227, 242; VHD to JD, 12 Dec. 1866, 16

Dec. 1866, JD Papers, AL; VHD to W. Preston Johnston, 25 Aug. 1866, 27 Sept. 1866, Johnston Papers, TL.

17. Thomas Reed Turner, *Beware the People Weeping: Public Opinion and the Assassination of Abraham Lincoln* (Baton Rouge: Louisiana State University Press, 1982), 133–134; Rembert W. Patrick, *Jefferson Davis and His Cabinet* (Baton Rouge: Louisiana State University Press, 1944), 363–364; Richard H. Abbott, *Cobbler in Congress: The Life of Henry Wilson, 1812–1875* (Lexington: University Press of Kentucky, 1972), 163; *Memoir*, 2:794–797; Charles O'Conor to VHD, 2 May 1867, JD Family Coll., MC; Cooper, *Jefferson Davis*, 564–565; "Arrival of Mr. Davis," *Baltimore Sun*, 13 May 1867, p. 1; Constance Cary Harrison, *Recollections Grave and Gay* (New York: Charles Scribner's Sons, 1911), 264–267; Copy of Jefferson Davis's bond, 13 May 1867, JD Family Coll., MC; Gary Collison, *Shadrack Minkins: From Fugitive Slave to Citizen* (Cambridge, Mass.: Harvard University Press, 1997), 204–205; VHD to John Garrett, 3 June 1867, Robert Garrett Family Papers, LC.

18. VHD to John Garrett, 3 June 1867, Robert Garrett Family Papers, LC; VHD to William Preston, 3 July [1867], Wickliffe-Preston Family Papers, University of Kentucky-Lexington; VHD to John Garrett, n.d. May 1867, Robert Garrett Family Papers, LC.

19. VHD to Burton Harrison, 1 Nov. 1867, Burton Norvell Harrison Family Papers, LC; *Memoir*, 2:797–799; JD to VHD, n.d. [1867], JD Papers, AL; VHD to John Garrett, 3 June 1867, Robert Garrett Family Papers, LC; "Mr. Jefferson Davis's Family," *Times* (London), 14 Nov. 1865, p. 1; "The Davis Family," *New York Times*, 11 Oct. 1866, p. 2; VHD to JD, 7 Nov. 1865, Billie Davis to JD, n.d. [1867], JD Papers, AL.

20. Jeffy D. Howell to Joseph Howell, 26 Feb. 1869, 21 Sept. [1868 or 1869], 5 Apr. 1869, Howell Family Papers, HL; *City Directory of New Orleans, 1870–1871* (n.p., n.p.), 305, New York Public Library; *JD Papers*, 2:333 n. 18; Federal Census of 1870, Virginia, Campbell County, Lynchburg, p. 68, dwelling 583; Christine I. De Wechmar Stoess, comp. Lorraine Chapman, "Episodes in the Life of Margaret Graham Howell," 50, JD Assoc., RU; *Memoir*, 2:800; JD to VHD, 29 May 1881, White House Assoc. of Alabama, White House of the Confederacy, Montgomery.

21. VHD to S. S. Cummins, n.d. 1903, JD Family Coll., MC; VHD to Mary Ann Cobb, 6 Sept. 1867, Papers of Howell Cobb and Wife and Others, New-York Historical Society; George E. Carter, "A Note on Jefferson Davis in Canada—His Stay in Lennoxville, Quebec," *Journal of Mississippi History* 33 (May 1971): 134; *Memoir*, 2:804–805; Travel Diary of JD, 25 June 1868, JD Family Coll., MC; JD to Robert Ould, 2 May 1868, J. H. Carrington Papers, DU; VHD to Mary Ann Cobb, 6 July 1868, Howell Cobb Papers, UGA; Cooper, *Jefferson Davis*, 577.

22. JED to JD, 18 June 1868, JD Papers, AL; VHD to Mary Ann Cobb, 6 July 1868, Howell Cobb Papers, UGA; Travel Diary of JD, 25 July 1868, 4 Aug. 1868, JD Family Coll., MC; *Memoir*, 2:806–809; untitled article, *Times* (London), 6 Aug. 1868, p. 12; Judah Benjamin to JD, 6 Aug. 1868, JD Papers, AL; Eli N. Evans, *Judah P. Benjamin: The Jewish Confederate* (New York: Free Press, 1988), 333; "The Confederate Ex-President," *Times* (London), 17 Aug. 1868, p. 10; Lord Shrewsbury to JD, 28 Aug. 1868, JD Family Coll., MC.

23. *Memoir,* 2:807; Jeffy D. Howell to JD, 16 May 1868, JD Papers, AL; "Mr. Jefferson Davis," *Times* (London), 9 Sept. 1868, p. 5; Nannie Davis Smith, "Reminiscences of Jefferson Davis," *Confederate Veteran* 38 (May 1930): 181; VHD to JD, 28 Feb. 1870, JD Papers, AL.

24. David Cannadine, *The Decline and Fall of the British Aristocracy* (New Haven: Yale University Press, 1990), 4, 11–14, 19–21; R. J. M. Blackett, *Divided Hearts: Britain and the American Civil War* (Baton Rouge: Louisiana State University Press, 2001), 13–14, 61, 67–68; George Colayne, *The Complete Peerage,* ed. Geoffrey H. White (London: St. Catherine Press, 1949), 9:728–729; Bernard Burke, *A Genealogical and Heraldic Dictionary of the Peerage and Baronetage, Together with Memoirs of the Privy Councillors and Knights,* 49th ed. (London: Harrison and Sons, 1887), 1250–55, 123–124; Lord Shrewsbury to JD, 28 Aug. 1868, JD Family Coll., MC; Leslie Stephen and Sidney Lee, eds., *The Dictionary of National Biography: From the Earliest Times to 1900* (1917; repr., London: Oxford University Press, 1967), 9:1203–1205; Lady Mildred Hope to VHD, 16 Aug. 1868, JD Family Coll., MC.

25. *Memoir,* 2:808–809; Roy Porter, *London: A Social History* (Cambridge, Mass.: Harvard University Press, 1995), 207–208, 187–188, 225–227; Demographia, Greater London, www.publicpurpose.com, accessed 3 Aug. 2000; Hippolyte Taine, *Taine's Notes on England,* trans. and intro. by Edward Hyams (London: Thames and Hudson, 1957), 13–14; Wirt Adams to JD, 1 Sept. 1868, Travel Diary of JD, 24 Oct. 1868, 26 Oct. 1868, JD Family Coll., MC; JD to VHD, 22 Nov. 1868, JD Papers, AL; Cooper, *Jefferson Davis,* 582.

26. Burton Harrison to VHD, 16 July n.d. [1864], Pritchard von David Coll., Center for American History, University of Texas–Austin; C. J. McRae to VHD, 25 Sept. 1865, JD Papers, AL; Statements by Varina Davis, 11 Mar. 1868, MC; Blackett, *Divided Hearts,* 14, 62–63, 138–140; Cash Accounts in Travel Diary of JD, JD Family Coll., MC; JD to VHD, 26 Feb. 1870, JD Papers, AL; VHD to Lise Mitchell, 20 Apr. 1869, Lise Mitchell Papers, TL; JD to VHD, 9 Aug. 1869, JD Papers, AL; VHD to Mary Ann Cobb, 22 Oct. 1868, Howell Cobb Papers, UGA.

27. Travel Diary of JD, 31 Dec. 1868, JD Family Coll., MC; VHD to Mrs. Howell Cobb, 22 Oct. 1868, Howell Cobb Papers, UGA; Patrice Higonnet, *Paris: Capital of the World,* trans. Arthur Goldhammer (Cambridge, Mass.: Harvard University Press, 2002), 170–194, 328; JD to VHD, 7 Feb. 1869, JD Papers, TU; JD to Cora Ives, 25 Apr. 1869, JD Papers, DU; www.carte.com/carteparis/html, accessed 3 Aug. 2000; JD to VHD, 27 Jan. 1869, Dudley Mann to "Dear and Good Friend," 15 Mar. 1869, JD Papers, AL.

28. Travel Diary of JD, 2 Jan. 1869 [misdated 1868], JD Family Coll., MC; JD to VHD, 7 Feb. 1869, JD Papers, TU; *Memoir,* 2:809.

29. Albert Guerard, *Napoleon III: A Great Life in Brief* (New York: Alfred A. Knopf, 1955), 177, 195–200; *Memoir,* 2:809–810; JD to VHD, 7 Feb. 1869, JD Papers, TU; "A Paragraph," *Memphis Daily Appeal,* 12 July 1869, p. 2.

30. Untitled article, *Southern Opinion,* 9 Jan. 1869, p. 1; JD to VHD, 27 Jan. 1869, JD Papers, AL; "Local & General," Stratford-upon-Avon, 4 Dec. 1868, n.p., Marie Corelli, "Harvard House Guide Book," 36, Shakespeare Birthplace Trust; JD

to VHD, 30 July 1869, 9 Feb. 1869, 9 Aug. 1869, VHD to JD, 17 Aug. 1869, JD to Maggie Davis, 6 Aug. 1869, JD Papers, AL; VHD to Cora Ives, 3 Mar. 1869, JD Papers, DU.

31. Lord Shrewsbury to JD, 15 Mar. 1869, A. Beresford-Hope to JD, 18 July 1869, JD Family Coll., MC; Lord Henry Percy to VHD, 10 July n.d. [1869], JD Papers, AL; Spencer Ponsonby to Lord Abinger, 6 Apr. 1869, JD Family Coll., MC; Jeff Davis Jr. to VHD, 15 May 1869, JD Papers, AL; S. W. Jackman, *The People's Princess: A Portrait of H.R.H. Princess Mary, Duchess of Teck* (Shooter's Lodge, UK: Kensal Press, 1984); Stanley Weintraub, *Albert, Uncrowned King* (London: John Murray, 1997), 415.

32. VHD to JD, 20—25 Dec. 1869, JD Papers, AL; www.cv81pl.freeserve.co .uk/stoneleigh.html, accessed 1 Mar. 2004; H. T. Cooke, *Cooke's Guide to Warwickshire* (Warwick: H. T. Cooke and Son, 1888), 281—309; VHD to Lady Leigh, 24 Apr. 1898, JD Papers, AL; VHD to Lise Mitchell, 20 Apr. 1869, Lise Mitchell Papers, TL; VHD to JD, 16 Oct. 1869, JD Papers, AL.

33. VHD to [Mrs. L. G. Young?], 15 Aug. 1903, JD Papers, Robert W. Woodruff Library, Emory University; VHD to JD, 16 Oct. 1869, JD Papers, AL; *Memoir*, 2:808; VHD to Lise Mitchell, 20 Apr. 1869, Lise Mitchell Papers, TL.

34. David Kynaston, *The City of London*, vol. 1, *A World of Its Own, 1815—1890* (London: Chatto and Windus, 1994), 217, 226—227; "Mrs. Jefferson Davis," *Times* (London), 17 May 1866, p. 10; VHD to Mary Ann Cobb, 22 Oct. 1868, Howell Cobb Papers, UGA; James P. Shenton, *Robert John Walker: A Politician from Jackson to Lincoln* (New York: Columbia University Press, 1961), 14—15, 102, 195—198; JD to A. M. Clayton, 15 Apr. 1870, Davis-Clayton Letters, UM; Judah Benjamin to JD, 20 Dec. 1868, JD to Editor of the *Standard*, n.d. Dec. 1868, JD Family Coll., MC; VHD to William Dodd, 10 Mar. 1905, William E. Dodd Papers, LC.

35. JD to Dudley Mann, 19 Apr. 1869, JD to VHD, 26 Aug. 1869, JD Papers, AL; JD to A. M. Clayton, 16 Sept. 1869, 23 Nov. 1869, Davis-Clayton Letters, UM; *Memoir*, 2:811; VHD to JD, 27 Sept. 1869, JD Papers, AL.

9. TOPIC OF THE DAY

1. JD to VHD, 3—4 Apr. 1870, JD Papers, AL; VHD to Helen Keary, n.d. [Jan. 1870], A Collection of Letters and Signatures Made by Mrs. C. E. Barrett-Lennard, Bodleian Library, Oxford University; VHD to JD, 3 Dec. 1869, 28 Feb. 1870, JD Papers, AL.

2. VHD to JD, 16 Oct. 1869, JD to VHD, 9 Nov. 1869, 23 Nov. 1869, JD Papers, AL; JD to Lise Mitchell, [20 or 30] Nov. 1869, JD Papers, New York Public Library.

3. JD to VHD, 23 Nov. 1869, JD Papers, AL; JD to VHD, 13—14 Mar. 1866, JD Papers, TU.

4. JD to VHD, 23 Nov. 1869, JD Papers, AL.

5. Untitled article, *Times* (London), 18 Nov. 1869, p. 5; "Ex-President Davis in the City," *Public Ledger* (Memphis), 19 Nov. 1869, p. 2, Newspaper Clipping File, Special Colls., Memphis Public Library; Gerald M. Capers Jr., *The Biography of a*

River Town: Memphis, Its Heroic Age (Chapel Hill: University of North Carolina Press, 1939), 114; JD to VHD, 23 Nov. 1869, JD Papers, AL; "Hon. Jefferson Davis," *Memphis Daily Appeal,* 26 Feb. 1870, p. 4; Elizabeth Meriwether to Minor Meriwether, 19 Nov. 1869, Meriwether Family Papers, UM; JD to Mary Stamps, 10 Nov. 1869, Mary Stamps Papers, UNC.

6. Ruth Ketring Nuermberger, *The Clays of Alabama: A Planter-Lawyer-Politician Family* (Lexington: University of Kentucky Press, 1958), 82–83; Virginia Clay-Clopton, *A Belle of the Fifties: Memoirs of Mrs. Clay of Alabama, Covering Social and Political Life in Washington and the South, 1853–66,* ed. Ada Sterling (New York: Doubleday, Page and Co., 1904), 3–9, 19, 128, 132–135, 176–177; Bell Irvin Wiley, *Confederate Women* (Westport, Conn.: Greenwood Press, 1975), 54; Mary Boykin Chesnut, *Mary Chesnut's Civil War,* ed. C. Vann Woodward (New Haven: Yale University Press, 1981), 559, 654, 774, 541; VHD to JD, 23 Mar. 1867, JD Family Coll., MC; JD to VHD, 25 Dec. 1869, JD Papers, AL; JD to VC, 30 Aug. 1874, C. C. Clay Papers, DU; George P. Rawick, ed., *The American Slave: A Composite Autobiography* (Westport, Conn.: Greenwood Press, 1977), suppl. ser. 1, vol. 8, Mississippi, pt. 3, pp. 1004–1005, Florida Hewitt.

7. Clay-Clopton, *Belle of the Fifties,* 346–347; *Memphis City Directory for 1870* (n.p., no pub.), 77, *Edwards's Memphis Directory,* Vol. 8, 1870 (n.p., no pub.) 92, Archives, Memphis Public Library; JD to Mary Stamps, 10 Nov. 1869, Mary Stamps Papers, UNC; JD to Anna E. Carroll, 22 Dec. 185[7], 26 Mar. 1860, Anna Ella Carroll Papers, H. Furlong Baldwin Library, Maryland Historical Society; JD to VC, 23 Jan. 1870, 2 Feb. 1870, 16 Feb. 1870, Clay Papers, DU.

8. VHD to JD, 3 Dec. 1869, 20–25 Dec. 1869, 28 Dec. 1869, JD Papers, AL.

9. Carl de Wechmar Stoess to VHD, 26 Feb. 1870, JD Papers, AL; Obituary of Charles D. W. Stoess, *Times* (London), 3 Apr. 1891, p. 9; Margaret Howell to VHD, 27 Feb. 1870, VHD to JD, 4 Mar. 1870, JD to VHD, 3–4 Apr. 1870, JD Papers, AL.

10. Lady Abinger to VHD, 26 Apr. 1870, JD Family Coll., MC; JD to VHD, 19 May 1870, VHD to JD, 28 Feb. 1870, 4 Mar. 1870, JD to VHD, 3–4 Apr. 1870, JD Papers, AL.

11. JD to VHD, 17–18 Jan. 1870, 26 Feb. 1870, VHD to JD, n.d. [1870], JD Papers, AL; VHD to JD, 1 Apr. 1870, JD and Family Papers, MS.

12. VC to C. C. Clay, 11 Jan. 1870, Clay Papers, DU; Elizabeth Meriwether to Minor Meriwether, 19 Nov. 1869, Meriwether Family Papers, UM; VC to JD, 10 Apr. 1870, JD to VHD, 2 Apr. 1870, JD to VC, 31 May 1870, Clay Papers, DU.

13. JD to WD, 1 June 1870, JD to VHD, 3–4 Apr. 1870, 3–4 June 1870, n.d. 1870, JD Papers, AL; VHD to JD, 22 June 1870, JD Assoc., RU.

14. JD to VC, 23 Apr. 1870, 31 May 1870, 15 June 1870, 30 June 1870, 8 July 1870, Clay Papers, DU.

15. C. J. McRae to VHD, 25 Sept. 1865, JD Papers, AL; VHD to Mr. DeRosset, n.d. May 1870, Maggie Davis to Mr. DeRosset, 23 July [misdated 3 July] 1870, Louis DeRosset to Mrs. Gaston Meares, 3 July 1870, Mrs. Gaston Meares to Louis DeRosset, 19 June 1870, DeRosset Papers, UNC; VHD to JD, 22 June 1870, JD Assoc., RU; "Winnie's Table Talk," JD Family Coll., MC.

16. JD to VC, 8 Aug. 1870, 14 Aug. 1870, Clay Papers, DU.

17. Judah Benjamin to JD, 6 Sept. 1870, JD Family Coll., MC; JD to VHD, 19 Sept. 1870, JD Papers, AL; JD to Lady Wilde, 21 Sept. 1870, JD Assoc., RU; JD to VHD, 23 Sept. 1870 [misdated 1871], JD Papers, AL; Joy Melville, *Mother of Oscar: The Life of Jane Francesca Wilde* (London: John Murray, 1994), 7, 56, 60, 84, 111; Janet Sharp Hermann, *Joseph E. Davis: Pioneer Patriarch* (Jackson: University Press of Mississippi, 1990), 164; *Memoir*, 2:811; JD to JED, 22 July 1867, JD to Lise Mitchell, 24 Oct. 1870, Mitchell Journal and Letters, TL, copy at UNC.

18. Untitled article, *Times* (London), 3 Nov. 1870, p. 4; JD to Carl de Wechmar Stoess, 9 Oct. 1870, copy at JD Assoc., RU; JD to VHD, 30 June 1871, JD Papers, AL; *Memoir*, 2:811–812; Capers, *River Town*, 44, 47, 125, 149, 163–164, 180–183; Lafcadio Hearn, *Occidental Gleanings,* comp. Albert Mordell (New York: Dodd, Mead, and Co., 1925), 156–158.

19. JD to VC, 14 Feb. 1871, JD Papers, AL; Memphis Tax Book, n.p., 1871, Archives, Memphis Public Library; *Boyle and Chapman's City Directory,* 1874, p. 120; Wiley, *Confederate Women,* 75–77; C. C. Clay to JD, 30 Nov. 1870, JD Family Coll., MC.

20. JD to VHD, 22 May 1871, VHD to JD, 11 June 1871, JD Papers, AL.; JD to William L. Davis, 12 June 1871, JD Letter, unprocessed ms., MS; *The Secret Eye: The Journal of Ella Gertrude Clanton Thomas, 1848–1889,* ed. Virginia Ingraham Burr, intro. by Nell Irvin Painter (Chapel Hill: University of North Carolina Press, 1990), 372–373; JD to VC, 10 June 1871, 27 June 1871, Clay Papers, DU.

21. JD to Maggie Davis, 29 June 1871, JD Papers, AL; Burke Davis, *The Long Surrender* (New York: Random House, 1985), 243–245; "Jeff Davis' Woman Troubles," *Albany Evening Journal,* 26 July 1871, p. 2; "Jeff and the Herald," *New York Herald,* 27 July 1871, p. 6; "The Jeff Davis Slander," *Courier-Journal* (Louisville), 18 July 1871, p. 2; "The Jeff Davis Scandal," *Courier-Journal* (Louisville), 19 July 1871, p. 4; "A Scandalous Story about Jeff Davis," *New York Times,* 17 July 1871, p. 6; "Hon. Jefferson Davis," *Baltimore Sun,* 18 July 1871, p. 1.

22. "A Scandalous Story about Jeff Davis," *New York Times,* 17 July 1871, p. 6; "Academy of Music," *New Orleans Times-Picayune,* 4 Apr. 1871, p. 4; "Jeff Davis' Woman Troubles," *Albany Evening Journal,* 26 July 1871, p. 2; Davis, *Long Surrender,* 245, 247; "Jeff and the Herald," *New York Herald,* 27 July 1871, p. 6; "The Jeff Davis Scandal," *Courier-Journal* (Louisville), 19 July 1871, p. 4; "Jeff-O! Jeff!!," *New York Herald,* 26 July 1871, p. 7; "Mr. Jefferson Davis," *New York Herald,* 31 July 1871, p. 6.

23. "Jeff and the Herald," p. 6; "The Davis Scandal," *Courier-Journal* (Louisville), 22 July 1871, p. 1; "Card from Jefferson Davis," *Chicago Tribune,* 22 July 1871, p. 1; "A Card," *Boston Daily Advertiser,* 22 July 1871, p. 1; "Hon. Jefferson Davis," *Natchez Weekly Democrat,* 9 Aug. 1871, p. 1; "A Card from Jefferson Davis," *Baltimore Sun,* 22 July 1871, p. 1; Davis, *Long Surrender,* 245; "Hon. Jefferson Davis," *Daily Dispatch* (Richmond), 20 July 1871, p. 2; "Jefferson Davis," *Atlanta Constitution,* 23 July 1871, p. 2; "Hon. Jefferson Davis," *Weekly Clarion* (Jackson, Miss.), 27 July 1871, p. 2; "A Dirty Radical Slander Refuted," *Southern Recorder* (Milledgeville, Ga.) 8 Aug. 1871, p. 1; "Hon. Jefferson Davis," *Norfolk Virginian,* 21 July 1871, p. 2; "A Scandalous

Story about Jeff Davis," p. 6; "Jeff Davis' Woman Troubles," p. 2; "Jeff Davis Denies Having Insulted a Lady," *Albany Evening Journal*, 22 July 1871, p. 2; "The Jeff Davis Scandal," *Nashville Union and American*, 25 July 1871, p. 1.

24. "The Jeff Davis Slander," *Courier Journal* (Louisville), 18 July 1871, p. 2; "Jeff Davis on a New Departure," *New York Herald*, 26 July 1871, p. 4; Collection description, C. C. Clay Papers, DU.

25. "Hon. Jefferson Davis," *Baltimore Sun*, 18 July 1871, p. 1; JD to C. C. Clay, 29 Dec. 1871, Clay Papers, DU.

26. Untitled article, *Daily Memphis Avalanche*, 15 July 1871, p. 1; "Personal," *Southern Opinion*, 1 Aug. 1868, p. 2; Hans L. Trefousse, *Andrew Johnson: A Biography* (New York: W. W. Norton, 1989), 361; "Items of Interest," *Colored Tennessian* (Nashville), 31 Mar. 1866, p. 1; VHD to John Meredith Read, n.d. [1880–1888], JD Family Coll., MC; Nannie Smith Davis, "Reminiscences of Jefferson Davis," *Confederate Veteran* 38 (May 1930): 180.

27. James H. Shankland, ed., *Public Statutes of the State of Tennessee since the Year 1858: A Supplement to the Code* (Nashville: Paul and Tavel, 1871), 168; VHD to JD, 7 Sept. 1871, JD Papers, AL.

28. JD to VC, 26 Oct. 1871, Clay Papers, DU; Wiley, *Confederate Women*, 51–52; JD to VC, 1 Nov. 1871, 5 Nov. 1871, Clay Papers, DU.

29. Clay-Clopton, *Belle of the Fifties*, 68; caption by Virginia Clay, photograph, *Confederate Veteran* 25 (June 1917): 253; JD to VC, 1 Apr. n.d. [1872], Clay Papers, DU.

30. Advertisement, *Daily Memphis Avalanche*, 4 Aug. 1871, p. 2; JD to VHD, 26 Aug. 1873, JD Papers, AL; JD to Maggie Davis, 26 Sept. 1871, JD Papers, TU; JD to WD, 22 Oct. 1871, VHD to JD, 17 Jan. 1874, JD Papers, AL; Hearn, *Occidental Gleanings*, 157; "A City's Progress," *Daily Memphis Avalanche*, 6 Sept. 1871, p. 4; Interview, Mary Hill and Olive Hill Grosvenor, 1919, pp. 5–6, Hill and Grosvenor Papers, UNC.

31. JD to VHD, 18 Sept. 1872, JD to VHD, 18 Jan. 1874, JD Papers, AL; JD to VC, 22 Aug. 1872, 2 Sept. 1872, Clay Papers, DU; JD to Mrs. Blandy, 6 Aug. 1872, Miscellaneous Bound Manuscripts, Massachusetts Historical Soc.; JD to Maggie Davis, 7 Sept. 1872, JD Papers, AL; JD to VC, 14 Sept. 1872, Clay Papers, DU; JD to VHD, 3 Oct. 1872, JD Papers, AL.

32. *Memoir*, 2:814; Interments, Elmwood Cemetery, William H. Davis, Special Colls., Memphis Public Library; "Gossip from Memphis," *Memphis Daily Appeal*, 9 June 1873, n.p.; "Death of Jeff Davis' Youngest Son," *Atlanta Constitution*, 18 Oct. 1872, p. 1; "By Mail and Telegraph," *New York Times*, 17 Oct. 1872, p. 1; Mary Custis Lee to VHD, 18 Nov. 1872, VHD to JD, 8 Mar. 1874, VHD, "Self life sketch," 3, JD to Maggie Davis, 1 Aug. 1873, JD Papers, AL.

33. JD to A. M. Clayton, 28 Aug. 1873, Davis-Clayton Letters, UM; Memphis Tax Books, Personal Property, 1873, p. 18, Archives, Memphis Public Library; JD to VHD, 23 July 1873, JD Papers, AL; *Memoir*, 2:812–815; JD to VHD, 25 Aug. 1873, JD Papers, AL; JD to Elizabeth Meriwether, 6 Sept. 1873, Minor L. Meriwether Pa-

pers, West Tennessee Historical Society, at UM; JD to VHD, 28 Aug. 1873, JD Papers, AL.

34. JD to VHD, 26 Apr. 1874, 29 Mar.—2 Apr. 1874, 26 Feb.–3 Mar. 1874, 15 Mar. 1874, JD Papers, AL.

35. JD to VC, 9 Sept. 1873, Clay Papers, DU; JD to VHD, 26 Feb.–3 Mar. 1874, 29 Mar.–2 Apr. 1874, 15 Mar. 1874, JD Papers, AL; "Mr. Jefferson Davis," *Times* (London), 5 June 1874, p. 8.

36. VHD to JD, 8 Mar. 1874, JD Papers, AL; *Memoir,* 2:812; Interview, Mary Hill and Olive Hill Grosvenor, 1919, pp. 5–6, Hill and Grosvenor Papers, UNC; Memo by unknown roommate, Jefferson Davis Jr., Alumni Files, Virginia Military Institute Archives; VHD to JD, 1 Jan. 1874, 24 June 1875, JD Papers, AL.

10. CROWD OF SORROWS

1. VHD to JD, 1 Jan. 1874, JD Papers, AL; VHD to J. U. Payne, 12 Apr. 1867, Charles Erasmus Fenner Papers, UNC; VHD to Clare de Graffenreid, 7 Mar. 1887, Varina Davis Letters, MS; JD to VHD, 25 Aug. 1873, JD Papers, AL; JD to C. C. Clay, 29 Dec. 1871, C. C. Clay Papers, DU; Memphis Tax Books, Supplemental Assessment, 1872, pp. 21, 50, Archives, Memphis Public Library; Probate Records, no. 2606, Joseph E. Davis, Davis Papers, taxes received by Collector's Office, Prairie Co., Arkansas, Old Court House Museum, Vicksburg; Memphis Tax Books, Personal Property, 1873, pp. 3, 31, 34, Archives, Memphis Public Library; JD to Mary Stamps, 2 Apr. 1873, Mary Stamps Papers, UNC.

2. Jane Turner Censer, *The Reconstruction of White Southern Womanhood, 1865–1890* (Baton Rouge: Louisiana State University Press, 2003), 185–186; VHD to Joseph Pulitzer, 1 Feb. 1887, Joseph Pulitzer Papers, Rare Book and Manuscript Library, Columbia Univ.; "Gentlemen and Ladies," 4 Dec. 1874, by Mrs. Jefferson Davis and Mrs. Thomas H. Allen, Varina Jefferson Davis Papers, Alabama Archives; Jack S. Blocker Jr., *"Give to the Wind Thy Fears": The Women's Temperance Crusade, 1873–1874* (Westport, Conn.: Greenwood Press, 1985), 136; Marsha Wedell, *Elite Women and the Reform Impulse in Memphis, 1875–1915* (Knoxville: University of Tennessee Press, 1991), 4, 31–32, 36–39, 150 n. 36; Frances Willard, *How to Win: A Book for Girls* (Chicago: W.C.T.U. Publishing Assoc., 1886), 76.

3. VHD to JD, 1 Jan. 1874, JD Papers, AL; Lee Meriwether, *My Yesteryears: An Autobiography* (Webster Groves, Mo.: International Mark Twain Society, 1942), 58, 82–83; Wedell, *Elite Women,* 14, 22–25; JD to Elizabeth Meriwether, 17 Feb. 1872, Elizabeth Meriwether to her sons, 15 May 1876, JD to Elizabeth Meriwether, 5 Jan. 1876, Meriwether Family Papers, West Tennessee Historical Society, at UM; Lee Meriwether, *Afterthoughts: A Sequel to My Yesteryears* (Webster Grove, Mo.: International Mark Twain Society, 1945), 8.

4. Annette E. Church and Roberta Church, *The Robert E. Churches of Memphis: A Father and Son Who Achieved in Spite of Race* (Ann Arbor, Mich.: Edwards Bros., 1974), 31; Willard B. Gatewood, *Aristocrats of Color: The Black Elite, 1880–1920* (Bloomington: Indiana University Press, 1990), 89; Mary Church Terrell, *A Colored*

Woman in a White World, introduction by Nellie Y. McKay (New York: G. K. Hall, 1996), 58–59; VHD to JD, 1 Jan. 1874, JD Papers, AL.

5. Will of Joseph E. Davis, 18 Mar. 1869, Exhibit D, Jefferson Davis v. J. H. D. Bowmar et. al, MS; Janet Sharp Hermann, *Pursuit of a Dream* (New York: Oxford University Press, 1981), 103–111, 152–157, 201; JD to VHD, 14 Jan. 1873, 10 Nov. 1873, 29 Dec. 1873, JD Papers, AL; JD to Lise Hamer, 6 Jan. 1887, JD and Family Papers, MS; JD to VHD, 16 Feb. 1878, JD Papers, AL.

6. Lise Mitchell Journal, Mitchell Journal and Letters, 18 May 1876, TL, copy at UNC; JD to VHD, 30 Mar. 1878, JD and Family Papers, MS; JD to Addison Hayes, 18 June 1878, JD to VHD, 15 May 1875, JD to VHD, 5 June 1875, 9 June 1875, JD Papers, AL; Hermann, *Pursuit of a Dream,* 204.

7. JD to VHD, 10 Mar. 1875, JD Papers, AL; JD to Addison Hayes, 4 June 1877, JD to VHD, 20 Oct. 1865, JD Papers, TU; JD to Mary Stamps, 7 Jan. 1870, Mary Stamps Papers, UNC.

8. JD to VHD, 14 June 1875, JD Papers, AL; Deposition of John Perkins, 470, Davis v. Bowmar; VHD to MBC, 25 Mar. 1885, Williams-Chesnut-Manning Papers, USC; JD to VHD, 6 May 1875, JD Papers, AL; Pittman & Pittman to VHD, 18 June 1875, JD Family Coll., MC; Deposition of Varina Howell Davis, 344–376, Davis v. Bowmar.

9. JD to VHD, 22 Oct. 1875, JD Papers, AL; Lee Ann Whites, *The Civil War as a Crisis in Gender: Augusta, Georgia, 1860–1890* (Athens: University of Georgia Press, 1995), 149–150; "Jefferson Davis: His Address at the Texas State Fair," *New York Times,* 18 May 1875, p. 8.

10. William F. Howell to VHD, 12 Dec. 1884, Jeffy D. Howell to VHD, 28 Sept. 1874, JD Papers, AL; William Harwar Parker, *Recollections of a Naval Officer, 1841–1865,* intro. and notes by Craig L. Symonds (Annapolis: Naval Institute Press, 1985), 346; VHD to Minor Meriwether, 18 Nov. 1875, Minor L. Meriwether Papers, West Tennessee Historical Society, at UM; *Memoir,* 2:819–822; JD to Mary Stamps, 25 Dec. 1875, Mary Stamps Papers, UNC.

11. VHD to JD, 7 Nov. 1865, JD Papers, AL; "Joel Addison Hayes, Jr.," 1, JD and Family Papers, MS; *Boyle and Chapman's Memphis Directory* (n.p.: n.p., 1876), 205, New York Public Library; VHD to JD, 9 Sept. 1877, JD Papers, AL; JD to Maggie Hayes, 19 Jan. 1876, JD and Family Papers, MS; VHD to Minor Meriwether, 18 Nov. 1875, Minor L. Meriwether Coll., West Tennessee Historical Society, at UM; JD to VHD, 9 Nov. 1875, JD Papers, AL; "Miss Maggie H. Davis," *New York Times,* 21 Jan. 1876, p. 1; *Memoir,* 2:823; JD to VHD, 31 Jan. 1876, JD Papers, AL.

12. "Died," *Wheeling Daily Register,* 7 Jan. 1876, p. 2, West Virginia Archives; Register of Deaths, vol. 2, 1871–1881, p. 68, West Virginia Archives; Ohio County Deeds Index, Grantors, W: 1778–1935, Reel 358, pp. 586–588, West Virginia Archives; Deed Book, Section G, Lot 75, Greenwood Cemetery, West Virginia; "Death of A Sister of Mrs. Jefferson Davis," *Lynchburg Daily Virginian,* 13 Jan. 1876, p. 3, Jones Memorial Library, Lynchburg.

13. VHD to John Garrett, 2 Dec. 1874, Robert Garrett Family Papers, LC; M. Morse to VHD, 11 June 1875, VHD to JD, 18 June 1875, JD Papers, AL; VHD to

Dudley Mann, 15 Sept. 1875, *The Collector: A Magazine for Autograph and Historical Collectors* 850 (1977): 18; Addison Hayes to JD, 11 Mar. 1876, JD Family Coll., MC; VHD to Elizabeth [Minna] Blair, 24 July 1883, Blair Family Papers, LC.

14. Bell Irvin Wiley, *Confederate Women* (Westport, Conn.: Greenwood Press, 1975), 76–77; JD to VC, 8 Sept. 1874, 16 July 1875, 3 Jan. 1875, 4 Mar. 1875, Clay Papers, DU; VC to JD, 2 Sept. 1874, JD Family Coll., MC.

15. JD to VHD, 22 Jan. 1876, 28 Jan. 1876, 7 Mar. 1876, 25 Mar. 1876, JD to J. William Jones, 17 Apr. 1876, JD Papers, AL.

16. Thomas J. Brown, *Dorothea Dix: New England Reformer* (Cambridge, Mass.: Harvard University Press, 1998), 74; JD to VHD, 25 Mar. 1876, JD to Maggie Hayes, 25 May 1876, JD Papers, AL; "Mr. Jefferson Davis," *Times* (London), 14 June 1876, p. 7; *Memoir,* 2:823–824; JD to WD, 21 Sept. 1876, JD Papers, AL; F. W. Tremlett to JD, 3 June 1876, JD Family Coll., MC; M. S. Nagasaki to JD, 21 July 1876, JD Papers, AL.

17. *Memoir,* 2:824; JD to Dudley Mann, n.d. [12 Aug. 1876], William P. Palmer Coll., Western Reserve Historical Society; JD to WD, 21 Sept. 1876, Jeff Davis Jr. to VHD, 1 Dec. 1876, JD Papers, AL; Robert Seager II, *And Tyler Too: A Biography of John and Julia Gardiner Tyler* (New York: McGraw-Hill, 1963), 523; Dudley Mann to JD, 13 Sept. 1876, JD Family Coll., MC; JD to VHD, 31 Oct. 1876, VHD to JD, 24 June 1875, 3 June 1875, JD Papers, AL; Meriwether, *My Yesteryears,* 19.

18. "Mr. Jefferson Davis," *Times* (London) 18 Nov. 1876, p. 11; *Memoir,* 2:824; JD to Addison Hayes, 1 Mar. 1877, 29 June 1877, JD and Family Papers, MS; VHD to Elizabeth [Minna] Blair, 24 July 1883, Blair Family Papers, LC; Elbert B. Smith, *Francis Preston Blair* (New York: Free Press, 1980), 437; JD to VHD, 1 May 1877, JD to WD, 24 Apr. 1877, WD and VHD to JD, 18 Feb. 1877, VHD to JD, 2 Aug. 1877, JD to VHD, 26 Feb. 1877, 24 Dec. 1876, JD Papers, AL.

19. *Memoir,* 2:823–824; JD to VHD, 9 Dec. 1876, 24 Dec. 1876, JD Papers, AL; JD to Elizabeth Meriwether, 5 Jan. 1876, Meriwether Family Papers, UM.

20. JD to VHD, 24 Dec. 1876, JD to Maggie Hayes, 1 Feb. 1877, JD Papers, AL; Sarah Dorsey to Leonidas Polk, 20 Feb. 1862, Leonidas Polk Papers, University of the South–Sewanee; Bertram Wyatt-Brown, *The House of Percy: Honor, Melancholy, and Imagination in a Southern Family* (New York: Oxford University Press, 1994), 119–158; Filia [Sarah Dorsey], *Lucia Dare* (n.p.: n.p., 1867).

21. JD to VHD, 24 Dec. 1876, JD Papers, AL; Jeff Davis Jr. to VHD, 1 May 1877, JD and Family Papers, MS; Michael Fellman, *Citizen Sherman: A Life of William Tecumseh Sherman* (New York: Random House, 1995), 348–351, 385–386; JD to VHD, 1 Jan. 1877, JD Papers, AL; Wyatt-Brown, *House of Percy,* 159; JD to Maggie Hayes, 1 Feb. 1877, JD Papers, AL; Hilton Howell Railey, *Touch'd with Madness* (New York: Carrick and Evans, 1938), 13.

22. Wiley, *Confederate Women,* 132; JD to VHD, 1 May 1877, JD to Maggie Hayes, 1 Feb. 1877, JD to VHD, 11 June 1877, JD Papers, AL.

23. VHD to JD, 2 Aug. 1877, JD Papers, AL; VHD to Elizabeth [Minna] Blair, 24 July 1883, Blair Family Papers, LC; Wiley, *Confederate Women,* 132.

24. JD to WD, 17 Oct. 1877, JD to Addison Hayes, 29 Sept. 1877, Maggie

Hayes to VHD, 9 June 1877, JD Papers, AL; VHD to C. C. Harrison, 7 Nov. 1877, Burton Norvell Harrison Family Papers, LC.

25. VHD to W. T. Walthall, 16 Dec. 1877, W. T. Walthall Papers, MS; VHD to JD, 3 Mar. 1878, JD to Maggie Hayes, 25 Feb. 1878, JD to WD, 30 Mar. 1878, JD Papers, AL; VHD to JD, 18 Apr. 1878, Louisiana Historical Society, New Orleans.

26. JD to Dudley Mann, 25 Apr. 1878, William P. Palmer Coll., Western Reserve Historical Society; JD to Crafts Wright, 4 Sept 1878, JD Papers, AL; *Memoir,* 2:826; JD to Addison Hayes, 22 Mar. 1878, JD Papers, AL; JD to W. T. Walthall, in Dorsey's hand, 24 Mar. 1878, W. T. Walthall Papers, MS; Sarah Dorsey to JD, 1 Nov. 1877, JD Family Coll., MC; Ledger, Estate, S. A. Dorsey account with Payne Kennedy & Co, 26 Dec. 1878 to 12 Apr. 1880, JD Family Coll., MC; JD to WD, 27 Nov. 1878, JD Papers, AL; JD to Addison Hayes, 29 June 1877, JD and Family Papers, MS.

27. Wyatt-Brown, *House of Percy,* 165–166, 168–169, 160.

28. Will of Sarah Dorsey, written 4 Jan. 1878, probated 15 July 1879, Louisiana State Museum; JD to Eliza O. Cochran, 24 June 1879, JD Family Coll., MC; Exhibit A, filed 12 Dec. 1879, Stephen Percy Ellis et al. v. Jefferson Davis, Equity Case No. 8934, RG21, U.S. District Courts, General Case Files, Eastern District of New Orleans, National Archives, Fort Worth; Sarah Dorsey to Dudley Mann, 25 Apr. 1878, JD Family Coll., MC.

29. Wyatt-Brown, *House of Percy,* 164; JD to VHD, 15 Mar. 1879, JD and Family Papers, MS; *Memoir,* 2:826; VHD to W. T. Walthall, 8 Sept. 1878, W. T. Walthall Papers, MS.

30. JD to VHD, 26 Feb. 1877, JD Papers, AL; Jeff Davis Jr. to VHD, 1 May 1877, JD and Family Papers, MS; "Jeff Davis Once More," *New York Times,* 30 May 1875, p. 9; "Jefferson Davis Speaks Again," *New York Times,* 12 Sept. 1875, p. 1; JD to WD, 13 Nov. 1874, W. T. Walthall to VHD, 15 Oct. 1878, JD Family Coll., MC; JD to Stephen D. Lee, 17 July 1878, Stephen Dill Lee Papers, UNC.

31. Francis H. Smith to JD, 23 Feb. 1875, Superintendent's Correspondence, Jefferson Davis Jr., Dropped 11 May 1875, Superintendent's Order Books, Virginia Military Institute Archives; JD to Jeff Davis Jr., 21 July 1874, TL; J. M. Greer to WD, 31 Aug. 1876, JD Family Coll., MC; Interview, Mary Hill and Olive Hill Grosvenor, 1919, p. 6, Hill and Grosvenor Papers, UNC; VHD to JD, 14–16 Apr. 1866, JD to WD, 17 Oct. 1877, JD Papers, AL; Jeff Davis Jr. to JD, 5 Sept. 1878, JD Family Coll., MC; Jeff Davis Jr. to JD, 19 Sept. 1878, JD Family Coll., MC; JD to VHD, 26 Feb. 1877, JD Papers, AL; Arthur Marvin Shaw, *William Preston Johnston: A Transitional Figure of the Confederacy* (Baton Rouge: Louisiana State University Press, 1943), 116.

32. Margaret Humphreys, *Yellow Fever and the South* (Baltimore: Johns Hopkins University Press, 1999), 5, 28, 60–61; Thomas H. Baker, "Yellowjack: The Yellow Fever Epidemic of 1878 in Memphis, Tennessee," *Bulletin of the History of Medicine* 42 (1968): 243–250, 261; Terrell, *Colored Woman in a White World,* 36–37; Jeff Davis Jr. to JD, 5 Sept. 1878, JD Family Coll., MC; VHD to W. T. Walthall, recd. 12 Oct.

1878, W. T. Walthall Papers, MS; *Memoir,* 2:827–828; Addison Hayes to JD, 14 Oct. 1878, S. C. Harvey to JD and VHD, 17 Oct. 1878, W. T. Walthall to VHD, 17 Oct. 1878, JD Family Coll., MC; "Jefferson Davis' Son," *New York Times,* 21 Oct. 1878, p. 2; Interments, Elmwood Cemetery, Jeff Davis Jr., Special Colls., Memphis Public Library.

33. JD to Addison Hayes, 18 Oct. 1878, JD Papers, AL; VHD to Col. Ellyson, 5 Mar. 1895, JD Family Coll., MC; VHD to Hartley Graham, 22 Jan. 1887, JD Papers, AL; VHD to Catherine Thompson, 26 Mar. 1885, MC; VHD to C. C. Harrison, 5 Apr. 1880, Harrison Family Papers, UVA; VHD to W. T. Walthall, recd. 21 Oct. 1878, in JD's hand, W. T. Walthall Papers, MS; "Jefferson Davis' Son," *New York Times,* 21 Oct. 1878, p. 2; Sally A. Menken to VHD, 1 Nov. 1878, Frederick and Ellen McGuiness to JD and VHD, 22 Oct. 1878, JD Family Coll., MC; JD to WD, 27 Nov. 1878, JD Papers, AL.

34. JD to VHD, 12 Jan. 1879, JD Papers, TU; JD to VHD, 7 Apr. 1879, JD Papers, AL; JD to W. T. Walthall, 26 Feb. 1879, W. T. Walthall Papers, MS; VHD to Mrs. Hayes, 12 Mar. 1879, JD Assoc., RU; VHD to JD, n.d. [27 Mar.] 1879, JD Papers, AL; JD to Dudley Mann, 3 Sept. 1879, JD Assoc., RU; Payne Kennedy & Co. to Sarah Dorsey, 4 Feb. 1879, JD Family Coll., MC; Indenture between Sarah Dorsey and JD, 19 Feb. 1879, May Wilson McBee Papers, Greenwood-Leflore Public Library, Greenwood, Mississippi; JD to Eliza O. Cochran, 24 June 1879, JD Family Coll., MC; *Memoir,* 2:29.

11. FASCINATING FAILURES

1. VHD to JD, 4 Feb. 1878, JD Papers, AL.

2. "Jefferson Davis," *Memphis Weekly Appeal,* 9 Apr. 1879, p. 4; "Mrs. Jefferson Davis," *Memphis Weekly Appeal,* 16 Apr. 1879, p. 2.

3. "Mrs. Jefferson Davis," *Memphis Weekly Appeal,* 16 Apr. 1879, p. 2; "President Davis," *New Orleans Picayune,* 13 June 1879, n.p.

4. J. U. Payne to JD, 30 Apr. 1879, JD Family Coll., MC; JD to Dudley Mann, 3 Sept. 1879, JD Assoc., RU; JD to VHD, 4 July 1879, JD Papers, TU; JD to W. T. Walthall, 4 July 1879, W. T. Walthall Papers, MS; JD to Eleanor Wells, 2 Aug. 1879, JD Family Coll., MC; VHD to Owen Dorsey, 14 Oct. 1894, Varina Howell Davis Letter, MS.

5. JD to "Mary," 4 Aug. 1879, JD Papers, AL; Herschel Gower, *Charles Dahlgren of Natchez: The Civil War and Dynastic Decline* (Washington, D.C.: Brasseys', 2002), 193; Summons, filed 19 Dec. 1879, Stephen Percy Ellis et al. v. Jefferson Davis, Equity Case No. 8934, RG21, U.S. District Courts, General Case Files, Eastern District of New Orleans, National Archives, Fort Worth [hereafter cited as Ellis et al. v. Davis]; Exhibit A, filed 12 Dec. 1879, Bill of Complaint, [page torn] 1879, pp. 1–24, 27, Ellis et al. v. Davis.

6. Demurrer of Defendant, filed 15 Jan. 1880, pp. 1–6, Decree Dismissing Bill, filed 8 Mar. 1880, Petition for Appeal, filed 17 Sept. 1880, Ellis et al. v. Davis; J. C. Derby to JD, 11 Dec. 1883, JD Family Coll., MC; Bertram Wyatt-Brown, *The House of Percy: Honor, Melancholy, and Imagination in a Southern Family* (New York: Oxford

University Press, 1994), 169; J. D. S. Newell to JD, 23 Dec. 1881, JD to J. D. S. Newell, 31 Dec. 1883, JD Family Coll., MC.

7. Janet Sharp Hermann, *The Pursuit of a Dream* (New York: Oxford University Press, 1981), 205, 207, 210–212, 220–222; JD to VHD, 9 Dec. 1884, JD Papers, AL; Will of JD, 18 Sept. 1879, JD and Family Papers, MS.

8. VHD to Owen Dorsey, 14 Oct. 1894, Varina Howell Davis Letter, MS; VHD to WD, 16 Feb. 1880, VHD to Maggie Hayes, 11 Apr. 1884, VHD to Nan Davis Smith, 29 Feb. 1880, JD Papers, AL; VHD to Maggie Hayes, n.d. [12 June] 1883, JD and Family Papers, MS; George P. Rawick, ed., *The American Slave: A Composite Autobiography* (Westport, Conn.: Greenwood Press, 1977), suppl. ser. 1, vol. 10, Mississippi, pt. 5, p. 2330, John Williams; VHD to Mr. Secor, 23 Feb. 1887, Davis Family Papers, Historic New Orleans Coll.; VHD to Maggie Hayes, n.d. [12 June] 1883, JD and Family Papers, MS; Edward L. Ayers, *The Promise of the New South: Life after Reconstruction* (New York: Oxford University Press, 1992), 20–22, 55–103, 310–316; *House-keeping in the Sunny South,* ed. Mrs. E. R. Tennett (Atlanta: Jas. P. Harrison and Co., 1885), 229.

9. *Memoir,* 2:829; E. Merton Coulter, *William Montague Browne: Versatile Anglo-Irish American, 1823–1883* (Athens: University of Georgia Press, 1967), 250–251; JD to J. C. Derby, 22 Feb. 1880, JD Papers, DU; W. T. Walthall to Wirt Adams, 27 Jan. 1881, W. T. Walthall Papers, MS; VHD to J. C. Derby, Apr. 15 and 23, 1880, Miscellaneous Mss., Historical Society of Pennsylvania; VHD to Maggie Hayes, n.d. [Dec. 1880], JD Papers, AL.

10. VHD to WD, 22 Apr. 1880, JD Papers, AL; *Memoir,* 2:829–830; JD, *The Rise and Fall of the Confederate Government,* 2 vols., foreword by Bell I. Wiley (1881; repr., New York: Thomas Yoseloff, 1958), 2:764.

11. Davis, *Rise and Fall,* 2:629, 708, 496–497, 683, 702; Davis, *Rise and Fall,* 1:1–2, 57, 2:1–2, 159–160, 582, 707, 718, dedication page; D. K. McRae to VHD, 3 Aug. 1881, JD Family Coll., MC; James M. Merrill, *William Tecumseh Sherman* (Chicago: Rand McNally, 1971), 385–386; "New Publications," *New York Times,* 26 June 1881, p. 10; W. T. Walthall to Wirt Adams, 27 Jan. 1881, W. T. Walthall Papers, MS; JD to VC, 20 July 1882, C. C. Clay Papers, DU; George Cary Eggleston, *Recollections of a Varied Life* (New York: Henry Holt and Co., 1910), 164–165; Albert Janin to JD, 9 Sept. 1879, JD Family Coll., MC.

12. JD to Gertrude Thomas, 28 Aug. 1879, JD Papers, DU; VHD to Maggie Hayes, n.d. [12 June] 1883, JD and Family Papers, MS; VHD to Dudley Mann, 26 Nov. 1879, William P. Palmer Coll., Western Reserve Historical Society; JD to L. B. Northrup, 14 Jan. 1880, A. Conger Goodyear Coll., Sterling Memorial Library, Yale University; John McIntosh Kell, *Recollections of a Naval Life* (Washington, D.C.: Neale Co., 1900), 295; Mary Craig Sinclair, *Southern Belle,* with a foreword by Upton Sinclair and an introduction by Peggy Whitman Prenshaw (Jackson: University Press of Mississippi, 1999), 20; [Winnie Davis], "Jefferson Davis in Private Life," *New York Herald,* 8 Aug. 1895, pp. 1–2; JD to VHD, 29 May 1881, White House Assoc. of Alabama, White House of the Confederacy, Montgomery; JD to William Mickle, 10 Jan. 1887, Sam Richey Coll., Miami Univ. of Ohio.

13. JD to "Mary," 4 Aug. 1879, JD to VHD, 9 Dec. 1884, JD Papers, AL; J. William Harris, *Deep Souths: Delta, Piedmont, and Sea Island Society in the Age of Segregation* (Baltimore: Johns Hopkins University Press, 2001), 48, 52—53; VHD to C. C. Harrison, 23 Dec. 1886, Harrison Family Papers, UVA; J. U. Payne to JD, 9 July 1881, JD Family Coll., MC; To the Circuit Court of Prince William County, 11 Oct. 1881, Kempe v. Kempe (1873–1881), Chancery Court, file box 11, Office of the Clerk of Circuit Court, Manassas, Va.; Transaction of 13 Mar. 1884, Joseph R. Davis to VHD, Harrison County Deeds, vol. 20, p. 15, MS; VHD to Thomas Roach, 29 July 1883, JD Papers, DU; VHD to Addison and Maggie Hayes, 1 Jan. 1887, JD and Family Papers, MS.

14. VHD to JD, 18 Apr. 1878, Louisiana Historical Society, New Orleans; Rosalie Friedlander to JD, 11 Nov. 1879, JD Family Coll., MC; WD to VHD, postmarked 30 July 1880, JD Papers, AL; VHD to WD, 20 Sept. 1880, JD and Family Papers, MS; Dudley Mann to JD, 5 Aug. 1880, JD Family Coll., MC; Rosalie Friedlander to JD, 10 July 1879, WD to JD, 28 Nov. 1879, WD to VHD, 27 Sept. 1880, JD Papers, AL; Interview, Mary Hill and Olive Hill Grosvenor, 1919, p. 6, Hill and Grosvenor Papers, UNC; VHD to WD, 20 Sept. 1880, JD and Family Papers, MS; VHD to C. C. Harrison, 5 Apr. 1880, Harrison Family Papers, UVA.

15. JD to VHD, n.d. [15 Sept. 1881], JD Papers, AL; JD to Dudley Mann, 30 Sept. 1881, William P. Palmer Coll., Western Reserve Historical Society; *Memoir,* 2:831; Judah Benjamin to VHD, 25 Apr. 1881, JD Papers, AL; JD to Mary Stamps, 11 Oct. 1881, Mary Stamps Papers, UNC; JD to Dudley Mann, 16 July 1880, William P. Palmer Coll., Western Reserve Historical Society; VHD to JD, n.d. [14 Sept.] 1881, JD Papers, AL; Entry by VHD, 21 Nov. n.d. [1881], n.p., Winnie Davis's Essay Journal, JD Family Coll., MC; Dudley Mann to JD, 15–16 Jan. 1882, JD Family Coll., MC.

16. VHD to JD, 8 Mar. 1874, JD Papers, AL; Jane Kempe to "My Dear Nannie," 6 June 1876, Richardson and Farrar Papers, UNC; JD to VHD, 5 Jan. 1874, JD Papers, AL; J. D. Howell to "My Darling Sister," 1 Aug. [n.d., 1879–1880], J. D. Howell to Addison Hayes, 29 Apr. 1880, Jefferson Davis–Hayes Coll., UM; VHD to Lydia Purnell, 10 Apr. 1881, typescript, JD Assoc., RU; Becket Howell to VHD, 26 Mar. n.d. [1881], JD Family Coll., MC; "Capt. Becket Kempe Howell," *New Orleans Sunday Picayune,* n.d. [1882], p. 64, Mrs. Frances Sprague Scrapbook, MS.

17. William F. Howell to VHD, 20 Nov. 1882, Charles Clark to VHD, 18 Dec. 1884, William F. Howell to VHD, 12 Dec. 1884, JD Papers, AL; VHD to John Meredith Read, n.d., Becket Howell to VHD, 26 Mar. n.d. [1881], JD Family Coll., MC.

18. VHD to WD, 20 Sept. 1880, JD and Family Papers, MS; VHD to WD, n.d. [May 1881], Jennie Bass to VHD, 13 May 1885, VHD to Maggie Hayes, 27 July 1881, JD Papers, AL; George T. Denison, *Soldiering in Canada: Recollections and Experiences* (Toronto: George N. Morang and Co., 1901), 70–72; Minor Meriwether to Elizabeth Meriwether, 7 Mar. 1887, Meriwether Family Papers, UM.

19. VHD to J. C. Derby, Apr. 15 and 23, 1880, Miscellaneous Mss., Historical Society of Pennsylvania; Anna Farrar Goldsborough, "Notes on Varina Howell Da-

vis," 7–8, JD Assoc., RU; VHD to Mr. Robbins, 15 July 1886, William M. Robbins Papers, UNC; VHD to D. H. Maury, 16 Nov. 1886, copy at JD Assoc., RU; VHD to Mrs. Jeremy F. Gilmer, 22 Nov. 1883, Jeremy Frances Gilmer Papers, UNC; VHD to Elizabeth [Minna] Blair, 24 July 1883, Blair Family Papers, LC; VHD to MBC, 25 Mar. 1885, Williams-Chesnut-Manning Papers, USC; VHD to C. C. Harrison, 5 Apr. 1880, Harrison Family Papers, UVA.

20. JD to Addison Hayes, 28 July 1882, JD Papers, TU; JD to VHD, 19 Dec. 1879, VHD to Maggie Hayes, 8 Nov. 1889, JD Papers, AL; VHD to Joseph Pulitzer, 1 Feb. 1887, Joseph Pulitzer Papers, Rare Book and Manuscript Library, Columbia University; VHD to J. C. Derby, Apr. 15 and 23, 1880, Miscellaneous Mss., Historical Society of Pennsylvania; VHD to C. C. Harrison, 5 Apr. 1880, Harrison Family Papers, UVA; VHD to Mrs. James Smith, 21 Jan. 1888, David Colin Humphreys Papers, MS.

21. Charles Reagan Wilson, *Baptized in Blood: The Religion of the Lost Cause, 1865–1920* (Athens: University of Georgia Press, 1980), 1; Mrs. S. W. Price to JD, 3 July [1881 or 1886], Varina Jefferson Davis Papers, Alabama Archives; JD to Annie McCardle, 18 Jan. 1885, Old Court House Museum, Vicksburg; JD to James Lyons, 15 May 1879, James Lyons Papers, UNC; "To the Confederate Dead," *New York Times,* 30 Apr. 1886, p. 5; "The Revival of Jeff Davis," *Chicago Tribune,* 5 May 1886, p. 9; "A Response to Mr. Davis," *New York Times,* 30 Apr. 1886, p. 1; "Mr. Davis's Southern Tour," *New York Times,* 4 May 1886, p. 5.

22. William A. Blair, *Cities of the Dead: Contesting the Memory of the Civil War in the South, 1865–1914* (Chapel Hill: University of North Carolina Press, 2004), 115, 121–126; Wilson, *Baptized in Blood,* 38; Gaines M. Foster, *Ghosts of the Confederacy: Defeat, the Lost Cause, and the Emergence of the New South, 1865–1913* (New York: Oxford University Press, 1987), 67–68, 73–74; Stuart McConnell, *Glorious Contentment: The Grand Army of the Republic, 1865–1900* (Chapel Hill: University of North Carolina, 1992), 167–168, 189–190; David W. Blight, *Race and Reunion: The Civil War in American Memory* (Cambridge, Mass.: Belknap Press of Harvard University Press, 2001), 338–380; JD to Robert N. Scott, 27 Nov. 1882, W. Flanagan Coll., San Jacinto Museum of History; JD to W. Preston Johnston, 6 Oct. 1883, Johnston Papers, TL; Eggleston, *Recollections of a Varied Life,* 240–241; "The Lost Cause," *New York Times,* 16 May 1886, p. 6; "A Confederate Officer" to JD, 20 May 1887, JD Family Coll., MC.

23. J. D. Renfroe to WD, 13 Nov. 1887, JD Family Coll., MC; Foster, *Ghosts of the Confederacy,* 95–96; Omer Bartov, *Mirrors of Destruction: War, Genocide, and Modern Identity* (New York: Oxford University Press, 2000); David Goldfield, *Still Fighting the Civil War: The American South and Southern History* (Baton Rouge: Louisiana State University Press, 2002), 1–28, 41; Kirk Savage, *Standing Soldiers, Kneeling Slaves: Race, War, and Monument in Nineteenth-Century America* (Princeton: Princeton University Press, 1997), 130–148; Wilson, *Baptized in Blood,* 50; JD to E. G. W. Butler, 13 May 1884, Allyn K. Ford Coll., Minnesota Historical Society; Rawick, ed., *American Slave,* suppl. ser. 1, Mississippi, vol. 10, pt. 5, p. 2330, John Williams.

24. VHD to Maggie Hayes, 11 Apr. 1884, JD Papers, AL; Neneas Mendenhall to

WD, 29 Oct. 1887, JD Family Coll., MC; VHD to JD, 9 Feb. 1885, JD Papers, TU; VHD to Mr. Robbins, 15 July 1886, William M. Robbins Papers, UNC; Goldsborough, "Notes on Varina Howell Davis," 8, JD Assoc., RU; VHD to [Mr. Posey], 7 Sept. 1883, Varina Jefferson Davis Papers, Alabama Archives.

25. Claude S. Fischer, *America Calling: A Social History of the Telephone to 1940* (Berkeley: University of California Press, 1992), 93–94; JD to W. S. Lovell, 22 June 1883, JD to Edward Owen, 31 Jan. 1889, JD Family Coll., MC; VHD to Thomas Hines, 11 Dec. 1886, Thomas H. Hines Papers, Filson Historical Society; JD to W. Preston Johnston, 11 Feb. 1882, Johnston Papers, TL; JD to David P. Secor, 15 Jan. 1885, Davis Family Papers, Historic New Orleans Coll.; inscription, 14 Aug. 1886, in Henry D. Capers, *Belleview: A Story of the Past and Present* (New York: E. J. Hale and Son, 1880), Beinecke Library, Yale University.

26. B. H. Catching to JD, 31 Aug. 1885, JD Family Coll., MC; VHD to Varina Davis Bonney, 6 June 1884, Subject File, Varina Howell Davis, MS; Thomas T. Munford to JD, 22 Feb. 1884, JD Papers, DU; "Jeff Davis and His Wife," *Ashtabula Weekly Telegraph,* 21 July 1882, p. 4.

27. VHD to Thomas Hines, 11 Dec. 1886, Thomas H. Hines Papers, Filson Historical Society; VHD to Mr. Posey, 31 July 1883, Varina Jefferson Davis Papers, Alabama Archives; VHD to Lydia Purnell, 10 Apr. 1881, typescript, JD Assoc., RU; VHD to MBC, 25 Mar. 1885, Williams-Chesnut-Manning Papers, USC; Elisabeth Muhlenfeld, *Mary Boykin Chesnut: A Biography,* foreword by C. Vann Woodward (Baton Rouge: Louisiana State University Press, 1981), 218, 222; VHD to Varina Davis Bonney, 6 June 1884, Subject File, Varina Howell Davis, MS.

28. "Jeff Davis: A Visit to the Ex-Chieftain at Beauvoir," *Baltimore Sunday Herald,* 10 July 1887, n.p.; VHD to JD, 9 Feb. 1885, JD Papers, TU; VHD to Elizabeth [Minna] Blair, 29 July 1883, Blair Family Papers, LC; Obituary for Daniel Agnew, *New York Times,* 10 Mar. 1902, p. 9; Daniel Agnew, "A Biographical Sketch of Governor Richard Howell of New Jersey," *Pennsylvania Magazine of History and Biography* 22 (1898): 221–230; Daniel Agnew to VHD, 19 Oct. 1880, JD Family Coll., MC.

29. Frances E. Willard, *Glimpses of Fifty Years: The Autobiography of an American Woman* (New York: Source Book Press, 1889, 1990), 566; Ruth Bordin, *Frances Willard* (Chapel Hill: University of North Carolina Press, 1986), xiv, 82, 14–24, 37–39, 53, 100–115; Lydia Jones Trowbridge, *Frances Willard of Evanston* (Chicago: Willett, Clark and Co., 1938), 140–141; Emily Apt Geer, *First Lady: The Life of Lucy Webb Hayes* (Kent, Ohio: Kent State University Press and the Rutherford B. Hayes Presidential Center, 1984), 237; Belle Kearney, *A Slaveholder's Daughter* (1900; repr., New York: Negro Universities Press, 1969), 135, 140, 185; Sallie F. Chapin, *Fitz-Hugh St. Clair, the South Carolina Rebel Boy* (Philadelphia: Claxton, Remsen and Haffelfinger, 1872), 250–252.

30. Frances Willard, *How to Win: A Book for Girls* (Chicago: WCTU Publishing Assoc., 1886), 76; Eleanor Flexner, *Century of Struggle: The Woman's Rights Movement in the United States,* rev. ed. (Cambridge, Mass.: Belknap Press of Harvard University Press, 1975), 188; Bordin, *Frances Willard,* 44, 46, 103, 108, 110, 112, 154.

31. Bordin, *Frances Willard,* 112, 117; VHD to Frances Willard, 24 Mar. 1882,

Temperance and Prohibition Papers, Woman's Christian Temperance Union Series, Historical Files of the National Headquarters; VHD to JD, 8 Mar. 1874, JD Papers, AL; Willard, *How to Win,* 76; Frances E. Willard, *Woman and Temperance, Or, The Work and the Workers of the Woman's Christian Temperance Union* (repr., New York: Arno Press, 1972), 557.

32. H. Montgomery Hyde, *Oscar Wilde: A Biography* (New York: Da Capo Press, 1975), 51-76; Mary Warner Blanchard, *Oscar Wilde's America: Counterculture in the Gilded Age* (New Haven: Yale University Press, 1998), xi-43; "Oscar Wilde," *Frank Leslie's Illustrated Newspaper,* 1 July 1882, p. 11; "Oscar Wilde," *Daily Picayune,* 17 June 1882, p. 3, "Arrival of Mr. Oscar Wilde," *Times-Democrat,* 17 June 1882, p. 3, "Oscar Wilde," *Atlanta Constitution,* 4 July 1882, n.p., Ellmann Coll., University of Tulsa.

33. Richard Ellmann, *Oscar Wilde* (New York: Alfred A. Knopf, 1988), 197; "Oscar Wilde," *Cleveland Herald,* 11 July 1882, p. 4; "Oscar Wilde," *Atlanta Constitution,* 4 July 1882, n.p., Ellmann Coll., University of Tulsa; Oscar Wilde, *The Complete Letters of Oscar Wilde,* ed. Merlin Holland and Rupert Hart-Davis (New York: Henry Holt, 2000), 175-176.

12. THE GIRDLED TREE

1. Charles Clifton Ferrell, "'The Daughter of the Confederacy'—Her Life, Character, and Writings," in *Publications of the Mississippi Historical Society,* ed. Franklin L. Riley (Oxford, Miss.: Mississippi Historical Society, 1899), 72; Helen Keary to JD, 4 Nov. 1882, JD Family Coll., MC; Mary Craig Sinclair, *Southern Belle,* with a foreword by Upton Sinclair and an introduction by Peggy Whitman Prenshaw (Jackson: University Press of Mississippi, 1999), 58; WD to Gaston Robbins, 10 Apr. 1887, William M. Robbins Papers, UNC; WD to VHD, n.d. May 1884, VHD to WD, 28 Jan. 1886, JD Papers, AL; VHD to C. C. Harrison, 20 Dec. 1886, Harrison Family Papers, UVA.

2. Inscription, *The Merry Old Dame Who Sings Fiddle De Dee* (London: Dean and Son, n.d.), Davis Rare Books, MC; Maggie Hayes to WD, 27 June 1880, JD Papers, AL; WD to Joseph Pulitzer, 20 Oct. 1887, Joseph Pulitzer Papers, Rare Book and Manuscript Library, Columbia University; VHD to WD, 27 June 1880, JD Papers, AL; JD to Maggie Hayes, 18 July 1881, JD and Family Papers, MS; VHD to Maggie Hayes, 27 July 1881, JD Papers, AL; VHD to Mrs. Jeremy Gilmer, 22 Nov. 1883, Jeremy Francis Gilmer Papers, UNC; VHD to W. H. Morgan, n.d. 1889, JD Papers, LC; *JD Papers,* 4:415-416; VHD to C. C. Harrison, 23 Dec. 1886, Harrison Family Papers, UVA; VHD to Maggie Hayes, 1 Jan. 1883, JD and VHD to Addison Hayes, 2 June 1883, JD Papers, AL; JD to O. H. Peck, 16 Dec. 1885, JD Coll., Chicago Historical Society; VHD to WD, 28 Jan. 1886, JD Papers, AL; "Clever Daughters of Clever Men: Jefferson Davis's Daughter," *Ladies' Home Journal,* Dec. 1891, p. 8; Ferrell, "Daughter of the Confederacy," 73; WD to Gaston Robbins, 30 Jan. 1888, William M. Robbins Papers, UNC.

3. WD to Bradley T. Johnson, 13 Mar. 1885, McGregor Coll., UVA; "Shouting for Jeff Davis," *Chicago Tribune,* 28 Apr. 1886, p. 1; "The Utterances of Ex-Rebel

President Jeff Davis," *Chicago Tribune,* 30 Apr. 1886, p. 1; *Memoir,* 2:831, misdated 1882.

4. "Davis in Montgomery," *New York Times,* 2 May 1886, p. 4; "Mr. Davis in Savannah," *New York Times,* 3 May 1886, p. 1; "Jefferson Davis at Atlanta," *New York Times,* 1 May 1886, p. 1; *Memoir,* 2:831, misdated 1882; "The Confederate Yell," *Chicago Tribune,* 3 May 1886, p. 1; Henry Grady to JD, 15 Nov. 1886, JD Family Coll., MC; "Jeff Davis Going Home," *Courier-Journal* (Louisville) 9 May 1886, p. 5; VHD to David A. Secor, 15 May 1886, JD Papers, DU.

5. JD to I. B. Watson, 24 June 1886, I. B. Watson Ms., USC; Mr. and Mrs. Louis Flatan to WD, 20 Jan. 1887, N. J. Lewis to WD, 30 Oct. 1888, Nellie R. Folsom to WD, 9 Nov. 1888, JD Family Coll., MC; Mrs. H. C. Lynch to WD, 5 Apr. 1887, MC; WD, "Babies Named After Me," volume dated 1885–1890, JD Family Coll., MC; "Flo" to WD, n.d. Mar. 1887, and Mrs. Molliet to WD, 20 Mar., 1887, MC; [Dabney] Maury to JD, 6 June 1887, JD Family Coll., MC; WD to Mrs. Adam, n.d., Apr. 1887, Varina A. J. Davis Coll., Chicago Historical Society; Thomas W. Herringshaw, *Prominent Men and Women of the Day* (n.p.: A. B. Gehman and Co., 1888), n.p.; "Winnie Davis at Jackson," *New York Times,* 25 May 1888, p. 1; M. W. Phillips to JD, 26 May 1888, JD Family Coll., MC; Henry A. Lewis to JD, 29 Aug. 1886, Varina Jefferson Davis Papers, Alabama Archives.

6. Scrapbook belonging to WD, in author's possession, purchased in 1997; "Miss Winnie Davis Dead," *New York Times,* 19 Sept. 1898, p. 4; WD to VHD, n.d. May 1884, JD Papers, AL; WD to Bradley T. Johnson, 13 Mar. 1885, McGregor Coll., UVA.

7. "The Daughter of the Confederacy," *New York Sun,* 19 Feb. 1887, repr., *Southern Reveille,* JD Family Coll., MC; "Miss Winnie Davis Dead," *New York Times,* 19 Sept. 1898, p. 4; W. H. Morgan to VHD, 29 Nov. [1883], JD Family Coll., MC; Lee Meriwether to Elizabeth Meriwether, 7 Mar. 1887, Meriwether Family Papers, West Tennessee Historical Society, at UM, infrared copy; Leo Braudy, *The Frenzy of Renown: Fame and Its History,* with a new afterword (New York: Vintage Books, 1997), 9; Gaines M. Foster, *Ghosts of the Confederacy: Defeat, the Lost Cause, and the Emergence of the New South* (New York: Oxford University Press, 1987), 97, 136–137; Virginia S. Hilliard to JD, 21 July 1887, R. W. McBride to WD, 8 June 1887, JD Family Coll., MC.

8. "Winnie Davis in Syracuse," "Miss Davis' First Sleigh-Ride," in George W. Jones to JD, 25 Nov. 1886, JD Family Coll., MC; VHD to C. C. Harrison, 20 Dec. 1886, Harrison Family Papers, UVA; John Meredith Read to VHD, 8 Oct. 1888, JD Family Coll., MC; untitled article, *Syracuse Herald,* 1 Oct. 1899, n.p., Biographical Files, "Howard G. White," Onondaga Historical Assoc.; James E. Jouette to WD, n.d. [1887], JD Family Coll., MC; WD to Manton Marble, n.d. [1880s], Manton Marble Papers, LC.

9. VHD to Gaston Robbins, 17 Oct. 1888, William M. Robbins Papers, UNC; Ferrell, "Daughter of the Confederacy," 73–74; "Don Quixote" to WD, 11 Oct. 1888, C. E. McKernan to WD, 14 Mar. 1887, F. M. Sterrett to JD, 16 July 1888,

E. W. Ruth to JD, 28 Apr. 1889, JD Family Coll., MC; "Winnie Davis, the Daughter of the Confederacy, Dead," *New York World,* 19 Sept. 1898, JD Family Coll., MC.

10. W. A. Swanberg, *Pulitzer* (New York: Charles Scribner's Sons, 1967), 38, 3–12, 32, 37–44, 58, 69, 114–115, 124, 147, 193; VHD to Kate Pulitzer, 13 June 1888, Pulitzer Papers, Rare Book and Manuscript Library, Columbia Univ.; George Juergens, *Joseph Pulitzer and the New York World* (Princeton: Princeton University Press, 1966), 3–7; Joseph Pulitzer to WD, 17 Mar. 1887, JD Family Coll., MC; "Miss Davis in Maine," *New York Times,* 15 Aug. 1888, p. 4; VHD to Joseph Pulitzer, 1 Feb. 1887, Pulitzer Papers, Rare Book and Manuscript Library, Columbia Univ.; "Miss Davis Hears the News," *Chicago Tribune,* 7 Dec. 1889, p. 1; VHD to Joseph Pulitzer, 10 Dec. 1887, Pulitzer Papers, Rare Book and Manuscript Library, Columbia Univ.; "Jefferson Davis at Home," *New York World,* 6 Oct. 1886, Scrapbook of Minor Meriwether, Meriwether Family Papers, West Tennessee Historical Society, at UM.

11. VHD to Joseph Pulitzer, 4 May 1887, Pulitzer Papers, Rare Book and Manuscript Library, Columbia Univ.; Denis Brian, *Pulitzer: A Life* (New York: John Wiley, 2001), 5, 87, 103–104; VHD to Joseph Pulitzer, 10 Dec. 1887, 1 Feb. 1887, Pulitzer Papers, Rare Book and Manuscript Library, Columbia Univ.

12. VHD to D. H. Maury, 16 Nov. 1886, copy at JD Assoc., RU; VHD to C. C. Harrison, 20 Dec. 1886, Harrison Family Papers, UVA; VHD to Charles Dudley Warner, 26 Dec. 1886, Charles Dudley Warner Papers, Watkinson Library, Trinity College, Hartford, Conn.

13. VHD to Mrs. Jeremy F. Gilmer, 24 Dec. 1885, 22 Nov. 1883, Jeremy Francis Gilmer Papers, UNC; VHD to Addison Hayes, n.d. May 1905, JD and Family Papers, MS; VHD to Charles Dudley Warner, 26 Dec. 1886, Charles Dudley Warner Papers, Watkinson Library, Trinity College, Hartford, Conn.; Edward L. Ayers, *The Promise of the New South: Life after Reconstruction* (New York: Oxford University Press, 1992), 351–352; WD to Charles Dudley Warner, 23 Apr. 1888, Charles Dudley Warner Papers, Watkinson Library, Trinity College, Hartford, Conn.; Grace King to WD, 7 July 1888, JD Family Coll., MC.

14. Jane Turner Censer, *The Reconstruction of White Southern Womanhood, 1865–1890* (Baton Rouge: Louisiana State University Press, 2003), 212–233; H. S. Edwards to WD, 18 Mar. 1888, Daniel Agnew to WD, 9 Mar. 1888, JD Family Coll., MC; WD to Gaston Robbins, 30 Jan. 1888, William M. Robbins Papers, UNC; E. C. Wharton to JD, 31 May 1888, Sam H. James to WD, 12 Feb. 1889, T. H. Lewis to WD, n.d. [1886–1888], JD Family Coll., MC; VHD to Clare de Graffenreid, 7 Mar. 1887, Varina Davis Letters, MS; Ferrell, "Daughter of the Confederacy," 74; Dudley Mann to WD, 21 Feb. 1888, JD Family Coll., MC.

15. Varina Anne Davis, "Serpent Myths," *North American Review* 146 (1888): 161–171; Daniel Agnew to WD, 9 Mar. 1888, JD Family Coll., MC; Ferrell, "Daughter of the Confederacy," 74–75; VHD to Mr. Secor, 14 Aug. 1888, Davis Family Papers, Historic New Orleans Coll.; Sidney Root to WD, 24 Dec. 1887, JD Family Coll., MC.

16. Miss Willard to WD, 6 Feb. 1888, JD Family Coll., MC; *Memoir,* 2:889; Mrs. M. W. Bartlett to JD, 17 Apr. 1889, JD Family Coll., MC; VHD to Miss Willard, 21

May 1887, WCTU Papers, Ohio Historical Society and Michigan Historical Colls.; Lydia Jones Trowbridge, *Frances Willard of Evanston* (Chicago: Willett, Clark and Co., 1938), 104–105; S. F. Chapin, "Southern Echoes," *Union Signal,* 25 Aug. 1887, p. 4, Willard Memorial Library, Evanston, Illinois; Frances E. Willard, *Glimpses of Fifty Years: The Autobiography of an American Woman* (New York: Source Book Press, 1990, 1889), 566, 373; WD to Miss Willard, 7 Sept. 1887, WCTU Papers, Ohio Historical Society and Michigan Historical Colls..

17. F. R. Lubbock to JD, 12 July 1887, 6 Aug. 1887, W. B. Montgomery to JD, 16 July 1887, JD Family Coll., MC; Mark E. Neely Jr., *Southern Rights: Political Prisoners and the Myth of Confederate Constitutionalism* (Charlottesville: University Press of Virginia, 1999), 37–41; John H. Reagan to JD, 29 July 1887, Jefferson Davis Reagan Coll., Dallas Historical Society; *Memoir,* 2:895, 888–889; JD to W. M. Leftwich, 24 Aug. 1887, JD Family Coll., MC; VHD to John A. Parker, 7 Sept. 1887, George R. Wendling Papers, TL; *The Handbook of Texas,* ed. Walter Prescott Webb (Austin: Texas State Historical Assoc., 1952), 2:414–415; JD to J. William Jones, 29 July 1888, Acc. 21294, Personal Papers, Library of Virginia.

18. Willard, *Glimpses of Fifty Years,* 566; Ruth Bordin, *Frances Willard: A Biography* (Chapel Hill: University of North Carolina Press, 1986), 103, 99; Eleanor Flexner, *Century of Struggle: The Woman's Rights Movement in the United States,* rev. ed. (Cambridge, Mass.: Belknap Press of Harvard University Press, 1975), 109–111; Joan D. Hedrick, *Harriet Beecher Stowe: A Life* (New York: Oxford University Press, 1994), 354, 362–363; Elisabeth Griffith, *In Her Own Right: The Life of Elizabeth Cady Stanton* (New York: Oxford University Press, 1984), 129; Ayers, *Promise of the New South,* 317; Susan B. Anthony to VHD, 6 Feb. 1888, JD Family Coll., MC.

19. VHD to Col. Marchant, 8 June 1889, Varina Howell Davis Letters, VHS; Foster, *Ghosts of the Confederacy,* 54–55; Gary W. Gallagher, *Lee and His Generals in History and Memory* (Baton Rouge: Louisiana State University Press, 1998), 199–212; JD and VHD to Jubal Early, 18 Apr. 1889, VHD to Jubal Early, 23 May 1888, VHD to Jubal Early, 13 Oct. 1885, Jubal Early Papers, LC.

20. VHD to Joseph Pulitzer, 4 May 1887, Pulitzer Papers, Rare Book and Manuscript Library, Columbia Univ.; VHD to Hartley Graham, 22 Jan. 1887, JD Papers, AL.

21. Daniel Agnew to VHD, 2 May 1889, John Meredith Read to VHD, 13 Dec. 1889, VHD to John Meredith Read, n.d., JD Family Coll., MC; VHD to C. C. Harrison, 20 Dec. 1886, Harrison Family Papers, UVA; VHD to D. H. Maury, 16 Nov. 1886, copy at JD Assoc., RU; VHD to Elizabeth [Minna] Blair, 24 July 1883, Blair Family Papers, LC.

22. "The Week," *Public Opinion,* 5 Nov. 1887, p. 73; "Mr. Davis at Macon," unknown newspaper, 26 Oct. 1887, n.p.; "Townsend," "Our Washington Letter," unknown newspaper, n.d., Scrapbook Coll., MC; "The Cheering of Jeff Davis," *Chicago Tribune,* 29 Oct. 1887, p. 1; VHD to Joseph Pulitzer, 10 Dec. 1887, Pulitzer Papers, Rare Book and Manuscript Library, Columbia Univ.

23. JD to Thomas W. Colley, 16 Mar. 1888, JD Family Coll., MC; VHD to Miss Tschudi, 21 Jan. 1888, Varina Anne Howell Davis Coll., UGA; VHD to James

Redpath, n.d. [c. 1889], Gilder-Lehrman Coll., Pierpont-Morgan Library, copy at New-York Historical Society; JD to Lise Hamer, 6 Mar. 1887, JD Papers, AL; VHD to James Redpath, 1 Oct. 1888, copy at JD Papers, MS; Stacy Schiff, *Vera (Mrs. Vladimir Nabokov)* (New York: Random House, 1999), 237–238, 245, 281; VHD to John A. Parker, 7 Sept. 1887, George R. Wendling Papers, TL; JD and VHD to Jubal Early, 18 Apr. 1889, Jubal Early Papers, LC; JD to A. J. Hayes, 26 Apr. 1889, JD and VHD to Varina Hayes, 17 May 1888, JD Papers, AL; "Jeff Davis, a Visit to the Ex-Chieftain at Beauvoir," *Baltimore Sunday Herald,* 10 July 1887, p. 1; "The Home of Jefferson Davis," *Frank Leslie's Illustrated Newspaper,* n.d. [c. 1888], Mrs. Frances Sprague Scrapbook, MS; VHD to Mrs. Jeremy F. Gilmer, 22 Nov. 1883, Jeremy Francis Gilmer Papers, UNC.

24. JD to VC, 11 Oct. 1878, JD to VC, 12 Jan. 1882, VC to JD, 16 Feb. 1882, JD to VC, 25 Feb. 1882, 15 June 1882, 12 July 1882, VC to JD, 15 July 1882, JD to VC, 10 Aug. 1882, C. C. Clay Papers, DU.

25. JD to VC, 19 Dec. 1882, 13 Mar. 1883, 4 May 1884, 20 June 1883, 2 Jan. 1884, Clay Papers, DU; "The Utterances of Ex-Rebel President Jeff Davis," *Chicago Tribune,* 30 Apr. 1886, p. 1; "Dixie Reigns Supreme," *New York Times,* 29 Apr. 1886, p. 1; VC to JD, 14 Jan. 1887, JD Family Coll., MC.

26. J. S. M. Curry to David Clopton, 12 Dec. 1887, Clay Papers, DU; "Ancestry of the Cloptons," 161–162, UM; Willie Clopton to David Clopton, 28 Aug. 1887, Clay Papers, DU; JD to VHD, 20 Oct. 1865, JD Papers, TU; JD to VC, 21 Nov. 1887, Clay Papers, DU.

27. JD to Editor of *Mobile Register,* 24 May 1884, William T. Walthall Papers, MS; JD to VHD, 29 May 1885, 14 Mar. 1883, JD Papers, AL.

28. Sinclair, *Southern Belle,* 21; *Memoir,* 2:927; JD to Lee Willis, 13 Apr. 1889, JD Assoc., RU; VHD to W. H. Morgan, n.d. 1889, JD Papers, LC; JD, "Autobiography of Jefferson Davis," *Belford's Magazine* 4 (Dec. 1889–May 1890): 255, 266.

29. VHD to Mrs. Jeremy Gilmer, 24 Dec. 1885, Jeremy Francis Gilmer Papers, UNC; *Memoir,* 1:30; JD to VHD, 22 Sept. 1881, JD Papers, AL; VHD to Catherine Thompson, 26 Mar. 1885, MC; VHD to Jubal Early, 7 May 1888, Jubal Early Papers, LC.

30. "Miss Davis in Maine," *New York Times,* 15 Aug. 1888, p. 4; George Lewis to WD, 31 Dec. 1888, Albert de Foresta to WD, 24 Dec. 1888, Mary R. E. Robins to JD, 17–18 Feb. 1884, JD Family Coll., MC; VHD to JD, 7 Nov. 1865, JD Papers, AL.

31. "Biographical Sketch," Biographical Files, "John Wilkinson," Onondaga Historical Assoc.; "A Notable Betrothal," *Syracuse Standard,* 17 Apr. 1890, n.p., Onondaga Historical Assoc.; "Death," *Syracuse Standard,* 5 May 1889, p. 4, WPA Notes, Onondaga County Public Library; "Death of Alfred Wilkinson," *Syracuse Standard,* 8 July 1886, p. 4, WPA Notes, Onondaga County Public Library; "Republican County Convention," *Syracuse Standard,* 2 Oct. 1861, p. 2, WPA Notes, Onondaga County Public Library; "Alfred Wilkinson, Delegate," 23 June 1876, *Syracuse Journal,* Biographical Files, "Mrs. Charlotte Wilkinson," Onondaga Historical Assoc.; VHD to

W. H. Morgan, n.d., 1889, JD Papers, LC; *Boyd's Syracuse Directory,* 1884–1885, p. 401, Syracuse University.

32. "The Bank of Wilkinson & Co. Closed," *New York Tribune,* 12 Dec. 1884, n.p., Banking Files, "Wilkinson Bank," Onondaga Historical Assoc.; "The Wilkinson Failure," *Syracuse Journal,* 22 Dec. 1884, n.p., Biographical Files, "J. Forman Wilkinson," Onondaga Historical Assoc.; "Sale of Wilkinson & Co.'s Effects," *Syracuse Standard,* 26 Feb. 1885, n.p., Biographical Files, "J. Forman Wilkinson," Onondaga Historical Assoc.; "The Wilkinson Case," *Syracuse Standard,* 20 Jan. 1885, n.p., Biographical Files, "J. Forman Wilkinson," Onondaga Historical Assoc.; National Butchers and Drovers' Bank v. J. Forman Wilkinson et al., Banking Files, "Wilkinson Bank," Onondaga Historical Assoc.; Loos et al. v. Wilkinson et al., 2 Oct. 1888, 110 N.Y. 195, 18 N.E. 99, Law Library, Onondaga County Courthouse; "Where the Money Went," *Syracuse Standard,* 17 Jan. 1885, n.p., Biographical Files, "J. Forman Wilkinson," Onondaga Historical Assoc.; "Syracuse Block 450," *Syracuse Courier,* n.p., 5 Aug. 1886, WPA Notes, Onondaga County Public Library.

33. "A Notable Betrothal," *Syracuse Standard,* 17 Apr. 1890, n.p., Biographical Files, "Alfred Wilkinson, Jr.," Onondaga Historical Assoc.; VHD to W. H. Morgan, n.d., 1889, JD Papers, LC; VHD to Jubal Early, 27 Apr. 1890, Jubal Early Papers, LC.

34. VHD to W. H. Morgan, n.d. 1889, JD Papers, LC; Harvard College Class of 1880, Report of 1890, p. 81, Harvard University Archives.

35. VHD to W. H. Morgan, n.d., 1889, JD Papers, LC; VHD to Jubal Early, 20 Apr. 1890, Jubal Early Papers, LC; VHD to "My very dearly beloved old Friend," 26 Apr. 1890, JD to Dudley Mann, 22 Oct. 1889, JD Papers, AL; VHD to Ellen Woodbury, 19 Feb. 1890, Levi Woodbury Family Papers, LC; VHD to Maggie Hayes, 8 Nov. 1889, JD Papers, AL.

13. DELECTABLE CITY

1. John C. Trainor to VHD, 10 Nov. 1889, JD Family Coll., MC; "Jefferson Davis," *Atlanta Constitution,* 7 Dec. 1889, p. 1; Maggie Hayes to VHD, 17 Nov. 1889, JD and Family Papers, MS; "Jefferson Davis," *Atlanta Constitution,* 7 Dec. 1889, p. 1; *Memoir,* 2:932; Death Certificate, 8 Dec. 1889, JD Papers, New York Public Library; VHD to Mrs. Jeremy F. Gilmer, 5 Apr. 1890, Jeremy Francis Gilmer Papers, UNC; "Second Edition: True to His Colors," *Chicago Tribune,* 7 Dec. 1889, p. 1; *Memoir,* 2:930; E. H. Farrar to Maggie Hayes, 6 Dec. 1889, JD and Family Papers, MS.

2. "The National Shame," *Atlanta Constitution,* 7 Dec. 1889, p. 1; "Jefferson Davis," *New York Times,* 12 Dec. 1889, p. 2; "Passing by the Bier of Jefferson Davis," *New York Times,* 9 Dec. 1889, p. 1; "Davis Dead," *Atlanta Constitution,* 6 Dec. 1889, p. 1; "Jefferson Davis's Life," *New York Times,* 6 Dec. 1889, p. 2; "Miss Davis Hears the News," *Chicago Tribune,* 7 Dec. 1889, p. 1; W. Gray to the Editor, *Times* (London), 7 Dec. 1889, p. 10; "From Washington: Reminiscences of Mr. Davis's Career at the Capital," unknown newspaper, n.d. Dec. 1889, n.p.

3. "Passing by the Bier of Jefferson Davis," *New York Times,* 9 Dec. 1889, p. 1; "At

Mr. Davis's Grave," *New York Times,* 13 Dec. 1889, p. 1; Statement by VHD to the Associated Press, unknown newspaper, 7 Dec. 1889, n.p.; "The Funeral of Jefferson Davis," *Frank Leslie's Illustrated Weekly,* 21 Dec. 1889, p. 7; VHD to Mr. Saussy, 8 Jan. 1890, George N. Saussy Papers, GHS; Frederick McGuinesss to VHD, 22 July 1891, JD Family Coll., MC; VHD to Ellen Woodbury, 19 Feb. 1890, Levi Woodbury Family Papers, LC; VHD to James Redpath, 10 Dec. 1889, Autograph File: D, Houghton Library, Harvard Univ.

4. Jonathan Coss to the author, 14 Aug. 2001, AXA Archives, Death Claim Records, Equitable Insurance Co.; "Jefferson Davis's Will," *New York Times,* 18 Dec. 1889, p. 1; Jane Turner Censer, *The Reconstruction of White Southern Womanhood, 1865–1895* (Baton Rouge: Louisiana State University Press, 2003), 101–102; Robert Seager II, *And Tyler Too: A Biography of John and Julia Gardiner Tyler* (New York: McGraw-Hill, 1963), 549; untitled article, *Frank Leslie's Illustrated Weekly,* 28 Dec. 1889, p. 7; Index to Mexican War Pension Files, 1877–1926, Cooley-Elmore, Roll 4, T-317, NA; "To Pension Mrs. Davis," *New York Times,* 19 Nov. 1891, p. 2; "A Monument To Jefferson Davis," *Chicago Tribune,* 10 Dec. 1889, p. 3; VHD to "The Citizens of the Confederate States," 8 Mar. 1890, Johnston Papers, TL; VHD to Mrs. Jeremy F. Gilmer, 5 Apr. 1890, Gilmer Papers, UNC; VHD to John Reagan, 30–31 May 1891, Jefferson Davis Reagan Coll., Dallas Historical Society.

5. *Memoir,* 2:194–195, 814, 207–208, 508–516, 807–810; *Memoir,* 1:676–677, 380–408, 3–29, 262; Hannah Tillich, *From Time to Time* (New York: Stein and Day, 1973); Brenda Maddox, *Nora: The Real Life of Molly Bloom* (Boston: Houghton Mifflin, 1988); Shirley A. Leckie, *Elizabeth Bacon Custer and the Making of a Myth* (Norman: University of Oklahoma Press, 1993), 102; Candace Falk, *Love, Anarchy, and Emma Goldman* (New York: Holt, Rinehart and Winston, 1984), 3–6, 377.

6. *Memoir,* 1:1–2, 265, 408, 523, 439, 198–199, 78–79, 409; 2:925, 41–47, 12, 919, 810–811, 823–826, 923–925.

7. *Memoir,* 1:311–312, 423–424, 683, 262; 2:40, 35.

8. *Memoir,* 1: dedication page; 2:1–2, 210, 536–574, 848–881, 87–91, 925, 182–183, 220–221.

9. Untitled article, *Biloxi Herald,* 25 Jan. 1890, p. 1; VHD to Mrs. Jeremy F. Gilmer, 5 Apr. 1890, Gilmer Papers, UNC; VHD to A. R. Lawton, 4 July 1890, Alexander Robert Lawton Papers, UNC; VHD to Mrs. L. W. Norwood, postmarked 6 May 1887, copy at JD Assoc., RU; VHD to Joseph Pulitzer, 20 Sept. 1887, Joseph Pulitzer Papers, Rare Book and Manuscript Library, Columbia University; VHD to John Reagan, 30–31 May 1891, Jefferson Davis Reagan Coll., Dallas Historical Society; VHD to Burton Harrison, 26 Jan. 1890, Harrison Family Papers, UVA; "Mrs. Davis's Explanation," *New York Times,* 6 Nov. 1890, p. 9; "Mrs. Jefferson Davis," *Biloxi Herald,* 20 Dec. 1890, p. 4; VHD to W. Preston Johnston, n.d. [Mar. 1890], Johnston Papers, TL; VHD to Maggie Hayes, n.d. [May 1890], JD Papers, TU.

10. VHD to John Reagan, 17 Sept. 1892, Jefferson Davis Reagan Coll., Dallas Historical Society; Daniel E. Sutherland, *The Confederate Carpetbaggers* (Baton Rouge: Louisiana State University Press, 1988), 31–41 69–70; George J. Lankevich, *Ameri-*

can Metropolis: A History of New York City (New York: New York University Press, 1998), 126, 120; VHD to Maggie Hayes, n.d. [1892], JD Papers, AL.

11. "The Gerard," *New York Herald,* 31 Mar. 1895, p. 16; VHD to Mrs. Cohen, 17 Jan. 1894, Cohen-Phillips Papers, GHS; *New York City Directory,* 1894, p. 314, New York Public Library; "The Girard," *New York Times,* 26 Aug. 1894, p. 21; VHD to Mrs. Howe, 28 Nov. 1893, P. C. Wright Coll., UVA; VHD to Maggie Hayes, n.d. [1892], JD Papers, AL; VHD to Jefferson Hayes-Davis, 20 May 1894, JD and Family Papers, MS; VHD to Margaret S. Winchester, 25 Mar. 1895, Varina Davis Letter, MS; VHD to Jane F. J. Nicholson, 11 May 1898, Janin Family Papers, HL; VHD to John B. Lillard, 8 Feb. 1893, Harrodsburg Historical Society, Harrodsburg, Ky.; VHD to Jefferson Hayes-Davis, 20 May 1894, JD and Family Papers, MS.

12. "Miss Davis's Story," 16 Oct. 1890, unknown newspaper, Biographical Files, "Alfred Wilkinson, Jr.," Onondaga Historical Assoc.; "Mrs. Davis Was Not There," *New York Times,* 26 July 1891, p. 3; VHD to Anne Grant, 27 Nov. 1899, JD Family Coll., MC; Anna Farrar Goldsborough, "Notes on Varina Howell Davis," 15, JD Assoc., RU; VHD to Mr. Ellyson, 22 Sept. 1892, VHD to Anne Grant, 12 July 1894, 25 Apr. 1898, JD Family Coll., MC; VHD to Gov. Stone, 12 May 1891, John M. Stone Papers, MS; VHD to Margaret S. Winchester, 25 Mar. 1895, Varina Davis Letter, MS; "Aunt Bettie" to Lise Hamer, 14 Nov. n.d. [1900], Mitchell Family Papers, TL; W. Preston Johnston to VHD, 18 Apr. 1899, JD Papers, AL.

13. Harvard College Class of 1880, Report of 1890, p. 81, Harvard Univ. Archives; "A Notable Betrothal," *Syracuse Standard,* 17 Apr. 1890, n.p., Biographical Files, "Alfred Wilkinson, Jr.," Onondaga Historical Assoc.; "Winnie Davis's Engagement," *New York Times,* 7 Oct. 1890, p. 5; "Winnie Davis to Be Married," *New York Times,* 27 Apr. 1890, p. 3; "Mr. Alfred Wilkinson," *Frank Leslie's Illustrated Newspaper,* 7 June 1890, p. 372; W. A. Swanberg, *Pulitzer* (New York: Charles Scribner's Sons, 1967), 134–135.

14. Theodore Nunn to VHD, 1 Apr. 1887, James S. Richardson to WD, 17 Aug. 1888, JD Family Coll., MC; Mary Craig Sinclair, *Southern Belle,* with a foreword by Upton Sinclair and an afterword by Peggy Whitman Prenshaw (1957; repr., Jackson: University Press of Mississippi and Banner Books, 1999), 60; VHD to Jubal Early, 27 Apr. 1890, Jubal Early Papers, LC; VHD to Editor of the *Constitution* (Weatherford, Texas), 6 May 1890, n.p.; VHD to Gabrielle DeRosset, 5 June 1890, DeRosset Papers, UNC.

15. VHD to Jubal Early, 27 Apr. 1890, W. H. Payne to Jubal Early, 6 Dec. 1889, R. L. Dabney to Jubal Early, 19 June 1889, L. L. Lomax to Jubal Early, 3 Apr. 1890, Jubal Early Papers, LC.

16. "Miss Davis's Story," 16 Oct. 1890, unknown newspaper, Biographical Files, "Alfred Wilkinson, Jr.," Onondaga Historical Assoc.; "The Engagement Off," *Utica Globe,* 18 Oct. 1890, n.p., Biographical Files, "Alfred Wilkinson, Jr.," Onondaga Historical Assoc.; "Winnie Davis's Engagement," *New York Times,* 7 Oct. 1890, p. 5; "Explosion of Benzine," *Syracuse Standard,* 22 Aug. 1890, n.p., WPA Notes, Onondaga County Public Library.

17. "Miss Davis's Marriage Postponed," *New York Times,* 10 Aug. 1890, p. 6; "Winnie Davis's Engagement," *New York Times,* 6 Oct. 1890, p. 1; "The Engagement Off," *Utica Globe,* 18 Oct. 1890, Biographical Files, "Alfred Wilkinson, Jr.," Onondaga Historical Assoc.; "Winnie Davis's Engagement," *New York Times,* 14 Oct. 1890, p. 1; "Miss Winnie Davis," *Atlanta Constitution,* 18 Oct. 1890, p. 1; untitled article, *Frank Leslie's Illustrated Weekly,* 1 Nov. 1890, p. 225; "Winnie Davis's Engagement," *New York Times,* 12 Oct. 1890, p. 2; "Miss Davis's Story," 16 Oct. 1890, unknown newspaper, Biographical Files, "Alfred Wilkinson, Jr.," Onondaga Historical Assoc.; "Death of Miss Davis," *Washington Post,* 19 Sept. 1898, p. 1.

18. "Winnie Davis's Engagement," *New York Times,* 14 Oct. 1890, p. 1; "Miss Davis's Story," 16 Oct. 1890, unknown newspaper, Biographical Files, "Alfred Wilkinson, Jr.," Onondaga Historical Assoc.; VHD to Ellen Woodbury, 19 Feb. 1890, Levi Woodbury Family Papers, LC; VHD to JD, 2 Aug. 1877, JD Papers, TU; "Miss Davis's Story," 16 Oct. 1890, unknown newspaper, n.p., Biographical Files, "Alfred Wilkinson, Jr.," Onondaga Historical Assoc.; Harvard College Class of 1880, Report of 1895, pp. 83–84, Report of 1920, p. 206, Harvard Univ. Archives; VHD to W. H. Morgan, n.d. 1889, JD Papers, LC.

19. "Mr. Davis's Burial Place," *New York Times,* 27 Dec. 1889, p. 1; VHD to Gov. Stone, 11 July 1891, John M. Stone Papers, MS; VHD to Major Morgan, n.d. [spring] 1891, BR; VHD to W. Preston Johnston, 21 June 1891, Johnston Papers, TL; "The Last Resting Place," *Biloxi Herald,* 11 July 1891, p. 2; VHD to Mr. Ellyson, 3 May 1892, JD Family Coll., MC; Goldsborough, "Notes on Varina Howell Davis," 9, JD Assoc., RU; VHD to Charles Howry, 10 Oct. 1905, Howry Family Papers, LC.

20. VHD to Charles Herbst, 7 Feb. 1895, Kentucky Historical Society, Frankfort; VHD to John Reagan, 30–31 May 1891, Jefferson Davis Reagan Coll., Dallas Historical Society; VHD to Anne Grant, 26 Feb. n.d. [1898], JD Family Coll., MC; VHD to Margaret S. Winchester, 25 Mar. 1895, Varina Davis Letter, MS; *JD Papers,* 4:120 n. 5; VHD to Mrs. Huston, 27 Apr. 1904, Miscellaneous Albums–Varina Davis, UNC; VHD to Addison Hayes, 20 June n.d. [1894], JD and Family Papers, MS; Sinclair, *Southern Belle,* 59; VHD to S. A. Cunningham, 5 July 1892, Varina Howell Davis Letters, Tennessee State Library and Archives; Hilton Howell Railey, *Touch'd with Madness* (New York: Carrick and Evans, 1938), 12–13; J. William Harris, *Deep Souths: Delta, Piedmont, and Sea Island Society in the Age of Segregation* (Baltimore: Johns Hopkins University Press, 2001), table 22, 365.

21. VHD to J. F. Cappleman, 12 Feb. 1904, catalog of Cohasco, photocopy in author's possession; VHD to Charles Dudley Warner, 23 Sept. 1892, Charles Dudley Warner Papers, Watkinson Library, Trinity College, Hartford, Conn.; VHD to C. C. Harrison, postmarked 9 Dec. 1890, Burton Norvell Harrison Family Papers, LC; Swanberg, *Pulitzer,* 217, 277, 95–96; George Juergens, *Joseph Pulitzer and the New York World* (Princeton: Princeton University Press, 1966), vii, xi, 133, 145, 157, 172.

22. Joseph Pulitzer to WD, 17 Mar. 1887, JD Family Coll., MC; Swanberg, *Pulitzer,* 110, 119, 217; "Mrs. Jefferson Davis at Port Colborne, Ont.," unknown newspaper, n.d. [1896], n.p.; VHD to Joseph Pulitzer, 23 Dec. 1902, Pulitzer Papers, Rare

Book and Manuscript Library, Columbia University; VHD, "Christmas in the Confederate White House," *New York World Sunday Magazine,* 13 Dec. 1896, pp. 25, 40, JD Family Coll., MC; Nicholson Baker and Margaret Brentano, *The World on Sunday: Graphic Art in Joseph Pulitzer's Newspaper (1898–1911)* (New York: Bulfinch Press, 2005), 7; Mary E. M. White, ed., *Etiquette for All Occasions* (Boston: Allston Station, 1900); VHD to Mrs. Gregory, 12 Mar. 1892, Varina Davis Miscellaneous Manuscripts, New-York Historical Society; VHD to Joseph Pulitzer, 9 Feb. n.d. [1900], 2 Dec. 1902, Pulitzer Papers, Rare Book and Manuscript Library, Columbia University.

23. Joseph R. Davis to J. U. Payne, 20 Feb. 1893, JD Papers, AL; VHD to Addison Hayes, 20 June n.d. [1894], JD and Family Papers, MS; VHD to W. Preston Johnston, 21 June 1891, Johnston Papers, TL; VHD to Margaret S. Winchester, 25 Mar. 1895, Varina Davis Letter, MS; "Aunt Bettie" to Lise Hamer, 14 Nov. n.d. [1900], Mitchell Family Papers, TL; VHD to Gov. Stone, 25 July 1891, John M. Stone Papers, MS; VHD to Mr. Ellyson, 22 Sept. 1892, JD Family Coll., MC; VHD to Mahala Roach, 28 June 1901, JD Papers, DU.

24. VHD to Mrs. Cohen, 22 Jan. 1893, Cohen-Phillips Papers, GHS; Mrs. Jefferson Davis, "The Widow of Stonewall Jackson," *Ladies' Home Journal,* Sept. 1893, p. 5; "General U.D.C. Convention," *Confederate Veteran* 17 (Dec. 1909): 590; Jessie Drew Beale, "New York State Division," *Confederate Veteran* 24 (Mar. 1916): 108–109; "Chapter at Galveston Texas," *Confederate Veteran* 10 (Oct. 1898): 460; CMLS Minute Books, 18 Apr. 1898, MC; *White House of the Confederacy: An Illustrated History* (Richmond: Cadmus Marketing, n.d.), 24–25.

25. "A Confederate Dinner," *Biloxi Herald,* 28 Jan. 1893, p. 1; VHD to Anne Grant, 21 Oct. n.d. [1896], JD Family Coll., MC; VHD to Stephen D. Lee, 23 Oct. 1896, Stephen Dill Lee Papers, UNC; VHD to Mr. Ellyson, 13 May 1893, JD Family Coll., MC; Programme of Ceremonies, Jefferson Davis Re-interment, 30–31 May 1893, Noxubee County Historical Society; VHD to Anne Grant, 26 May 1893, JD Family Coll., MC; VHD to Anne E. Snyder, 9 May 1897, Autograph File D, Houghton Library, Harvard Univ.; *Catalogue of the Confederate Museum of the Confederate Memorial Literary Society* (Richmond: Ware and Duke, Printers, 1905), 55, 169; Pierce Butler, *Judah P. Benjamin* (Philadelphia: George W. Jacobs and Co., 1906), 290 n. 1; VHD to William Dodd, 8 Mar., 10 Mar., 16 June 1905, William E. Dodd Papers, LC; William E. Dodd, *Jefferson Davis* (Philadelphia: George W. Jacobs and Co., 1907), 50, 67; VHD to John Reagan, 2 Aug. 1897, Jefferson Davis Reagan Coll., Dallas Historical Society.

26. VHD to Mrs. Oglesby, 19 June 1892, copy in Paul C. Richards Autographs; "Certain Parties," *Biloxi Herald,* 17 June 1893, p. 1; VHD to Major Morgan, n.d. [spring], 1891, BR; VHD to John T. Browne, 2 Apr. 1895, copy at Confederate Museum, Austin; VHD to Mrs. A. H. Thomas, 13 Apr. 1895, John Herndon Coll., UVA; VHD to Hebert R. Robertson, 11 Dec. 1892, MC; VHD to Anne Grant, 21 Oct. n.d. [1896], JD Family Coll., MC.

27. VHD to J. U. Payne, 26 July 1895, Charles Erasmus Fenner Papers, UNC; VHD to Mary E. P. Anderson, 17 Apr. 1895, Pegram-Johnson-McIntosh Papers,

VHS; VHD to Richard Reed, 3 June 1898, copy at JD Assoc., RU; VHD to Mrs. Cohen, 22 Jan. 1893, Cohen-Phillips Papers, GHS; VHD to Elizabeth Goddard, n.d. [1890–1898], Lewis Cass Papers, William L. Clements Library, University of Michigan; Francis E. Willard and Mary A. Livermore, eds., *A Woman of the Century: Fourteen Hundred-Seventy Biographical Sketches Accompanied by Portraits of Leading American Women*, with a new introduction by Leslie Shepard (1893; repr., Buffalo: Charles Wells Moulton, 1967), 235; Certificate of the General Society of the United States Daughters, 1776–1812, 8 June 1892, JD Family Coll., MC; Web site of U.S. Daughters of 1812, www.iaw.on.ca/~jsek/usd1812.htm., accessed 15 July 2001; Mary Wright Woolton to VHD, 22 June 1898, JD Family Coll., MC; VHD to "Dear Ladies," 1 May 1899, Mount Vernon Ladies Assoc.; VHD to Mrs. Townsend, 5 Aug. 1899, Varina Davis Miscellaneous Mss., New-York Historical Society.

28. Diary of Mary Ker, 11 Dec. 1889, Mary Susan Ker Papers, UNC; Sutherland, *Confederate Carpetbaggers*, 130; William Garrett Piston, *Lee's Tarnished Lieutenant: James Longstreet and His Place in Southern History* (Athens: University of Georgia Press, 1987), 104–170; Kevin Siepel, *Rebel: The Life and Times of John Singleton Mosby* (New York: St. Martin's Press, 1983), 159–277; "The Selection of Richmond," *Biloxi Herald*, 1 Aug. 1891, p. 2; "To Be in Hollywood," *New York Times*, 6 Nov. 1891, p. 1; "Personals," *New York Times*, 8 Sept. 1897, p. 6.

29. VHD to "My dear Friend," 7 Jan. 1892, Cohen-Phillips Papers, GHS; VHD to Mrs. Dial, 21 Nov. 1897, JD Family Coll., MC; VHD to Charles Aldrich, 6 May 1896, copy at Burlington Public Library, Burlington, Iowa; VHD to Mrs. Kimbrough, 12 Nov. 1894, JD Papers, LC; "A Home for Mrs. Jefferson Davis," *New York Times*, 9 Dec. 1891, p. 5.

30. "Celebrated Women Meet," *New York Times*, 25 June 1893, p. 1; "Widows of Renowned Leaders Meet," *Chicago Tribune*, 25 June 1893, p. 6; "Their Widows Met in Peace," *New York Herald*, 25 June 1893, p. 19; "She Will Drive with Mrs. Grant," *New York Herald*, 26 June 1893, p. 5.

31. O. W. Bennett to VHD, 1 July 1893, JD Papers, AL; "Celebrated Women Meet," *New York Times*, 25 June 1893, p. 1; "Mrs. Grant and Mrs. Davis," *New York Times*, 26 June 1893, p. 2; *New York City Directory*, 1892–1893, p. 542, New York Public Library; "She Will Drive with Mrs. Grant," *New York Herald*, 26 June 1893, p. 5; "Mrs. Davis at Narragansett," *New York Times*, 6 July 1893, p. 8; Julia Grant to VHD, 30 May 1894, 28 June n.d. [1894], 6 Mar. 1900, JD Papers, AL; "Now Rests in Hollywood," *Richmond News Leader*, 20 Oct. 1906, p. 6; "Honors to Mrs. Grant," *New York Times*, 28 Apr. 1897, p. 5; VHD to Julia Grant, 29 Apr. 1901, Ulysses S. Grant Papers, LC.

32. Julia Dent Grant, *The Personal Memoirs of Julia Dent Grant (Mrs. Ulysses Grant)*, ed. with notes and foreword by John Y. Simon, with introductions by Bruce Catton and Ralph G. Newman (New York: G. P. Putnam's Sons, 1975), 34, 42, 76, 83, 24, 175; Carl Sferrazza Anthony, *First Ladies: The Saga of the Presidents' Wives and Their Power, 1789–1961* (New York: William Morrow, 1990), 210, 216–217, 222; W. H. Crook, *Through Five Administrations: Reminiscences of Colonel William H. Crook, Body-Guard to President Lincoln,* comp. and ed. Margarita Spalding Gerry (New York:

Harper and Bros., 1910), 178–179; Memoir of Mildred M. H. Dewey, 130, Rutherford P. Hayes Presidential Center, Fremont, Ohio; Elbert B. Smith, *Francis Preston Blair* (New York: Free Press, 1980), 418; Brooks D. Simpson, *Ulysses S. Grant: Triumph over Adversity, 1822–1865* (Boston: Houghton Mifflin, 2000), 19, 404; *Memoir*, 2:768–769; "Celebrated Women Meet," *New York Times*, 25 June 1893, p. 1; VHD to Anne Grant, 12 July 1894, JD Family Coll., MC.

33. Simpson, *Ulysses S. Grant*, 440; Randall Blackshaw, "Mrs. Jefferson Davis," *Putnam's Magazine* 1 (Dec. 1906): 363; Ulysses S. Grant, *Personal Memoirs of U.S. Grant*, with an introduction and notes by James M. McPherson (New York: Penguin Books, 1999), 363, 623–624; *Memoir*, 2:487.

14. LIKE MARTHA

1. Marjorie Spruill Wheeler, *New Women of the New South: The Leaders of the Woman Suffrage Movement in the Southern States* (New York: Oxford University, 1993), xv, 13–14, 20; VHD, "Women of the '60's: Letter by Mrs. Jefferson Davis," *Atlanta Constitution*, n.d. 1893, pp. 9–10, Scrapbook Coll., MC; Carl Sferrazza Anthony, *First Ladies: The Saga of the Presidents' Wives and Their Power, 1789–1961* (New York: William Morrow, 1990), 246, 260, 219; "Certain Parties," *Biloxi Herald*, 17 June 1893, p. 1.

2. VHD, "Should Women Vote?" unknown newspaper, n.d. [1893–1894], n.p., JD Family Coll., MC; VHD to Addison Hayes, 7 Oct. 1896, JD and Family Papers, MS; Ruth Bordin, *Frances Willard: A Biography* (Chapel Hill: University of North Carolina Press, 1986), 190–201, 239.

3. VHD to Lord Roseberry, n.d. [Apr. 1898], JD Papers, AL; VHD to Mrs. Owen, 23 Feb. 1901, JD Family Coll., MC; Charles Reagan Wilson, *Baptized in Blood: The Religion of the Lost Cause, 1865–1920* (Athens: University of Georgia Press, 1980), 163–164; VHD to Anne Grant, 25 Apr. 1898, JD Family Coll., MC; VHD to James G. Holmes, 2 June 1898, Limestone College; VHD, "The White Man's Problem: Why We Do Not Want the Philippines," *Arena*, Jan.–June 1900, pp. 1–4; VHD to William H. McCabe, 17 Jan. 1896, William G. McCabe Papers, UVA.

4. Gaines M. Foster, *Ghosts of the Confederacy: Defeat, the Lost Cause, and the Emergence of the New South, 1865–1913* (New York: Oxford University Press, 1987), 149–152; Interview by Gilson Willets, n.d. [1898–1899], unknown newspaper, Scrapbook Coll., MC; Joel Williamson, *The Crucible of Race: Black-White Relations in the American South since Emancipation* (New York: Oxford University Press, 1984), 109–182; Ivan Hannaford, *Race: The History of an Idea in the West* (Washington, D.C.: Woodrow Wilson Center Press, 1996), 277–346; Leonard Dinnerstein, *Antisemitism in America* (New York: Oxford University Press, 1994), 35–57; Elisabeth Young-Bruehl, *Anatomy of Prejudices* (Cambridge, Mass.: Harvard University Press, 1996), 27, 37, 163; Louise Barnett, *Touched by Fire: The Life, Death, and Mythic Afterlife of George Armstrong Custer* (New York: Henry Holt, 1996), 94; Helen Lefkowitz Horowitz, *The Power and the Passion of M. Carey Thomas* (New York: Alfred A. Knopf, 1994), 3, 231–232, 264, 341–342, 381–382.

5. Peter R. DeMontravel, *A Hero to His Fighting Men: Nelson A. Miles, 1839–1925* (Kent, Ohio: Kent State University Press, 1998), 226, 361–362; Robert Wooster,

Nelson A. Miles and the Twilight of the Frontier Army (Lincoln: University of Nebraska Press, 1993), 54; VHD to [James M. Morgan], 30 June–1 July [1898], Varina Davis Letter, copy at VHS; Nelson Miles to Mr. Kirkman, 4 Feb. 1904, Nelson Miles Folder, Chicago Historical Soc.; VHD to Massa [Waller], 15 Feb. 1905, JD Papers, Robert W. Woodruff Library, Emory University; "Jefferson Davis's Imprisonment— Remembrances & justifications," [c. 1905], Nelson Miles Papers, U.S. Army Military History Institute, Carlisle Barracks, Pennsylvania; "Mrs. Davis concerning General Miles," *Confederate Veteran* 10 (Aug. 1902): 366; VHD to Mr. Scomp, 6 May 1904, Harrodsburg Historical Soc., Harrodsburg, Ky.; "Mrs. Davis to General Miles," *New York Times,* 21 Feb. 1905, p. 3; Nelson A. Miles, "My Treatment of Jefferson Davis," *Independent,* 1905, p. 415; VHD to Nelson Miles, n.d. [23 May 1865], Nelson Miles, "Open Letter to the Press," n.d. Feb. 1905, "Jefferson Davis's Imprisonment—Remembrances & justification," Nelson Miles Papers, Carlisle; VHD to Charles B. Howry, 9 Mar. 1905, Howry Family Papers, LC.

6. "A Monument to Jefferson Davis," *Chicago Tribune,* 10 Dec. 1889, p. 3; "Davis Dead," *Atlanta Constitution,* 6 Dec. 1889, p. 1; VHD to Dr. Stockton, postmarked 18 Aug. 1905, Varina Davis Letter, Schlesinger Library, Radcliffe College; *Catalogue of the Confederate Museum of the Confederate Memorial Literary Society* (Richmond: Ware and Duke, Printers, 1905), 79; Frances E. Willard and Mary A. Livermore, eds., *A Woman of the Century: Fourteen Hundred-Seventy Biographical Sketches Accompanied by Portraits of Leading American Women in All Walks of Life* (Buffalo: Charles Wells Moulton, 1893), 234–235; "Mrs. Julia Ward Howe and Mrs. Jefferson Davis," *Harper's Weekly,* 4 Sept. 1897, p. 875; VHD to Anne Grant, 26 Feb. n.d. [1898], JD Family Coll., MC; "Very Much of an Invalid," *New York Times,* 25 Apr. 1893, p. 1.

7. VHD to Anne Grant, 26 Feb. n.d. [1898], JD Family Coll., MC; VHD to Mary E. P. Anderson, 17 Apr. 1895, Pegram-Johnson-McIntosh Papers, VHS; VHD to Anne Grant, 21 Oct. n.d. [1896], VHD to "My dear John," 27 Apr. 1895, JD Family Coll., MC; VHD to James W. Eldridge, 16 Feb. 1891, Eldridge Coll., HL; VHD to Chevalier Reynolds, 29 Nov. 1894, copy in Sotheby's Printed Books and Manuscripts, Sale Number 5021; "Second Edition: Jeff Davis is Dead," *Chicago Tribune,* 6 Dec. 1889, p. 1; VHD to Philip H. Ward, n.d. [1892–1898], Frederick C. Schang Coll., Rare Book and Manuscript Library, Columbia University; Isoline M. Moses to VHD, 5 Nov. 1891, 11 Nov. 1891, VHD to Isoline M. Moses, 7 Nov. 1891, JD Family Coll., MC; O. W. Bennett to VHD, 1 July 1893, JD Papers, AL; William I. Rasin to VHD, 11 Apr. 1891, JD Family Coll., MC.

8. "Mrs. Davis Dies of Pneumonia," *New York World,* 17 Oct. 1906, p. 9, JD Family Coll., MC; VHD to Anne Grant, 12 July 1894, 25 Apr. 1898, 15 Aug. 1899, JD Family Coll., MC; VHD to Maggie Hayes, n.d. 1892, JD Papers, AL; "Mrs. Davis to Rest by Husband," *Evening Bulletin* (Philadelphia) 17 Oct. 1906, p. 1; VHD to Varina Hayes, 15 June 1895, JD and Family Papers, MS; VHD to Margaret S. Winchester, 25 Mar. 1895, Varina Davis Letter, MS; VHD to "My dear John," 27 Apr. 1895, JD Family Coll., MC.

9. VHD to Anne Grant, 15 Nov. 1891, 3 May 1895, 15 Aug. 1899, 29 Nov. 1898, JD Family Coll., MC; VHD to Mrs. Cohen, 7 Jan. 1892, 11 June 1890, 17 Jan.

1894, Cohen-Phillips Papers, GHS; VHD to Margaret S. Winchester, 25 Mar. 1895, Varina Davis Letter, MS; VHD to C. C. Harrison, 7 Sept. 1898, Harrison Family Papers, UVA; VHD to Mrs. A. R. Lawton, 27 Nov. 1895, Alexander Robert Lawton Papers, UNC.

10. VHD to John Reagan, 16 Apr. 1895, Jefferson Davis Reagan Coll., Dallas Historical Society; Lee Meriwether, *My Yesteryears: An Autobiography* (Webster Grove, Mo.: International Mark Twain Society, 1942), 20; Charles Clifton Ferrell, "'The Daughter of the Confederacy'—Her Life, Character, and Writings," in *Publications of the Mississippi Historical Society,* ed. Franklin L. Riley (Oxford, Miss.: Mississippi Historical Society, 1899, 1919), 75, 69 n.1, 81; Jane Turner Censer, *The Reconstruction of White Southern Womanhood, 1865–1890* (Baton Rouge: Louisiana State University Press, 2003), 258–260; Varina Anne Jefferson Davis, *The Veiled Doctor: A Novel* (New York: Harper and Bros., 1895); Davis, *A Romance of Summer Seas: A Novel* (New York: Harper and Bros., 1898); "Books by Varina Anne Jefferson-Davis," *Harper's Weekly* 10 (1898): 976; VHD to J. U. Payne, 26 July 1895, Charles Erasmus Fenner Papers, UNC; Varina Anne Davis, "Jefferson Davis in Private Life," *New York Herald,* 8 Aug. 1895, pp. 1–2; Varina Anne Davis, "The American Girl Who Studies Abroad," *Ladies' Home Journal,* Feb. 1892, p. 9; idem, *Ladies' Home Journal,* Mar. 1892, p. 6.

11. Poultney Bigelow to WD, 17 Sept. 1898, JD Papers, AL; Stanley Weintraub, *The London Yankees: Portraits of American Writers and Artists in England, 1894–1914* (New York: Harcourt Brace Jovanovich, 1979), 19; Appointment by John T. Dickinson, 25 Apr. 1890, JD Family Coll., MC; Ferrell, "Daughter of the Confederacy," 71; VHD to Anne Grant, 26 Feb. n.d. [1898], JD Family Coll., MC; John Sherman to "Gentlemen," 28 Jan. 1898, JD Papers, AL; WD to Gen. Anderson, 9 Feb. 1891, JD Family Coll., MC; VHD to Margaret S. Winchester, 25 Mar. 1895, Varina Davis Letter, MS; VHD to Mrs. Cohen, 17 Jan. 1894, Cohen-Phillips Papers, GHS; Mary Craig Sinclair, *Southern Belle,* with a foreword by Upton Sinclair and an afterword by Peggy Whitman Prenshaw (1957; repr., Jackson: University Press of Mississippi and Banner Books, 1999), 55.

12. WD to C. Aldrich, 22 May 1892, Charles Aldrich Autograph Coll., State Historical Society of Iowa; VHD to Mr. Block, n.d. [Aug. 1897], Museum of the City of Mobile; W. M. David to WD, 27 July 1890, JD Family Coll., MC; VHD to John T. Browne, 2 Apr. 1895, copy at Confederate Museum, Austin; VHD to C. C. Harrison, 28 May 1895, Burton Norvell Harrison Family Papers, LC; Fitzhugh Lee to VHD, 7 Apr. 1897, JD Papers, AL; WD to Frederick F. Bowen, 11 June 1893, Frederick Fillison Bowen Papers, VHS; "Ex-Governor Lubbock," *Biloxi Herald,* 5 Oct. 1895, p. 7; VHD to Anne Grant, 24 Feb. 1896, JD Family Coll., MC.

13. VHD to [James M. Morgan], 30 June–1 July [1898], Varina Davis Letter, copy at VHS; VHD to Stephen D. Lee, 20 July 1898, Stephen Dill Lee Papers, UNC; VHD to Anne Grant, 29 Aug. 1898, JD Family Coll., MC; Ferrell, "Daughter of the Confederacy," 84; VHD to C. C. Harrison, 7 Sept. 1898, Harrison Family Papers, UVA; W. A. Swanberg, *Pulitzer* (New York: Charles Scribner's Sons, 1967), 253; VHD to Belle [Morgan], n.d. [fall 1898], BR.

14. Kate [Pulitzer] to VHD, 18 Sept. 1898, Max Winchester to VHD, 19 Sept.

1898, Sallie Howell Oglesby to VHD, 18 Sept. 1898, "Rachel" to VHD, 19 Sept. 1898, Julia Dent Grant and Nellie Grant to VHD, 20 Sept. 1898, Adolph S. Ochs to VHD, 19 Sept. 1898, Thomas Nelson Page to VHD, 20 Sept. 1898, J. Hoge Tyler to VHD, 21 Sept. 1898, JD Family Coll., MC; VHD to Mrs. Clopton, 13 Oct. 1898 [misdated 1899], C. C. Clay Papers, DU; Percy M. Emory to VHD, 18 Sept. 1898, JD Family Coll., MC.

15. "Her Body Is at Rest," *Richmond Dispatch,* 24 Sept. 1898, n.p.; "Great Scene in Hollywood," *Evening Leader,* 24 Sept. 1898, n.p.; E. H. Farrar to VHD, n.d. [21] Sept. 1898, U.D.C., Pelham Chapter, Birmingham, to VHD, 12 Oct. 1898, JD Family Coll., MC; "Dr. J. William Jones, Chaplain General of the U.C.V.," *Confederate Veteran* 6 (Oct. 1898): 470–471; "Winnie Davis, the Daughter of the Confederacy, Dead," *New York World,* 19 Sept. 1898, p. 2, JD Family Coll., MC.

16. VHD to Mr. Secor, 8 Nov. 1898, Davis Family Papers, Historic New Orleans Coll.; VHD to Mrs. Clopton, 13 Oct. 1898 [misdated 1899], Clay Papers, DU; "Aunt Bettie" to Lise Hamer, 20 Mar. 1899, Mitchell Family Papers, TL; VHD to Emma J. Stovall, 19 Sept. 1899, copy at Confederate Museum, Austin; VHD to Varina Mitchell, 15 Sept. 1899, BR; Sinclair, *Southern Belle,* 55, 75; VHD to Harry Stillwell Edwards, 28 Oct. 1899, copy at JD Assoc., RU; VHD to Mr. Saussy, 13 July 1903, George N. Saussy Papers, GHS; no author, *St. Peter's By the Sea* (Narragansett: St. Peter's By the Sea, 2001), window 12.

17. "Mrs. V. Jefferson Davis," *Confederate Veteran* 8 (Dec. 1900): 469; VHD to Mrs. E. M. Durham, 19 Mar. 1902, Davis Family Papers, Historic New Orleans Coll.; A. M. Kimbrough to VHD, 10 Sept. 1905, JD Papers, AL; VHD to A. M. Kimbrough, 1 Aug. 1906, A. McC. Kimbrough and Family Papers, MS; VHD, Eulogy for John Taylor Wood, 29 July 1904, Thomas E. Buchanan Papers, DU; VHD to J. Mack Moore, 4 Apr. 1903, Old Court House Museum, Vicksburg; VHD to Mrs. Austin, 1 Mar. 1905, JD Family Coll., MC; VHD to John Reagan, 12 Oct. 1901, Jefferson Davis Reagan Coll., Dallas Historical Society; VHD to Charles B. Howry, 4 May 1903, Howry Family Papers, LC; VHD to "My Dear Boy," 13 Jan. 1899, Varina Davis Miscellaneous Mss., New-York Historical Society.

18. VHD to Mrs. Houston, 20 May 1899, 27 Apr. 1904, Miscellaneous Albums-Varina Davis, UNC; Anna Farrar Goldsborough, "Notes on Varina Howell Davis," 7–8, JD Assoc., RU; Kate Doyle to Mrs. Carey, 6 May 1907, Virginia Room Accession Papers, MC; "Weaned from South," unknown newspaper, n.d. [1902–1906], JD Family Coll., MC.

19. VHD to Anne Grant, 29 Nov. 1898, 2 Nov. [misdated 2 Dec.] , 1899, n.d. Feb. 1899, 19 Feb. 1899, JD Family Coll., MC; Kirk Savage, *Standing Soldiers, Kneeling Slaves: Race, War, and Monument in Nineteenth-Century America* (Princeton: Princeton University Press, 1997), 135–148; "Davis Memorials Dedicated," *New York Times,* 9 Nov. 1899, p. 5; "Winnie Davis Honored," *New York Times,* 10 Nov. 1899, p. 4; "United Daughters of the Confederacy," *Confederate Veteran* 12 (Dec. 1899): 532.

20. Foster, *Ghosts of the Confederacy,* 163–167, 171–173; Sarah E. Gardner, *Blood and Irony: Southern White Women's Narratives of the Civil War, 1861–1937* (Chapel Hill: University of North Carolina Press, 2004), 127, 118; Wilson, *Baptized in Blood,* 160,

38, 1, 18, 32; Mrs. L. H. Raines to Mrs. M. C. Goodlett, n.d., p. 76, in *Historical Records of the United Daughters of the Confederacy,* vol. 1, *Origin of the Daughters of the Confederacy and the U.D.C.,* U.D.C. Coll./Rutherford Scrapbooks, MC; Anastatia Sims, *The Power of Femininity in the New South: Women's Organizations and Politics in North Carolina, 1880–1930* (Columbia: University of South Carolina, 1997), 147; David Goldfield, *Still Fighting the Civil War: The American South and Southern History* (Baton Rouge: Louisiana State University Press, 2002), 4, 30, 33–34; Williamson, *Crucible of Race,* 259–261; VHD to Anne Grant, 19 Feb. 1899, 29 Nov. 1898, 2 Nov. 1899, 15 Aug. 1899, JD Family Coll., MC.

21. John H. Reagan to Editor of *New Voice,* 6 Mar. 1899, VHD to John Reagan, 16 Mar. 1899, Jefferson Davis Reagan Coll., Dallas Historical Society; John Reagan to VHD, 21 Mar. 1899, JD Papers, AL; John Reagan to VHD, 20 Feb. 1897, VHD to John Reagan, 2 Aug. 1897, Jefferson Davis Reagan Coll., Dallas Historical Society; Pierce Butler, *Judah P. Benjamin* (Philadelphia: George W. Jacobs and Co., 1906), 234.

22. John Sergeant Wise, *The End of an Era,* ed. and annotated by Curtis Carroll Davis (New York: Thomas Yoseloff, 1899, 1965), 401–403; VHD to John S. Wise, 4 Jan. 1900, John S. Wise to VHD, 8 Feb. 1900, Varina Howell Davis File, VHS.

23. Randall Blackshaw, "Mrs. Jefferson Davis: The Record of Two Conversations," *Putnam's Magazine* 1 (Dec. 1906): 362; Mary E. M. White, ed., *Etiquette for All Occasions* (Boston: Allston Station, 1900), 98, 98–99, 36, 91, 159, 94, 91–92; JD to VHD, 18 Apr. 1848, E 187 Manuscripts, Massachusetts Historical Society; VHD to Margaret S. Winchester, 25 Mar. 1895, Varina Davis Letter, MS.

24. White, *Etiquette for All Occasions,* 102, 118–119, 155.

25. VHD to Mr. and Mrs. Kimbrough, 8 July 1902, A. McC. Kimbrough and Family Papers, MS; "Jefferson Davis not a Keeper of Bloodhounds," *Century Magazine* 64 (Sept. 1902): 806–807; Burgess Montgomery to VHD, 7 Jan. 1895, JD Papers, AL; Janet Sharp Hermann, *The Pursuit of a Dream* (New York: Oxford University Press, 1981), 233; Isaiah Montgomery to VHD, 25 Apr. 1902, JD Papers, AL; George P. Rawick, ed., *The American Slave: A Composite Autobiography* (Westport, Conn.: Greenwood Press, 1977), suppl. ser. 1, vol. 9, Mississippi, pt. 4, pp. 1546–47, Isaiah Montgomery; Burgess Montgomery to VHD, 7 Jan. 1895, JD Papers, AL; Thornton Montgomery to VHD, 13 Oct. 1890, JD Family Coll., MC; James H. Jones to VHD, 28 Oct. 1893, JD Papers, AL; VHD to Senators Daniel and Martin, 8 Dec. 1899, JD Family Papers, Hill Memorial Library, Louisiana State University; "Now Rests in Hollywood," *Richmond News-Leader,* 20 Oct. 1906, p. 6.

26. Paul Avrich, *Anarchist Portraits* (Princeton: Princeton University Press, 1988), 53–78, 95–98; P. A. Kropotkin, *Kropotkin's Revolutionary Pamphlets: A Collection of Writings by Peter Kropotkin,* ed. with introduction, biographical sketch, and notes by Roger N. Baldwin (1927; repr., New York: Dover, 1970), 26–27; "Booker T. Washington," *The Freeman* (Indianapolis), 30 Mar. 1901, p. 4; Louis R. Harlan, *Booker T. Washington: The Making of a Black Leader, 1856–1901* (New York: Oxford University Press, 1972), 204, 227–229, 284–286.

27. Goldfield, *Still Fighting,* 242; Harlan, *Washington, Making of a Black Leader,*

304–316; Louis R. Harlan, *Booker T. Washington: The Wizard of Tuskegee, 1901–1915* (New York: Oxford University Press, 1983), 176; VHD to Mrs. E. M. Durham, 16 Mar. 1906, Davis Family Papers, Historic New Orleans Coll.; VHD to Mrs. J. M. Bennett, 6 Apr. 1906, West Virginia and Regional History Coll., West Virginia University Libraries.

28. VHD to Julia Dent Grant, 11 Apr. 1901, Ulysses S. Grant Papers, LC; Owen Wister, *Ulysses S. Grant* (Boston: Small, Maynard and Co., 1900); Blackshaw, "Mrs. Jefferson Davis," 363; VHD, "The Humanity of Grant," *New York World,* 21 Apr. 1901, n.p., JD Family Coll., MC. Cf. Sutherland, *Confederate Carpetbaggers,* 254–255, who portrays the widow Davis as an ardent defender of the Confederacy to the end of her life.

29. VHD to Julia Dent Grant, 29 Apr. 1901, Ulysses S. Grant Papers, LC; "Mrs. Jefferson Davis Regrets," *Loyal Legion Bulletin* 21 (July 1966): 3; Blackshaw, "Mrs. Jefferson Davis," 363; JD to Jubal Early, 30 Apr. 1888, Jubal Early Papers, LC; Mary Soames, *Clementine Churchill,* rev. ed. (London: Doubleday, 2002), 260–261, 553, 569.

30. "Southern Veterans Dine," *New York Times,* 20 Jan. 1900, p. 7; "Revolutionary Sons Dine," *New York Times,* 2 May 1900, p. 7; "Divinity–Dewey–Destiny," unknown newspaper, 1 May 1900, n.p., copy at John Preston Davis Papers, Schomburg Center for Research in Black Culture, New York Public Library; VHD to Mrs. Owen, 23 Feb. 1901, JD Family Coll., MC; VHD to Varina D. Howell, 1 Oct. 1905, BR; VHD to Mary Mitchell White, 19 Feb. 1905, in White, "Interludes," JD Assoc., RU.

31. VHD to Mr. and Mrs. Kimbrough, 8 July 1902, A. McC. Kimbrough and Family Papers, MS; VHD to Addison Hayes, n.d. [May 1902], JD Papers, AL.

32. VHD to J. F. Cappleman, 12 Feb. 1904, catalog of Cohasco, p. 22, photocopy in author's possession; VHD to Mrs. Houston, 27 Apr. 1904, Misc. Albums–Varina Davis, UNC; VHD to William Dodd, 16 June 1905, William E. Dodd Papers, LC.

33. VHD to J. A. Palfrey, 24 Apr. 1899, TL; Thomas Bender, *New York Intellect: A History of Intellectual Life in New York City, from 1750 to the Beginnings of Our Own Time* (New York: Alfred A. Knopf, 1987), 275–277; VHD to Mrs. J. M. Bennett, 1 May 1906, West Virginia and Regional History Coll., West Virginia University Libraries; VHD to Varina Mitchell, 22 June 1905, BR.

34. VHD to Mrs. E. M. Durham, 28 Mar. 1902, 16 Mar. 1906, Davis Family Papers, Historic New Orleans Coll.; VHD to "My dear Mary," 15 Aug. 1903, JD Papers, Robert W. Woodruff Library, Emory Univ.; VHD to Mary Craig, 1 Feb. 1904, M. C. K. Sinclair Papers, IU; VHD to "My very Dear Friend," 18 Aug. 1906, JD Papers, LC; Will of Varina Anne Davis, 11 Feb. 1898, VHD to Addison Hayes, n.d. May 1905, JD and Family Papers, MS; "Mrs. Davis Declines Gift," *New York Times,* 22 May 1904, p. 1; VHD to Samuel Hayward, 11 Dec. 1902, BR; VHD to "My dear little Bettie," 22 Sept. 1901, JD Papers, AL; Fredericke Ogden to Austin Smith, 28 Nov. 1902, Mary Frederike Quitman Ogden Smith Papers, MS.

35. VHD to Varina Hayes, 23–25 Feb. 1906, undated newspaper clipping, n.p., gift of Davis Gaillard to the author; VHD to Mr. and Mrs. A. M. Kimbrough, 4 Mar. 1902, A. McC. Kimbrough and Family Papers, MS; Lucy B. Mitchell to Lise Hamer,

26 Feb. 1902, Mitchell Family Papers, TL; "Mrs. Davis Is Dead," *Washington Post,* 17 Oct. 1906, p. 3; John W. Burgess, *Reminiscences of an American Scholar: The Beginnings of Columbia University,* with a foreword by Nicholas Murry Butler (New York: Columbia University Press, 1934), 292; Blackshaw, "Mrs. Jefferson Davis," 362—364; VHD to William Dodd, 8 Mar. 1905, 16 June 1905, Dodd Papers, LC.

36. VHD to William Dodd, 8 Mar. 1905, Dodd Papers, LC; VHD to Mr. Kimbrough, 28 May 1902, A. McC. Kimbrough and Family Papers, MS; VHD to Mrs. Austin, 1 Mar. 1905, JD Family Coll., MC; VHD to Mary C. Kimbrough, 26 Mar. 1905, M. C. K. Sinclair Papers, IU; VHD to George Barksdale, 18 June 1903, Miscellaneous Manuscripts, Valentine Richmond History Center; VHD to Frederick Bancroft, 14 Feb. 1900, Frederick Bancroft Papers, Rare Book and Manuscript Library, Columbia Univ.; S. S. [Benner] to VHD, 22 Feb. 1905, notation by VHD, Varina Jefferson Davis Papers, Alabama Archives.

37. VHD to Mrs. J. M. Bennett, 2 Apr. 1906, West Virginia and Regional History Coll., West Virginia University Libraries; VHD to Mary Kimbrough, 15 Oct. 1902, A. McC. Kimbrough and Family Papers, MS; VHD to Bessie Perkins, 17 May 1905, JD Papers, AL; VHD to "My dear Mary," 15 Aug. 1903, JD Papers, Robert W. Woodruff Library, Emory Univ.; VHD to Mr. Kimbrough, 19 May 1902, A. McC. Kimbrough and Family Papers, MS; VHD to Mrs. L. G. Young and family, 13 May 1903, JD Papers, Robert W. Woodruff Library, Emory Univ.; VHD to W. Preston Johnston, 4 Apr. 1899, Tucker Family Papers, UNC; "Frederike" to "My dearest Husband," 11 Apr. 1903, Mary Frederike Quitman Ogden Smith Papers, MS; Elizabeth Waller to Anne Grant, n.d. [Oct. 1899], JD Family Coll., MC; VHD to Mrs. Houston, 23 Aug. 1904, Misc. Albums–Varina Davis, UNC; VHD to Mary Bateson, 27 Nov. 1900, 3 Oct. 1902, n.d. Dec. 1904, gift of Davis Gaillard to the author; Goldsborough, "Notes on Varina Howell Davis," 3, 15, JD Assoc., RU.

38. VHD to Varina Mitchell, 9 July 1903, BR; VHD to Charles B. Howry, 4 May 1903, Howry Family Papers, LC; VHD to "My very dear Friend," n.d., JD Papers, LC; notation on VHD to Dr. Stockton, postmarked 18 Aug. 1905, Varina Davis Letter, Schlesinger Library, Radcliffe College; "Mrs. Davis On Visit Here," unknown newspaper, n.d. [1901], p. 1, JD Family Coll., MC; Burgess, *Reminiscences,* 292–293; VHD to Varina Mitchell, 9 July 1903, BR; VHD to J. F. Cappleman, 11 Mar. 1904, catalog of Cohasco, photocopy in author's possession; VHD to C. C. Harrison, 16 May 1904, Harrison Family Papers, UVA; VHD to Mrs. J. P. Anderson, 26 Feb. 1906, James Patton Anderson Coll., George A. Smathers Libraries, University of Florida.

39. VHD to Joseph Pulitzer, 3 Apr. 1905, Joseph Pulitzer Papers, Rare Book and Manuscript Library, Columbia Univ.; VHD to Mrs. E. M. Durham, 16 Mar. 1906, Davis Family Papers, Historic New Orleans Coll.; VHD to Mrs. Walter Charleston, n.d. [Feb. 1905], JD Papers, Robert W. Woodruff Library, Emory Univ.; VHD to Mr. Kimbrough, 5 Aug. 1906, A. McC. Kimbrough and Family Papers, MS; VHD to Joseph R. Davis, 27 Aug. 1896, copy at JD Assoc., RU; "Mrs. Jefferson Davis Passes Away," *Richmond Times-Dispatch,* 17 Oct. 1906, p. 1; "Mrs. Davis to Rest by Husband," *Evening Bulletin* (Philadelphia), 17 Oct. 1906, p. 1.

15. AT PEACE

1. "Obituary," *New York Tribune*, 17 July 1882, p. 5; "'First Lady' of Confederacy," *Los Angeles Times*, 17 Oct. 1906, p. 1; "Mrs. Davis Dead," *Boston Globe*, 17 Oct. 1906, pp. 1–6; "Mrs. Jefferson Davis Laid to Rest," *Afro-American Ledger*, 20 Oct. 1906, p. 2; "Obituary," *Times* (London), 18 Oct. 1906, p. 6; "Richmond People on Death of Mrs. Davis," *Richmond Evening Journal*, 17 Oct. 1906, p. 7; James Pickett Jones, *John A. Logan: Stalwart Republican from Illinois* (Tallahassee: Florida State University, 1982), 8, 12–13, 215–216; "Mrs. Gen. Logan Writes on Mrs. Jefferson Davis," *Richmond Evening Journal*, 20 Oct. 1906, p. 6; "Corporal Tanner Pays a High Tribute," *Richmond Times-Dispatch*, 18 Oct. 1906, p. 2; Photograph, *Richmond News-Leader*, 20 Oct. 1906, p. 1; "Many Societies Will Take Part," *Richmond Evening Journal*, 17 Oct. 1906, p. 1.

2. "Mrs. Davis Dead," *Boston Globe*, 17 Oct. 1906, pp. 1, 6; "Funeral of Mrs. Davis," *New York Tribune*, 18 Oct. 1906, p. 5; "Mrs. Jeff Davis Dead at the Majestic," *New York Times*, 17 Oct. 1906, p. 1; "Mrs. Davis Is Dead," *Washington Post*, 17 Oct. 1906, p. 3; "Mrs. Jefferson Davis," *Atlanta Constitution*, 17 Oct. 1906, p. 6; "Mrs. Jefferson Davis Dead; Succumbs to Pneumonia," *Virginian-Pilot* (Norfolk), 17 Oct. 1906, pp. 1, 7; "Mrs. Varina Jefferson Davis," *Confederate Veteran* 14 (Nov. 1906): 485–486; untitled article, *Richmond Evening Journal*, 17 Oct. 1906, p. 9; "Our Tribute to Mrs. Davis," *Richmond Times-Dispatch*, 20 Oct. 1906, p. 2.

3. Will of Varina Davis, 26 Mar. 1901, Old Court House Museum, Vicksburg; VHD to "My dear Friend," 4 Sept. 1906, JD Papers, LC; VHD to Addison Hayes, n.d. May 1905, JD and Family Papers, MS.

4. "Brief Service for Mrs. Davis in New York," *Virginian-Pilot* (Norfolk), 19 Oct. 1906, p. 1; "Federal Escort at Davis Funeral," *New York Herald*, 19 Oct. 1906, p. 9; "The Funeral of Mrs. V. J. Davis," *Roanoke Times*, 20 Oct. 1906, p. 1; "Mrs. Davis Laid to Rest in Richmond," *New York World*, 20 Oct. 1906, p. 9, JD Family Coll., MC; "Mrs. Davis Now at Rest," *Richmond Times-Dispatch*, 20 Oct. 1906, p. 1; "Mrs. Davis Laid to Rest," *Baltimore Sun*, 20 Oct. 1906, p. 2; "Rests in Grave near President of Confederacy," *Virginian-Pilot* (Norfolk), 20 Oct. 1906, p. 1; "Now Rests in Hollywood," *Richmond News-Leader*, 20 Oct. 1906, p. 6; "Mrs. Davis Laid to Rest in Richmond," *New York World*, 20 Oct. 1906, p. 9, JD Family Coll., MC; Davis plot, Hollywood Cemetery, author's visit, 1994.

5. Mary Craig Sinclair, *Southern Belle,* with a foreword by Upton Sinclair and an introduction by Peggy Whitman Prenshaw (1957; repr., Jackson: University Press of Mississippi, 1999), 14, 20–21, 17, 55, 180; VHD to A. M. Kimbrough, 21 Aug. 1902, A. McC. Kimbrough and Family Papers, MS; A. M. Kimbrough to VHD, 10 Sept. 1905, JD Papers, AL; VHD to Mary C. Kimbrough, 26 Mar. 1905, M. C. K. Sinclair Papers, IU; VHD to Mr. Kimbrough, [16 Oct.] 1894, VHD to "My very dear Friend," 1 Oct. 1905, JD Papers, LC.

6. Mrs. Kimbrough to Mrs. Kimbrough [*sic*], n.d. [1906], JD Papers, LC; "Davis Letter Led to Sensation," *News Leader*, 21 Nov. 1906, Kimbrough Family Papers Addition, Mississippi State Univ.; Sinclair, *Southern Belle*, 14; Mary Kimbrough to "Dear Sirs," 9 Feb. 1913, VHD to Mr. Kimbrough [16 Oct.] 1894, JD Papers, LC.

7. "Criticised Mississippi," *Washington Post,* 21 Nov. 1906, p. 4; "Post Mortem Letter of Mrs. Davis Stirred Daughters of Confederacy," *Atlanta Constitution,* 21 Nov. 1906, p. 1; T. C. DeLeon, *Belles, Beaux and Brains of the 60's* (New York: G. W. Dillingham Co., 1907, 1909), 458; S. D. Lee to Maggie Hayes, 17 Dec. 1906, JD Papers, AL; "'Post-Mortem Statement' of Mrs. Davis," *Confederate Veteran* 15 (Jan. 1907): 42.

A NOTE ON SOURCES

THE DOCUMENTATION on Varina Howell Davis's life is huge, which helps explain why this book is the first biography by a professional scholar. The best previous work, by the journalist Ishbel Ross, *First Lady of the South: The Life of Mrs. Jefferson Davis* (New York: Harper and Brothers, 1958), draws on a thin research base and presents a sanitized view of Davis's life; moreover, Ross published four biographies between 1953 and 1958. In my research, I examined dozens of manuscript collections, as well as census reports, government records, city directories, newspapers, magazines, memoirs, and interviews. The sources are scattered through many archives, from Massachusetts to California. Davis received and replied to letters from people all over the United States, so that quite a few institutions possess one or two of her letters. The same is true for Varina's daughter Winnie Davis, who became a household name in the 1880s and has sometimes been confused with Varina herself.

Certain aspects of the Davis correspondence present special challenges to scholars. Many letters by Varina's mother, Margaret Howell, are undated or incorrectly dated, so I dated them when possible according to their contents. Because the Davises were famous, a few forgeries have surfaced (bad forgeries, easy to spot). For obvious reasons, I did not cite those letters. Nor did I cite any publications on the Davises by Hudson Strode, who altered manuscripts, deleting and rearranging passages within individual letters. I avoided notoriously unreliable memoirs such as LaSalle Corbell Pickett's *Across My Path: Memories of People I Have Known* (New York: Brentano, 1916).

Regarding the war-related controversies in Varina Davis's life, most of her letters from 1860 and 1861, such as the one to her mother in June 1861, have been omitted from other books or published in expurgated form. Other works

393

neglect her vacillating comments about the Confederacy during the war and her meditations in 1865 on the causes of the war and the future of regional politics. As I composed the narrative on the much-debated 1865 flight from Richmond, I took into account the many inconsistencies in the sources on such questions as how many times the Davises met on the road, where the capture took place, what Varina was wearing, and what Jefferson was wearing.

Some letters from the Davis correspondence have disappeared under idiosyncratic circumstances. Several missives in the Confederate Museum in Austin evidently were not transferred to the Helen Marie Taylor Museum in Waco after the Austin museum closed in the 1990s. The Taylor Museum ceased operation in about 2000, and those letters are now lost, so I cited them as "copy at Confederate Museum, Austin." A few institutions have sold Varina Davis's letters or donors reclaimed yet others after I read them on research trips, so in those cases I cited the letters as "copy at" or "copy in" the respective institutions. I did the same with some documents of unknown provenance that are currently on deposit with various other institutions.

ACKNOWLEDGMENTS

NOW THAT THIS BOOK IS DONE, I am delighted to thank the many people who helped me along the way. The National Endowment for the Humanities furnished two grants from the Travel to Collections Program, and the Charles Warren Center at Harvard University and the Humanities Institute at the University of Virginia provided fellowships with precious time to write.

Among the many dedicated archivists and curators I worked with, these individuals were especially helpful: Virginia Beatty of the Willard Memorial Library; Jonathan Coss of the AXA Archives; Gordon Cotton of the Old Court House Museum in Vicksburg; John Dougan at the Archives Department of Memphis Public Library; Katherine Hall of the Howell, New Jersey, Historical Society; Patrick Hotard of Beauvoir, The Jefferson Davis Home & Presidential Library; Patrick Kerwin of the Library of Congress; Sarah Millard of the Archives Section of the Bank of England; Mimi Miller of the Historic Natchez Foundation; Tommy O'Bierne of the Chancery Court in Natchez; and Robin Reed and Tucker Hill of the Museum of the Confederacy. Ed Frank of Special Collections at the University of Memphis allowed me to make an infrared image of a letter in the collections. John Coski and Ruthann Coski of the Museum of the Confederacy were most generous with their expertise on the Davises and the Civil War era. Thoroughly modern in their outlook on history, they extended every courtesy, and I very much appreciated their assistance.

These descendants of the Davis, Grant, Howell, and Tyler families kindly corresponded with me, provided copies of manuscripts, or granted permission to cite manuscripts: Genevieve Barksdale, Ulysses Grant Dietz, Jayne Eannarino, Davis Gaillard, Ellen Gilchrist, Bertram Hayes-Davis, Julia S. Mills,

Harrison Tyler, and Barbara Palmer Webb. Marka Stewart, Varina Davis's great-granddaughter, allowed me to interview her, and her son Charles Bennett graciously arranged the interviews.

These good folk alerted me to the existence of certain manuscripts or gave copies of them to me: Joseph Arnold, Mary Blanchard, Jane Turner Censer, Cita Cook, William Cooper, Dorothy E. Cox, Lee and Debbie Cravens, Wayne Cutler, Michael Davis, Cliff Dickinson, Cynthia Earman, Cammie East, Steve Engle, Arline Fleming, Barrett Freedlander, Jean Friedman, Gary Gallagher, Elizabeth Glade, Joseph Glatthaar, David Heiden, Randolph Hollingsworth, Virginia Laas, Thomas Lowry, Robert May, Mark Pitcavage, George Rable, Scott Sandage, Lee Shepard, Eric Walther, Bertram Wyatt-Brown, and Robert Zalimas. I owe a cordial thanks to William C. Davis, who sent me manuscripts on several occasions as he forged ahead on his various projects. To all of these individuals, I am grateful for their generosity.

My research assistants Michelle Ehlert, Bogac Ergene, Jason Moyer, Mark Pitcavage, Megan Real, Leonard Sadosky, Anna Travis, and John Yaggi tracked down leads on topics in social, economic, and political history. Erica Puntel and Doug Paul, both tireless, highly skilled detectives, read old issues of obscure newspapers and found some rare literary references.

I am indebted to the colleagues who shared their knowledge about specific aspects of the research: John Burnham, for the medical history of nineteenth-century America; Ted DeLaney, for the genealogy of the Tyler-Waller family; Brian Joseph, for translating the Sanskrit in Winnie Davis's letters; and Russell Kelm and Daniel Kornstein, for their counsel about the law. David Herbert Donald shared his great wisdom about writing biography and kept faith in the project to the end.

Three colleagues, Jane Turner Censer, William Harris, and George Rable, gave the entire manuscript a close reading. I deeply appreciate their shrewd analysis of the argument and the style. True intellectual comrades, they saved me from many errors and outbreaks of bad writing. Thomas LeBien and Brooks Simpson read several chapters and made numerous perceptive comments. At Harvard University Press, Joyce Seltzer was a thoughtful, careful editor. I am of course responsible for the completed book, including any remaining mistakes or instances of poor prose.

Finally, I wish to thank the loved ones who sustained me with the right mix of timely encouragement, acute observation, and patient interest: Aron, Beverly, Charles, Frederick, and most of all Michael.

INDEX

Porter, David Dixon, 94–95, 158
Presidential election of 1860, 90–92
Prisoners of war, 133–134, 169, 311
Public figures. *See* Fame
Puerperal fever, 76–78, 86, 215
Pulitzer, Joseph, 249–250, 254, 255, 263, 271, 274–275
Pulitzer, Kate, 249–250, 263, 265, 271, 288, 290, 305, 307

Race, 2–4; in antebellum era, 28–29, 62–63, 97; during war, 112, 119; postwar, 169–170, 210–211, 228, 282, 284–285, 296–297, 311–312. *See also* African Americans; Slavery; Slaves
Reconciliation between North and South, postwar, 7–8, 237, 282, 299, 306, 311
Reform, 7, 68, 209–210, 242, 248. *See also* Temperance; Woman suffrage; Woman's Christian Association; Woman's Christian Temperance Union
Regional identity, 3, 11, 13; in antebellum era, 29, 42–43, 60, 81–82, 88–92; in secession crisis, 92–100; wartime, 114–115, 119; postwar, 194, 267–268, 299, 307, 311–312. *See also* North, perceptions of the; South, perceptions of the
Religious faith, 24, 84, 210, 287, 305
Republican Party: in antebellum era, 66–68, 88–90; in secession crisis, 98; wartime, 152; postwar, 165, 176, 237, 296–297. *See also* Democratic Party; Lincoln, Abraham; Political culture; Presidential election of 1860; Whig Party
Rowley, Jane Kempe Girault. *See* Kempe, Jane

Scott, Sir Walter, works by, 18, 70, 75, 186, 217
Scott, Winfield, 81–82, 85
Secession. *See* Confederacy; Davis, Jefferson; Davis, Varina Howell
Seward, William, 67, 77, 97, 286
Sexuality, 27–28, 38, 70, 172, 200–201, 260
Shakespeare, William, works by, 75, 158, 167, 179, 208, 288
Slavery: as economic system, 28–29, 61–63, 97, 133; as political issue, 28–29, 267, 282; as moral issue, 29, 63, 169–170. *See also* African Americans; Plantation economy; Race; Slaves
Slaves, 2, 137–138, 267; as household workers, 28–29, 38–40, 62, 97, 116, 132–133, 143, 145, 228; as plantation workers, 38–40, 61–63, 133; as fugitives, 126–127, 143–144, 180. *See also* African Americans; Plantation economy; Race; Slavery
South, perceptions of the, 2, 29, 194, 267. *See also* North, perceptions of the; Regional identity
Spanish-American War, 284–285
Sprague, Frances Kempe, 16, 236, 291
Sprague, Margaret. *See* Winchester, Margaret ("Missy") Sprague
Sprague, Sturges, 16, 21
Stanton, Edwin, 143, 146, 162, 177, 179
Sterne, Laurence, 19, 52, 80, 121
Stowe, Harriet Beecher, 6, 37, 213, 253
Strickland, Agnes, works by, 1, 70, 131–132

Taylor, Margaret Smith, 55–56, 58, 96, 120
Taylor, Sarah Knox. *See* Davis, Sarah Knox Taylor
Taylor, Zachary, 33, 36, 55–58, 286
Temperance, 7, 241–242, 252–254. *See also* Chapin, Sallie; Willard, Frances; Woman's Christian Temperance Union
Thompson, Jacob, 87, 92
Tyler, Julia, 114, 120, 137, 217, 265–266

Unionists in the South, 5, 90, 95, 98, 115–116, 135, 301
United Daughters of the Confederacy (UDC), 276; and VHD, 277, 293–294, 300–303, 306, 308–310; and WD, 291, 306
Urban culture: VHD and, 8, 54, 87–88; in New York City, 9–10, 269–270, 279, 303; in Natchez, 14; in Philadelphia, 19, 23–24, 220; in Washington, D. C., 42–43, 87–88, 111; in Richmond, 111–127; in London, 185–189; in Paris, 185–186, 234–236; in Memphis, 199, 208